MW01716319

# Learn Access 97

## Annotated Instructor's Edition

*Dawn E. Wood*

*Valdosta Technical Institute*

QUE E&T

# Learn Access 97 Annotated Instructor's Edition



ISBN: 1-57576-890-9



02 01 00 99 4 3 2 1

Interpretation of the printing code: the rightmost double-digit number is the year of the book's printing: the rightmost single-digit number, the number of the book's printing. For example, a printing code of 99-1 shows that the first printing of the book occurred in 1999.

Screens reproduced in the book were created using Collage Plus from Inner Media, Inc., Hollis, NH.

*Learn Access 97* is based on Microsoft Access 97.

# Credits

**Publisher**
Robert Linsky

**Executive Editor**
Jon R. Phillips

**Director of Product Marketing**
Susan L. Kindel

**Operations Manager**
Christine Moos

**Acquisitions Editor**
Elizabeth D. Brown

**Development Editor**
Sydney Jones

**Software Coordinator**
Angela Denny

**Technical Editor**
Ed Metzger

**Senior Editor**
Karen A. Walsh

**Project Editor**
Nancy E. Sixsmith

**Indexer**
Sandy Henselmeier

**Proofreader**
John Etchison

**Layout**
Louis Porter, Jr.

**Team Coordinator**
Melody Layne

# About the Author

**Dawn Wood** is the Computer Coordinator/Lead Instructor for the Business & Industry Services division at Valdosta Technical Institute, Valdosta, GA. The majority of the courses she teaches are in continuing education. Dawn teaches customized courses to local businesses to upgrade employee skills and knowledge of computers. She has written materials for these specialized courses for her own use. Prior to teaching, Dawn worked as a technical support representative and technical writer for a software firm. She lives in Valdosta, GA, with her husband, Kenneth, and her two children.

## Trademark Acknowledgments

# To the Student:

Your *Learn* textbook may come with a Learn On-Demand CD-ROM. Learn On-Demand provides you with a unique way to learn and practice the material covered in the book. This CD-ROM can help make your learning experience more enjoyable and help you pass your tests by allowing you to learn in an interactive environment.

Learn On-Demand is available to you through your campus' computer lab or you can install it on your own computer. This section shows you how to install the software on your computer and how to use Learn On-Demand.

# System Requirements

The minimum system requirements that you need to install Learn On-Demand are

- An IBM-compatible PC with a minimum of 486SX CPU
- 8MB RAM (16MB recommended)
- Microsoft Windows 95
- Microsoft Office 97
- VGA display adapter and monitor (640×480 or better)
- Two-button mouse
- Audio sound card (optional, but recommended)
- 4x speed or faster CD-ROM

If you are taking a course that includes more than one *Learn* book, you will need additional hard drive space to install the software for those books. The following table will help you determine how much additional hard drive space you need.

| File Types | Estimated Hard Disk Space Requirements |
|---|---|
| Learn On-Demand program files | 2MB |
| Application support files | 1MB per application |
| Content files (for example, graphics and lesson files) | 3.5MB per lesson |
| Sound files | 20–25MB (optional) |

If you would like to access Learn On-Demand's audio, you can choose to run the sound directly from your CD-ROM, which will lower the memory requirements.

# To the Instructor:

The *Learn* textbook comes with a Learn On-Demand CD-ROM. These same files are also included on the Instructor's Resource CD-ROM that accompanies the *Annotated Instructor's Edition.*

Learn On-Demand can be installed on your school's network or you can install it on each computer in your campus' computer lab. This section shows you how to install the software on your computer and how to use Learn On-Demand.

# System Requirements

The minimum system requirements that you need to install Learn On-Demand are

- An IBM-compatible PC with a minimum of 486SX CPU
- 8MB RAM (16MB recommended)
- Microsoft Windows 95
- Microsoft Office 97
- VGA display adapter and monitor (640x480 or better)
- Two-button mouse
- Audio sound card (optional, but recommended)
- 4x speed or faster CD-ROM

**Pothole:** A CD-ROM is not required to access Learn On-Demand from a network server, but one is required to complete the installation process.

If you are teaching a course that includes more than one *Learn* book, you will need additional hard drive space to install the software for those books. The following table will help you determine how much additional hard drive space you need.

| File Types | Estimated Hard Disk Space Requirements |
|---|---|
| Learn On-Demand program files | 2MB |
| Application support files | 1MB per application |
| Content files (for example, graphics and lesson files) | 3.5MB per lesson |
| Sound files | 20–25MB (optional) |

If you would like to access Learn On-Demand's audio, you can choose to run the sound directly from your CD-ROM, which will lower the memory requirements.

## Network Security Settings

Network security settings for the Learn On-Demand directory/folder should be configured according to the information in the following table.

| Network Type | Privileges to Set |
|---|---|
| Novell NetWare | Read, File Scan, Write, and Modify rights to the directory/folder where Learn On-Demand is installed. Create or Delete rights should not be set. |
| Microsoft network | Read, Write, and Execute rights. |

## Working with the Files from the CD-ROM

If you are working on a computer in a lab, verify that you can save the files to the hard drive. Some schools and universities do not allow you to save files to the computers in the computer labs. If the files have been installed on a network or by a lab assistant, your instructor will inform you where the files are located.

After inserting the CD-ROM, an installation screen will appear. The screen has two options:

- Install—This option allows you to install the student data files that accompany the text and the Learn On-Demand software.
- Exit—This option closes the installation window and returns you to the Windows desktop.

## Installing the Files to Your Hard Drive

If you have been instructed to install the files on a lab computer or if you are installing them on your home computer, follow these steps:

**1** From the installation screen, click the **Install** button.

**2** The **Install** dialog box is displayed. Click the **OK** button.

**3** The **Select Destination Directory** dialog box is displayed. This dialog box applies only to the student data files. If you install Learn On-Demand, you will see a similar screen during that installation. Unless instructed otherwise by your instructor, the default location is recommended. Click **OK**. When you install the student data files, a directory named lrnpptst is created on your hard drive where the student files will be installed. The installation of the student data files allows you to access the data files from the **Start** menu programs. To access the student data files from the **Start** menu, click **Start**, click **Programs**, and then click **Learn Access 97**. The student data files are located in the Student folder and arranged by lesson.

**4** The **Select Program Group** dialog box opens. The default group name is Learn Access 97. To override the default, highlight the text, type the new name, and click **OK**. The program group name you entered will appear in the **Start** menu after the installation is complete.

**5** The Readme.txt appears. The Readme.txt gives you important information regarding the installation. Make sure you use the scrollbar to view the entire Readme.txt file. When you are finished reading the Readme.txt, click **OK**.

**6** A dialog box appears confirming that the installation is complete. Click **OK** to exit the Installation screen.

**7** To install the On-Demand software, click the **Start** button.

**8** Click **Program**

**9** Point to **Learn Access 97**.

Follow the directions as they appear on your screen. You have three installation options: Minimal Install, Standard Install, and Full Install. Minimal Install copies the basic program files to your computer, but requires the CD for graphics and sound. Standard Install copies all program files to your computer, but requires the CD for sound. Full Install copies all program and sound files to your computer. If you accept the default directory\folder to install Learn On-Demand, all Learn On-Demand files are placed in Learn\Ondemand. If you choose another location to install Learn On-Demand, all the files are copied to the directory\folder you specify. Files are not copied to any other location during the install. Learn On-Demand appears automatically in the Start menu programs after installation. The Learn On-Demand shortcut appears in the item's submenu.

**10** Select **Install Access 97 On Demand**.

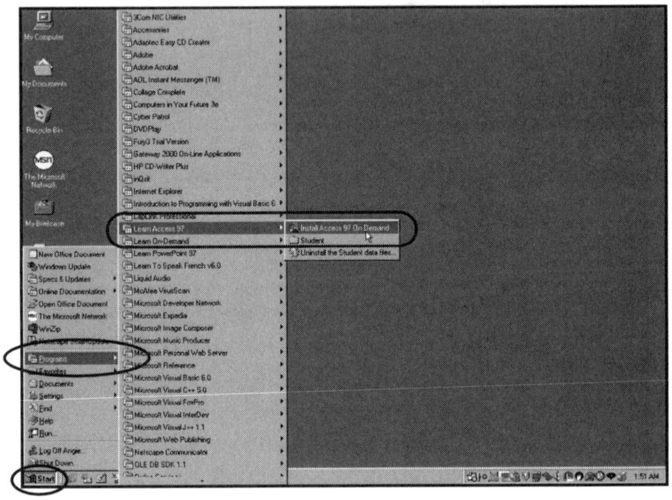

# Uninstalling Files from the CD

When you have completed the course, you may decide you don't need Learn On-Demand or the student data files anymore. If that's the case, you have the capability to uninstall them. This section covers the uninstall process for both Learn On-Demand and the student data files.

## Uninstalling Learn On-Demand

Learn On-Demand includes an uninstall program. You can use this program to remove specific titles from Learn On-Demand. If all titles are removed from Learn On-Demand, most program files will be removed from your computer, as will the shortcuts from the Programs submenu; however, the Learn\Ondemand directory structure where Learn On-Demand was originally installed will still exist.

Use the following procedure to uninstall a title from Learn On-Demand:

**1** Click **Start**.

**2** Click **Find**.

**3** Click **Files or Folders**.

**4** In the **Named** text box, type **Uninst.exe**.

**5** In the **Look in** box, type the drive where Learn On-Demand is installed.

**6** Click the **Find Now** button.

**7** When the file is displayed in the results list, double-click **Uninst.exe** that is located in the Learn\On-Demand folder.

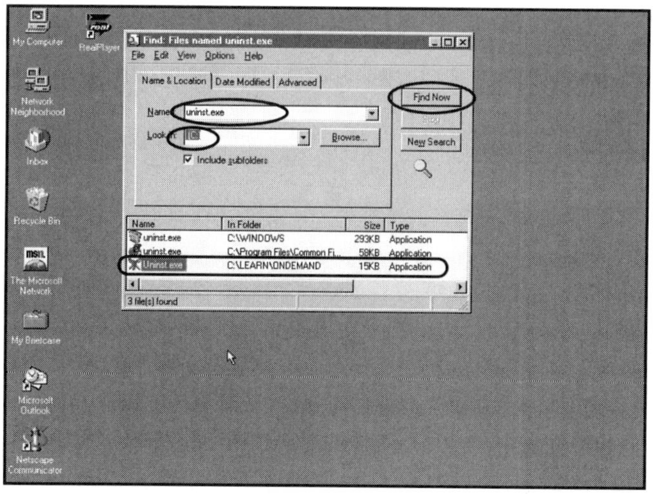


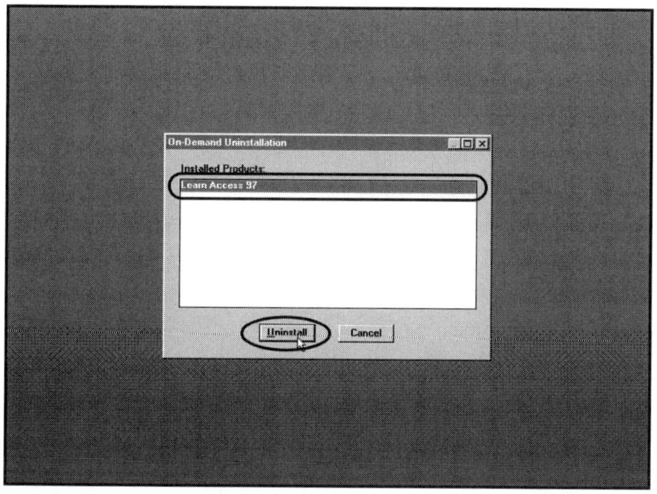


**8** From the **On-Demand Uninstallation** dialog box, select the title you want to uninstall and click the **Uninstall** button.

## Uninstalling the Student Data Files

There is also a program to uninstall the student data files. The following steps walk you through the process:

**1** Click on the **Start** menu and then click **Programs**.

**2** Click **Learn Access 97**.

**3** Click **Uninstall Learn Access 97**.

**4** Click one of the Uninstall methods listed:

- Automatic—This method deletes all files in the directory and all shortcuts created.
- Custom—This method allows you to select the files you want to delete.

**5** Click **Next**.

**6** The **Perform Uninstall** dialog box appears. Click **Finish**. The Student data files and directories will be deleted.

# Starting Learn On-Demand

To start Learn On-Demand, do the following:

1. From the taskbar, click the **Start** button. The **Start** menu appears.
2. Click **Programs**. The **Programs** menu appears.
3. Click the **Learn On-Demand** program group. The **Learn On-Demand** sub-menu appears.

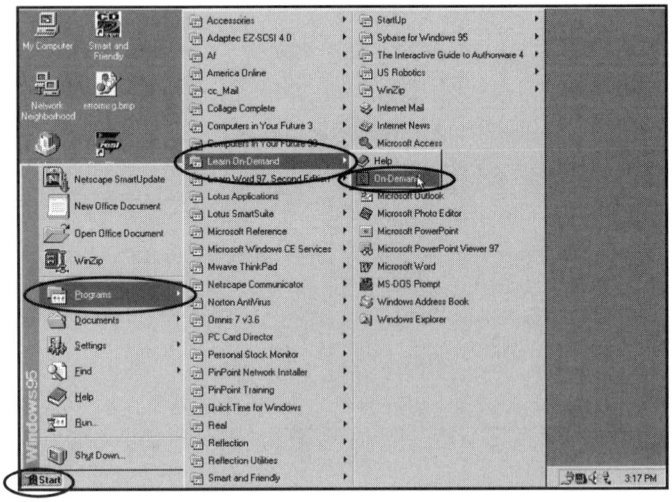


Learn On-Demand toolbar

4. Click **On-Demand**. The Learn On-Demand toolbar floats on the Windows desktop.

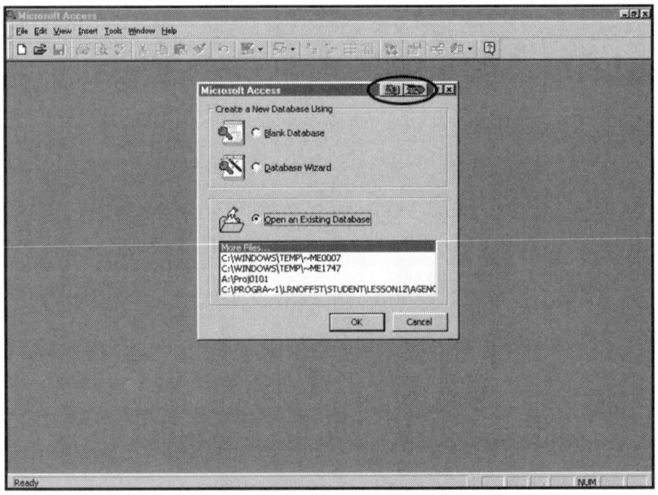


5. The Teacher button appears when you are in an application for which you have a Learn On-Demand title installed. At this point, you need to open Access.
6. The Learn On-Demand toolbar appears on Access' opening dialog box. After selecting the option and clicking **OK**, the Learn On-Demand toolbar appears on the application title bar.

# Using Learn On-Demand

Through interactive training, Learn On-Demand teaches students how to use a software program's features to complete tasks. This process makes students more productive because they can get the training they need when they need it. Specific tasks are covered in *topics*. You can learn about a topic using any of the four Learn On-Demand playback modes: Concept, Concurrent, Teacher, or Demo. These modes are covered individually later in this tutorial.

The **Interactive Training—Lesson Selection** dialog box is the central location from which you can find and view available training modules, lessons, and topics. From this location, you can launch a desired topic in any of Learn On-Demand's training modes. The dialog box contains three tabbed pages: **Contents**, **Search**, and **Topics for**. The purpose of each page is to help you view and locate training relevant to your specific needs, which are reviewed later in this tutorial.

Click the **Teacher** button on the application title bar to open the **Interactive Training—Lesson Selection** dialog box. You are now ready to select the desired topic and training mode.

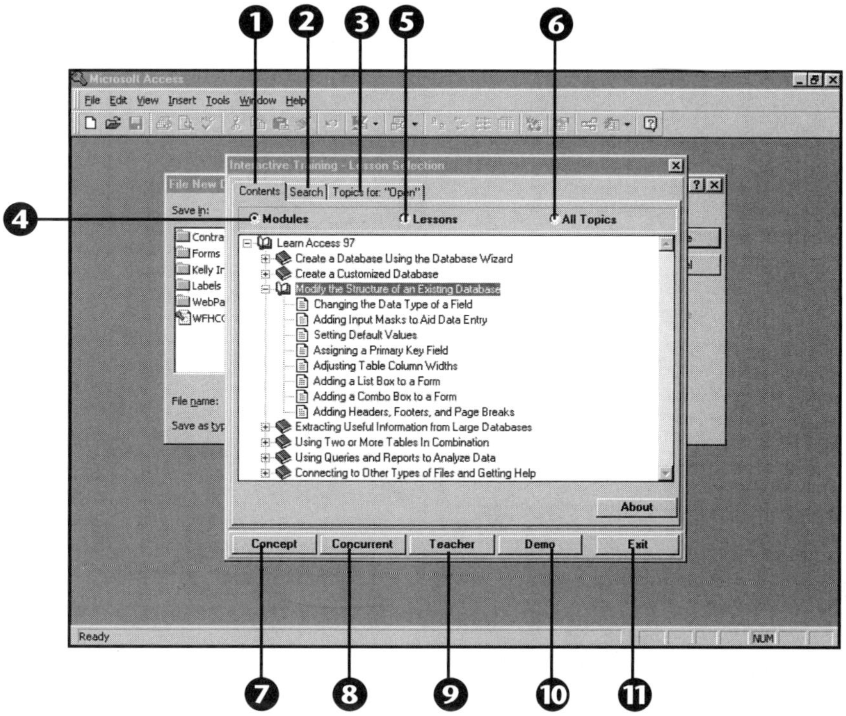


❶ Displays all the modules, lessons, or topics available. Click the plus (+) box to expand the listings and click the minus (–) box to contract the listings. A description of each selected topic appears below the list box.

❷ Enables you to quickly locate topics of interest. You can enter a keyword to find all related topics.

❸ Displays only those topics that relate to your working application. A description of each selected topic appears below the list box.

❹ When selected, displays the Learn On-Demand titles (modules) that are applicable to the working application. Expanding modules displays the lessons within them. The lessons can then be further expanded to display the individual topics.

❺ When selected, groups by lesson the topics that are applicable to the working application. Expanding lessons displays the topics within them.

❻ When selected, displays all topics that are applicable to the working application.

❼ Provides a description of the key concept of the current topic.

❽ Enables you to learn while you work.

❾ Prompts you to enter mouse clicks or keystrokes as you complete tasks in a simulated environment.

❿ Displays an animated demonstration of the task being completed in a simulated environment.

⓫ Closes the **Interactive Training—Lesson Selection** dialog box and returns you to your application. This button does not close Learn On-Demand. The Learn On-Demand icon still appears on your application title bar.

# Using Concept Mode

Although it is important to learn how to perform a task, it is also important to learn when and why a task is performed. Learn On-Demand's *Concept mode* displays the key concept of a topic to help students gain a better understanding of how the topic relates to everyday uses of the application.

Use the following procedure to learn how to use Learn On-Demand's Concept mode:

1 Select a topic describing the task you want to learn how to complete. Click the **Concept** button.

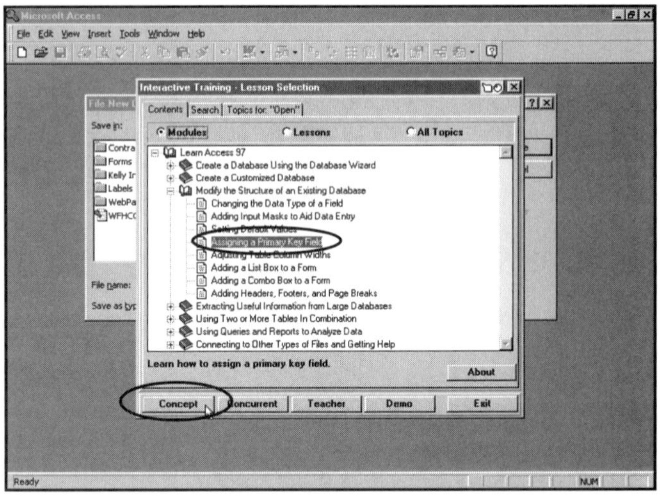

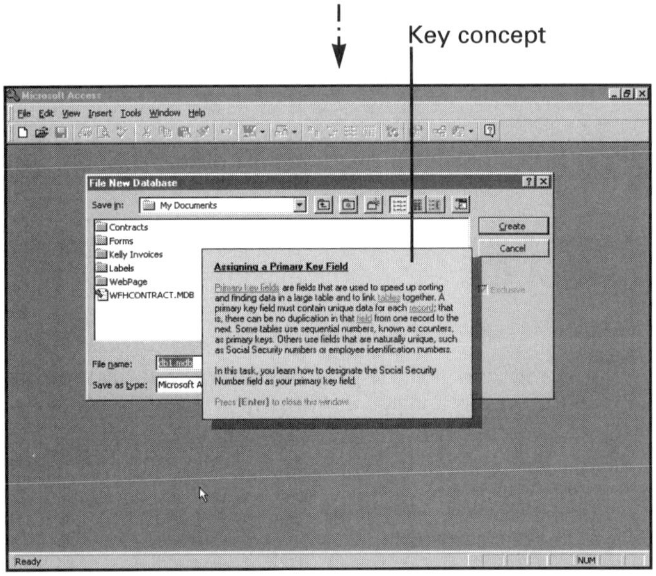


2 Learn On-Demand displays the key concept for the topic. When you have finished viewing the topic, click anywhere or press any key. The concept information disappears from your screen and returns you to the **Interactive Training—Lesson Selection** dialog box.

# Using Concurrent Mode

With Learn On-Demand's *Concurrent mode*, students can learn interactively while working with the "live" application and data. This unique mode makes it possible for students to accomplish real tasks with actual data.

When Concurrent mode is selected, the **Topic** dialog box opens within the application. This dialog box includes a series of steps that need to be followed in sequence to complete the selected task. A red check mark appears when a step has been completed. Note: You must follow these steps exactly as directed.

**1** Concurrent mode prompts the student with a *hotspot* around the area of the screen needing action.

**2** The hotspot is outlined with a red marquee.

**3** The red line drawn from the hotspot to the current step provides easy and clear onscreen directions.

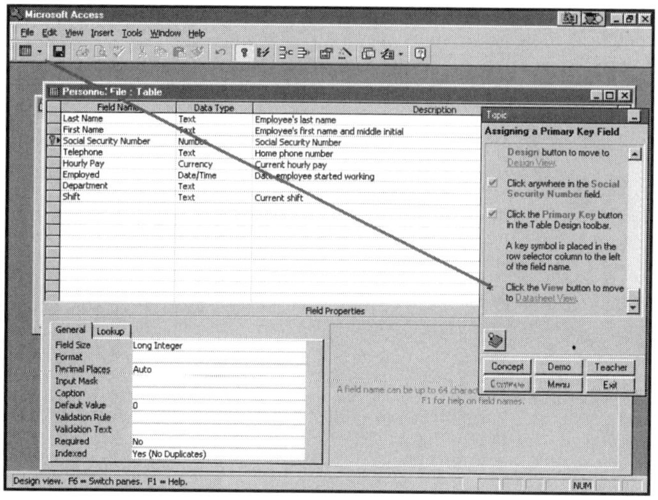


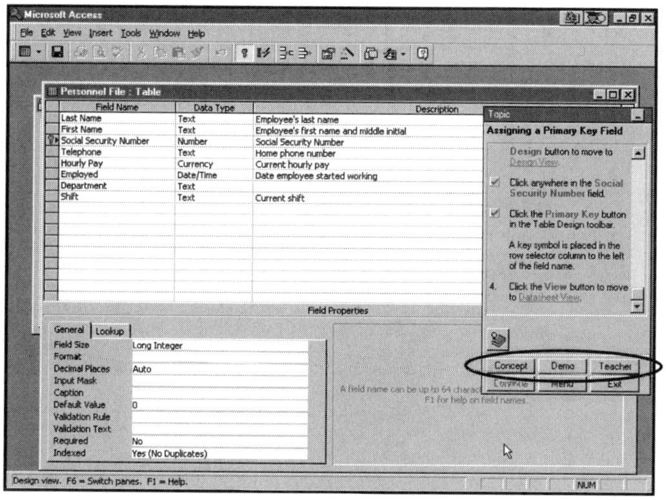


If you need further assistance during your concurrent training session, you can switch to another training mode by clicking the **Concept**, **Demo**, or **Teacher** mode buttons.

# Using Teacher Mode

*Teacher mode* prompts students to enter the necessary mouse clicks or keystrokes to complete tasks in a simulated environment. When you are working in Teacher mode, Learn On-Demand places a hotspot over the location where you need to complete an action. The hotspot is outlined with a red marquee. If you make a mistake, Learn On-Demand prompts you to try again. Notice that Teacher mode provides a simulated environment, so active data and system settings in your application are protected. You can control Teacher mode by using the buttons that appear at the bottom of the Teacher mode screen. Use the following procedure to learn how to complete a task in Learn On-Demand's Teacher mode:

**1**  Click the **Teacher** button to open the **Interactive Training—Lesson Selection** dialog box, if necessary.

**2** Select a topic describing the task you want to learn how to complete. With the topic selected, click the **Teacher** button.

**3** Learn On-Demand displays an opening screen with the objective of the topic in Teacher mode.

4 Click the **Forward** button to begin training. The training for the selected topic appears in Teacher mode.

Buttons appear at the bottom of the **Topic** dialog box. You can use the buttons, which are described in the following figure, to perform additional Learn On-Demand functions.

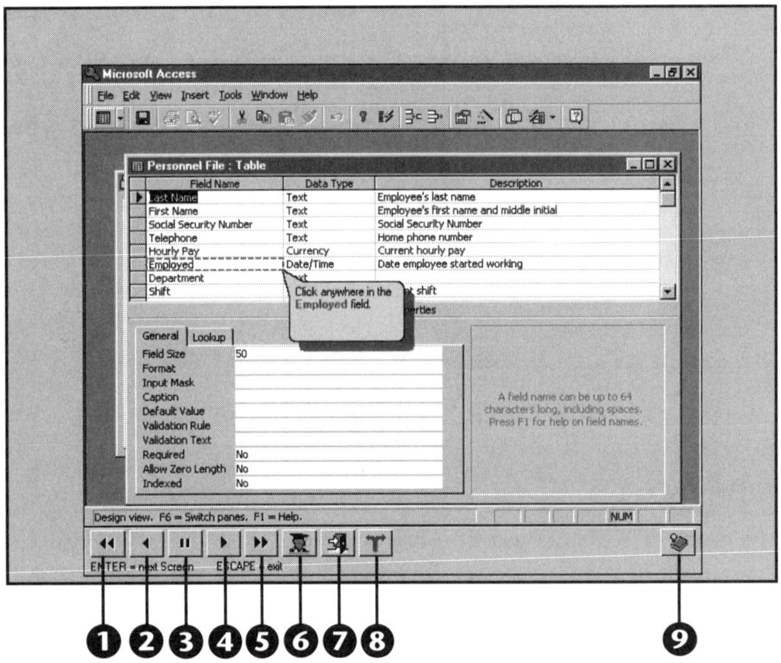


❶ Enables you to move to the beginning screen within a topic. (Applicable for multiple-step topics only.)

❷ Enables you to move backward one step at a time.

❸ Pauses Teacher mode.

❹ Enables you to move forward one step at a time.

❺ Enables you to move to the last screen within a topic.

❻ Returns you to the **Interactive Training—Lesson Selection** dialog box. From this dialog box, you can select another topic.

❼ Exits Teacher mode.

❽ Alternative button. If this button is black, it will show an alternative way to complete a task.

❾ Displays the key concept for the selected topic. Tells you when you would use a software function and why.

In addition to the buttons, pressing the ↵Enter key advances Teacher mode one frame at a time. Pressing the Esc key exits Teacher mode.

**Pothole:** Whenever text input is required in Teacher mode, the requested text must be entered exactly as suggested.

# Using Demo Mode

*Demo mode* enables students to learn by watching an animated demonstration of operations being performed. All required activities, such as moving the mouse and selecting menu items, are completed automatically.

When students are working in Demo mode, they can stop the demonstration at any time by pressing the Esc key. They can also pause the animation by holding the ⇧Shift key. Releasing the ⇧Shift key resumes the demonstration.

Use the following procedure to learn how to complete a task in Learn On-Demand's Demo mode:

1. Click the **Teacher** button to open the **Interactive Training—Lesson**. The **Interactive Training—Lesson Selection** dialog box opens.
2. Select the topic describing the task you want to learn how to complete. Click the **Demo** button. Learn On-Demand displays an animation that demonstrates how to complete the task.
3. You can obtain more information about a topic at any time while using Demo mode by pressing the F1 key to display the **Concept** button. Clicking this button once displays conceptual information about the task, and clicking it again removes the information from your screen. Pressing the Esc key removes the button. Depending on the topic being viewed, other buttons may also appear, including the **In Depth**, **Quick Tip**, or **Pothole** buttons.

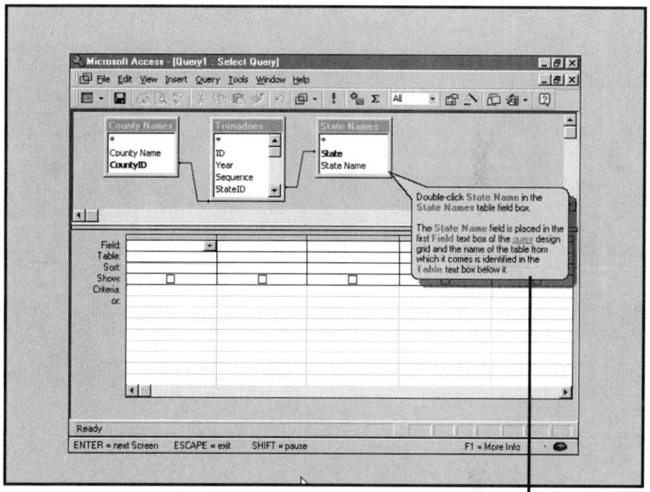


Step-by-step animation

# Searching by Topic

After you have started Learn On-Demand and are in the application (with your file open) for which you want training, you can select a topic. Simply choose a selection from the list of available modules, lessons, or topics from the **Search** tab in the **Interactive Training—Lesson Selection** dialog box.

**1** Click the **Search** tab. The **Search** page appears.

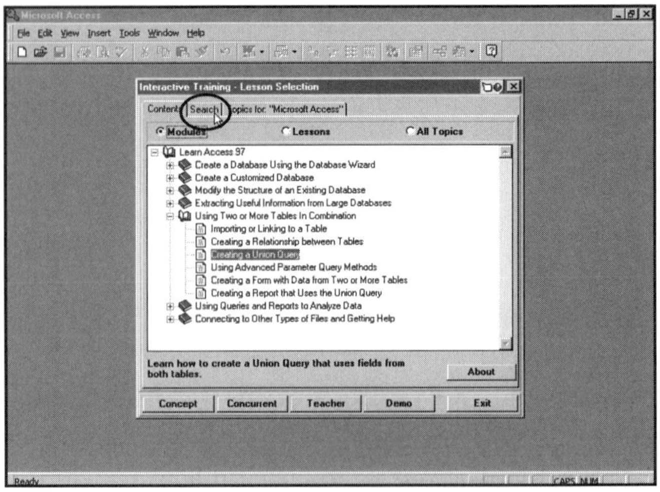


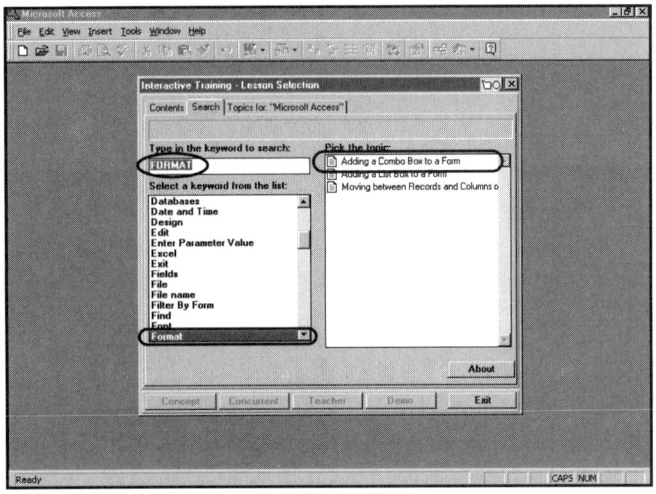


**2** Type the keyword **<u>FORMAT</u>**.

**3** Related keywords of **format** appear in the **Select a keyword from the list** box. Select **Format** from the list.

**4** Related topics appear in the **Pick the topic** list box.

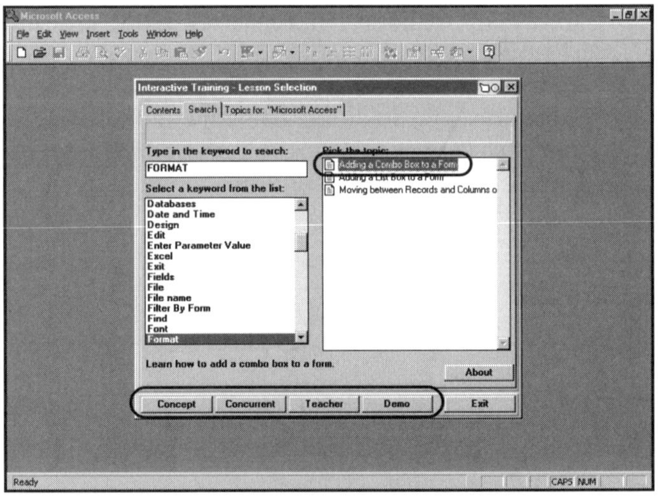


**5** Select a topic from the **Pick the topic** frame.

**6** Select your desired mode: **Concept, Concurrent, Teacher**, or **Demo**. Follow the steps as outlined on your screen.

## Exiting Learn On-Demand

Use the following procedure to exit Learn On-Demand:

**1** Click the **Learn On-Demand** button on the application title bar. The **Learn On-Demand** menu appears.

**2** Click the **Exit** command. The **On-Demand—Exit** dialog box opens.

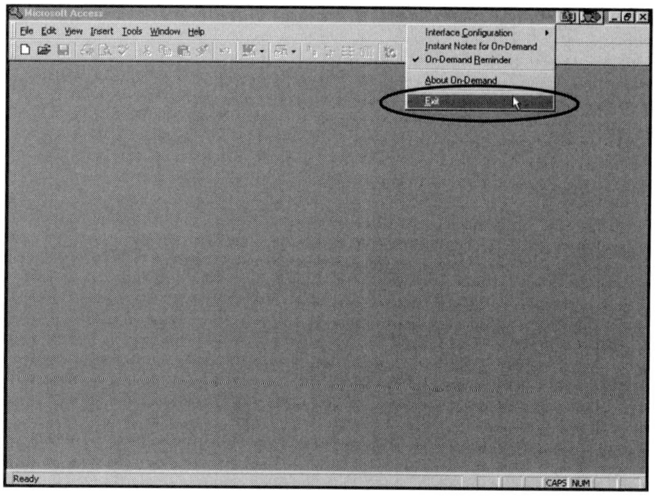


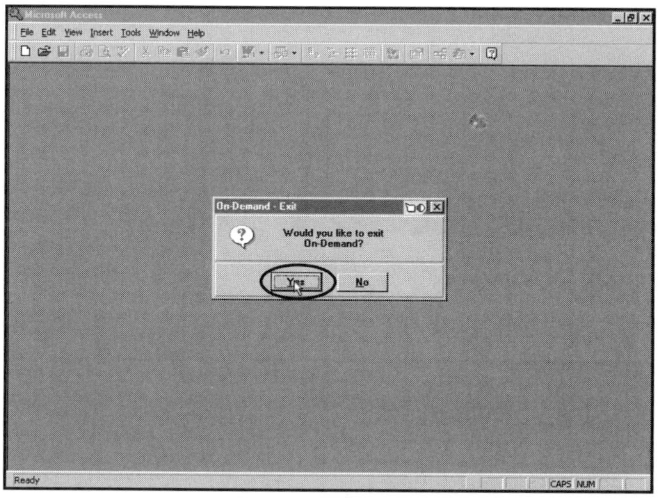


**3** Click **Yes**. Learn On-Demand closes.

# Technical Support

Should you need assistance installing or operating Learn On-Demand, email Technical Support at **support@mcp.com**.

# Glossary of Terms

**Concept mode** Learning mode displaying the key concept of a topic. Explains when, where, and why you would use a program's features, as well as any other important conceptual information about a topic.

**Concurrent mode** Learning mode enabling you to learn interactively while you work without leaving your "live" application.

**Content files** Graphics and lesson files associated with Learn On-Demand.

**Demo mode** Learning mode enabling you to learn by watching an animated demonstration of operations being performed in a simulated application environment.

**Hotspot** Area where user input is required.

**Keyword** A word or phrase used to find a specific training topic. Users enter keywords on the **Search** page in the **Interactive Training—Lesson Selection** dialog box.

**Teacher mode** Learning mode enabling you to learn interactively by prompting you to enter mouse clicks or keystrokes as you complete tasks in a simulated application environment.

**Topic** The most specific level of organization within PTS courseware titles. Each topic provides all the information required to complete a specific task within an application.

# Table of Contents at a Glance

# Table of Contents

## Lesson 3: Modify the Structure of an Existing Database 64



## Lesson 4: Extracting Useful Information from Large Databases 94



## Lesson 5: Using Two or More Tables In Combination 128

# Introduction

As computer technology advances at lightning speed, more and more people turn to Que Education and Training. It is easy to get lost in the technoshuffle of software releases, hardware upgrades, new operating systems, and online technology. We've published more than 500 titles written by people who are the absolute best in their field. With a strong network of experts, Que Education and Training knows how to provide readers with support, guidance, and insight they can trust.

We do more than just look nice on your bookshelf.

You'll find Que Education and Training books in offices, classrooms, and homes across the United States and abroad. Our books are easy to find. They are the ones that are highlighted and marked with pages turned down. Most likely, you'll find them right beside the computer—ready to help in troubleshooting and problem solving. We do more than just look nice on your bookshelf.

Que Education and Training is quickly becoming the leader in developing instructional materials. Our *Learn* courseware is anchored in the practical and professional needs of all types of students.

We were founded in the belief that people want to learn from experts. Just as your students expect you to be a pro, you should demand that the courseware you use is top of the line. You deserve expert advice and professional techniques, as well as thorough annotations, classroom exercises, and supplements that make your job easier while allowing you to teach the best possible course. You can trust Que Education and Training to deliver what you and your students need to take you wherever technology goes.

Our *Learn* courseware and accompanying *Annotated Instructor's Editions* are designed by instructors who understand the special challenges of providing computer instruction.

*Learn Access 97, Annotated Instructor's Edition* is designed for use by college instructors. The authors have made every effort to give you useful and practical information to ensure your teaching success. Our *Learn* courseware and accompanying *Annotated Instructor's Editions* (*AIEs*) are designed by instructors who understand the special challenges of providing computer instruction. The questions, tips, and examples used throughout the *AIE* provide students with instruction adapted to their needs, interests, and experience.

The *Annotated Instructor's Edition* can be used by instructors in various settings and with varying teaching experience. New instructors will make good use of the teaching tips and discussion questions that help them teach successfully the first time. Experienced instructors will value the fresh approaches and ideas for teaching familiar topics.

The *Annotated Instructor's Edition* includes several sections that will help you prepare for teaching the course, plan classes with the amount of time available, assess the students' skill levels before and after the course, and generally show you interesting and effective ways to present the information. Following is a brief description of the sections of the *Annotated Instructor's Edition*:

- **Preparation for Teaching Your Course.** This section suggests organization techniques, preparation ideas, teaching tips, and ideas for handouts and visuals.
- **Curriculum Guide.** This section provides guidance on how to teach the material within certain time constraints. You can easily adapt the material to one day, twelve hours, or twenty-five hours of instruction for the most effective use of the material.
- **Training Tips, Tricks, and Techniques.** This section gives you practical techniques and tactics from the *Computer Instructor's Personal Training Guide.* You'll get tips on dealing with student's expectations, objections, and hardware failure, as well as advice on body language and delivery.

- ***Annotated Instructor's Edition.*** The largest section of this manual, the *Annotated Instructor's Edition*, provides running commentary, assistance, and guidance during the class. The commentary provides tips, suggestions, and ideas for enhancing training. Annotations are marked clearly so that you can refer to them readily during class. Answers to all the questions and exercises at the end of each project are also included in the guide. You may want to customize and further annotate this part of the *Annotated Instructor's Edition* by adding your own tips in the margin.
- **Test Questions and Answers.** Additional true/false, multiple choice, and completion questions and answers are included in a special section. You may make photocopies of the tests or print the tests from the disc provided at the back of the *Annotated Instructor's Edition.*
- **PowerPoint Slides.** Slides of key points, objectives, and other information are included to supplement the text.

# Using the *Annotated Instructor's Edition*

The *Annotated Instructor's Edition* (*AIE*) is built around the corresponding *Learn* courseware, which assumes a classroom setting. The *AIE* reflects many hours of real-world teaching experience on the topic, offering you invaluable ideas, guidance, and advice to support your efforts in the classroom.

Each *Learn* workbook is designed to provide a great deal of hands-on use by the students. We believe that immersion in a topic is the best way to learn. Students prefer to be active doers rather than passive recipients of information. Whether you're a new or experienced instructor, the *Annotated Instructor's Edition* can help you provide effective instruction for all students in your class.

> We believe that immersion in a topic is the best way to learn. Students prefer to be active doers rather than passive recipients of information.

**Discovery-Based Training**

Students cannot be expected to respond to the basic "instructor lectures—student learns" training. Instead, they respond to discovering answers during hands-on exercises and practice. Don't just tell your students the answers. Allow them to find them with your support and guidance. Discovery-based training isn't rocket science. You provide the road map and let them reach their destination. If you are driving the entire time, they may get there—but they will have no idea how they did it.

Give students the freedom to make mistakes while you facilitate the learning experience. It's quite a difference from the "Do This, Do That" school of training, but it works. Just let the *Annotated Instructor's Edition* show you how.

## Personalizing the Manual

In addition to the numerous supplied examples and pointers, you'll want to add your own ideas to the material to make it your own. We encourage you to customize and personalize the *Annotated Instructor's Edition* as you adapt the material to your teaching style, experiences, and preferences.

Additionally, consider the following points as you teach or prepare to teach these lessons:

- **What was that?** When an unusual comment or question arises in class, make a note in the annotated area (margin) of the *AIE* for future reference.
- **Take notes.** Mark or make note of any methods of explaining a topic that work for you.
- **Prepare for the next time around.** Make copies of additional examples you have used and insert them into the *AIE.*
- **Mark it up.** Circle and highlight points that are important to you.

- **Once upon a time…** Note anecdotes about classroom experiences or personal experiences you have had with the program you're teaching—things that you can draw on in class to make your teaching more genuine.
- **Tell us about it.** Share your experiences with us so that all instructors using our materials can grow through each other's learning experiences.
- **Don't forget:** Relax and have fun!

## Anatomy of a Typical Lesson

Each *Learn* book typically is divided into six to eight lessons, concerning topics such as creating a customized database, extracting useful information from large databases, and using queries and reports to analyze data. Each lesson is then divided into a number of tasks related to that topic. For example, a lesson on extracting useful information from large databases is divided into tasks explaining how to find records, define a filter, and calculate values for a new column of data.

All *Learn* books include specific elements that help the student understand why the lesson is important and what to do if things go wrong.

Each element in *Learn Access 97* was designed to maximize learning and facilitate instruction. All *Learn* books include specific elements that help the student understand why the lesson is important and what to do if things go wrong. Additionally, step-by-step instructions make it easy for the student to complete tasks and follow procedures.

Following is a list of the *Learn* project elements and a description of how each element can help the student:

- **Lesson Objectives.** Starting with an objective gives a student a short-term, attainable goal. Using project objectives breaks the overwhelming prospect of learning the more advanced features of Access 97 into small, attainable, bite-sized tasks.

  Lesson objectives give the instructor a chance to stay focused and not get sidetracked. If questions come up that take away from the overall learning experience of the class, ask yourself whether the question relates to the lesson objective. If it does not, write down the question and save it for "off-line" time later.

**Using Off-Line Time**

Getting sidetracked by answering the wrong questions at the wrong time can leave you playing catch-up later. At the time, it may seem that swaying from your agenda won't be that big of a deal. If it happens enough, you'll find yourself so far from the topic at hand that you'll end the class without covering all the important material.

Creating "off-line" time is a great way to minimize the time you spend answering questions that don't relate to the topic you are covering or that apply to future lessons.

Explain to the class that there will be times that they will ask questions that you will label as off-line. Tell them that these questions will be written down and covered later. Then, as they pop up, write them on a white board or poster board. As you cover them, check them off. If you don't get to them, you can respond in a follow-up letter after the class. If they understand why it is important that you stick to the agenda, they can help you avoid getting sidetracked.

**Warning**: Do not confuse a "clarifying question" with an "off-line question." You always want to provide answers to the questions that directly relate to the subject matter in order to help students understand the material.

- **Why Would I Do This?** This section gives the student the reason these tasks or procedures are important to him. What can the student do with the knowledge? How can it be applied to everyday tasks?
- **Visual Summary.** A screen capture or printout of the results of the lesson is included at the beginning of the lesson to provide students an example of what will be accomplished in the lesson.

- **Step-by-Step Tutorial.** These numbered instructions guide the student to perform the procedures step-by-step. Each step has an accompanying figure placed to the right or left of the step. Each figure provides a visual reinforcement of the task at hand. Additionally, the student can refer to the stepped instructions later, when working on his own.
- **In Depth.** In Depth provides the student with a detailed look at a topic or procedure, or another way of doing something. It's one thing to show students how to do something; it's another issue to show them something "neat." In Depth might be lost on some of the more remedial students in the class; however, many students will take to this section as their favorite. They will walk away with a "better" way, a different insight.

It's one thing to show students how to do something; it's another issue to show them something "neat."

- **Quick Tip.** These provide students with a faster or more efficient way of doing something.
- **Pothole.** These short troubleshooting notes help students anticipate or solve common problems quickly and effectively.
- **Glossary.** New words or concepts are printed in italic the first time they are encountered. Definitions of these words or phrases are included in the glossary at the back of the book.
- **Student Exercises.** This section offers optional True/False, screen identification, and matching exercises designed to check comprehension and assess retention.
- **Application Exercises.** This section enables students to check their comprehension, evaluate their progress, and practice what they've learned. The exercises in this section build on and reinforce what has been learned in each lesson.

## Using the *Annotated Instructor's Edition*

The *Annotated Instructor's Edition* provides the instructor with the same text and elements as the student, but with a number of additions. Each lesson contains a wide variety of margin notes to assist the instructor in conducting a successful class. These notes give the instructor tips on directing the class, provide helpful tips and shortcuts on using the program, point out when slides should be shown, suggest questions to ask students, and provide additional guidance to new as well as experienced instructors.

Included within the *Annotated Instructor's Edition* are the following elements:

- **Lesson Time.** At the start of each project is an estimation of the typical time that it takes to complete that module.
- **On Your Mark.** Kickoff questions are provided that you can use to get students talking about what they expect to learn. These questions are useful for getting feedback from students on the connections they see between the topic and their "real work." They keep the instructor from just diving into a topic and help the students gain an understanding of what they are about to learn. It is the intent of the kickoff questions to create some association with and context for the topic.

Kickoff questions keep the instructor from just diving into a topic and help the students gain an understanding of what they are about to learn. They create some association with and context for the topic.

- **Tip for Instructors.** Each lesson in the *AIE* also contains tips to aid the instructor in presenting the topic. Their content includes such items as pedagogical tips; ideas on how to suggest other applications for a particular feature; deeper examples than those in the student courseware; real-life examples to connect a program feature or operation with a business scenario that students will recognize; discussion, where relevant, of how things are done in other programs (exporting data to WordPerfect instead of Word and QuattroPro instead of Excel); wrap-up discussion ideas ("Can you see yourself using this feature? How? In what situations?"); and suggestions for transition to the next topic.

> One key to students accepting your ability to teach is their belief that you are providing them with more than what is in their book.

- **Tip for Students.** These provide shortcuts for the instructor to share with the students. This gives the instructor the opportunity to share a new and unique tidbit of information not contained in the courseware. One key to students accepting your ability to teach (and therefore their learning acceptance threshold) is their belief that you are providing them with more than what is in their book. Many students leave traditional courseware-driven classes with the feeling that they could have read the book on their own—so why go to class? These sections provide tips for you to share to supplement the class. They make the class appear more of your own design until the time when you have made the class fully your own.
- **Quicksand.** These notes provide a "heads-up" for the instructor to things that are likely to cause problems: how to start using a feature by closing the Office Assistant, how to select a field text box rather than the label, and how to save a file into the proper folder, for example. Quicksand sections point out software problems and other things that might seem easy to you as the instructor, but won't seem easy or intuitive to students.
- **Concept Notes.** These notes shed new light on difficult or challenging concepts and present opportunities for trying out different analogies, metaphors, and examples.
- **Speedy Class.** Ideas for expanding on the material are provided in the Speedy Class notes, which contain comments and additional information to share with a class that is moving quickly and has the time and the ability to grasp the topic in more depth.
- **Q&A.** These sections offer questions designed to check for understanding concepts or procedures at critical junctures.

The elements provided in the *AIE* work in conjunction with the elements in the workbook to contribute to a well-rounded, easy-to-understand-and-use course of study for students. From planning and preparation to the evaluation of the course, the *Learn* method ensures a successful teaching experience for the instructor and the student.

## Preparation for Teaching Your Course

Whether you're wondering if you can be an instructor, or you know you can do the job but would appreciate some guidance, this section can help. Even if you're a seasoned instructor, you'll find some useful ideas in this section for teaching *Learn Access 97.* This section provides suggestions for preparing to teach the course, ideas for class organization and planning, and some tips and hints for teaching the class to your specific audience.

Even if you've never conducted a class before, you can successfully teach this course if you follow the guidelines in the *AIE.* The most important thing you need to know is your application. Become familiar with Access 97 and Windows 95 prior to class, go through the exercises as the student will, and read along in the *Annotated Instructor's Edition.* Experiment with the program and make sure that you're comfortable with it before you ever enter the classroom; then you'll be ready to help others learn Access 97.

Experiment with the program and make sure that you're comfortable with it before you ever enter the training room; then you'll be ready to help others learn Access 97.

## Teaching Experience

As part of the *Learn* series, *Learn Access 97* provides basic to intermediate skills in application training. You should expect your students to have a working knowledge of Windows 95. You may find, however, that some of your students may need a refresher on some aspects of Windows 95. You should be able to provide a basic understanding of Windows 95, as needed.

You will need to be very comfortable with Access 97. This text also covers some components of Excel, Word, and Internet access, so you should be somewhat familiar with each. Although this class is appropriate for an entry-level instructor, we highly recommend that you be well-versed in teaching principles and in the operating system.

Teaching a GUI (graphical user interface) class is much different from teaching a class on a character-based application or operating system such as MS-DOS. It is very important that you become sensitive to the motor skills required of the students that might be new to you. We recommend that you be familiar with using and teaching a GUI interface before teaching this class.

Obviously, the first step to being a successful instructor is to be prepared. Gather all the materials on the subject, organize them, and know where to find the answers to difficult questions. You don't have to know all the answers; no one does. But you should be able either to find the answer to a question or problem, or know where the student can go to find the answer. Reference materials, online Help, and the assistance of other experts in the field are invaluable. Do your research well before your class so that you feel prepared.

Accordingly, the more you know about your subject, the easier it will be to break down things and explain them on a very basic level for those who don't understand a concept or procedure. You also need to practice explaining things in a different way—trying various comparisons or correlations, for example. Your goal is to take advantage of those "teachable moments" and "aha!" experiences that every class contains.

Your goal is to take advantage of those "teachable moments" and "aha!" experiences that every class contains.

## Preparing to Teach *Learn Access 97* Checklist

- **Know your application.** Become familiar with the Access 97 topics to be covered prior to class, go through the exercises as the student will, and read along in the *Annotated Instructor's Edition.*
- **Experiment with the program.** Make sure that you're comfortable with the program before you ever enter the training room; then you'll be ready to help others learn Access 97.
- **Do your homework.** Research on a variety of topics will help prepare you to teach.
    - Get familiar with how the session's Access 97 topics are used in the "real world."
    - Be well-versed in teaching principles and in the operating system.
    - Be familiar with using and teaching a GUI interface before teaching this class.

## Presentation Skills

This course is best taught with a projection system hooked up to your computer. You can show the class what they are about to do, and the class can emulate what they see on the screen. Projection systems can represent a sizable investment on the part of the school. You should have practice using overhead projection systems or practice teaching from printed materials. The cheapest alternative to large-screen projection of the actual program is to use transparencies on an overhead projector, but this is not nearly as effective. If you don't have access to a projection system, plan on doing a lot of roaming around the classroom to examine screens.

> If you are new to teaching with a projection system we highly recommend several dry runs with no audience so that you can become familiar with the equipment.

There are considerations in teaching a GUI application that are not usually considered in training a character-based application. Be aware that the quality of most projection systems is geared for character-based displays. You will need to spend more time pointing to the screen, telling the students what they are looking for. The mouse pointer will frequently "get lost" on many of the less-expensive projection systems, forcing you to pay additional attention to what is happening on the screen, not just to what is on your monitor. If you are new to teaching with this type of media, we highly recommend several dry runs with no audience so that you can become familiar with the equipment.

## Resource CD-ROM

Included on the Resource CD-ROM is a set of PowerPoint slides that you can display onscreen within Windows or use as overhead transparency masters. These slides include summaries of important points, explanations of concepts, and support for discussion of significant interface features, such as toolbars or dialog boxes. Show these overheads as you teach each lesson and refer to them occasionally to vary the class.

You may want to create your own visuals to add to the class. Visuals can include posters, documents, overheads, slides, or any other props to help you get the point across.

## Setting Up the Classroom

> When teaching adults, enable and encourage them to "look at each other's work" for extra support, confirmation, and peer learning.

Each workstation must have Access 97 loaded on it or available on a network. We highly recommend one student per PC, but have successfully taught the class with two per PC, when necessary. Make sure that the computers are grouped so that you can easily move from one to another for individualized help during teaching, and so that each student can view at least one other student on his computer. When teaching adults, enable and encourage them to "look at each other's work" for extra support, confirmation, and peer learning.

> The way your classroom is configured can have an impact on the learning process.

The grouping of computers should face the same direction, toward any screen or board you might use to demonstrate or present visuals. Make sure that the distance from overhead screens, for example, is right for comfortable viewing. Make certain that the room is comfortable as far as temperature and lighting are concerned. All these issues make for a successful class.

You will need to install the Resource CD-ROM sample files on the server (or on each student's PC if the training room is not networked), create subdirectories on the server (or local hard drive) for each workstation, and then put a set of sample files in each subdirectory for each student. Check each computer to make sure that the program works and the files are where you say they will be.

Because each student has access to the PC, there is a constant problem of each PC looking different at the end of the class. You will need to reset each system for the same consistent look and feel to prepare to teach a new class. We strongly recommend that you reset the screens at the beginning of each class. Doing so will reduce any student confusion about screens that may not match.

## Training Resources

Even with excellent courseware and a thorough *Annotated Instructor's Edition*, you must have basic teaching ability to succeed as a computer instructor. Many people have a deep-seated fear of public speaking; you can overcome this fear only with practice. The more comfortable you are in front of an audience, the better you will be perceived by your students, and the more receptive they will be to learning. It is beyond the scope of this book to teach you the art of teaching or of public speaking. You might want to turn to the following resources if you are new to the teaching profession or want to improve your existing skills (much of the following list was downloaded from the CompuServe DPTRAIN forum):

- ***The Complete Computer Trainer.*** Clothier, Paul. McGraw-Hill, New York, NY. One of the outstanding authors of Que E&T's *The Computer Trainer's Personal Training Guide,* Paul Clothier helps veteran and novice instructors alike develop the interpersonal skills needed to be a successful computer instructor.
- ***The Complete Guide to Certification for Computing Professionals.*** Drake Prometric. McGraw-Hill, New York, NY. This comprehensive reference describes what certification is and isn't, and gives you full details on more than 25 certification programs nationwide.
- ***The Computer Trainer's Personal Training Guide.*** Brandon, Bill, et al. Macmillan Computer Publishing, 201 W. 103rd Street, Indianapolis, IN 46290 (1-800-428-5331). Cutting-edge training advice on traditional as well as "hot" topics from a team of experts.
- ***The Computer Training Handbook.*** The MASIE Center, P.O. Box 397, Saratoga Springs, NY 12866-0397 (1-800-98-MASIE or 518-587-3522). You can reach the MASIE Center on the World Wide Web at **http://www.masie.com**. Advice from a training visionary and the founder of the Computer Training & Support Conference.
- ***Games Trainers Play/More Games Trainers Play/Still More Games Trainers Play.*** Scannell, Ed. McGraw-Hill, New York, NY. This series contains icebreakers and other exercises.
- ***Instructional Design Strategies and Tactics.*** Leshin, Cynthia; Pollock, Joellyn; and Reigeluth, Charles. Educational Technology Publications, 700 Palisade Avenue, Englewood Cliffs, NJ 07632. A good primer on the basics of instructional design.
- ***The Internet Trainer's Guide.*** Kovacs, Diane K. Van Nostrand Reinhold Computer, New York, NY. From creating course outlines and conducting presentations to teaching methods and evaluation procedures, this book covers everything readers need to design Internet courses (including seminars, lectures, and hands-on labs).
- ***The Mager Six-Pack,*** a collection of basic books by Robert Mager, et al. You can purchase the following books individually or collectively from Lake Publishing Company, 500 Harbor Blvd., Belmont, CA 94002.

  *Making Instruction Work*: Planning, developing, teaching, and improving.

  *Analyzing Performance Problems* (with Peter Pipe): To train or not to train.

  *Preparing Instructional Objectives*: Mager's best-known work.

  *Measuring Instructional Results*: Criterion testing.

*Developing Attitudes Toward Learning*: Motivating students.

*Goal Analysis*: Why, when, and how to conduct educational goal analysis.

- ***101 Ways to Improve the Quality of Training.*** The MASIE Center, P.O. Box 397, Saratoga Springs, NY 12866-0397 (1-800-98-MASIE or 518-587-3522). You can reach the MASIE Center on the World Wide Web at **http://www.masie.com**. More advice from a training visionary and the founder of the Computer Training & Support Conference.

# Preparing Class Materials

Typically, a class will be set up with students having their own courseware book and their own PC. You'll find it helpful also to have nametags for them to put on top of the monitors.

You may want to review any of the additional exercises and Speedy Class tips in the *Annotated Instructor's Edition*, and then add some exercises of your own.

Consider preparing your own visual aids in addition to the slides and transparency masters included with the *AIE*.

If you need additional equipment, such as an overhead projector, flip chart, or chalkboard, make sure that it is in the room and working before class. Before each class, review discussion questions and other materials so that the subject is fresh in your mind. Gather your materials and organize them so that you can quickly find overheads, reference notes, or any other supplementary items while you teach.

Develop and give your own presentation that introduces the class and instructor, and gives the basic agenda for the course. Pop in and out of it during the course as you introduce each lesson. Build some of the features that the class uses into your presentation.

You need to keep in mind the hardware that the presentation will be running on.

## Opening the Class

At the beginning of class, introduce yourself, and list some of your credentials and background. Even if you work with the students or know them personally, you should take a few minutes to give them some of your qualifications. You could mention other classes you teach, reference other companies you train, and any other information pertinent to this class. Keep this introduction short but informative.

How will Access 97 make the students' work easier, faster, and more efficient? How will mastery of Access 97 enable them to succeed professionally? Tie the application to the students' situation as much as possible. The *AIE* offers some "kickoff" questions ("On Your Mark") at the beginning of each project to encourage the students to make these associations.

Now you're ready to begin training.

## Closing the Class

You can come full circle with the opening class discussion by asking the students how they see themselves using their new skills.

At the end of each class, ask questions to make sure that the students have understood the key topics covered. The *AIE* includes question and answer sections at the end of each lesson. You can also add your own questions and comments. You can come full circle with the opening class discussion by asking the students how they see themselves using their new skills.

## Resource CD-ROM

A Resource CD-ROM has been included with your *Annotated Instructor's Edition.* This CD-ROM contains data files to be used by students as they work through the text. Also included on the CD-ROM are the solution files, which show the end result of students' work on the data files. In addition, there is a PowerPoint presentation, which can also be printed and used as handouts. The CD-ROM also includes additional test questions and answers.

The CD-ROM is set up with the following directories.

- SOLUTION, which contains the solution files that show how a student's file should look at the end of a tutorial. These files are named with the logical name the student was asked to assign at the beginning of a tutorial. Solution files are also provided for the "Application" exercises at the end of each lesson.
- PPTSLIDE, which includes the "Visual Summary," lesson objectives, concepts, and other information to augment your instruction.
- STUDENT, which contains the data files your students will use to complete the tasks in the textbook and the "Application" exercises provided at the end of each textbook lesson. The filenames correspond to the filenames called for in the textbook, such as LESS0101, LESS0102, and so on.
- TESTQA, which includes test questions and answers.
- ADDEXER, which includes additional exercises to accompany the lessons.
- PPTVIEW, which contains PowerPoint Viewer 97.

## The Successful Instructor's Checklist

- **Get organized.** Gather all the materials on the subject, organize them, and know where to find the answers to difficult questions.

  You should be able either to find the answer to a question or problem, or know where the student can go to find the answer. Reference materials, online Help, and the assistance of other experts in the field are invaluable.
- **Do some research.** Do your research well before your class so that you feel prepared.
- **Practice.** Try explaining things in a different way, trying various comparisons or correlations.
- **Prepare your classroom.** Hook up your projection system to the instructor's computer. Set up the classroom so the computers face your projection area. Make sure that the distance from overhead screens, for example, is right for comfortable viewing.
  - If you don't have access to a projection system, plan on doing a lot of roaming around the classroom to examine screens.
  - Make sure additional equipment, such as an overhead projector, flip chart, or chalkboard, is in the room before class.
- **Test the equipment.** Make sure the above-mentioned equipment is in working condition.

- **Conduct dry runs.** We highly recommend several dry runs with no audience so that you can become familiar with the equipment.
- **Create your own supplements.** You may want to create your own visuals to add to the class. Visuals can include posters, documents, overheads, slides, or any other props to help you get the point across.
- **Prepare the equipment.** Do not wait until the last minute to install software and check the equipment.
  - Load Access 97 on each workstation. Make sure that each application works.
  - Install the Resource CD-ROM sample files on the server (or on each student's PC if the classroom is not networked).
  - Create subdirectories on the server (or local hard drive) for each workstation.
  - Put a set of sample files in each subdirectory for each student.
  - Check each computer to make sure that the program works and the files are where you say they will be.
  - Reset each system for the same consistent look and feel to prepare to teach a new class.
- **Get ready for the class.** Having your classroom ready for students involves more than having equipment up to speed. The more comfortable your students are, the more they will be prepared to learn.

  Make certain that the room is comfortable as far as temperature and lighting are concerned.
- **Refresh your memory.** Don't wait until it's too late to make one last run-through.
  - Review discussion questions and other materials so that the subject is fresh in your mind.
  - Gather your materials and organize them so that you can quickly find overheads, reference notes, or any other supplementary items while you teach.

## Day-of-Course Checklist

- At the beginning of class, introduce yourself, and list some of your credentials and background.
- Refer often to and be familiar with the *Annotated Instructor's Edition* as you facilitate Discovery-Based Training.

# Curriculum Guide

The Curriculum Guide will enable you to give your class the best information in the amount of time available. Whether you are conducting an abbreviated class or using all the lessons, you won't have to walk out of the class kicking yourself for skipping an important component. We've clearly noted which projects and exercises are core units. You'll also be able to quickly see which projects are good to know, but not absolutely vital.

| Lesson | One Day of Instruction | 12 Hours of Instruction | 25 Hours of Instruction |
|---|---|---|---|
| 1 | Tasks 1–7 | Tasks 1–7, Application Exercises 1-4 | Tasks 1–7, all activities |
| 2 | Tasks 1–9 | Tasks 1–9, Application Exercise 1–5 | Tasks 1–9, all activities |
| 3 | Tasks 1–7 | Tasks 1–8, Application Exercise 1–3 | Tasks 1–8, all activities |
| 4 | Tasks 1–8 | Tasks 1–8, Application Exercises 3–4 | Tasks 1–8, all activities |
| 5 | Tasks 1–6 | Tasks 1-6, Application Exercises 1–3 | Tasks 1–6, all activities |
| 6 | Tasks 1, 4–8 | Tasks 1–8, Application Exercises 1–2 | Tasks 1–8, all activities |
| 7 | Tasks 1–4 | Tasks 1–8, Application Exercises 1–3 | Tasks 1–8, all activities |

# Training Tips, Tricks, and Techniques

Even a seasoned pro can benefit from the experience of others. The following section was condensed from *The Computer Trainer's Personal Training Guide,* written by Bill Brandon and a host of training experts. In this section, you'll hear practical advice about a variety of topics.

- Identifying student expectations
- Establishing a comfortable pace for the students
- Using body language to your advantage
- Making the learning process enjoyable
- Making differences in skill sets work
- Dealing with objections
- Avoiding disaster: When (not if) equipment fails

## Identifying Student Expectations (Why Are They Here?)

It is critically important for you to ask the students what they expect to gain from the course. The easiest, most natural time to do this is at the beginning of the first class session.

When you ask students what they expect to gain, there are several ways to have the students answer:

- Each student calls out his expectations and objectives.
- Students take time to list their expectations and objectives individually, combine lists with their immediate neighbor, and finally combine the list of that pair with

the list of another pair of students. A spokesperson for the group then reads the list out loud.

- Each student writes down on a small piece of paper one thing he hopes to learn in the class and crumbles it into a small ball. On a signal, each student tosses his paper across the room to another student (this can be done several times to get good mixing). After everyone has somebody else's objective, the items are read off the notes one at a time.

The last two methods generate much more activity than the first. They model the level of participation desired and generate a sense of fun and cooperation. The third method has the added benefit of protecting group members who may be shy about saying what they think is important. On the other hand, the first method is good to use when the group is comfortable together or already has a good sense of play and team spirit.

In each case, the instructor (or an assistant selected from the group) should record the expectations on a large piece of newsprint or a flipchart at the front of the room. When the list is complete, tear it off and tape it to the wall so that it remains visible throughout the class.

> There is no reason why the instructor should feel solely responsible for regulating the flow of the class.

## Give Students Control over the Pace

During a class, it is often hard for the instructor to judge whether people are satisfied with the pace of the class.

One interesting way to give control of the pace to the students is to hand out small paper ballots just before a break. On each ballot, students mark whether they feel the class is moving too slowly, too quickly, or about right. Collect these in a small receptacle at the door. Tally them on the marker board or on the newsprint pad so that students can see the results of the vote. Adjust your pace accordingly.

If you are lucky enough to be working in a classroom equipped with responder units, you can do the same thing without having to wait for a break. (In fact, you can use the responder units to ask whether students want to take a break.) A responder unit is a small box at the student's station that provides a variety of buttons for responding to true/false and multiple-choice questions. The results of the responses to a question are automatically tallied and displayed to the instructor on a separate monitor. Similar systems are sometimes used in distance-learning classrooms to give feedback to instructors who may be located miles away from their students.

> Proper body language can not only help the class understand the message you are conveying, but it can also help you stay in control and appear confident—even when you aren't!

## Body Language

Have you ever looked out in a class only to find a sea of blank faces? Have you ever wondered why the students aren't with you? Sometimes how you say something is as important as what you say.

- When you stand, keep your feet about shoulder-width apart, one foot slightly toward the students to whom you are speaking.
- Turn your whole head to look at students as you speak to them, not just your eyes.
- Use your hands to gesture and emphasize points; keep your elbows loose, not tucked into your ribs. Relax your shoulders and make your hand movements large and free.
- Move into the group of students as much as possible, rather than staying up behind a lectern or your own terminal.

- If you are using overhead slides or projected images, say a few words related to what is on the next image before you display it.
- Choose short words, action verbs, and active voice when you talk.

## Educational Entertaining

An appropriate amount of fun helps people learn without making them consciously aware of the fact that they are learning.

There is a fine line between being entertaining and being entertainment. You cross that line only when the students cease to be involved as active participants in the learning process. If you had the video camera running when the line was crossed, you would see students' behavior go from "using the software" to "watching the instructor" and stay there.

So how does an instructor stay entertaining, yet keep the focus and the activity out among the students?

**Do the expected in unexpected ways.** For example, if you need to "borrow" somebody from the class for a demonstration or to lead a group, ask for a volunteer. Say only that you need this person to do a very important job. Eventually someone will volunteer. Then tell this person that his important job is to pick the actual person who will be involved in the demonstration or lead the group. This is a very safe way to get a big laugh—much better than using a joke. It may also help you manage the person who would like to be the "teacher's pet" (you know—the one who always has his hand up first to answer a question).

**Do things in a way that requires people to move around.** When you review a step-by-step procedure, use a Koosh ball. Toss the ball to one of the students. This person must give the first step in the procedure and then toss the ball to another student. The second person gives the second step and throws the ball to someone who hasn't given a step yet. If someone misses a step, anyone who knows what comes next calls it out and gets the ball to pass on. This continues until the procedure is complete. Not only does this wake everyone up, it gets the know-it-alls to stop playing solitaire.

**Periodically award "fabulous prizes."** (Award prizes such as coffee mugs, mouse pads, or imprinted ballpoint pens for correct responses or performances. You should have a group that is fairly evenly matched if you plan to use this approach fairly.

The key word is appropriate. Should your classroom look like a three-ring circus? Absolutely not. Should people be smiling and looking as if they are having a great experience? Absolutely yes!

## Put Differences in Skill Sets to Work

Use the fact that there is a mixture of skill levels in the room to increase the level of participation by students.

It is neither necessary nor desirable to pair people up according to ability.

Most courseware is created with the assumption that everyone is at the same level. However, it is far more often the case that the group's skill levels are mixed. A strategy that works well is to deliberately place two people at one computer during the exercises that follow demonstration of a procedure. An effective way to do the pairing is to use a totally arbitrary personal characteristic. For example, individuals can only partner with someone who was born in the same season of the year or on the same day of the week as themselves.

While paired up for an exercise, each partner must complete the exercise, with coaching as necessary from his "buddy." Questions may be asked of the instructor, but both partners must each raise a hand, indicating that they could not solve the problem collectively. Change partners after each exercise.

## Dealing with Objections from Students

What's important isn't that you got an objection, but how you handle it.

Even in a well-planned, well-run course, everybody won't always be totally satisfied. In some classes, you will have a student who seems to have some problem with everything you are teaching. In other sessions, all is well until—bang! You get blindsided by a protest from a student.

This happens to every instructor. For any objection or question from a student, you have more than one way to respond so that everybody wins. The choice is yours.

**Meet the Objection.** The most basic, and perhaps natural, response is to meet the objection head on. Stick to your story and explain how your idea works. Sometimes this is effective. Sometimes it just starts a fight, makes you look defensive, and alienates class members.

If you decide to use the head-on response, using Ben Franklin's method: "It seems to me…" or "In my opinion…" helps to soften the response. It's better if you turn to face the other person squarely when you do this, but don't take a step toward or away from the person. Stepping toward the person can seem aggressive. Stepping back weakens your point.

Consider using the word "and" in your reply instead of "but." For example, saying, "I understand how it might seem that way to you and I believe you are overlooking…" keeps the other person listening to you and seems much less harsh than, "I understand what you're saying but you haven't considered…" By using "It seems to me…" or substituting "and" for "but," everybody wins.

**Accept the Objection.** Another basic response is to back off your point. Let the objector have it his way. If you realize that you were wrong, say so. The positive side of this choice is that you can come off looking better in the long run. The down side is that it may invite further attacks or undermine your credibility. Face the person squarely when you back off the point. If the other person is emotional about the objection, take a step back as you say, "You know, you're right." Then drop it and move on. Everybody wins.

**Deflect the Objection.** A third response is good to use when someone has made an objection you'd either like to check out or to discredit totally. Throw out a related question "overhead" to the group: "Has anyone else had an experience like this?" Take note of the answers and respond accordingly. If the question is discounted by the group, face the objector and say, "I'd like to understand the problem better. Are you willing to meet me on the break about this?" In most cases, this will be the last you'll hear about it, and you have helped the person save face. Everybody wins.

**Defer the Objection.** The fourth response is reserved for those times when you want to deal with the objection later. Perhaps someone brings up a point that you plan to address in another part of the program. Perhaps someone raises an objection that has an "agenda" attached. Smile, say you think that's a great question but you want to deal with it a little later in the course, and then write the objection on a piece of newsprint and hang it on the wall. You have acknowledged the point. You can get back to it when (and if) you want to. You are being fair and the objector has had his say. Everybody wins.

## Avoiding Disaster: When (Not If) Equipment Fails

Were Ben Franklin alive today, he would have to amend his famous saying about death and taxes. Hardware failure is now the third certainty in life.

In most classrooms, the weak link is the hardware. After that, the weakest link is the software on the instructor's system. As you plan your classes, keep this in mind. It is wise to have a Plan B for any eventuality.

> In most classrooms, the weak link is the hardware. After that, the weakest link is the software on the instructor's system.

The most commonly needed Plan B has to do with projector bulbs. If you are using an overhead projector or an LCD projector, have a spare bulb in the classroom where you can get to it quickly. Know how to replace the bulb. Remember to turn off the power to the projector before you make the replacement.

The most serious Plan B is the one that deals with the classroom network shutting down during the class. This is a Plan B you must think through carefully before every class. Will you cancel the course? Will you bring in a freestanding PC and a big monitor and continue to demonstrate until the system is restored? Will you shift to alternative media (a videotape or overheads)? You have plenty of choices, but they must be in place before disaster strikes.

.IDE 1–1

# Lesson 1

.IDE 1–2

# Create a Database Using the Database Wizard

LIDE 1–3

**Task 1** Creating an Address Database Using the Database Wizard

**Task 2** Using the Main Switchboard to View a Database Form and Add Text to a New Record

**Task 3** Entering Data in Fields that Use Input Masks and Special Data Types

**Task 4** Using the Reports Switchboard to Preview Database Reports

**Task 5** Examining the Database Table Using the Database Window

**Task 6** Using the "What's This?" Help Tool to Learn About the Design of a Form and a Report

**Task 7** Closing the Database and Exiting Access

LIDE 1–4

## Visual Summary

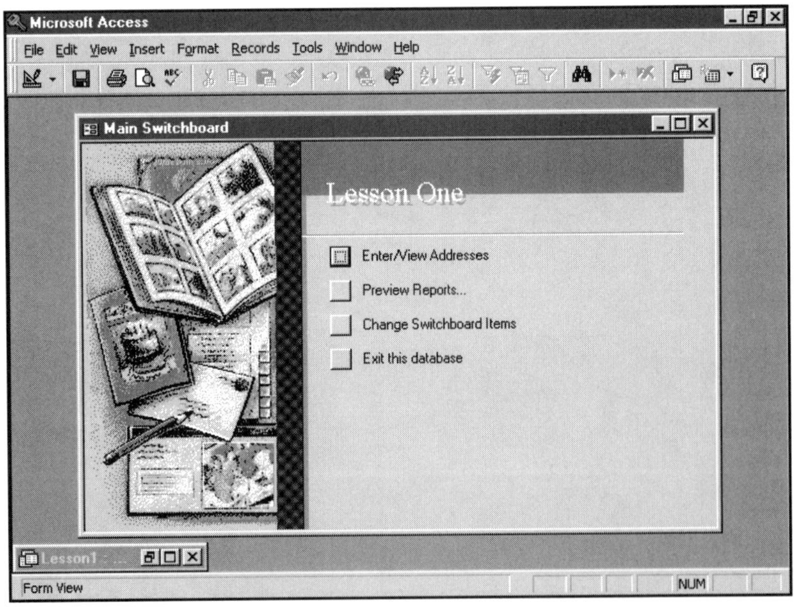


# Introduction

Access is a computerized *database* management system that allows you to store, retrieve, analyze, and print information. It is a system for managing large amounts of data. Companies use databases for many purposes: to manage customer files, to track orders and inventories, and for marketing purposes. An individual might set up a database to track household expenses or manage a list of family, friends, and business addresses. Teachers often set up a database to track students' grades and other class information. A database allows the user to access and manage thousands of pieces of data in an organized, efficient, and accurate manner.

To begin to use Access there are a number of terms that you need to understand. An Access database consists of *tables, queries, forms, reports, macros* and *modules* known generally as *objects.* These objects work together to store, search, input, report, and automate the data. The purpose of these objects is explained in the preface to this book. Please refer to this material for a more detailed overview. The objects of the database are viewed from the *Database window,* which is the window that opens when you open a database.

The approach used in this book emphasizes the coordination of the six objects so that you understand their interaction. The first lesson uses the Database Wizard to give you an overview of a database and each of the objects in the database. In later lessons each object in the database will be examined in more detail.

**On Your Mark**

What types of databases might you create in the real world? (Examples: inventory, sales, finances, accounting, teaching.)

When you are done with this entire lesson, you will have created a database that looks like this:

**Tip for Instructors**

The Learn on Demand Module that applies to Lesson 1 is found in the Create a Database Using the Database Wizard subfolder of Learn Access 97.

**Tip for Instructors**

Some of the features of this text require a custom installation. Be sure to review all of the text prior to teaching the course for the first time.

**Tip for Instructors**

Determine the mixture of jobs and work experiences of your class. Write them down for future reference during this course. Use real-world examples from those different areas.

**Lesson Time**
**60 minutes**

# Task 1

**Tip for Instructors**

The Learn on Demand Module/Lesson "Creating an Address Database Using the Wizard" applies to this task.

# Creating an Address Database Using the Database Wizard

## Why would I do this?

The Access *Database Wizard* is a program that helps you create a database, step by step, by presenting you with a series of options. In each of the steps you make selections that will be used to create your database. The advantage of using the Wizard is that it creates all of the necessary objects for you to be able to operate the database. For someone new to databases, this is a quick way to see how the different objects work together. Later in this book you will learn how to create each of the objects separately.

As you will see, Access contains 22 design templates of the most commonly used databases, including templates for addresses, inventory control, household inventory, a music collection, and students and classes. A design *template* is a pre-designed form or format that can be used instead of creating one of your own.

In this task, you learn how to use the Database Wizard to guide you through the process of creating an address database, using a design template.

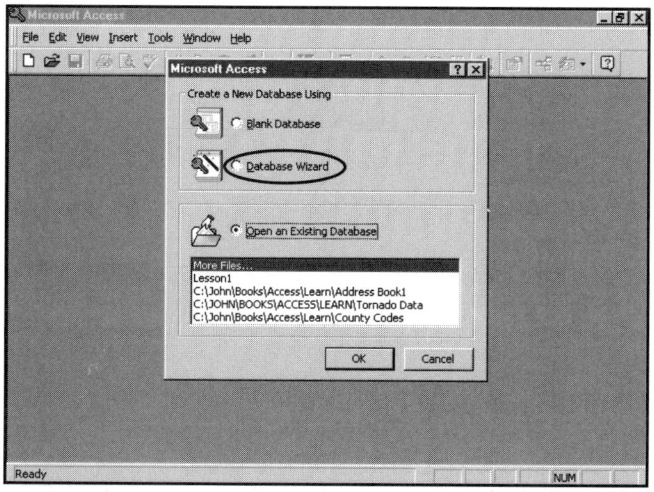


**1** Launch Microsoft Access. The Microsoft Access dialog box opens and provides three choices.

**Tip for Instructors**

Wizards provide a quick, easy setup of a particular feature or file. Some options are given as users are walked through the setup. However, some changes might be necessary to perfect the desired results. Students will learn how to make changes in this text.

**Tip for Instructors**

Explain database components and what they are used for. There is a thorough explanation in the preface of this text (pp. lx–xi).

**Quicksand**

The **Office Assistant** appears if this is the first time Access has been used since installation. Click **Start Using Access** to begin working.

**On Your Mark**

What type of database do you think is most common? *Answer:* **Address book**. Access provides 22 template databases that are commonly used.

**2** Click the **Database Wizard** option and click **OK**. The **New** dialog box opens.

**Tip for Instructors**

Explain the use of tabs in Windows 95 dialog boxes.

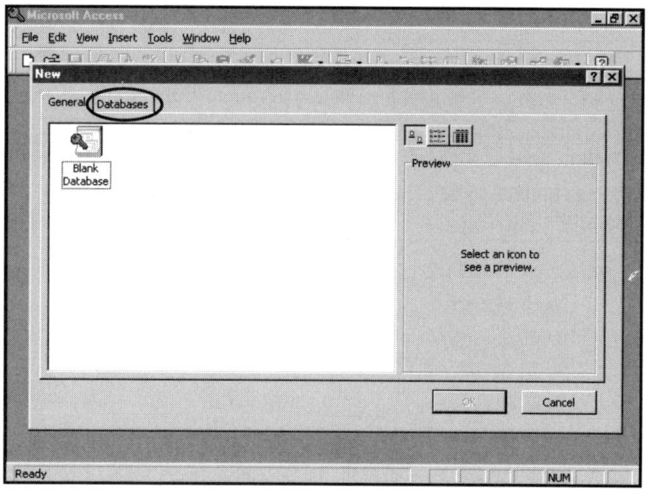

**3** Click the **Databases** tab, if necessary. The selection of existing database design templates is displayed. Click the **Address Book** icon.

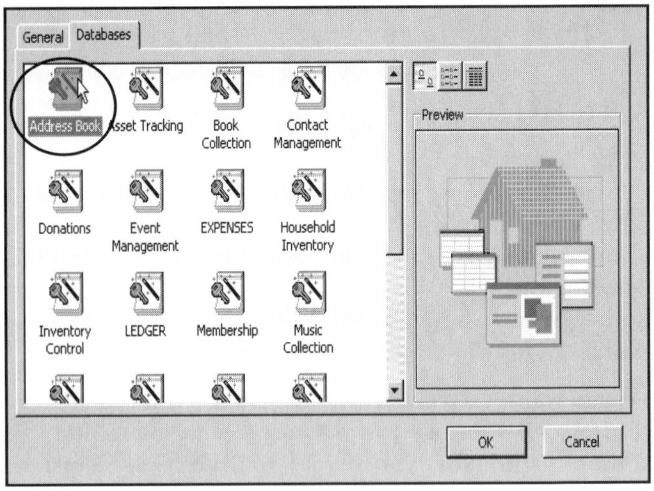


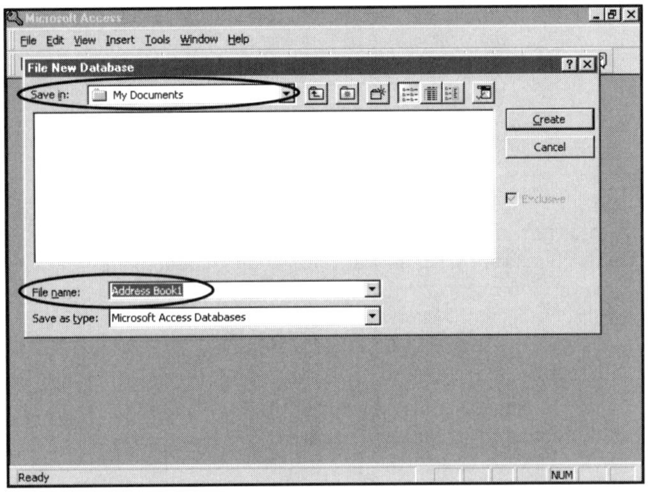


**Tip for Students**

This dialog box is used like the **Save As** dialog box. You must name the database before creating it.

**4** Click **OK**. The **File New Database** dialog box opens.

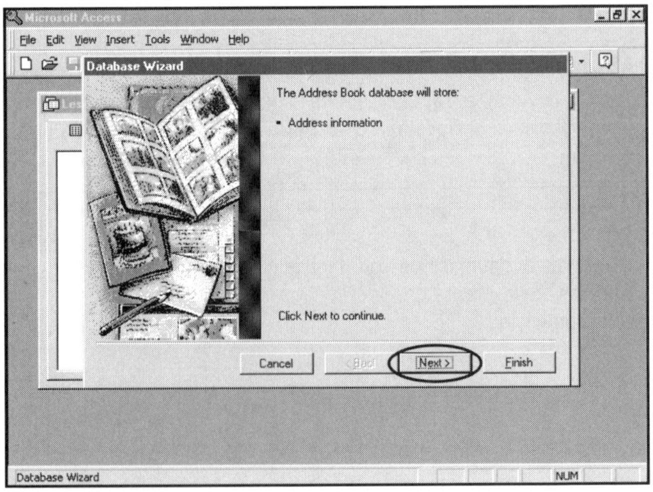


**Tip for Instructors**

An explanation of folders and file organization might be necessary.

**Quicksand**

Watch students to be certain they choose the correct folder for storage.

**5** Click the **File name** box and type **Lesson1**. Use the **Save in** box to locate the folder where your instructor has suggested that you save your files. Click **Create**. The **Database Wizard** dialog box opens.

**6** Click **N**ext. Another **Database Wizard** dialog box opens. Scroll down the list of fields in the **Fields in the table** box. These are the fields that will be included in your address database. The fields shown in italics are optional. Click the **Yes, include sample data** option at the bottom of the dialog box.

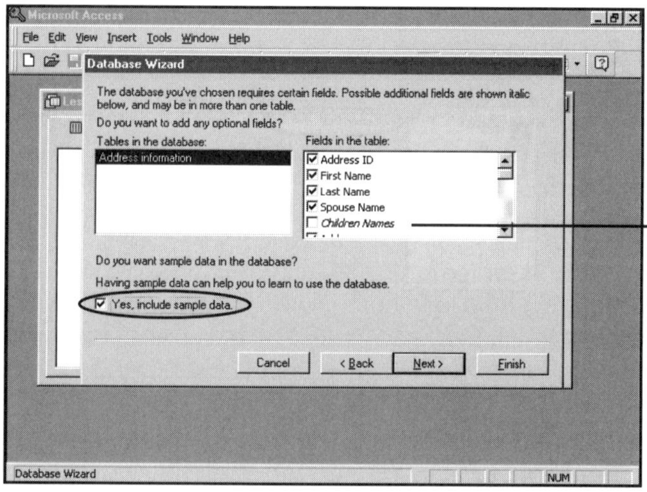


**Tip for Students**

When scrolling through the list, be careful not to click the field name items. You might accidentally deselect a field. If you do, simply click that field again to reselect it.

**Pothole:** If you did not click the "Yes, include sample data" box, your database will not include any data. Choose the Back button to return to the previous screen and click this option. This will ensure that data is included in your database.

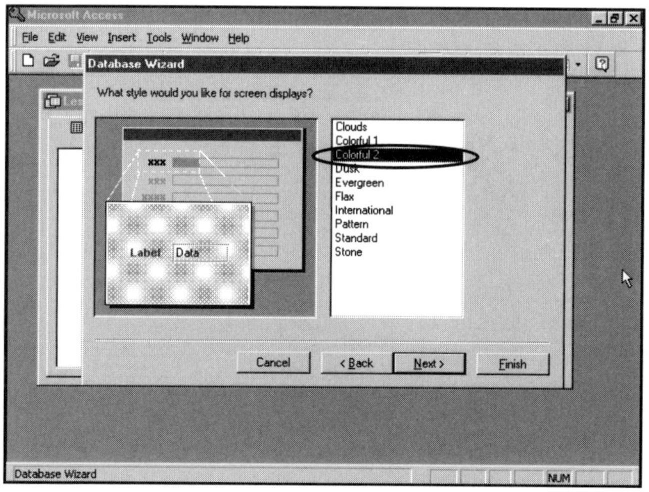


**7** Click **N**ext. A **Database Wizard** dialog box opens that allows you to pick from several backgrounds. **Click Colorful 2.**

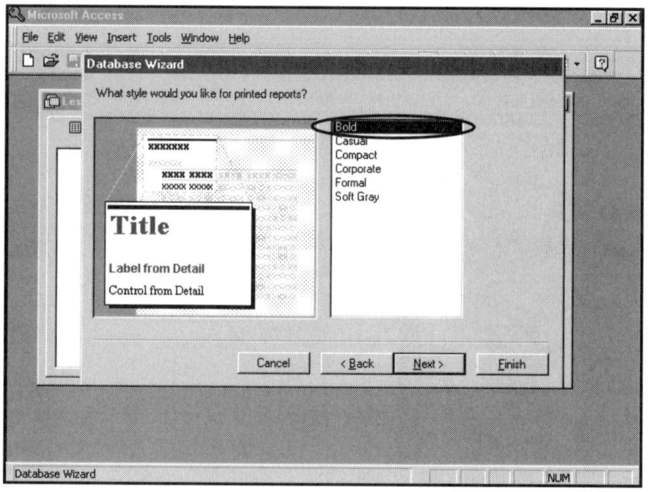


**8** Click **N**ext. A **Database Wizard** dialog box opens that allows you to pick a font style. Click **Bold**.

**Tip for Instructors**

The tab order will be discussed in Lesson 2, Task 7.

**3** Press Tab three times to advance to the **Home Phone** field. Notice that the selection jumped from the bottom of the first column of fields to the top of the second column. The sequence of fields on each page of the form the Tab key advances to is called the *tab order.*

**Tip for Students**

To move forward one field, press Tab. To move back one field, press Shift + Tab.

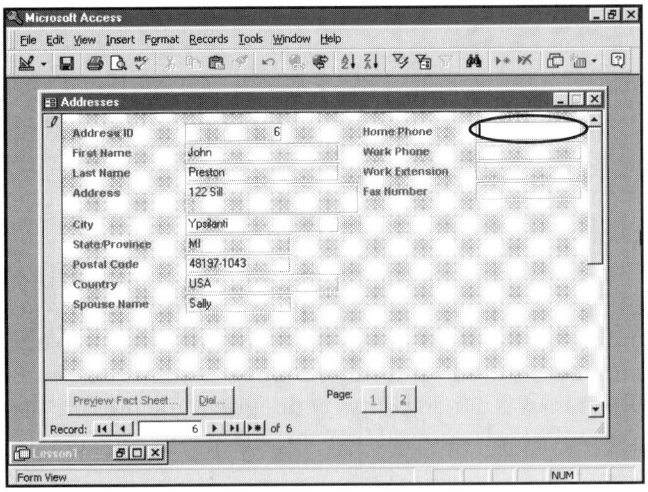


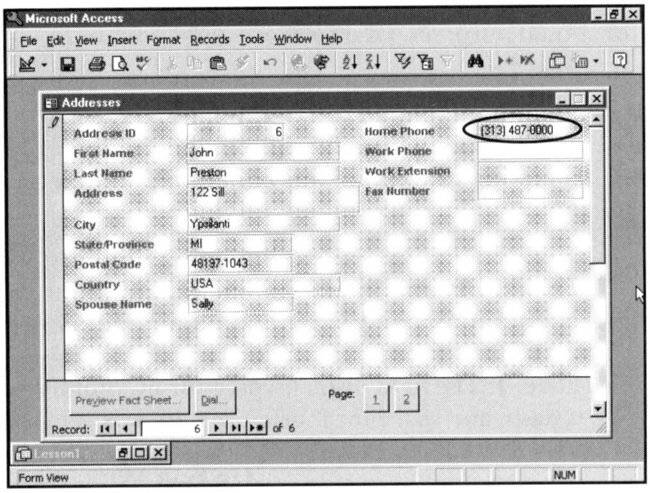


**Quicksand**

Some students may run out of room for their numbers because they did not start at the beginning of the field.

**4** Type <u>3134870000</u> and press Tab. Notice how the input mask automatically adds the parentheses and dashes.

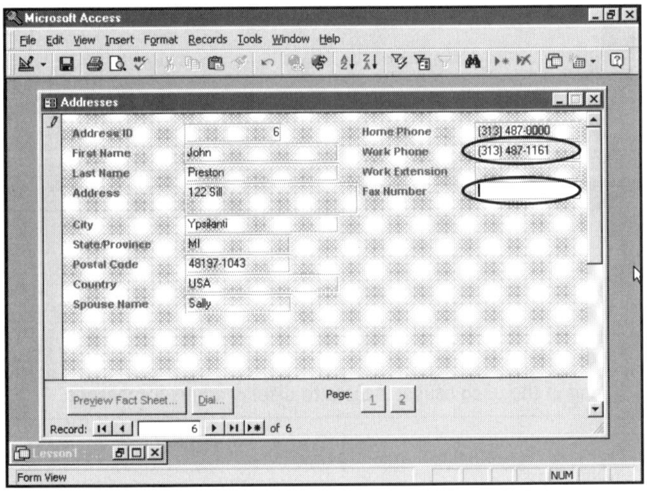


**5** Type <u>3134871161</u> to enter the work phone and press Tab. Press Tab once more to skip the Work Extension field. Your cursor is now in the **Fax Number** field.

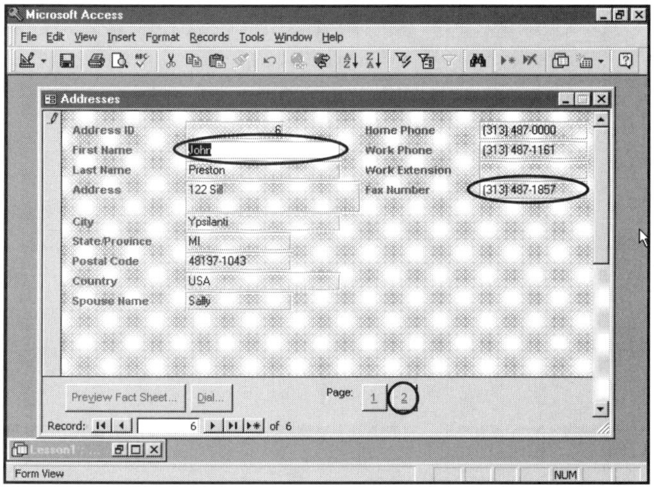


**6** Type **3134871857** to enter the Fax number and press Tab. The cursor will return to the **First Name** field on the form.

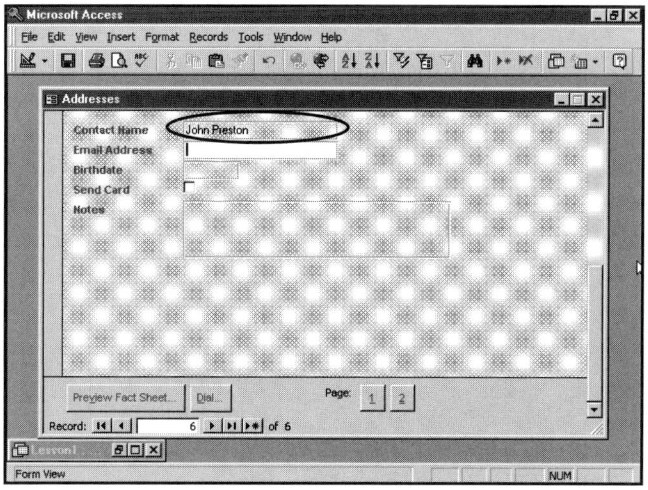


**7** Click the **2** button to go to the second page of the form. Notice that the **First Name** and **Last Name** fields have been combined to create **Contact Name**. This is an example of a *concatenated field.*

> **Concept**
>
> A *concatenated field* is field that combines two or more fields within a form to create a new field. It is created from the field properties in Design View.

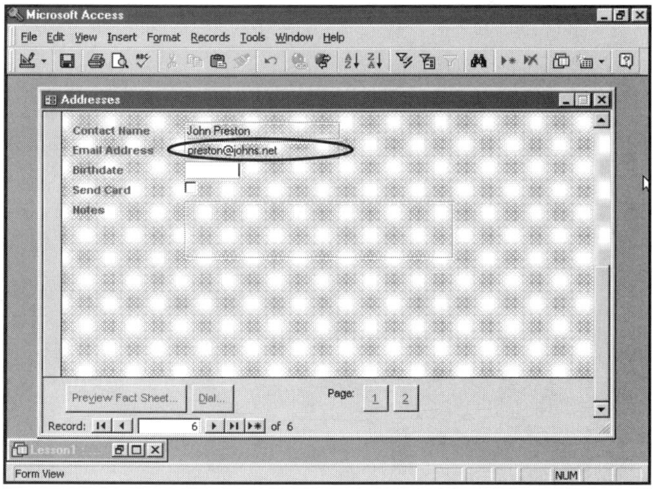


**8** Type **preston@johns.net** in the **Email Address** box and press Tab to advance to the **Birthdate** box.

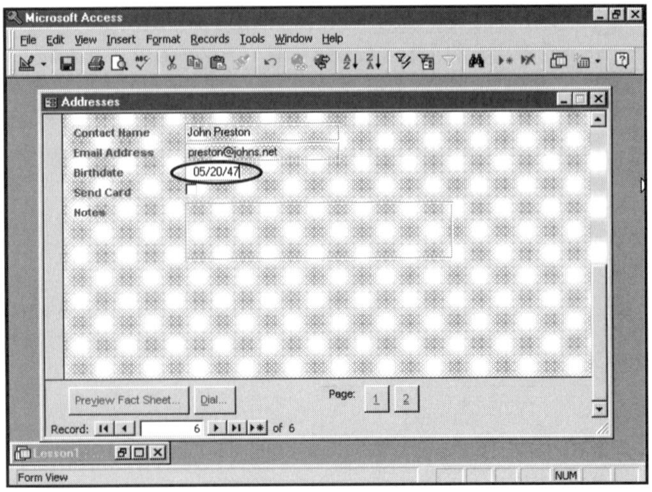


**9** Type **<u>052047</u>**. Notice that the input mask adds slashes and that the date requires a leading zero. This is an example of a field that uses *date* as the data type.

**10** Click the check box next to the **Send Card** label. This is an example of a field that uses the *Yes/No* data type. If you were to click it again, it would deselect it.

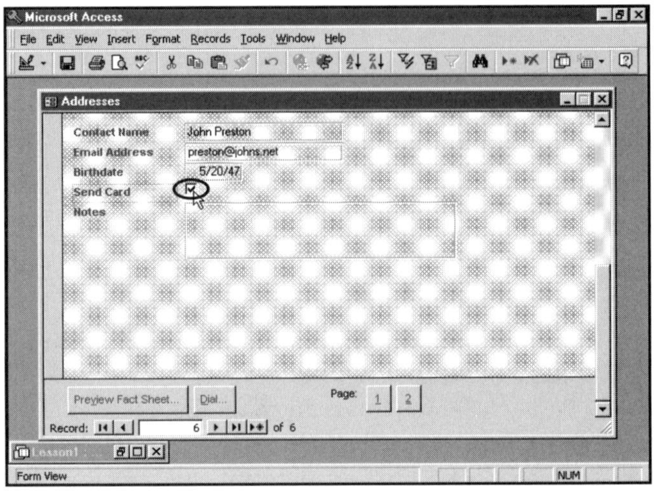


**Tip for Students** !

To select or deselect a check box by using the keyboard, press (Spacebar).

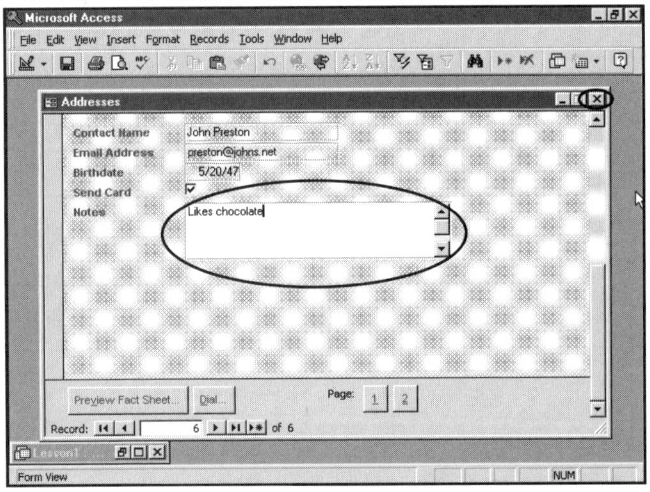


**11** Click in the **Notes** box and type **<u>Likes chocolate</u>**. This is an example of a field that uses the *memo* data type where unstructured and unlimited comments can be added.

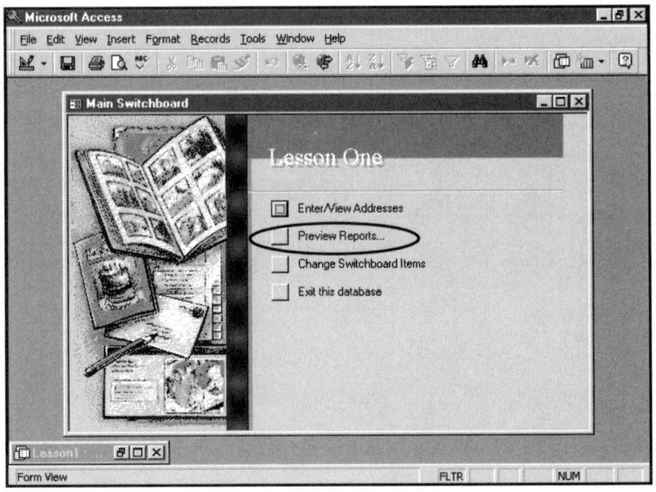


**Q & A** ?

*Question:* What is the purpose of an input mask? *Answer:* To apply a format to a field automatically and ensure that the correct data type is used.

*Question:* To what data type field can an input mask be added? *Answer:* Text.

**12** Click the **Close Window** button to return to the **Main Switchboard**.

# Task 4

## Using the Reports Switchboard to Preview Database Reports

**Tip for Instructors**

The Learn on Demand Module/Lesson "Using the Reports Switchboard" applies to this task.

**On Your Mark**

A telephone switchboard is used to direct calls. What might the **Reports Switchboard** be used for?

### Why would I do this?

The form you used in the previous task displayed records one at a time. In managing a database, you will also need to print several records at a time. When you need to print records you will want to use a report. Reports can be based on tables or queries and can consist of a simple listing of all the records, or they can consist of groups of selected or filtered records. A *filter* is used to limit records to those that meet certain requirements.

In this task, you learn how to use the Reports Switchboard to look at the different reports that were created as part of this database. Reports are viewed in a print preview mode so you can examine how the report will look before it is printed.

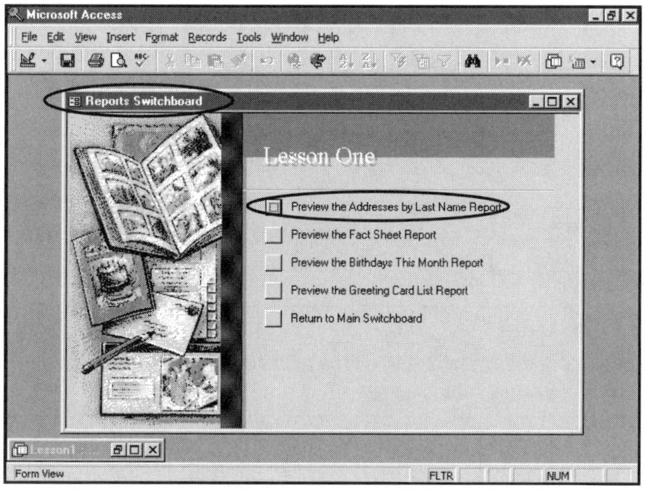


**1** Click the **Preview Reports** button. The **Main Switchboard** opens the **Reports Switchboard**, which displays several choices.

**Concept**

A *filter* extracts records for a temporary use; a *query* is used and saved for future use.

**Tip for Students**

Reports can be customized to reflect exactly the data needed in the format needed.

**2** Click the **Preview the Addresses by Last Name Report** button. A preview of the report opens and the pointer turns into a magnifying glass.

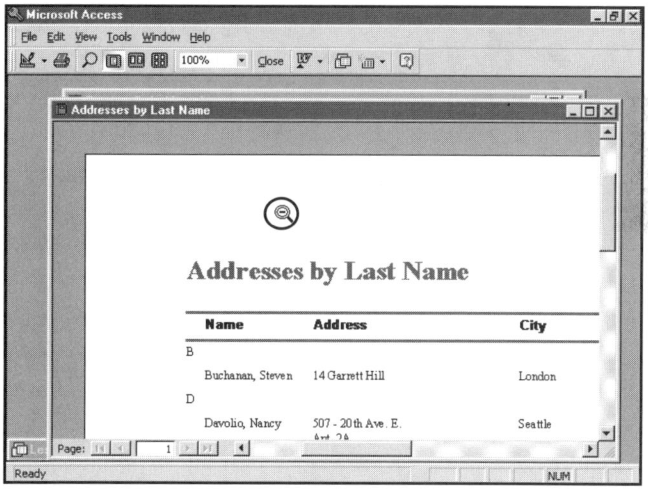


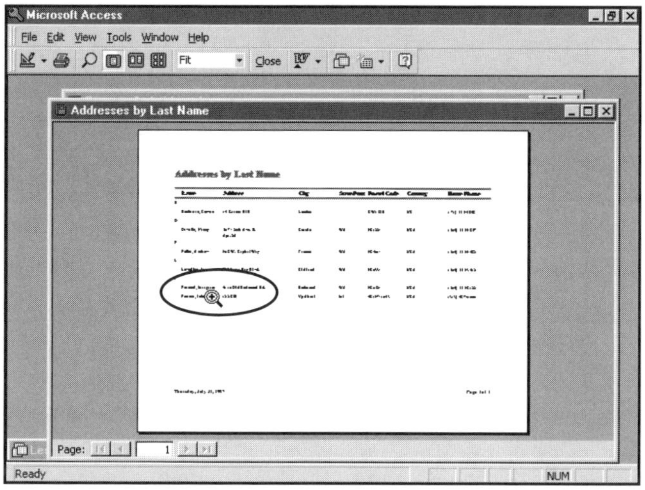


**3** Move the pointer onto the report and click. The view zooms out to show the whole page. Move the pointer onto the last record in the report.

**4** Click the mouse. The view zooms in on the last record. Notice that the record that you entered is now part of this report. This is an example of a report that groups records. In this case the groups are based on the first letter of the last name.

**Concept**

*Grouping* is a way of sorting records in a report. One report can have up to 10 grouping fields. Each new group is nested within the previous group as you add them.

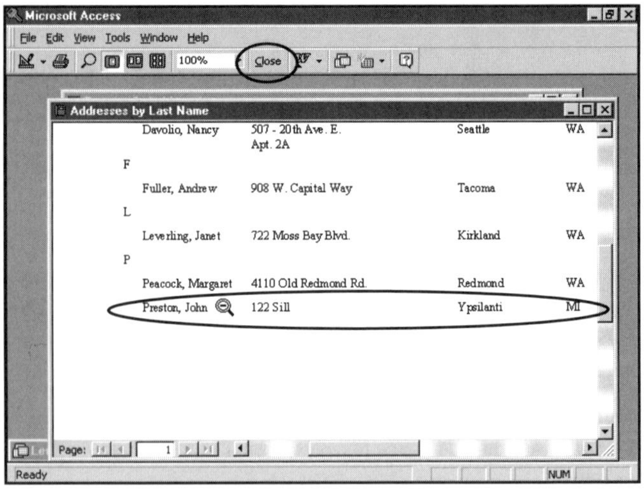


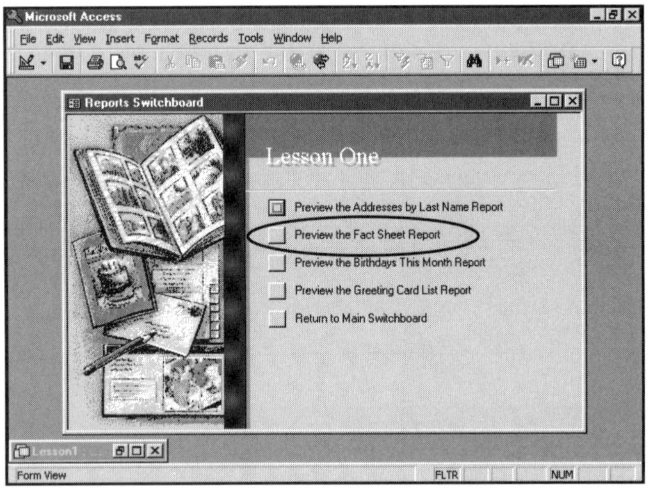


**5** Click the **Close** button on the toolbar to return to the **Reports Switchboard**.

**Quicksand**

Point out the **Close** button on the toolbar. Otherwise, students may click the Access Close button.

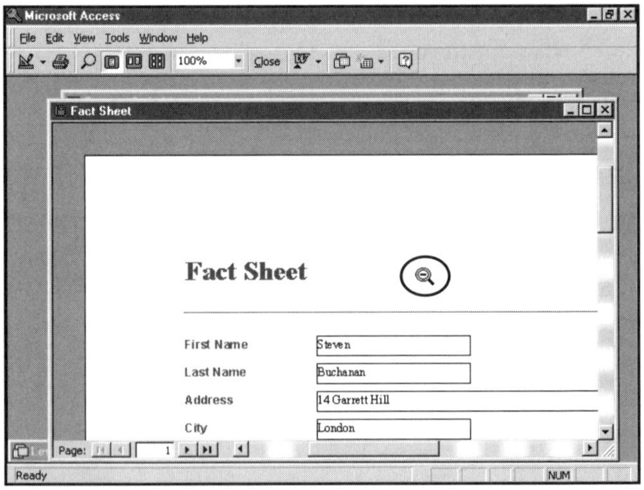


**6** Click the **Preview the Fact Sheet Report** button. The report is displayed and the cursor turns into a magnifying glass.

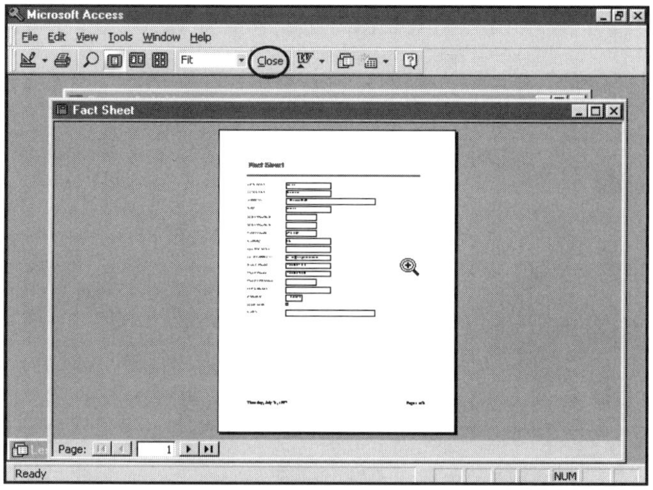


**7** Click anywhere in the report to switch the zoom to a full page view. This is an example of a *columnar report* which is designed to print one record per page in a single- column format.

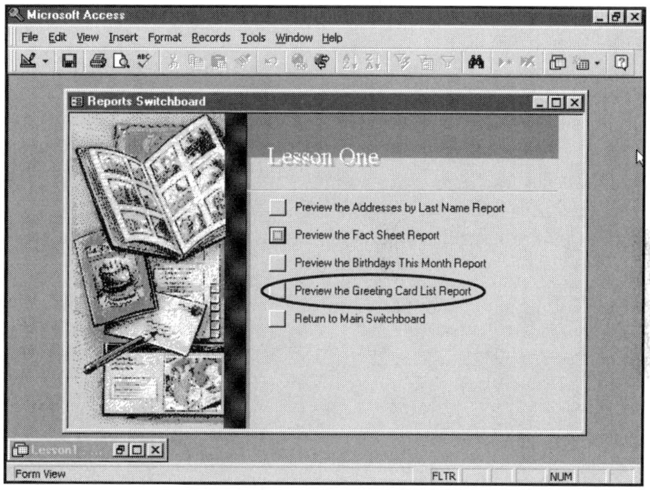


**8** Click the **Close** button on the toolbar to return to the **Reports Switchboard**.

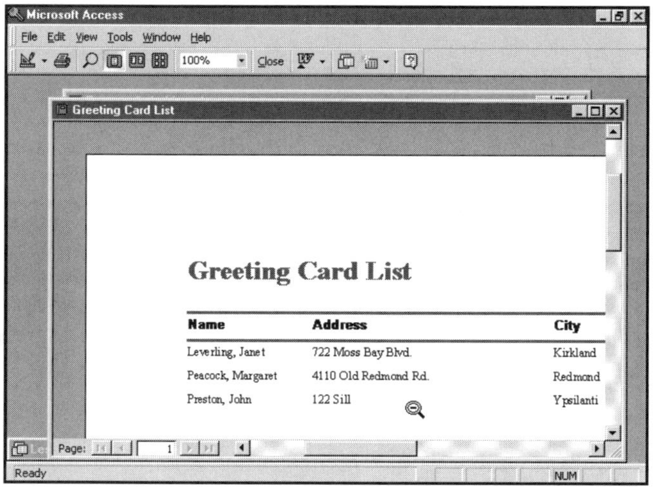


**9** Click the **Preview the Greeting Card List Report** button. This is an example of a report that uses a filter to restrict the records displayed to those that meet a certain criteria. In this case, the records shown are those that were checked for a greeting card.

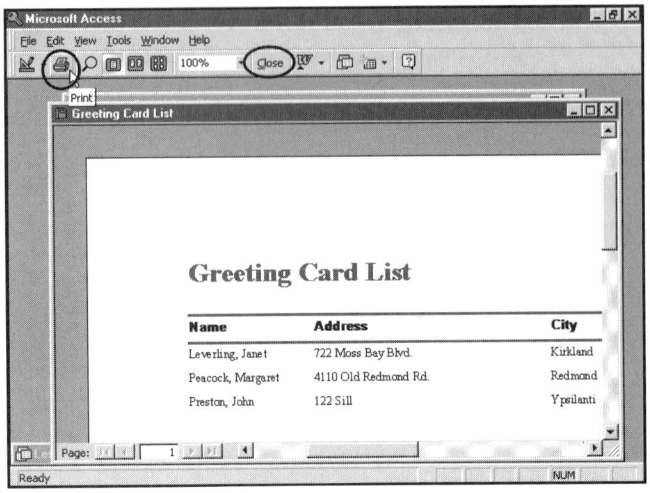


**10** Click the **Print** button on the toolbar to send this report to the printer.

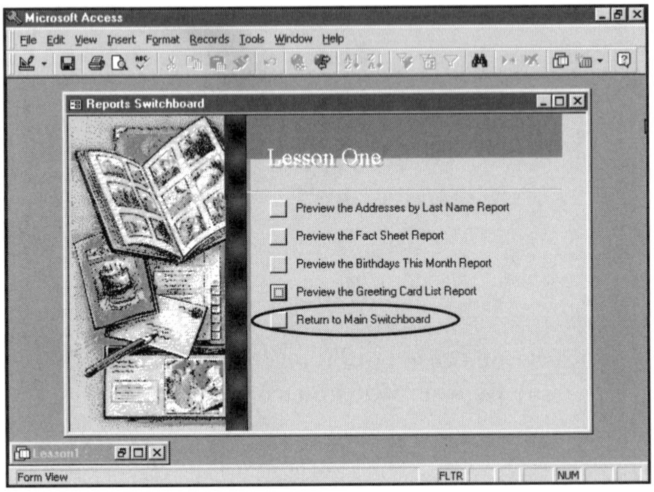


**11** Click the **Close** button on the toolbar to return to the **Reports Switchboard**.

**Quicksand**

Do not click the **Close** button on the **Reports Switchboard**. This action closes the entire switchboard. To return to the switchboard, click the **Maximize** button on the database (lower-left corner of screen) and open the Switchboard form.

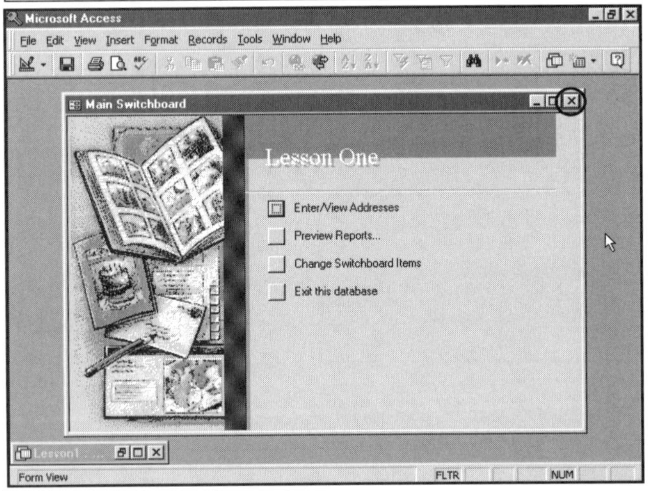


**12** Click **Return to Main Switchboard**. Do not exit the database at this time.

**Q & A**

*Question:* What are some of the different report types we looked at? *Answer:* A report with grouping options, a columnar report that shows only one record per page, and a report with the records restricted.

**13** Click the **Close Window** button at the corner of the **Main Switchboard** to close the switchboard but leave the database open.

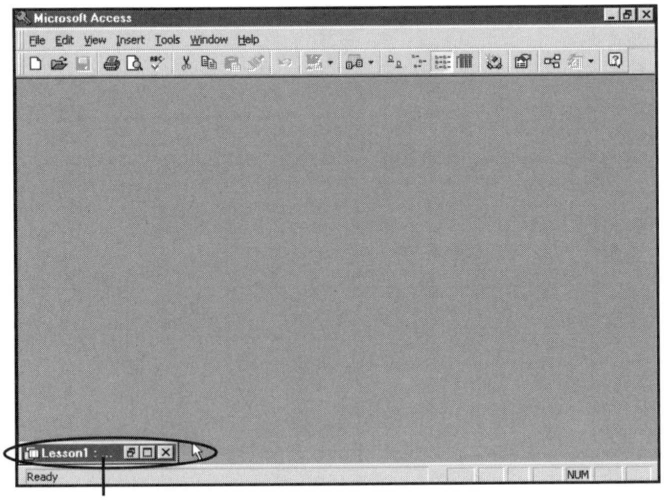


Reduced Database window

# Task 5

## Examining the Database Table Using the Database Window

**Tip for Instructors**

The Learn on Demand Module/Lesson "Using the Database Window" applies to this task.

**On Your Mark**

The **Table Wizard** is a helpful tool. Sometimes, however, it may not provide the table structure you need. What could you do to use the **Table Wizard** tool but also have the exact structure that you need?

### Why would I do this?

In this lesson, a Wizard was used to create a sample database. If you use Wizards to create databases, you may find that not all of the objects are exactly what you want or need. If you want to customize the database objects to fit your specific needs, you will need to use the Database window to modify the design of the objects. Likewise, when you create a database without using a Wizard you will use the Database window to create new objects, to open objects, or to change the design of objects. The Database window is similar to a switchboard in that it opens forms and reports you use to enter or print data. But the Database window also allows you to create or modify objects in your database. It is a central control window that gives you access to all areas of your database.

In this task, you will examine the table that was created for this database. You will learn how to add and then delete a record. You will look at the design of the table to see how an input mask property looks. In future lessons, you will use the table design window to create tables. This exercise gives you an introduction to the design and use of a table.

**1** Move the pointer to the **Maximize** button in the title bar of the Database window.

**Quicksand**

Take a moment to check each computer. Some students will have closed the entire database in the last lesson.

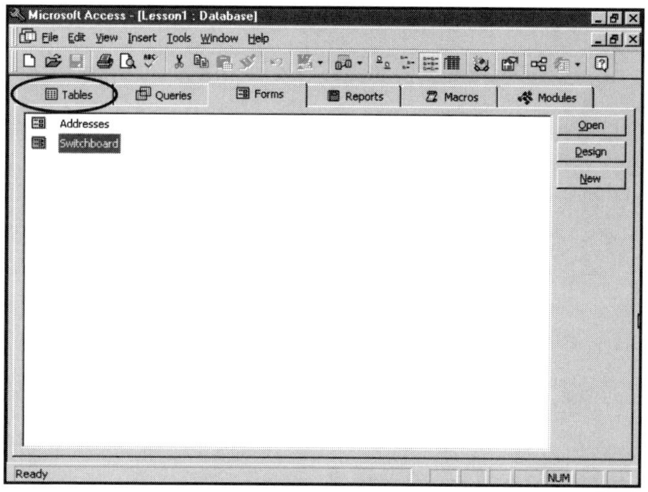


**Tip for Instructors**

Reiterate the use of tabs in Windows as well as the purpose of each component in the database.

**2** Click the **Maximize** button. The Database window displays six tabs showing the database objects: Tables, Queries, Forms, Reports, Macros, and Modules.

**3** Click the **Tables** tab. You see a list of the tables that were created for this database.

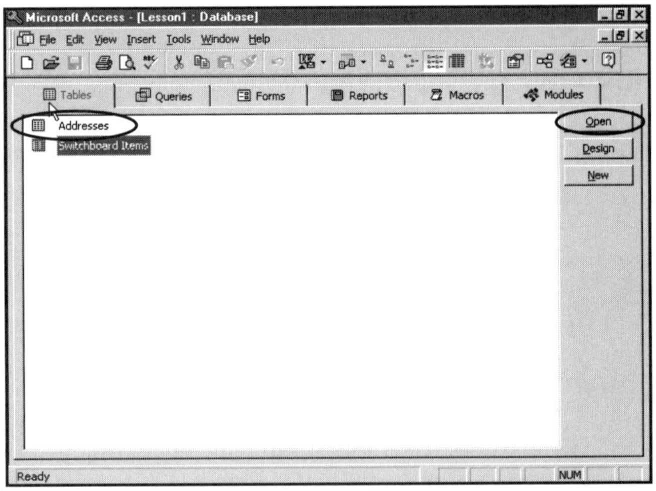


**Q & A** ?

*Question:* What is the purpose of the *Design View* and the *Datasheet View* in a table? *Answer:* The Design View enables the user to make changes to the database fields and properties; the Datasheet View enables the user to see the records in the database.

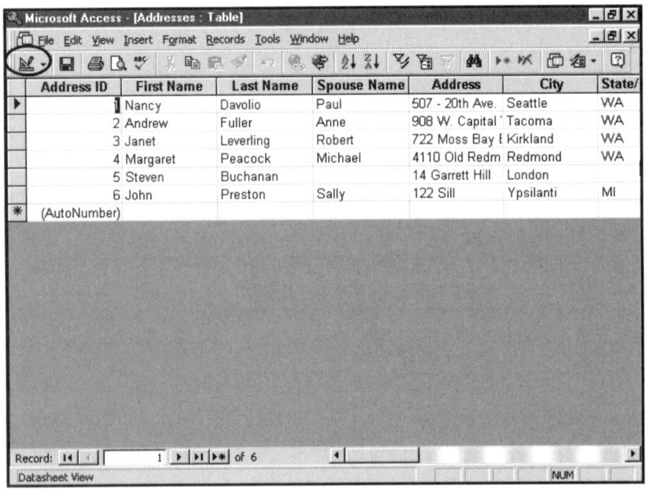


**4** Click **Addresses** and then click the **Open** button. The Addresses table opens in *Datasheet View.* This view shows the field names at the top of each column and the records in rows. Tables may be viewed in either of two ways: the Datasheet View you see, or the *Design View,* which is used to design or modify the table. The View button is used to switch between views.

Key field

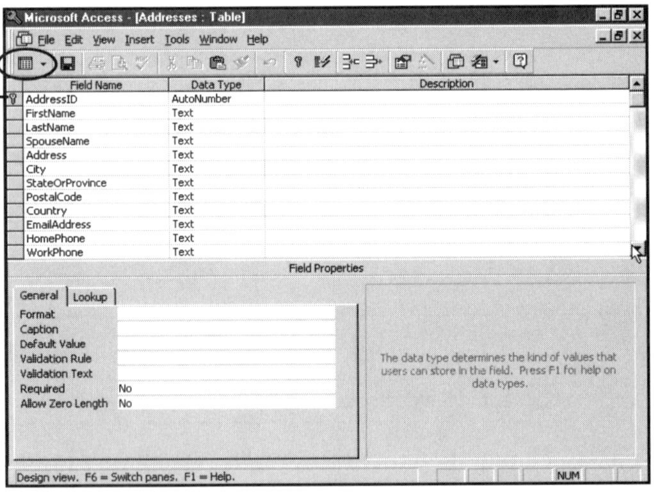


**Concept**

The **Open** button opens the selected table so that records can be manipulated. The **Design** button opens the selected table so the format or design can be changed.

**5** Click the **View** button. A list of fields is displayed. The bottom of the window contains properties that describe the currently selected field. A small key known as the *primary key* is placed next to the field to show that it has been designated as the field that contains a unique value for every record.

**Concept**

A *primary key* is a field that uniquely identifies each record in a table. Although primary keys are not essential, they do assist in indexing large databases.

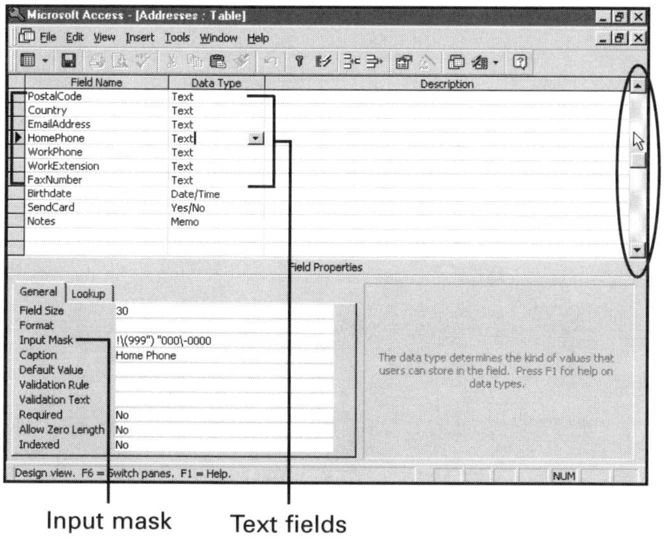


**6** Scroll down to see the last ten field names and click the **HomePhone** data type column. Notice that the **Field Properties** window displays the input mask that is used to insert the parentheses and dashes. Notice, too, that even though you entered numbers in the PostalCode and HomePhone fields, their data type is text. Number data types are generally used only for fields that have an intrinsic numeric value that may be used in a mathematical calculation.

**Concept**

The Text data type can contain any character. It must be used if an input mask is desired. Number data types are used if arithmetic will be used.

**7** Click the data type for the **Birthdate** field. Notice the input mask used for dates.

**Quicksand**

If you click the far right of the data type field, a drop-down list box appears. Be certain not to change the data type. It must be Text.

**In Depth:** Input masks look difficult, but you will learn how to use a wizard that will create them for you.

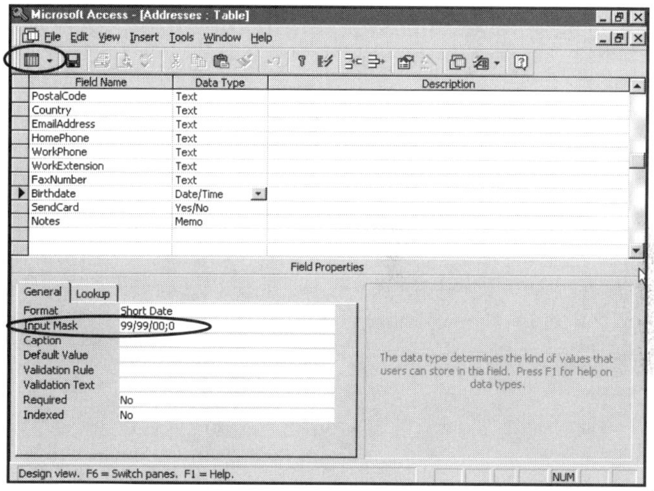


**Tip for Students**

In an input mask, a 9 represents any number, but an entry is not required. A 0 represents any number, but an entry is required.

**8** Click the **View** button to switch back to Datasheet View.

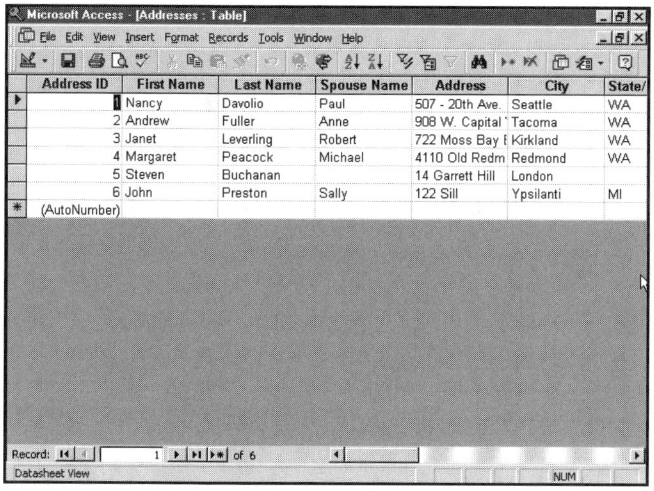

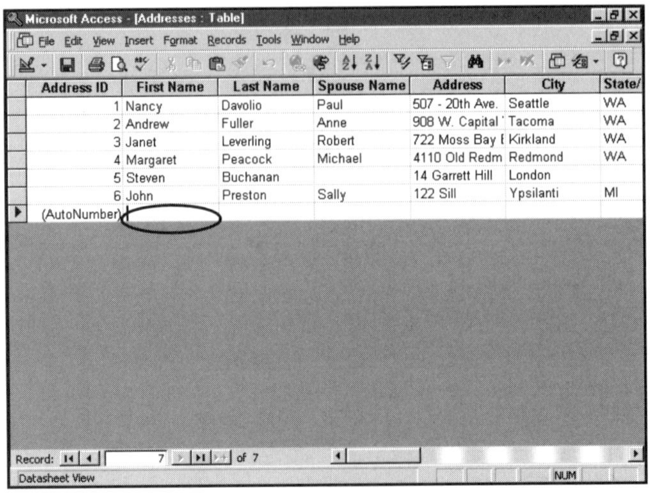


**9** Click the **First Name** field in the empty record at the bottom of the list of records.

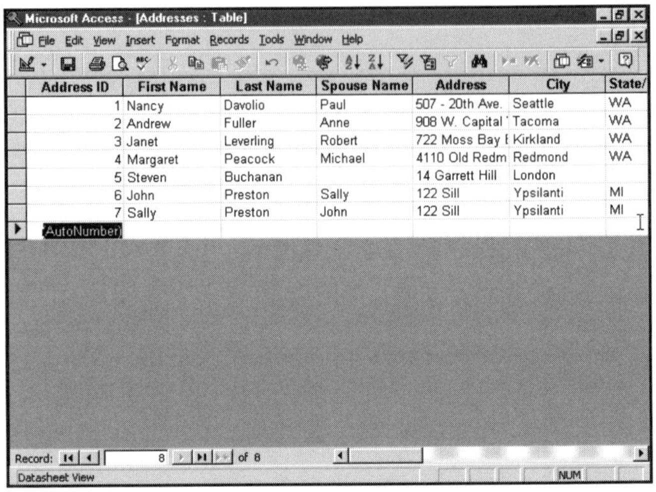


**10** Make up data for this record and enter it. Use Tab to advance from one field to the next as you move across the screen. After you enter the last field, press Tab again; the new record is saved and the cursor jumps back to the first field in the next record.

Record selector

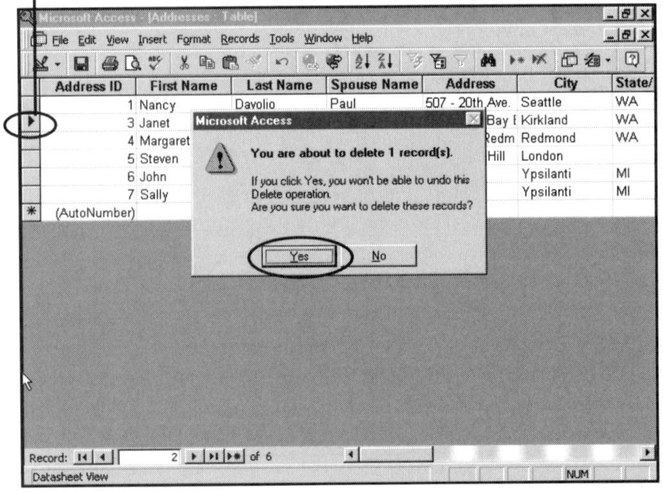


**11** Click the small box at the far left side of the second record. This box is called the *record selector.* Press Del to delete the record. A dialog box opens with a message warning you that the data will be deleted and there is no way to bring it back.

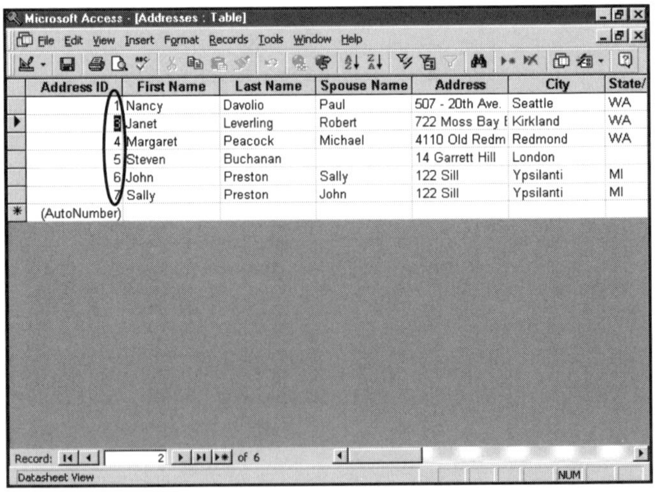


> **Tip for Students** !
> You cannot undo a record delete. If an important record is accidentally deleted, you can close the database without saving it and then reopen it. However, any work done since the last save will be lost.

**12** Click **Yes**. The record is deleted but the Address ID numbers in the other records do not change.

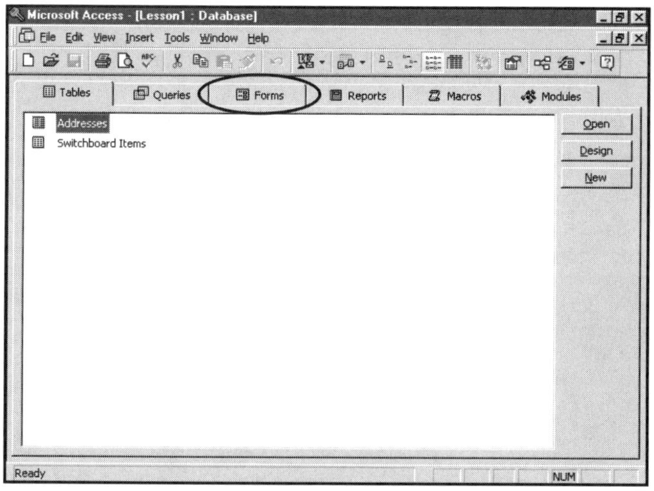


**13** Click the **Close Window** button to close the Datasheet View of the table to return to the Database window.

**Tip for Instructors**

The Learn on Demand Module/Lesson "Using the What's This? Help Tool" applies to this task.

**On Your Mark**

When learning how to use Access, what tools are available to you?

# Task 6

## Using the "What's This?" Help Tool to Learn About the Design of a Form and a Report

### Why would I do this?

You have seen how a table is displayed in rows and columns of data in Datasheet View. You have also seen the window that is used to design a table. Likewise, you can view data in your forms and reports, or you can look at the design of these objects to create or modify them.

In most cases, you will use a Wizard to create your forms or reports, but you may need to make some modifications after the object is created. This is done in Design View of the particular object you are changing. For example, if you are copying data from paper forms, you will find it easier to do if the fields on the screen are arranged in the same order as those on the paper forms. Similarly, you may wish to reorganize the fields in a report to create a different type of report. In order to customize reports or forms, you need to be familiar with how they are designed.

In Tasks 2, 3, and 4 you worked with the Form View of a form and the Preview View of reports. These views are used to display the data. In this task, you will examine the Design View of the forms and reports created for this database. To help you understand the different parts of these objects and how they are designed you learn how to use the "What's This?" help tool. This is a part of the Help options that will be examined in more detail in Lesson 7. In this task, the Help option is used to provide you with information about forms and reports.

**1** Click the **Forms** tab, click **Addresses**, and click the **Design** button. The **Addresses** form is displayed in Design View.

**Concept**

In order to customize reports or forms, you need to be familiar with how they are designed.

**Pothole:** When the Design View of a form or report opens, the Toolbox may also appear on the screen. To give you a better view of the design, simply close the Toolbox by clicking the Close button (**X**) in the upper right-hand corner of the Toolbox.

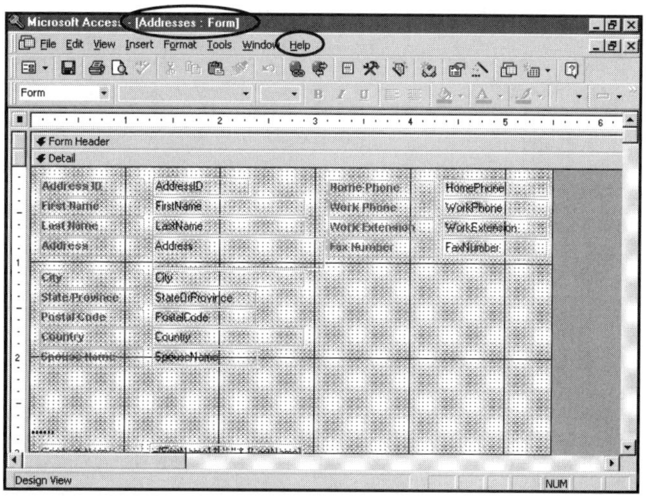

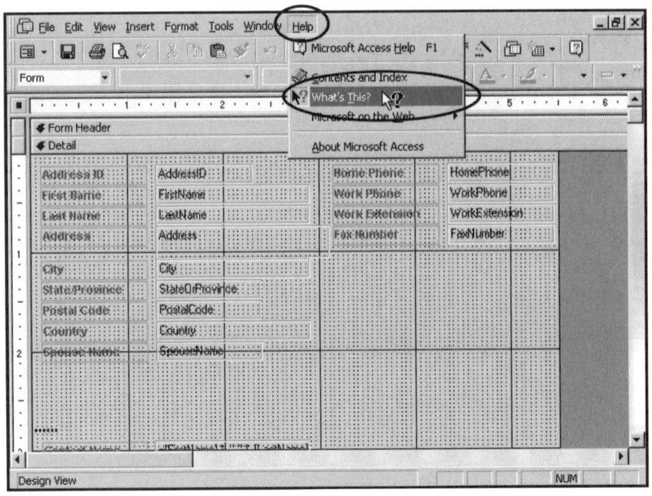

**2** Choose **Help** and **What's This?** from the menu. The pointer will turn into an arrow with a question mark attached.

> **Quicksand**
> The What's This? button appears in a dialog box when you right-click an object. This will not happen in a report or form unless you are in the Design view.

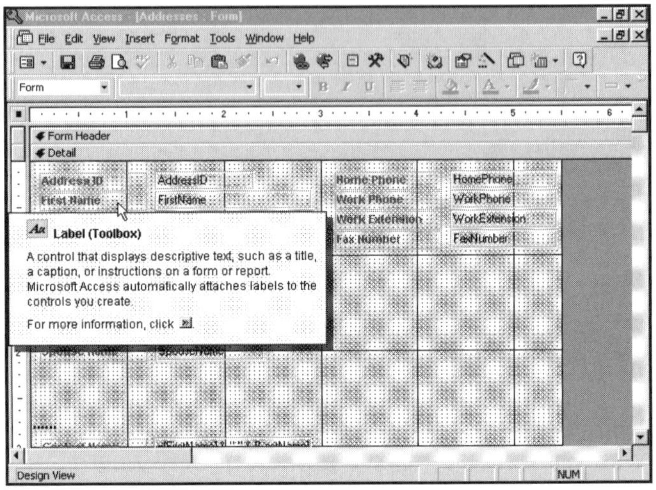


**3** Click the label for the **First Name** field. Read the message box that describes the *label box.* This is a control on a form or report that contains descriptive text such as a title or caption.

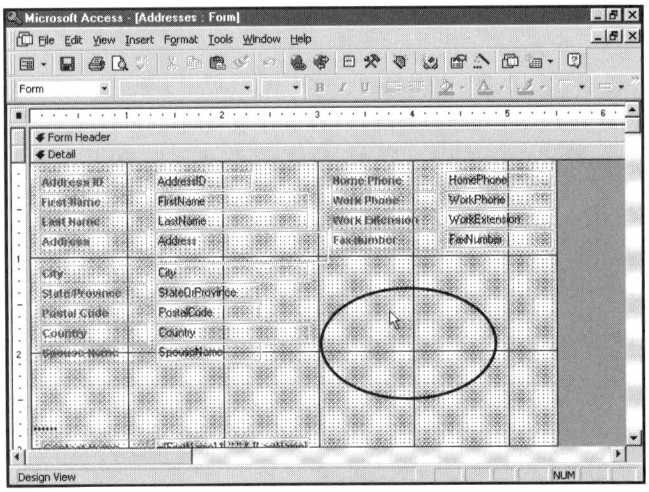

**4** Click an empty space in the form to close the message box.

> **Quicksand**
> The **What's This?** button works only once each time it is accessed.

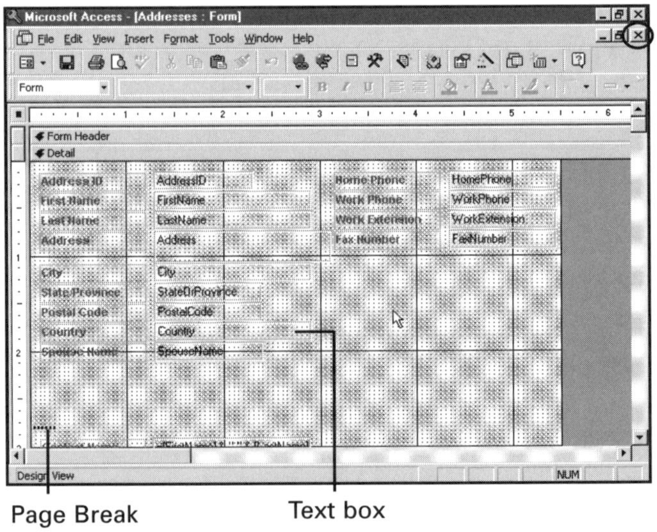


**5** Repeat steps 2 through 4 for a **text box** and the **page break**.

> **In Depth:** The design of a form or report contains many kinds of controls. A *control* is a graphical object on a form or report that is used to display data, perform an action, or make a form or report easier to read. You have just looked at a *text box,* which is a type of control that is bound to the database and is used to display the data. Another type of control is the page break. Controls like these help to make a form or report function the way you want.

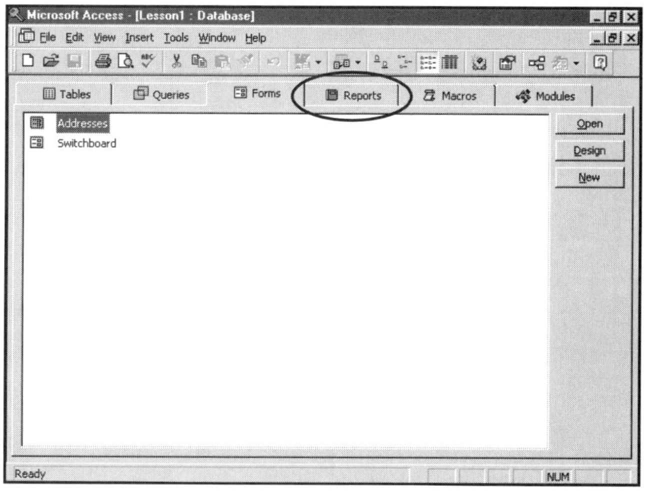


**6** Click the **Close Window** button to close the Form Design and return to the Database window.

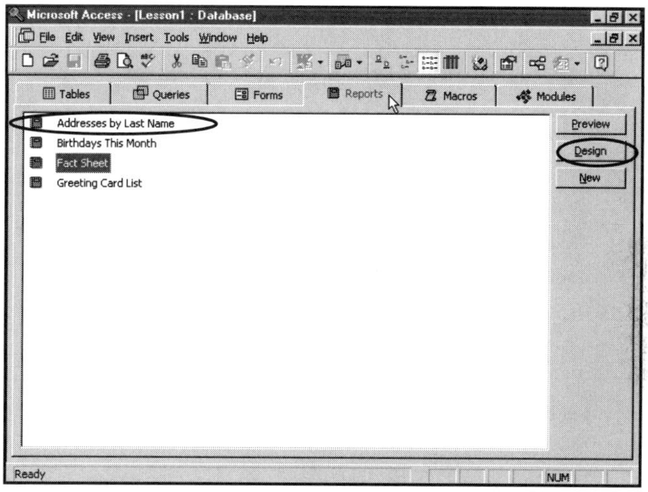


**7** Click the **Reports** tab to display the names of the reports.

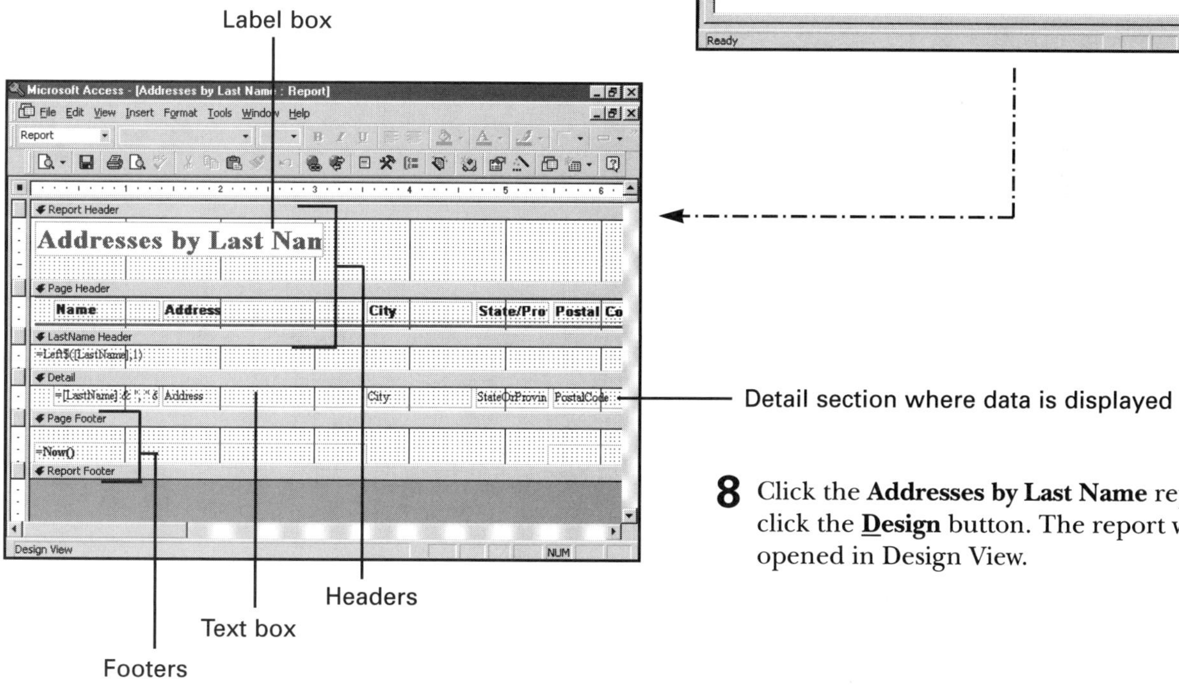


**8** Click the **Addresses by Last Name** report and click the **Design** button. The report will be opened in Design View.

**9** Choose **Help, What's This?** Click an empty space in the Report Header and read the description.

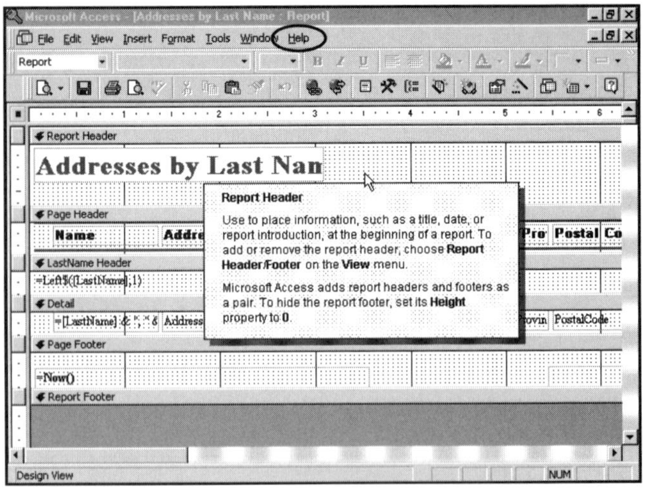


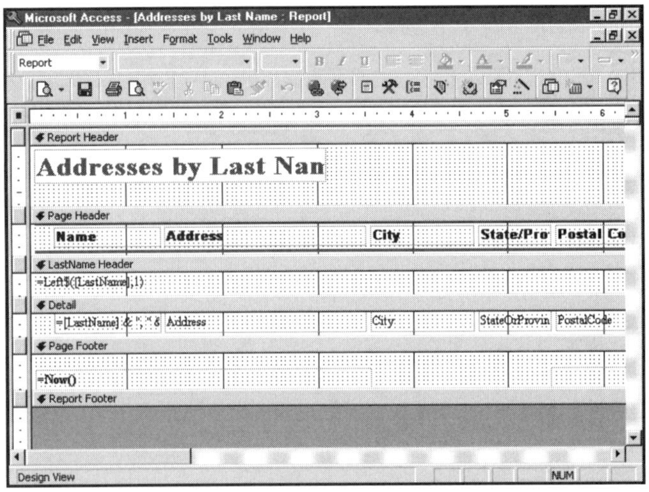

**10** Click an empty space on the screen to close the message box.

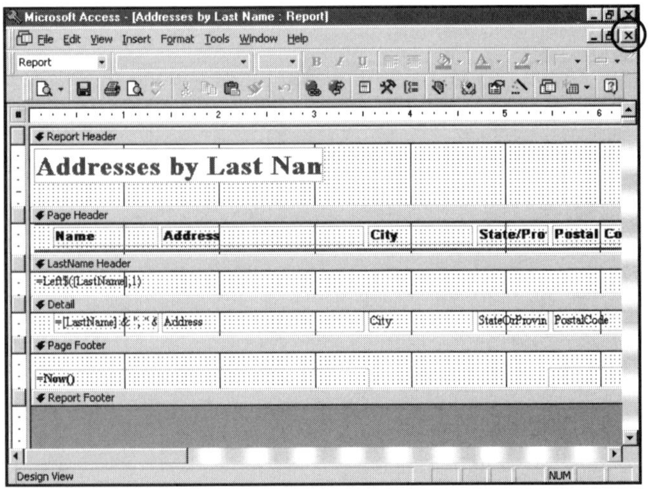

**Pothole:** When clicking in each area of the report design, it is important that you click in an open area and do not click on top of a text or label box. In the Page Header and Detail sections click to the left of the boxes. This open area will result in a description of the Page Header and the Detail sections of the report. When you click in the LastName Header you will see a description for Group Header. In this report, the Last Name field was used to group the data by the first letter of the last name, which resulted in this group header in the report design. In a report, you will see a group header for each field that you have grouped the data on.

**11** Repeat this process for the **Page Header**, **LastName Header**, **Detail**, and **Page Footer** sections.

2. Refer
parts
label i

1. __B_
2. __E_
3. __C_
4. __D_
5. __A_

A. Input
B. Non-t
C. Scroll
D. Field
E. View l

## Match

Match the st
is the best m
matching wc
the number.

1. _D_ Au
wh
2. _I_ Guic
dat
3. _K_ A l
allo
4. _E_ A ty
onl
5. _B_ Bu
oth
6. _A_ Inc
for
7. _J_ A ca
8. _G_ Col
eve
9. _F_ Use
ma
10. _C_ Wo

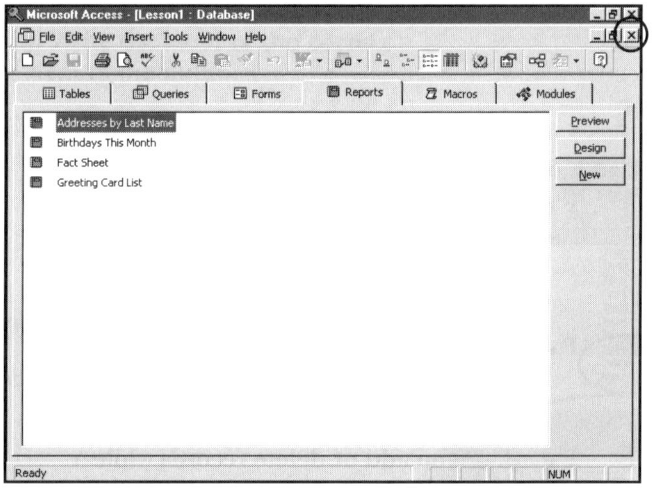


**12** Close the **Addresses by Last Name** report.

# Task 7

> **Tip for Instructors**
> The Learn on Demand Module/Lesson "Closing the Database and Exiting Access" applies to this task.

## Closing the Database and Exiting Access

### Why would I do this?

Access is designed to work with files that may be too large to fit in the computer's *RAM* memory, so most of the file remains on the disk while the program loads part of it into RAM memory. The program also assumes that the file is on your computer's hard disk. If you are storing a database on a floppy disk, it becomes very important that you are careful about closing a database properly and that you *never* swap floppy disks while a database is open. In this task, you learn how to close the database and then exit the Access program. If you simply turn off the computer while a database is open, you may corrupt the database beyond repair.

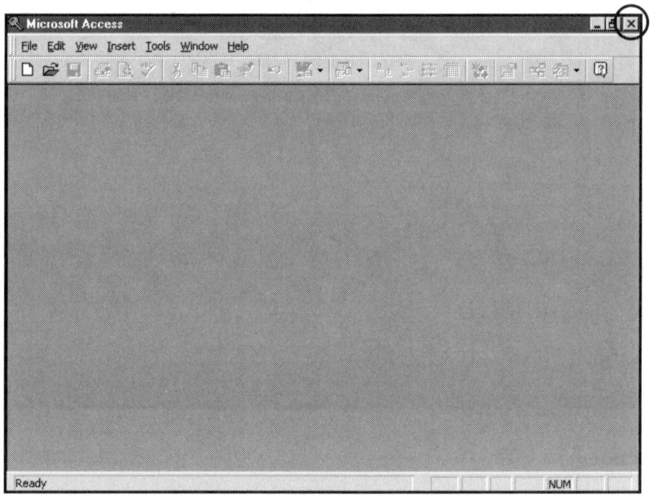


**1** Click the **Close Window** button on the Database window. Notice that it does not ask you if you want to save changes. Changes are made continuously to the database on the disk—they do not need to be saved.

> **On Your Mark**
> Why close Access before exiting Windows? (Computers use temporary files when a program is running. If you do not allow those files to be cleaned up by the software, it could cause future problems. Sometimes the database will even become unusable.)

**2** Click the **Close Window** button on the **Microsoft Access** title bar. The program closes.

# Stud

## True-F

Circle either

T F✓ 1.

T F✓ 2.

T✓ F 3.

T✓ F 4.

T F✓ 5.

T✓ F 6.

## Identif
## the Ac

1. Refer t
parts o
label i

1. _B_
2. _C_
3. _A_
4. _E_
5. _D_

A. Naviga
B. Labels
C. Fields
D. View b
E. Close V



**6** Type **Age** for the third field, then press ↵Enter. Click the arrow on the **Data Type** drop-down box to reveal all of the data types.

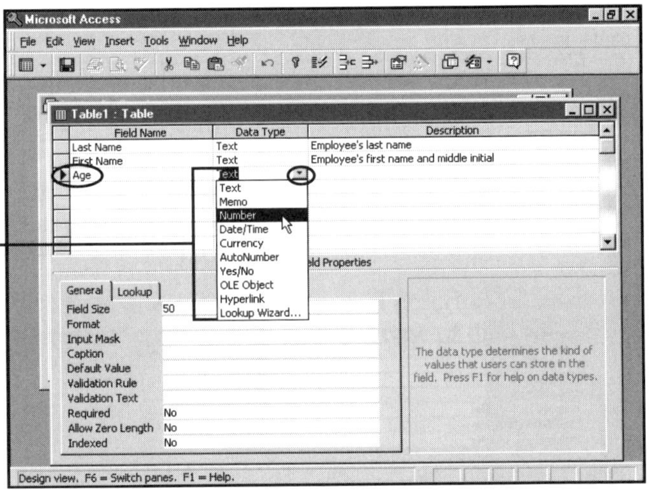


Data Type drop-down box

> **Tip for Students** !
>
> The drop-down arrow is visible only when the **Data Type** drop-down box is selected.

View button

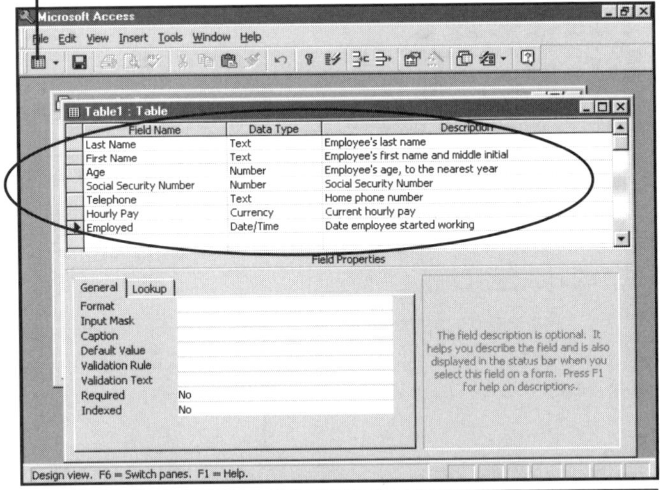


**7** Select the **Number** data type, then fill in the rest of the fields as shown in the figure.

> **Pothole:** If you click the drop-down arrow on the right side of the View button, you are given a choice of views. Choose Datasheet View. If you click directly on the View button it will change automatically to the view represented by the icon that is shown. In most cases, clicking the button will move you between a view of the design of an object and the view that shows that data in its most common form for that object. For example, in a table, the View button moves you between Design View and Datasheet View. In a form, the View button moves you between Design View and Form View. The View button is used in this book as the quickest and easiest way to switch back and forth between views.

> **Tip for Students** !
>
> If you know which data type you need, you can simply type the first letter of the data type without using the drop-down list. You can also press Alt and the down arrow to activate the drop-down list. Scroll down to highlight the entry you want and press ↵Enter to accept the entry and move to the next column.

> **Tip for Students** !
>
> Although the **Telephone** field and the **Social Security Number** field are both numbers, it is best to set the data type of the **Telephone** field to text. Remember that a number field cannot contain dashes.

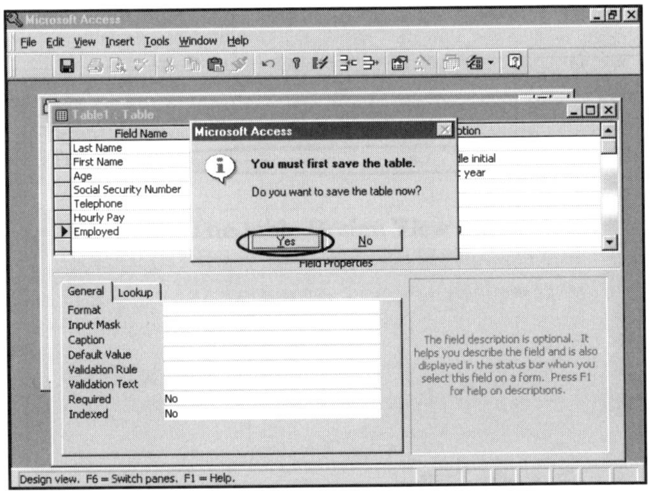


**8** Click the **View** button on the Standard toolbar to go to **Datasheet View**. A dialog box prompts you to save the table.

**9** Click **Yes**. The **Save As** dialog box opens. Type **Personnel File** in the Table Name box.

> **Q & A** ?
>
> *Question:* When does Access prompt you to save a table? *Answer:* Each time you modify its design and switch views or close.

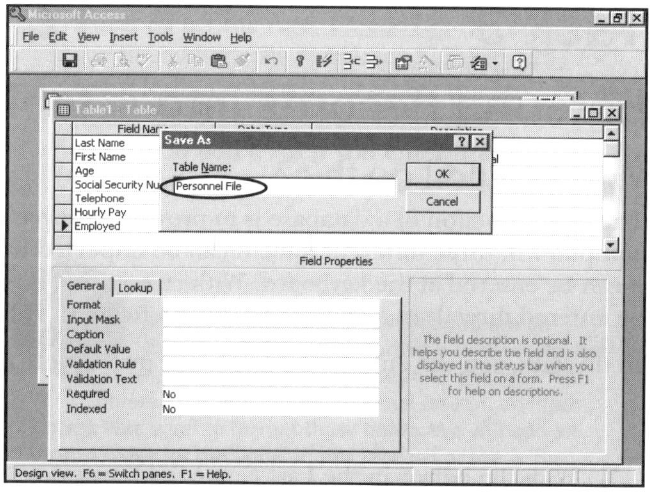


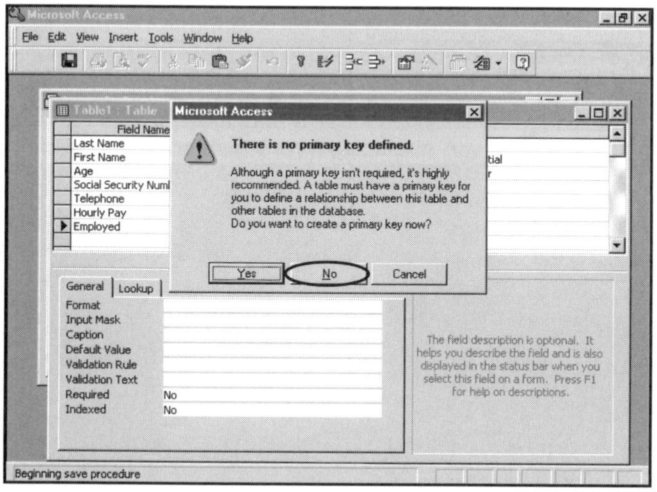


**10** Click **OK**. A dialog box warns you that you haven't selected a primary key and asks if you want to create one.

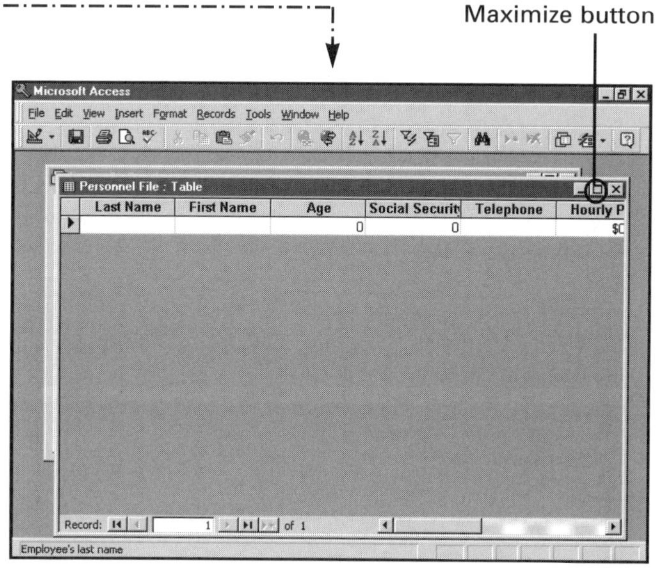


**11** Click **No**. You will deal with the primary key later. The table is now displayed in **Datasheet View** and is ready to accept data.

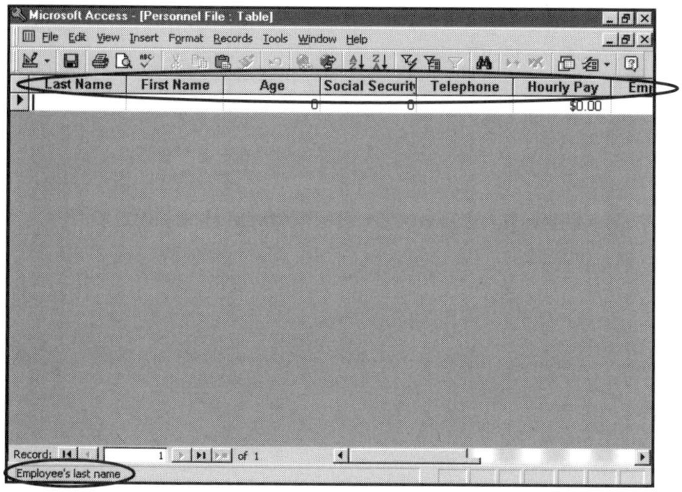


> **Tip for Students** !
>
> Each time a change is made in the design of a table, it needs to be saved. Access will prompt you to do so if you try to change views or change the table.

**12** Click the **Maximize** button to give you the full screen to work in. Notice the field names are shown as column headings, and the description of the field shows in the status bar.

**6** Click the **New Record** button on either the Standard toolbar or at the right end of the navigation buttons to move to an empty record. Use the AutoForm to enter the next four records listed below. Press Tab or Enter to move from field to field. After the last record is entered, the status bar will show that six records have been entered.

| | |
|---|---|
| Last Name | **Johnson** |
| First Name | **Deborah D.** |
| Age | **30** |
| SSN | **111223333** |
| Telephone | **(313)555-1234** |
| Hourly Pay | **9.50** |
| Employed | **5/25/95** |
| Last Name | **Abercrombie** |
| First Name | **Aaron A.** |
| Age | **16** |
| SSN | **222334444323232322** |
| Telephone | **(810)437-0000** |
| Hourly Pay | **5.00** |
| Employed | **6/12/97** |
| Last Name | **Prefect** |
| First Name | **Ford** |
| Age | **34** |
| SSN | **232323233** |
| Telephone | **(313)461-0000** |
| Hourly Pay | **9.00** |
| Employed | **10/1/90** |
| Last Name | **Dent** |
| First Name | **Arthur** |
| Age | **28** |
| SSN | **323232322** |
| Telephone | **(313)941-0000** |
| Hourly Pay | **9.00** |
| Employed | **10/1/90** |

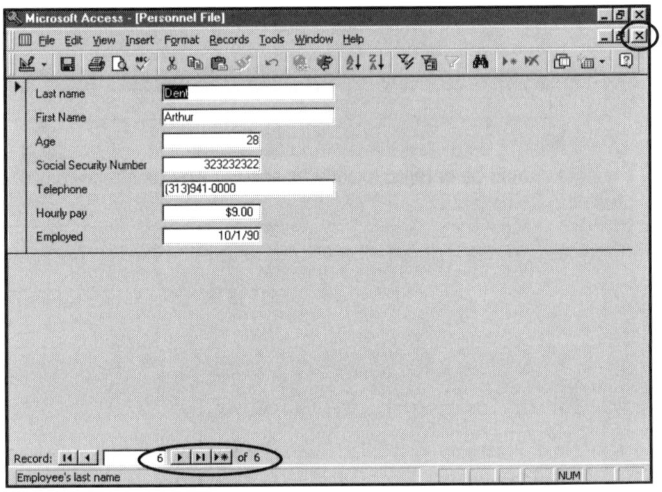


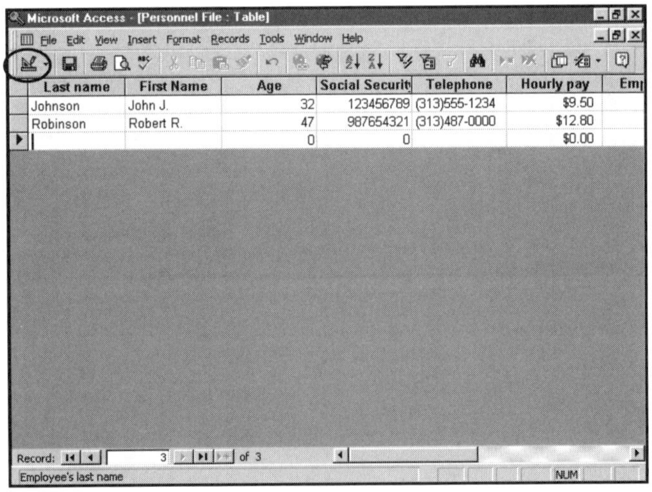


**Tip for Students**

If you press Tab on the last field entry, a new record automatically appears.

**Quicksand**

The table does not show the records entered in the AutoForm. Assure students that their data is not lost (see Step 8).

**7** Click the **Close Window** button to close the AutoForm. When it asks if you want to save the form, choose **No**.

**Tip for Students**

To display the new records without changing the view, press F5.

**8** The table datasheet that was opened when you created the AutoForm is now visible; however, only the first two records show. To see the rest of the records, you need to refresh the window. Click the **View** button to change to Design View.

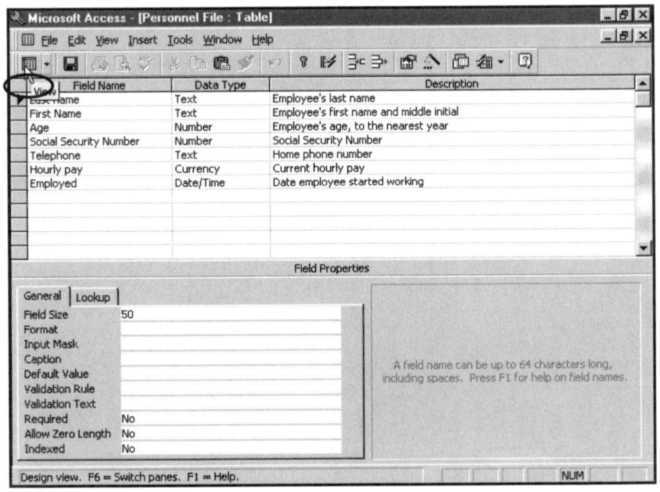

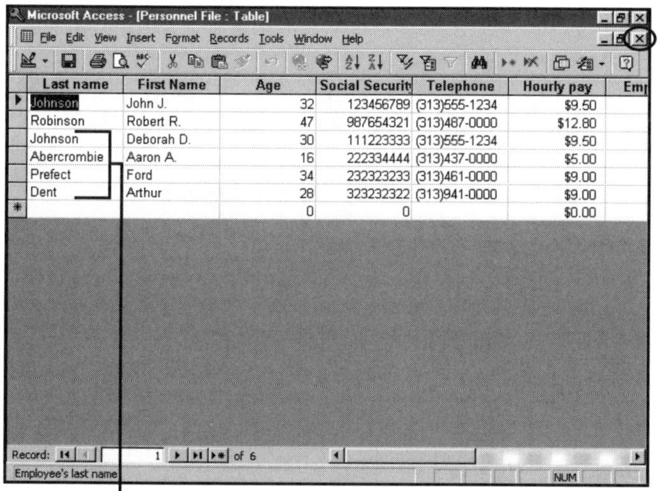


Records added by using Autoform

**9** Click the **View** button again to return to Datasheet View. Now you can see all of the records you have entered.

> **Q & A** ?
>
> *Question:* What is the purpose of the AutoForm? *Answer:* To display only one record at a time, as well as show all data fields on the screen at one time rather than using the Table View.

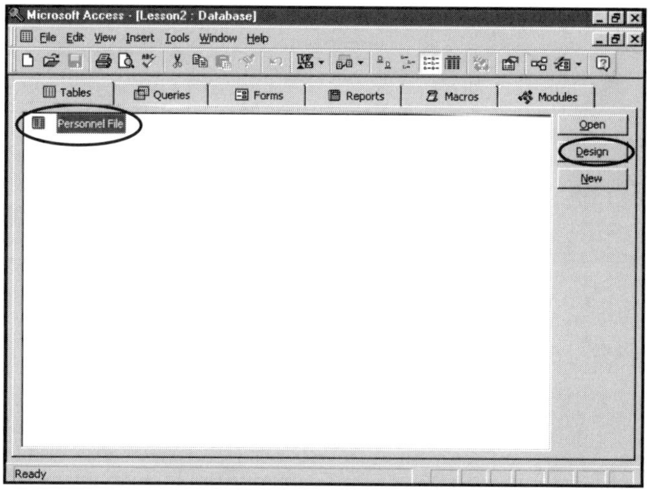


**10** Click the **Close Window** button. The **Tables** tab now shows the **Personnel File** table.

# Task 4

## Adding and Deleting Fields

### Why would I do this?

> **On Your Mark**
>
> Although planning is the most important step, you will make some errors in judgment and discover them later. What will you do the correct these errors? What consequences or impact do you think these changes will have on your table?

Prior planning is critical when designing a customized database. This helps to avoid problems at a later date. No matter how well you plan, however, there will be times when you need to add new fields to your database. You will also discover that some fields are extraneous and need to be removed.

In this task, you learn how to modify a table by adding new fields and deleting others. When you make changes to the design of a table after records have been entered, Access gives you warning messages that the changes may affect your data. For this reason, it is recommended that you back-up your file before you begin. If you know the content of your data you will be able to judge the impact of the warnings. Be aware of the following:

- If you delete a field, all of the data in that field will be deleted as well.
- If you delete a field from a table, it must also be removed from other objects. If you forget and do not remove the deleted field, any query that uses the field will not work and forms or reports will display an error message.
- If you rename a field in a table you must also rename it in any object that uses that field.
- If you resize a field to a smaller size, Access will warn you that data may be lost because it may not fit in the new smaller field.
- If you change a field's data type, Access will try to convert the data in that field.

> **Tip for Instructors**
>
> The Learn on Demand Module/Lesson "Adding and Deleting Fields" applies to this task.

> **Tip for Instructors**
>
> Go over the bulleted list very carefully for emphasis and clarification.

In this task, you learn how to add and delete fields and have the opportunity to see some of these warnings.

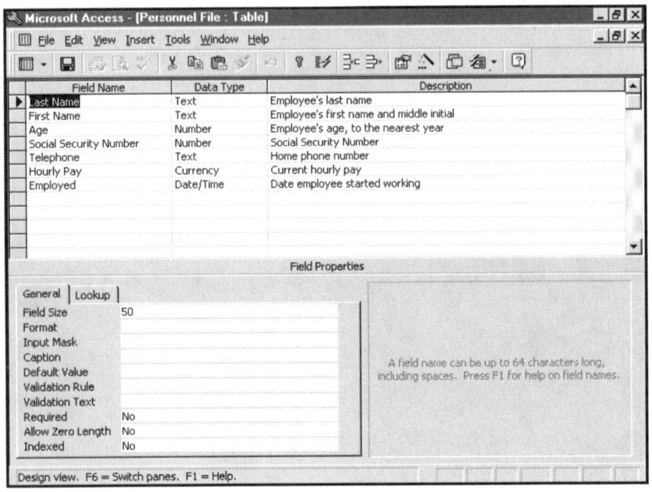


**1** Click the **Design** button to go to **Design View** of the Personnel File table. Because there is some question about whether it is legal to keep an employee's age, you will delete the **Age** field.

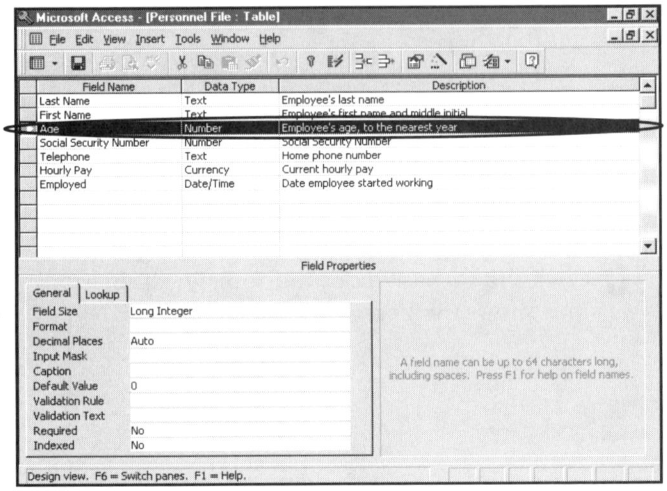


**2** Click in the **Row Selector** column to the left of the **Age** field. The entire row is now selected.

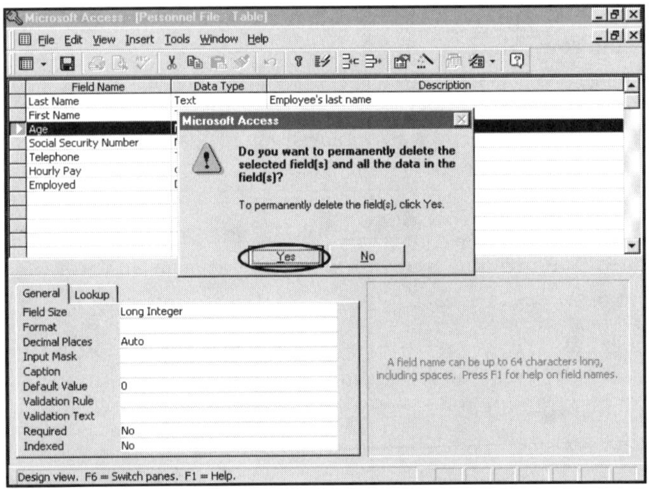


**3** Press Del. A dialog box warns you that the deletion will be permanent, and asks if you want to delete the field(s). Click **Yes**.

**Pothole:** When you delete a field, the deletion is final and all of the data in that field is lost. The Undo key will not work for this type of action.

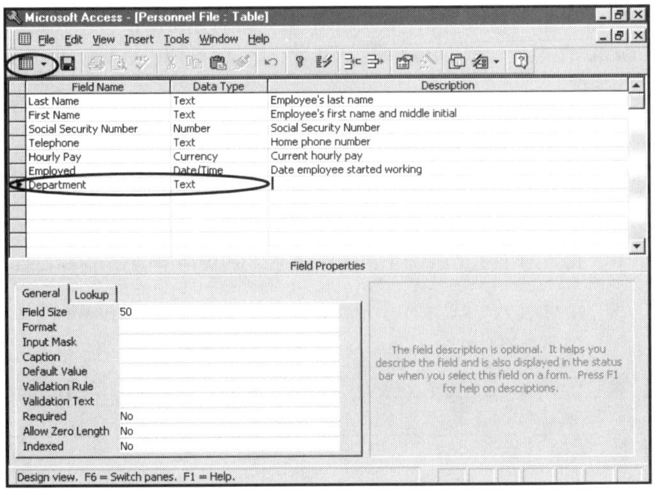


**4** To add another field, place the cursor in the Field Name box of the first blank row. Type **<u>Department</u>** as the new field name, accept the **Text** data type, and leave the Description area blank.

**5** Click the **View** button to change to **Datasheet View**. A dialog box opens and prompts you to save the table.

> **In Depth:** Anytime you change the structure of a database object, such as the change you made to the Personnel File table in step 4, you must save the change when it is made. You must save your changes before you go to Datasheet View, or they will be lost.

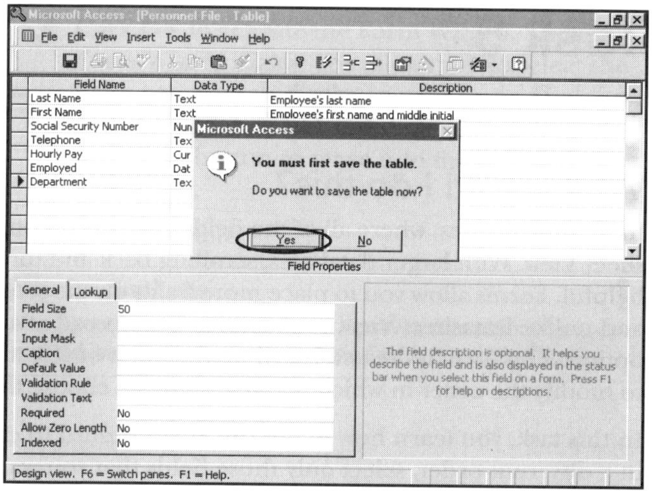


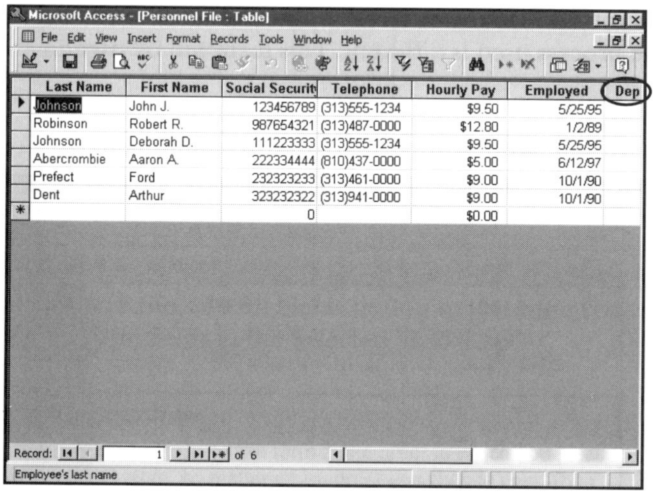


**6** Click **Yes** to save your changes. The datasheet no longer contains an Age field, but does show the **Department** field on the right.

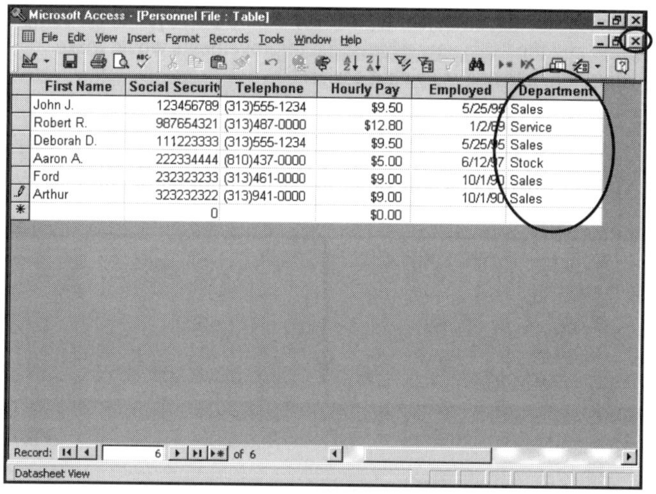


**7** Fill in the **Department** field as shown.

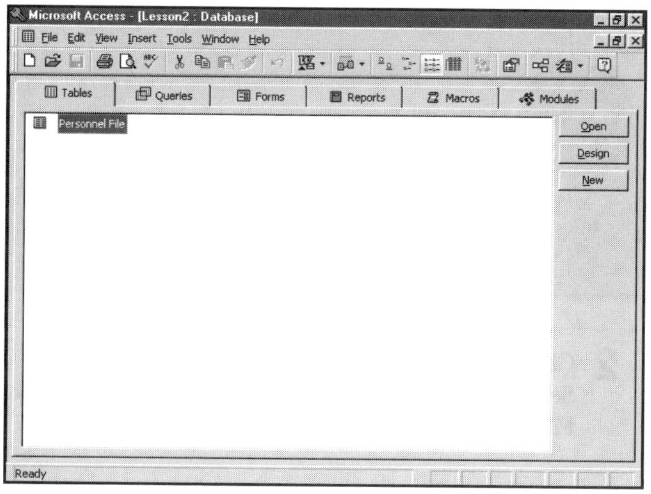


### Tip for Students !

When a new field is added after data records have been entered, that field will be empty for all records. Editing will be necessary to complete these fields.

### Q & A ?

*Question:* What happens when a field is deleted after data has been entered? *Answer:* All of the data in that field is deleted and any reports/ forms using that field will display an error until that field is removed from those objects.

**8** Click the **Close Window** button to close the table.

**6** Click **N**ext. The third **Form Wizard** dialog box prompts you to select a background style. Choose **Standard**, if necessary. A preview is shown on the left side of the dialog box.

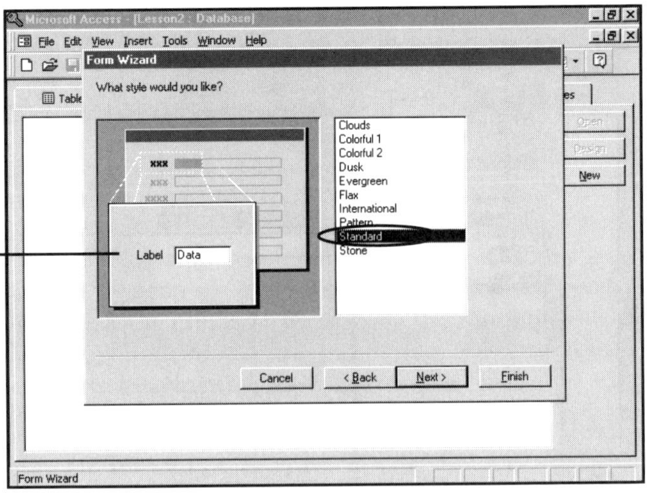


Preview box

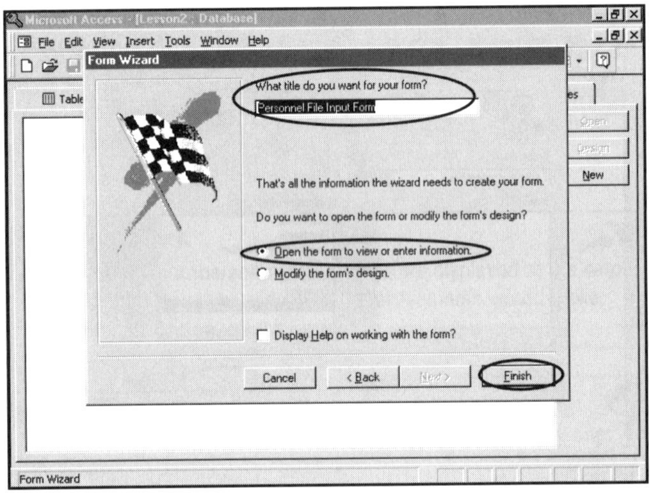


**Tip for Instructors**

Access chooses the same name as the table/query used if you do not specify a different name.

**7** Click **N**ext. The fourth (and final) **Form Wizard** dialog box prompts you to name the form. Type **Personnel File Input Form**. Make sure that the **Open the form to view or enter information** option is selected.

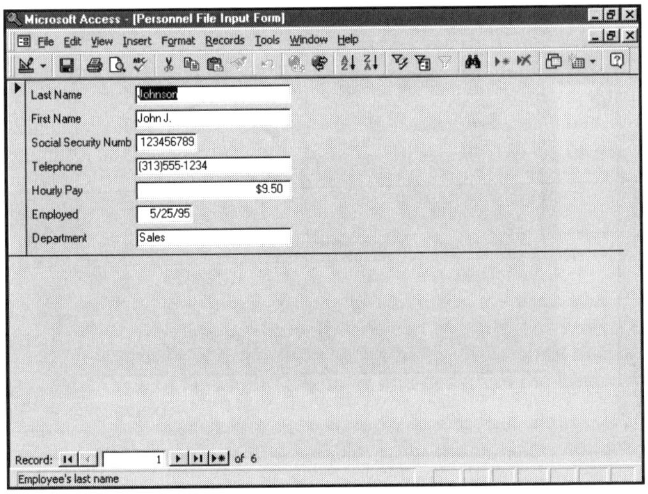


**8** Click **F**inish. Access generates the columnar form with the fields and background you selected. If your form is not maximized, click the **Maximize** button.

# Task 6

## Arranging Text and Label Fields in a Form and Adding a Label

> **Tip for Instructors**
> The Learn on Demand Module/Lesson "Arranging Text and Label Fields in a Form" applies to this task.

### Why would I do this?

When you use Form Wizard or AutoForm, Access arranges the data labels and the data boxes in a preset order. There will be many times when you would like to rearrange the fields to match the layout of a paper form. With practice you can design an Access form to look exactly like a printed form.

In this task, you learn how to move around in a form and change the layout of the text and label boxes.

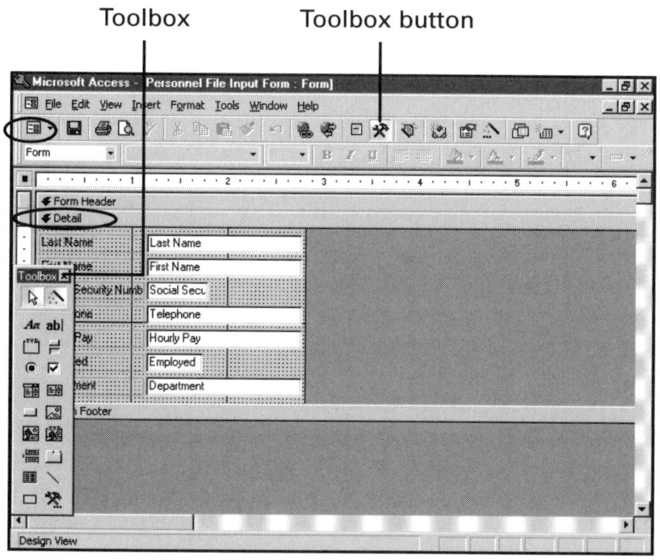


**1** Click the **View** button to move to **Design View**. The form design window is displayed, along with the Toolbox. (Note: If the Toolbox is not displayed on your screen, click the **Toolbox** button on the Standard toolbar.) All of the fields are shown in the ***Detail*** *section* of the form.

> **On Your Mark**
> When using the **Form Wizard**, the form is set up the way the wizard is preprogrammed. Looking at our form on the screen, how can you rearrange the form or add to its usefulness?

**SLIDE 2.4**

> **Tip for Instructors**
> The Form Design view can be intimidating to new users. Assure students that it will become clearer with usage.

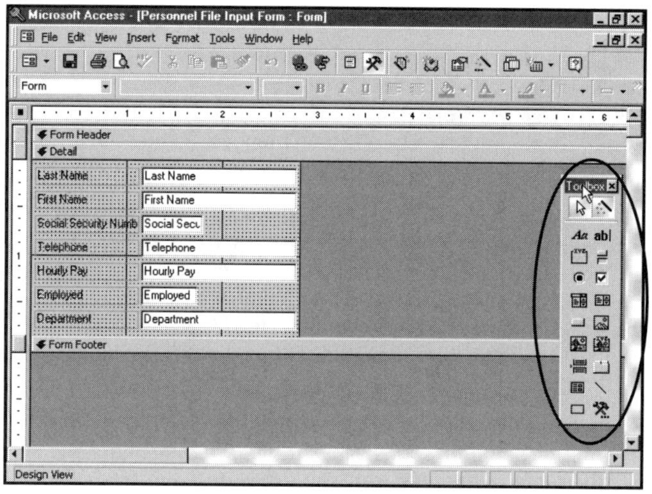


**2** Click the Toolbox title bar and drag the Toolbox to the right side of the screen.

**3** Click and drag the **First Name** field to the right of its current location, as shown in the figure.

> **In Depth:** While you are dragging the field, a hand replaces the arrow pointer. Field *placeholders* show where the field will be located when you release the mouse button. It doesn't matter whether you drag the field *label* (in this case, the field name) or the field *text box* (which contains the data).

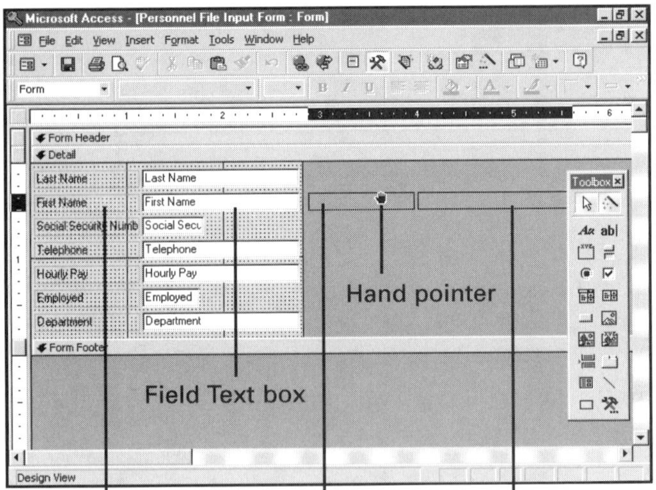


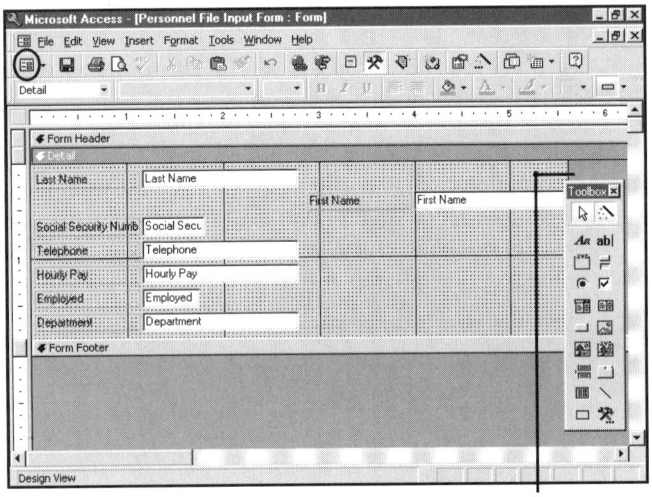


**4** Release the mouse button. The **First Name** field is now on the right half of the screen. The Detail work area automatically increased to accept the new field location.

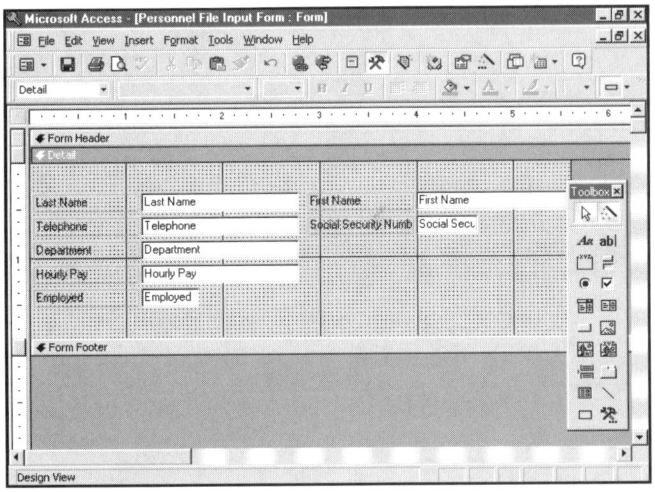


**5** Drag the other fields to match the illustration.

> **Pothole:** Be patient with yourself. Repositioning fields takes some practice. If you follow the steps below, you will find it easier to master the technique.
>
> To move a field with one motion, position the mouse pointer on top of the field you want to move. Click and hold down the left mouse button. The mouse pointer will turn into an open-hand symbol. When the mouse pointer is in the shape of a hand, drag the field to a new position.
>
> To move a field using two motions, position the mouse pointer on top of the field you want to move. Click and release the mouse to select the field. You can tell when a field is selected by the handles that surround the outer edges. Now, move the mouse around the edge of the field until the cursor turns into a hand. When you see the hand, click and drag the field to its new location. Do not release the mouse until the field is positioned where you want it.
>
> Whichever method you choose, the key is that the mouse pointer must be in the shape of a hand to move the field label and text box together.

**Speedy Class**

To move more than one field at a time, drag the mouse over at least a small portion of each field you want. Be sure to start in an empty space.

**Quicksand**

When dragging the fields, be sure not to drag the big handle on the upper-left corner of the **Field** text box. This handle moves the text box separately from the field label.

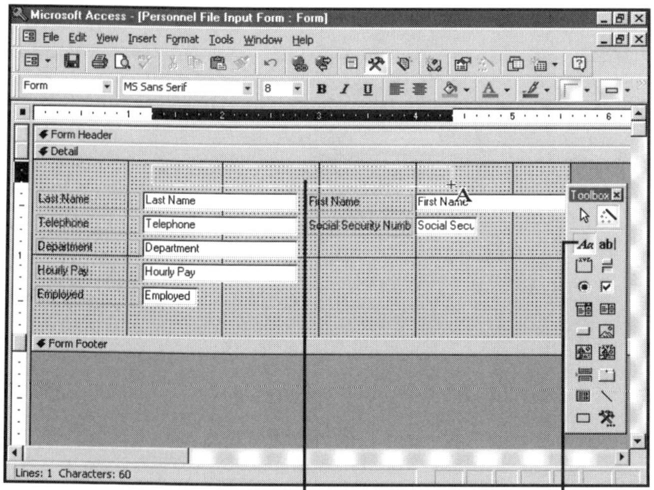


New label box

Label button

6 Click the **Label** button on the Toolbox toolbar. When you move the pointer to the **Detail** area, it changes to a crosshair with the letter **A** attached. Draw a new label box as shown in the figure.

**Pothole:** To begin drawing, click the mouse above the Last Name field and drag down and to the right above the First Name field. Do not release the mouse until you have finished drawing the new label box. If you release the mouse too soon, repeat the process and try again.

### Tip for Students

If the **Label** box is not large enough, it can be edited after the text has been added. (See the In Depth box below Step 8.)

### Concept

A *label* is text that appears in the form but is not connected to a table field. It will appear on every page of the form.

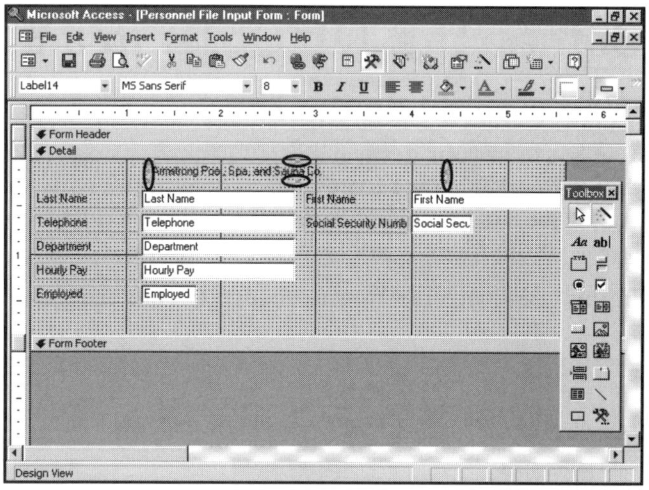


7 Type **Armstrong Pool, Spa, and Sauna Co.** in the label box. Click outside the new label, then click it again. Black handles surround the outer edge, showing that the box is selected.

### Quicksand

Before formatting can be added to a label, the **Label** box must be deselected and reselected. If a cursor is in the label, formatting can be done only by highlighting the text first.

### Quicksand

Dragging a corner handle can change two sides of the box. Dragging a middle handle changes only that side.

Font Size button

Bold button

Font button

Center button

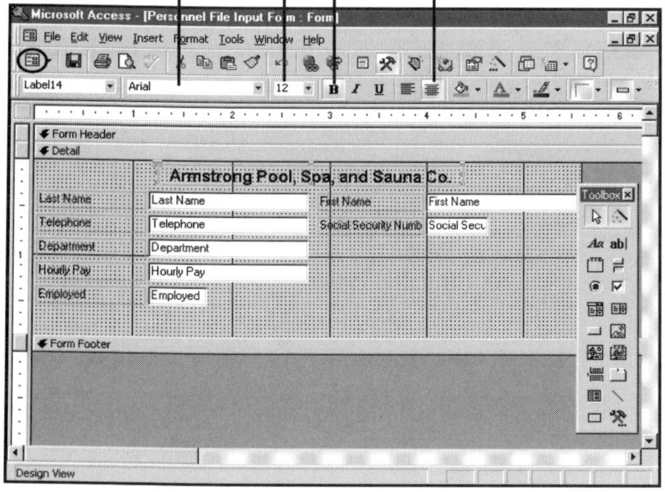


8 Click the **Bold** button and then the **Center** button on the Formatting toolbar. In the Font box, change the font to **Arial**, if necessary. Use the Font Size box to increase the font size to **12** point.

**In Depth:** If the formatted label no longer fits in the box, adjust the size of the box by clicking a black handle and then stretching the box to enlarge it. You may need to increase both the length and the height of the box.

**6** Click the **Print Preview** button. The forms created show in a print preview window. Click the **Print** button to print the forms.

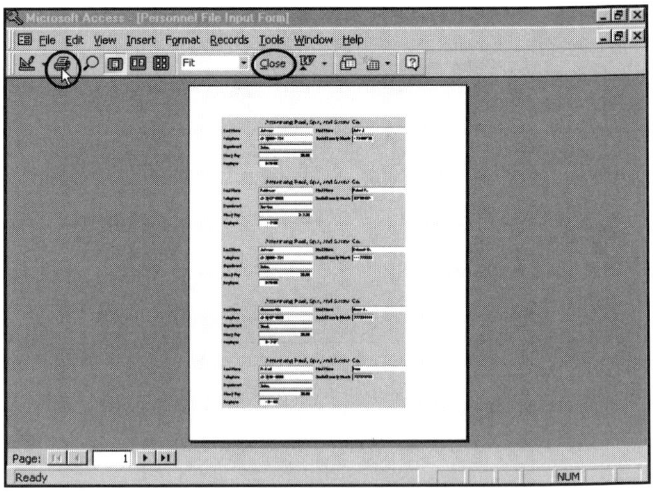


> **Tip for Students** !
>
> Printing from a form simply prints each record as it appears on the screen. Records follow one behind another. For a custom look, create a report from the database window, as shown in Task 8.

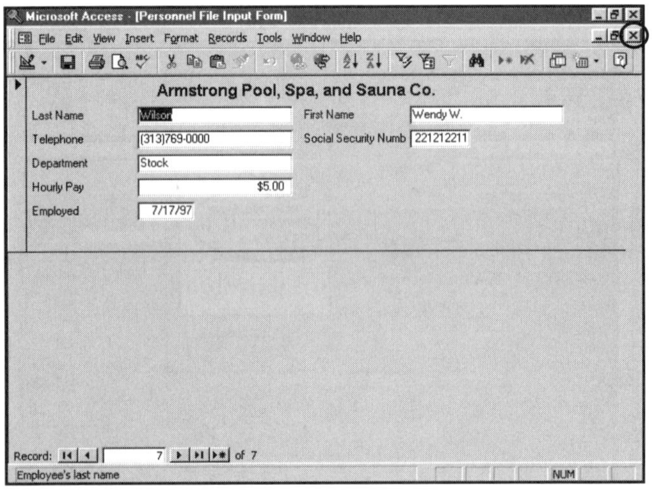


**7** Click the **Close** button to return to Form View.

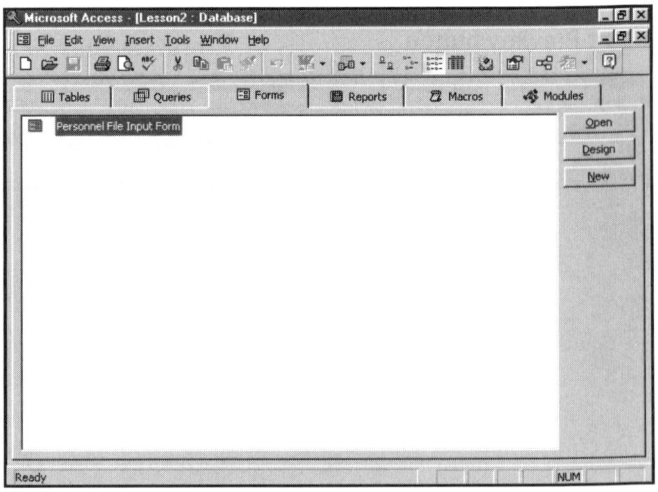


**8** Click the **Close Window** button to close the form and move to the database window. Save your changes when prompted.

# Task 8

**Tip for Instructors**

The Learn on Demand Module/Lesson "Creating a Report Using the Report Wizard" applies to this task.

## Creating a Report Using the Report Wizard

### Why would I do this?

When you have spent a great deal of time creating a database structure and entering data, you will want to print the information. A report gives you the flexibility to print the records and fields you select. You can also sort and group the records in a number of ways.

In this task, you use the Report Wizard. The Wizard helps you create a customized report that includes the fields you want, grouped and sorted in the manner you select. Reports, like forms, can be modified once they have been created. In this task, you will also create a report based on the Personnel File table that is grouped by department and sorted on last and then first name.

**1** Select the **Reports** tab. No reports are shown since none have been created in this database.

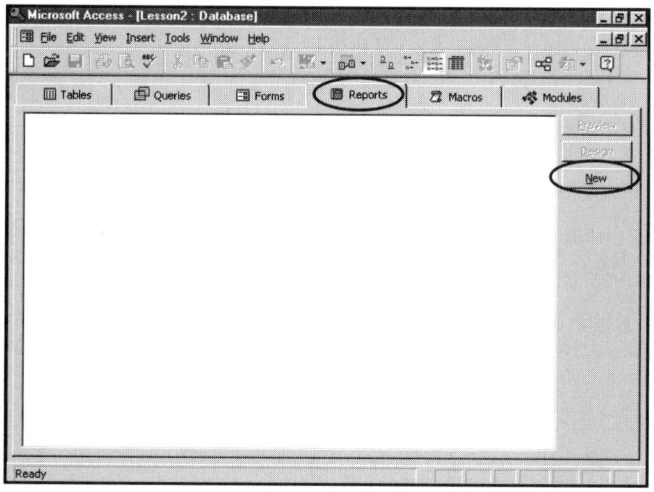


**On Your Mark**

Reports are an important function of a database. What is the easiest way to create a report?

**Tip for Students**

In most cases, it is easier to use a **Report Wizard** and modify the report than it is to create a report from scratch.

**2** Click the **New** button. The **New Report** dialog box opens. Select **Report Wizard** and select the **Personnel File** table from the drop-down box.

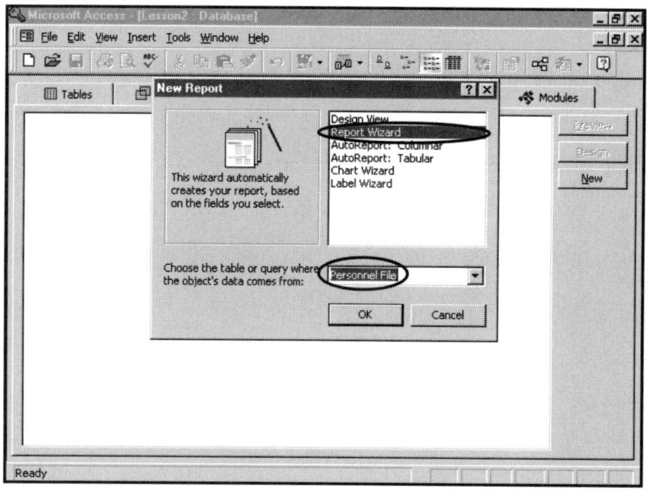


**Tip for Instructors**

A report based on a table prints all records in that table. To create a report for only specific records, a query should be created, as shown in Lesson 4, Task 6.

**3** Click **OK**. The first Report Wizard dialog box opens. Click the **Select All** button to move all of the fields from the **Available Fields** box to the **Selected Fields** box.

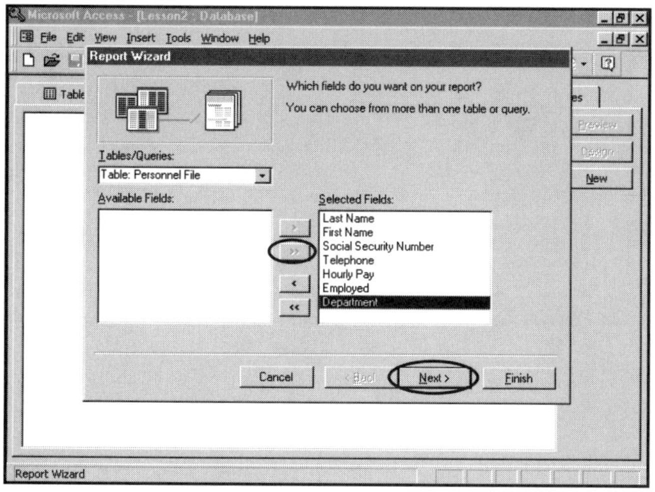

**4** Click **<u>N</u>ext**. The second Report Wizard dialog box allows you to group data. Select the **Department** field and click the **Select Field** button.

> **Concept**
>
> The field used for grouping appears as a heading with all matching records listed beneath that heading. That field is printed only one time for all records.

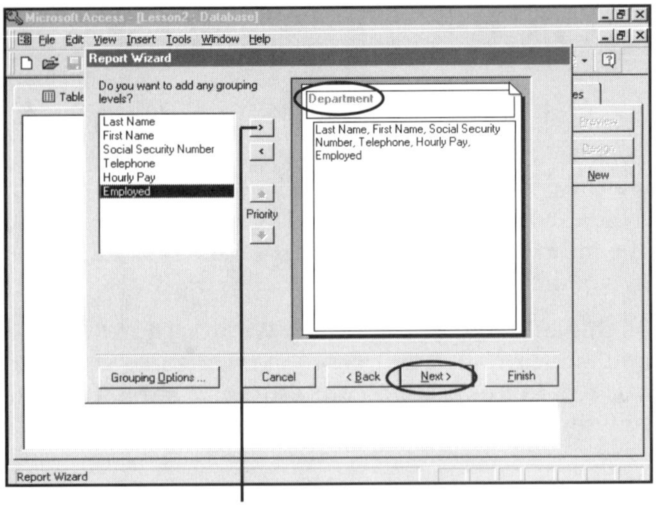


Select Field button

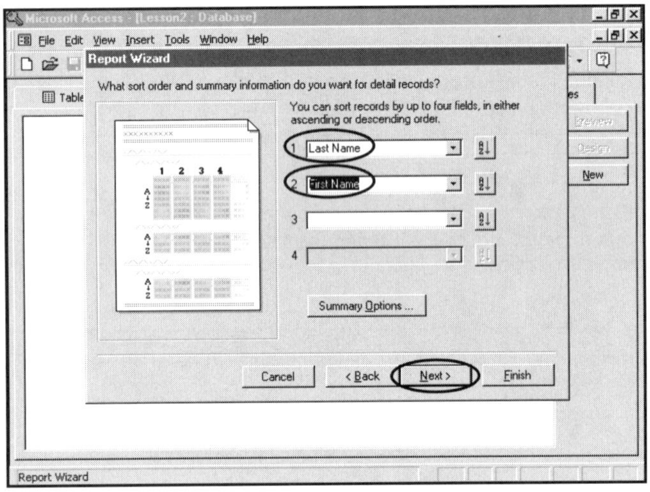


**5** Click **<u>N</u>ext**. The third Report Wizard dialog box allows you to sort data. You can sort on up to four fields. Select the **Last Name** field in the first sort drop-down box. Select the **First Name** field in the second drop-down box.

> **Concept**
>
> The data is sorted by the first field selected. The second field is then resorted if there is more than one of a specific first field. A phone book is a good example: the listings are sorted in alphabetical order by last name and then by first name.

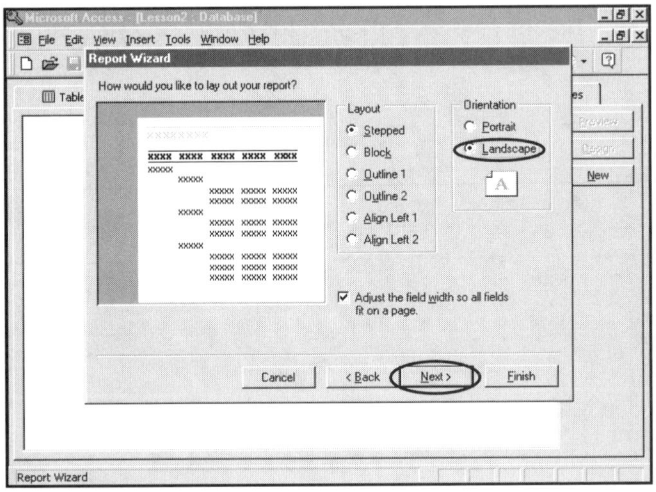


**6** Click **<u>N</u>ext**. The fourth Report Wizard dialog box allows you to choose the report layout. Select the **<u>L</u>andscape** button to print the report horizontally.

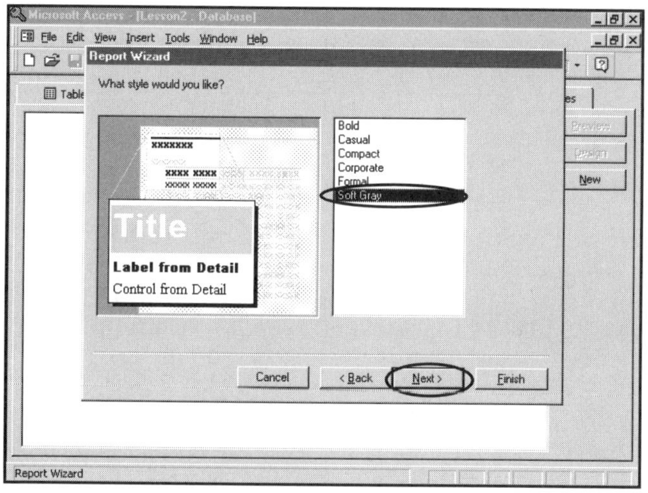


**7** Click **Next**. The fifth Report Wizard dialog box allows you to choose the report design. Select **Soft Gray**, if it is not already selected.

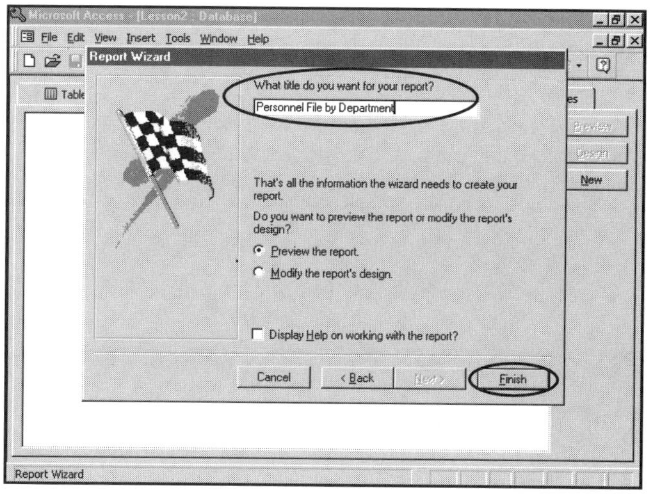


**8** Click **Next**. The sixth Report Wizard dialog box asks for a report name. Call the report **Personnel File by Department**.

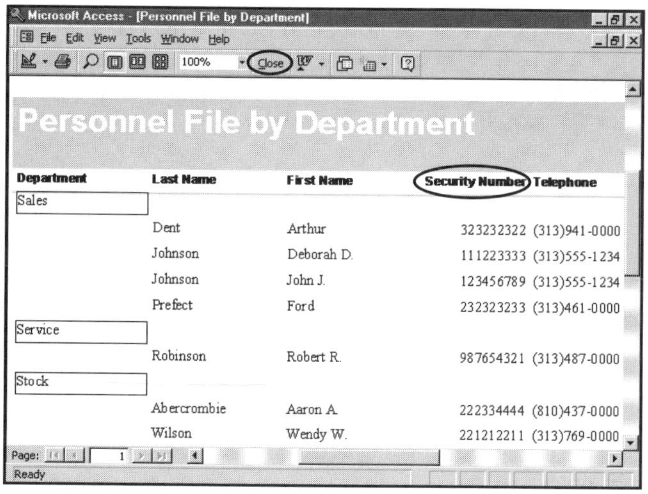


### Tip for Instructors

It is normal for reports to need editing, like this one. Some fields need more room, while others need to be shortened.

**9** Click **Finish**. A Report Preview is displayed. Notice that the form looks quite good, but still needs a little editing, because some of the field names are cut off and the spacing of the columns needs improvement.

# Task 9

> **Tip for Instructors**
> The Learn on Demand Module/Lesson "Modifying and Printing a Report" applies to this task.

## Modifying and Printing a Report

### Why would I do this?

The Report Wizard is a great tool to create the overall structure of a report. Often, however, the report may need some modifications to align fields under headings properly, or to show the full field name. In the report that was just created, the Social Security Number column heading is cut off on the left and only shows Security Number. Spacing between the columns is uneven, and the report would look better if the spacing was more evenly distributed. Once the report looks the way you want, it is easy to print a copy.

In this task, you learn a few techniques for modifying a report. The techniques used are similar to the ones used in Task 6 when you changed the design of the Personnel File Input Form. After modifying the report, you will print it.

**1** Click the **View** button to return to the Report Design window.

> **On Your Mark**
> Like the **Form Wizard**, the **Report Wizard** creates a report that might need modification. What changes do you see that need to be made in this report?

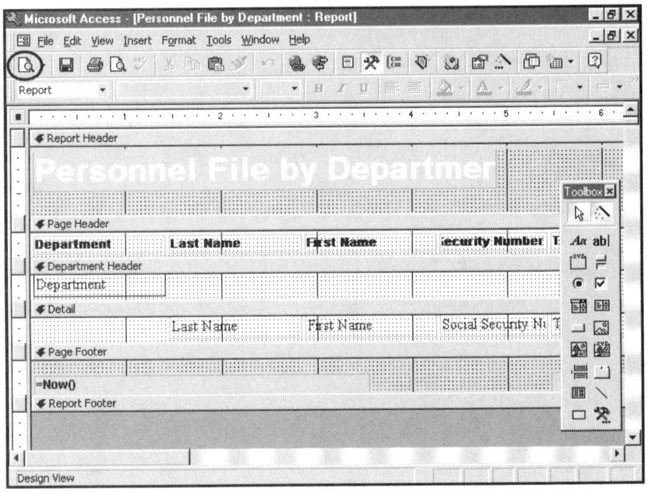


Handles

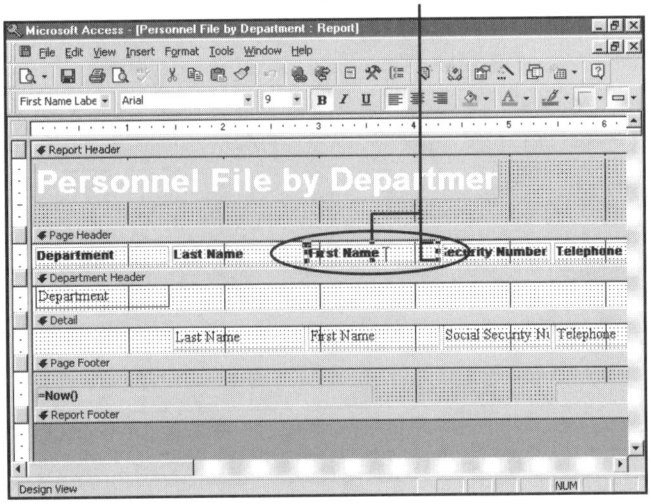


**2** Click the **First Name** label in the Page Header to select it. The small squares around the edge of the box are called handles. These are used to modify the size and shape of a label or text box.

> **Tip for Instructors**
> The items listed under either Header section are labels. The field names under the Detail section are actual data from your records. The Detail section might have multiple records, but the design does not require duplication of the fields.

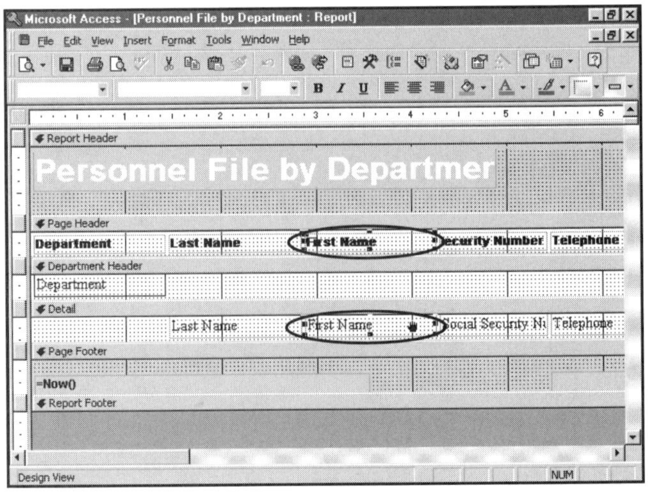


**3** Hold down the Shift key and click the **First Name** text box in the Detail section to select it. Both the label and the text boxes are now selected and can be modified together.

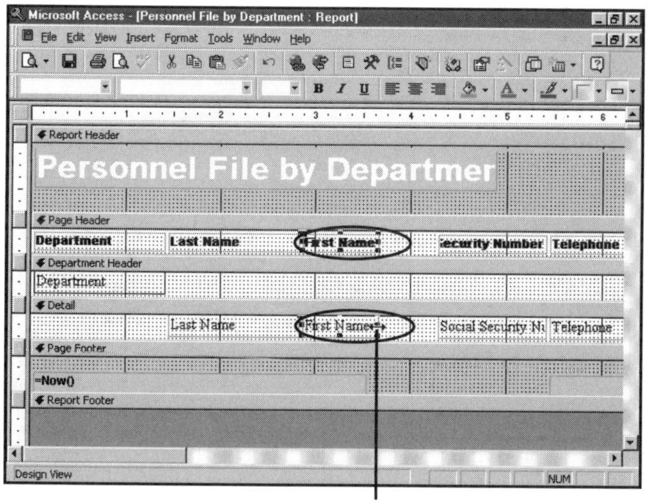


Double-headed arrow

**4** Point to the handle in the middle of the right end of the **First Name** text box. When the pointer turns into a double-headed arrow, click and drag the end of the box to the left to shorten the length of the box as shown in the figure. Now there is room to lengthen the size of the Social Security Number label.

### Quicksand

If the ⇧Shift key is not used, the labels will move alone and realignment will be required.

### Quicksand

If any of the corner handles are used to change the size of the field boxes, the box might become thinner or thicker vertically. Be sure to use the middle handle.

**5** Click the **Security Number** label to select it. Hold down the ⇧Shift key and click the **Social Security Number** text box to select it.

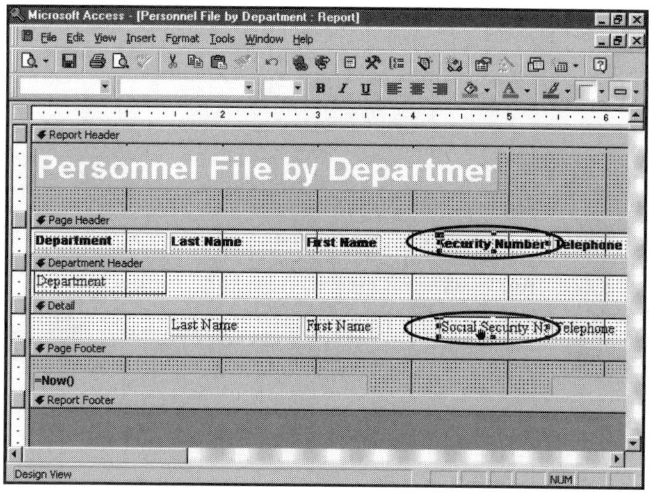


### Concept

Because the report is evenly spaced with the **Report Wizard**, it is necessary to shorten or move one field to lengthen another.

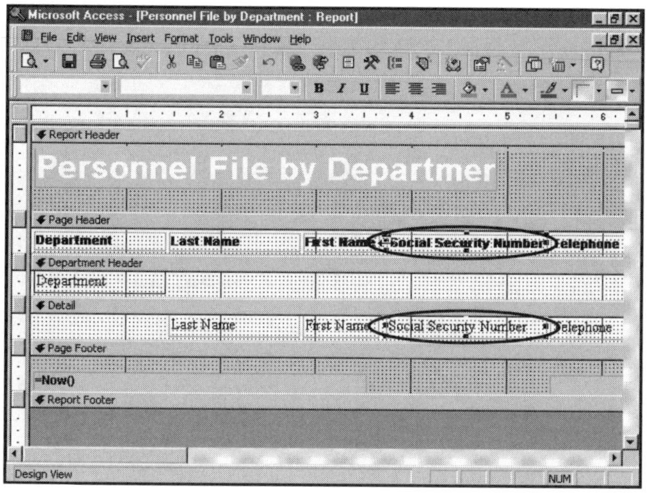


### Tip for Students

It is important to see all of the text in a field label in a header. However, the text of the field text box does not necessarily have to be seen in full, only the data. To check for correct width, switch to **Report View**.

**6** Point to the handle in the middle of the left end of the Security Number label box. Click and drag the end of the box to the left to lengthen it as shown in the figure.

**7** With both the label and text box still selected, click the **Center** alignment button on the Formatting toolbar. This centers the numbers under the label in the report.

Center button

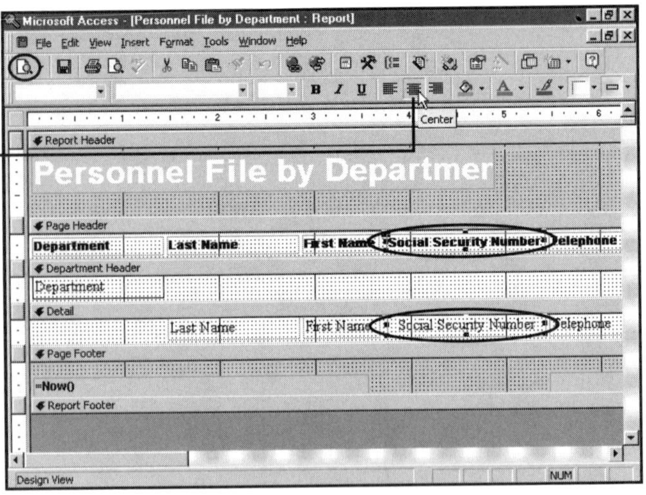


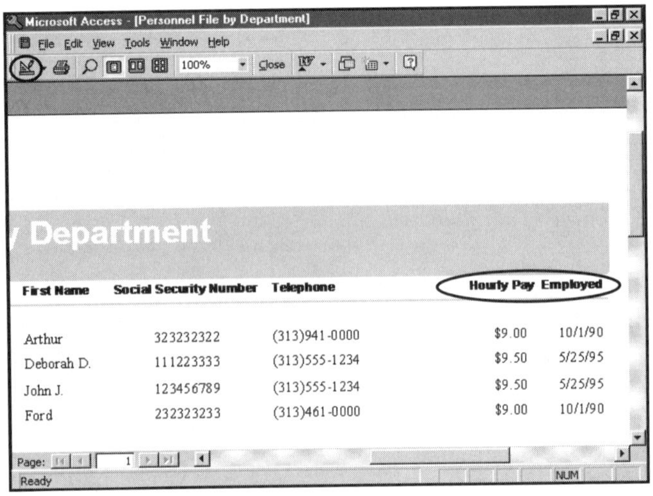


**8** Click the **View** button to see the effect of your changes. Scroll to the right and notice that the Hourly Pay and Employed fields are too close together.

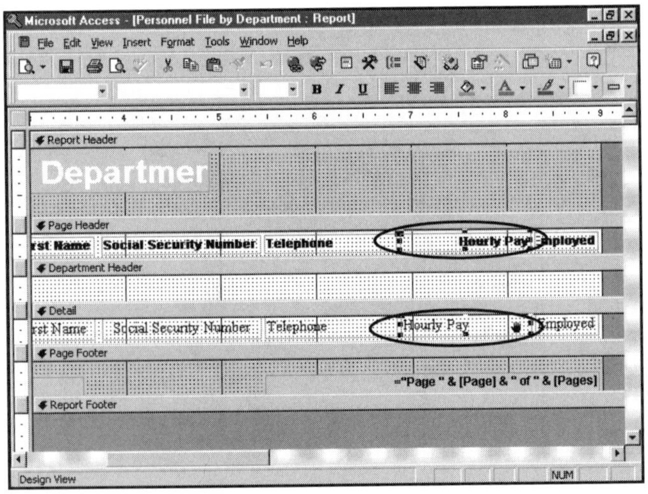


**Q & A** **?**

*Question:* How do you select the label and text box together?
Answer: press Shift as you click.

**9** Click the **View** button to return to **Design View**. Click the **Hourly Pay** label, hold down the Shift key, and click the **Hourly Pay** text box.

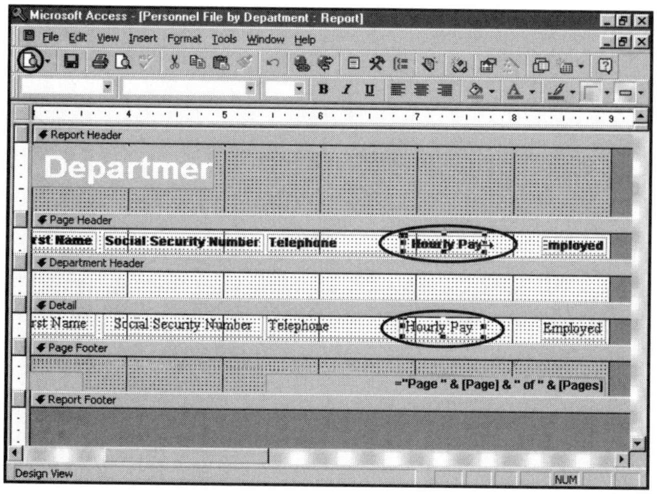


**10** Point to the handle on the right end of the **Hourly Pay** label box. Click and drag the end of the box to the left to shorten both the label and text box as shown in the figure.

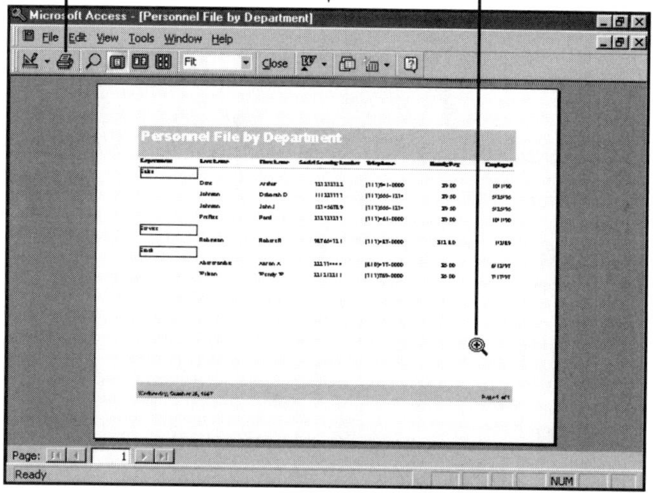


**11** Click the **View** button to see the effect of your changes. The mouse pointer is in the shape of a magnifying glass. Click the report to see a full-page view of the report. The columns are more evenly spaced now, and the column headings are fully displayed. If necessary, adjust the width of the Employed field so the title is fully displayed.

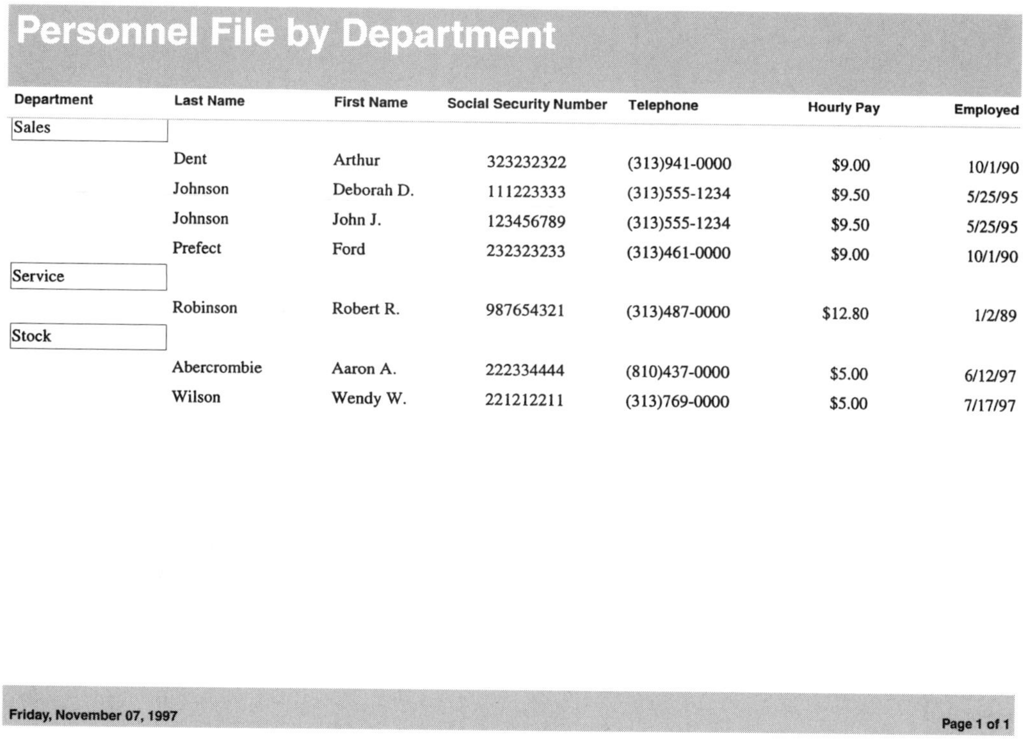

Personnel File by Department

| Department | Last Name | First Name | Social Security Number | Telephone | Hourly Pay | Employed |
|---|---|---|---|---|---|---|
| Sales | | | | | | |
| | Dent | Arthur | 323232322 | (313)941-0000 | $9.00 | 10/1/90 |
| | Johnson | Deborah D. | 111223333 | (313)555-1234 | $9.50 | 5/25/95 |
| | Johnson | John J. | 123456789 | (313)555-1234 | $9.50 | 5/25/95 |
| | Prefect | Ford | 232323233 | (313)461-0000 | $9.00 | 10/1/90 |
| Service | | | | | | |
| | Robinson | Robert R. | 987654321 | (313)487-0000 | $12.80 | 1/2/89 |
| Stock | | | | | | |
| | Abercrombie | Aaron A. | 222334444 | (810)437-0000 | $5.00 | 6/12/97 |
| | Wilson | Wendy W. | 221212211 | (313)769-0000 | $5.00 | 7/17/97 |

Friday, November 07, 1997 — Page 1 of 1

**12** Click the **Print** button to print a copy of the report.

**13** Click the **Close** button to return to **Design View**.

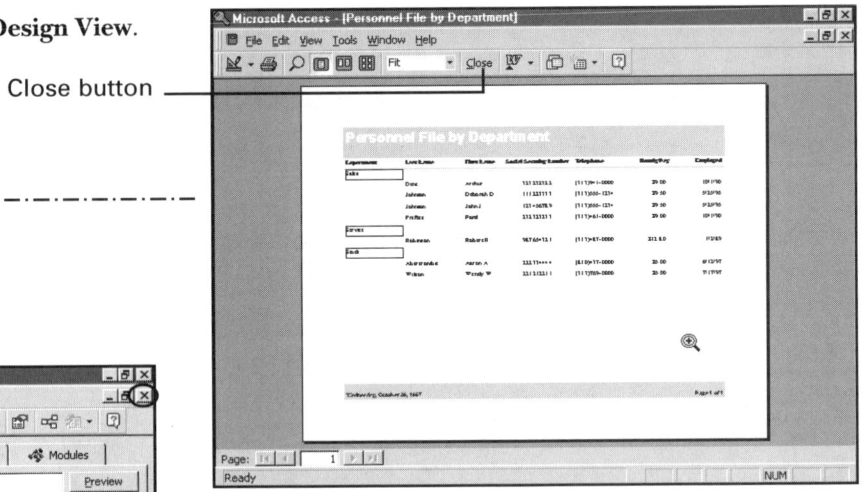


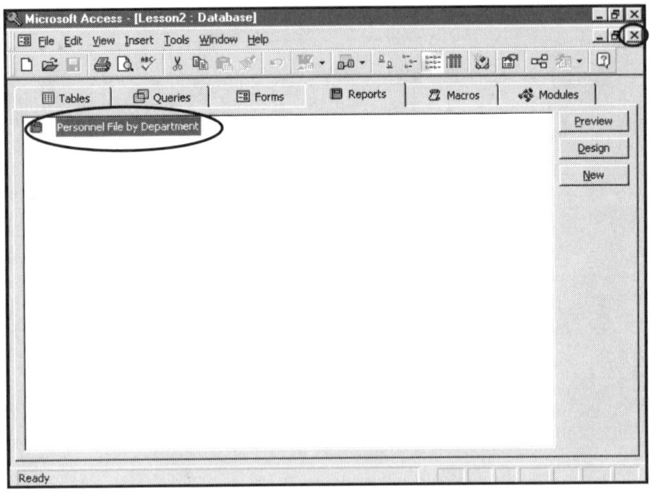


**14** Click the **Close Window** button and save the changes when prompted. The **Reports** tab of the database window shows the title of the report you created. Close the database.

# Student Exercises

## True-False

Circle either T or F.

(T) F **1.** To create a customized Access database you need to launch Access, choose Blank Database, name the file, and select a file location.

T (F) **2.** Once you have created a new database, the first thing you have to do is to create a form for data entry.

T (F) **3.** When creating a table in Design View, whatever you type in the Description column will appear in the Datasheet title bar.

(T) F **4.** When you make changes in the structure of a table, you need to save the table in order for your changes to take effect.

(T) F **5.** The first step in deleting a field is to click on the field's row selector.

T (F) **6.** If you delete a field, you can recover the data using the Undo button.

(T) F **7.** Data that you enter into a form or table is saved automatically.

(T) F **8.** You can see only one record at a time in a Columnar form.

T (F) **9.** The AutoForm: Columnar option gives you more control than the Form Wizard when creating a new form.

(T) F **10.** In a report, you can sort records up to four fields.

# Identifying Parts of the Access Screens

Refer to the figures and identify the numbered parts of the screen. Write the letter of the correct label in the space next to the number.

1. C
2. D
3. E
4. F
5. J
6. B
7. A
8. I
9. E
10. G

**A.** Label button
**B.** Toolbox button
**C.** View button
**D.** Undo button
**E.** Maximize button
**F.** Close Window button
**G.** Detail area
**H.** Text box
**I.** Label
**J.** Row selector

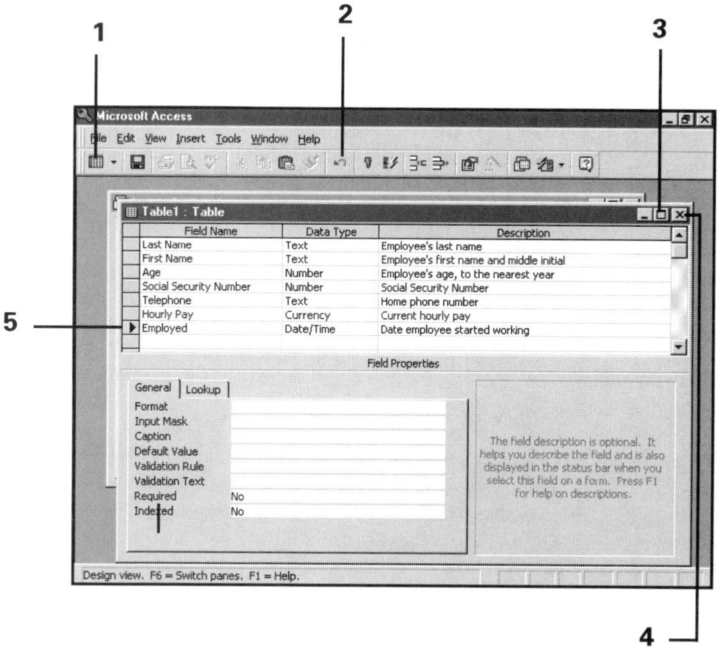


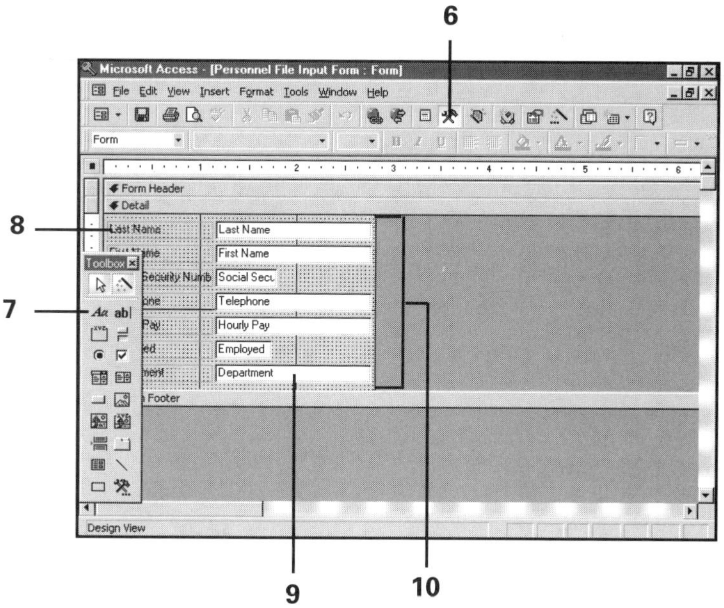

## Matching

Match the statements below to the word or phrase that is the best match from the list. Write the letter of the matching word or phrase in the space provided next to the number.

1. _D_ A toolbar of Access design tools
2. _F_ Option which allows you to create a customized database
3. _H_ Sets the tab order from left to right and top to bottom
4. _I_ Indicates you are editing a record that isn't saved yet
5. _A_ The shape of the pointer when you are moving a text box on a form
6. _G_ Indicates that a text box or label is selected
7. _B_ Indicates an empty record
8. _K_ Horizontal report orientation
9. _E_ The shape of the pointer when you are drawing a label box
10. _C_ Where the data is shown on a form

**A.** Hand pointer
**B.** Asterisk record selector
**C.** Text box
**D.** Toolbox
**E.** Crosshair pointer with an attached A
**F.** Blank Database
**G.** Handles
**H.** Auto Order
**I.** Pencil record selector
**J.** Portrait
**K.** Landscape

# Application Exercises

## Exercise 1 – Creating a Database and a Table

1. Launch Access. Choose the **Blank Database** option. Name the new database **EX0201**.
2. Use the skills that you have learned in this lesson to create the **Pool Parts Inventory** table as shown in the figure. See the steps below for more detail.
3. Make sure the **Table** tab is selected. Choose **New**.
4. Select the **Design View** option from the **New Table** dialog box.
5. Enter the fields as shown.
6. Click the **View** button to move to **Datasheet View**. Name the table **Pool Parts Inventory**.
7. Let Access create a **primary key** for you.

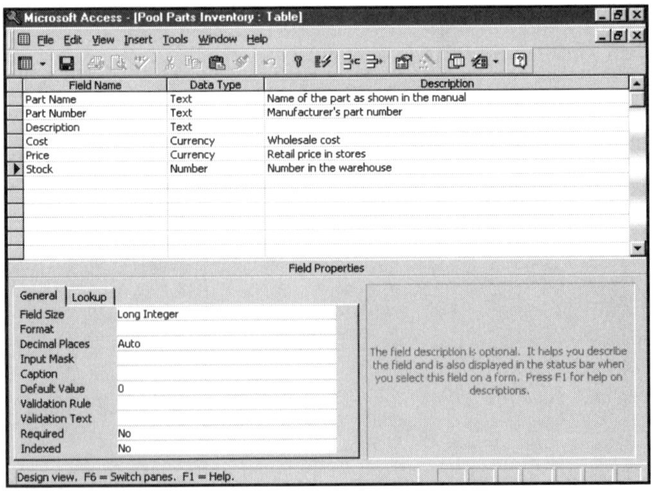

# Exercise 2 – Entering Records into the Inventory Table

1. Make sure you are in **Datasheet View** of the **Pool Parts Inventory** table.
2. Use the skills that you have learned in this lesson to enter the data into the table as shown in the figure. See the steps below for more detail. You can create an AutoForm to enter the data if you prefer. (Note: The widths of the columns in this table have been resized to show all of the fields.)
3. Enter the data for each field as shown. Press Tab or ↵Enter after each entry and at the end of each record.
4. Choose **File**, **Page Setup**, and **Landscape** orientation.
5. Choose **File**, **Print** to print a copy of the table.

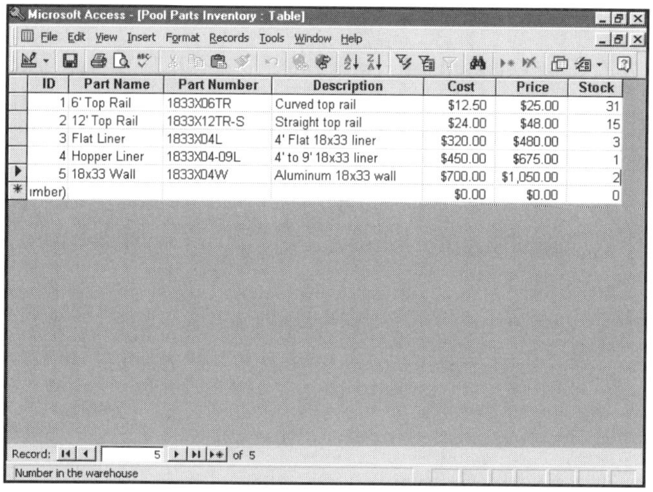


| ID | Part Name | Part Number | Description | Cost | Price | Stock |
|---|---|---|---|---|---|---|
| 1 | 6' Top Rail | 1833X06TR | Curved top rail | $12.50 | $25.00 | 31 |
| 2 | 12' Top Rail | 1833X12TR-S | Straight top rail | $24.00 | $48.00 | 15 |
| 3 | Flat Liner | 1833X04L | 4' Flat 18x33 liner | $320.00 | $480.00 | 3 |
| 4 | Hopper Liner | 1833X04-09L | 4' to 9' 18x33 liner | $450.00 | $675.00 | 1 |
| 5 | 18x33 Wall | 1833X04W | Aluminum 18x33 wall | $700.00 | $1,050.00 | 2 |
| ımber) | | | | $0.00 | $0.00 | 0 |

# Exercise 3 – Adding and Deleting Fields

1. Click the **View** button to return to **Design view**. Because this information is to be printed for a customer price list, you will remove the **Cost** field. You will also add a **Sale Price** field.
2. Use the skills that you have learned in this lesson to create the **Pool Parts Inventory** table as shown in the figure. See the steps below for more detail.
3. Click the **row selector** for the **Cost** field and press Del. Agree to permanently delete the data.
4. Move the cursor to the first blank row and type Sale Price. Choose the **Currency** data type. Type 10% off in the Description area.
5. Click the **View** button to move back to **Datasheet view**. Save the changes to the table.
6. Fill in the **Sale Price** field as shown.
7. Choose **File**, **Print** and print a copy of the table in **Landscape** orientation. Close the table.

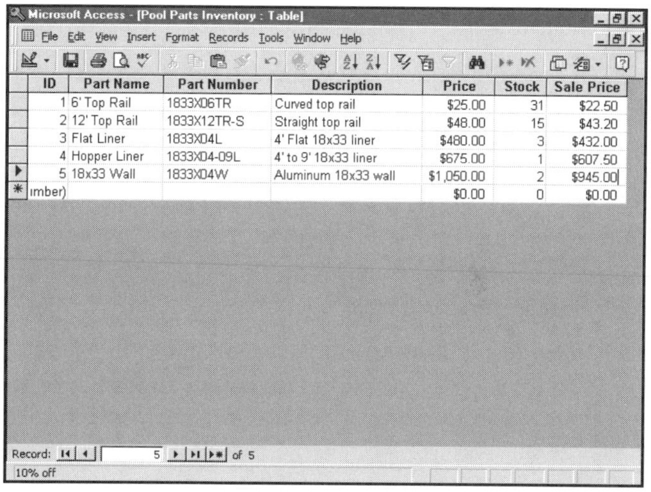


| ID | Part Name | Part Number | Description | Price | Stock | Sale Price |
|---|---|---|---|---|---|---|
| 1 | 6' Top Rail | 1833X06TR | Curved top rail | $25.00 | 31 | $22.50 |
| 2 | 12' Top Rail | 1833X12TR-S | Straight top rail | $48.00 | 15 | $43.20 |
| 3 | Flat Liner | 1833X04L | 4' Flat 18x33 liner | $480.00 | 3 | $432.00 |
| 4 | Hopper Liner | 1833X04-09L | 4' to 9' 18x33 liner | $675.00 | 1 | $607.50 |
| 5 | 18x33 Wall | 1833X04W | Aluminum 18x33 wall | $1,050.00 | 2 | $945.00 |
| ımber) | | | | $0.00 | 0 | $0.00 |

# Exercise 4 – Creating a Report Using the Report Wizard

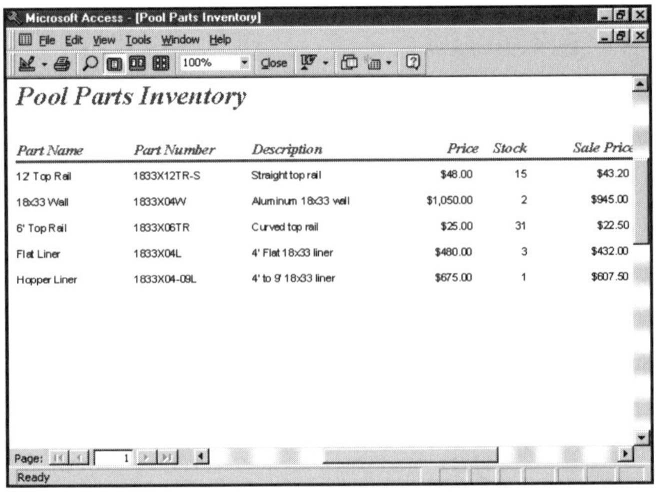


1. Click the **Reports** tab.
2. Use the skills that you have learned in this lesson to create the **Pool Parts Inventory** report as shown in the figure. See the steps below for more detail.
3. Click New. Choose **Report Wizard** and the **Pool Parts Inventory** table.
4. Select all of the fields, then highlight the **ID** field and remove it from the selected fields. (Note: To remove the ID field, click the < button. The ID field moves back to the Available Fields box.)
5. Do not group on any of the fields.
6. Sort by **Part Name**.
7. Select a **Tabular** report printed in the **Landscape** orientation.
8. Select the **Corporate** style.
9. Name the report **Pool Parts Inventory Report**.
10. Preview the report, then print it.
11. Close the report and return to the database window.

# Exercise 5 – Creating and Modifing a Form

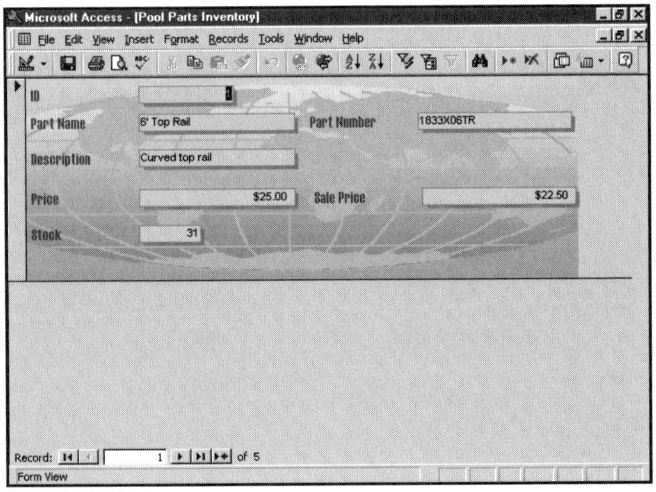


1. Click the **Forms** tab.
2. Use the skills that you have learned in this lesson to create the **Pool Parts Inventory Input Form** as shown in the figure. See the steps below for more detail.
3. Click **New**. Select the **AutoForm: Columnar** and the **Pool Parts Inventory** table. (Note: You may have a different background to your form.)
4. Click the **View** button to change to **Design View**. (Note: If necessary, click the Maximize button to enlarge the view.)
5. Rearrange the fields as shown. Choose **View**, **Tab Order**, **Auto Order** to reset the order of entry.
6. Return to **Form View**. Print a copy of the current record, Record 1, only.
7. Close the database and exit Access.

# Lesson 3
## Modify the Structure of an Existing Database



# Introduction

When you create a custom database, there are many modifications you can make so that the database is easier to read and more useful for the end-user. There are a number of field property changes you can make to improve the data-entry process. You can apply an input mask to format a field so it looks like the information you are entering, such as you saw with telephone numbers or Social Security numbers in Lesson 1. You can make common values appear in a field automatically, and you can create lists of common field entries so the user does not have to type the same information over and over. You can also add explanatory information to forms and reports to make them more useful.

In this lesson, you change some of the properties in a table and add a combo box, list box, header, footer, and a page break to a form.

**Tip for Instructors**
The Learn on Demand Module that applies to Lesson 3 is found in the Modify the Structure of an Existing Database subfolder of Learn Access 97.

**On Your Mark**
Thus far, we have learned how to create a simple database in which data is entered field by field by typing. What special features might help to automate a database?

## Visual Summary

When you have completed this entire lesson, you will have created a form in a database that looks like this:

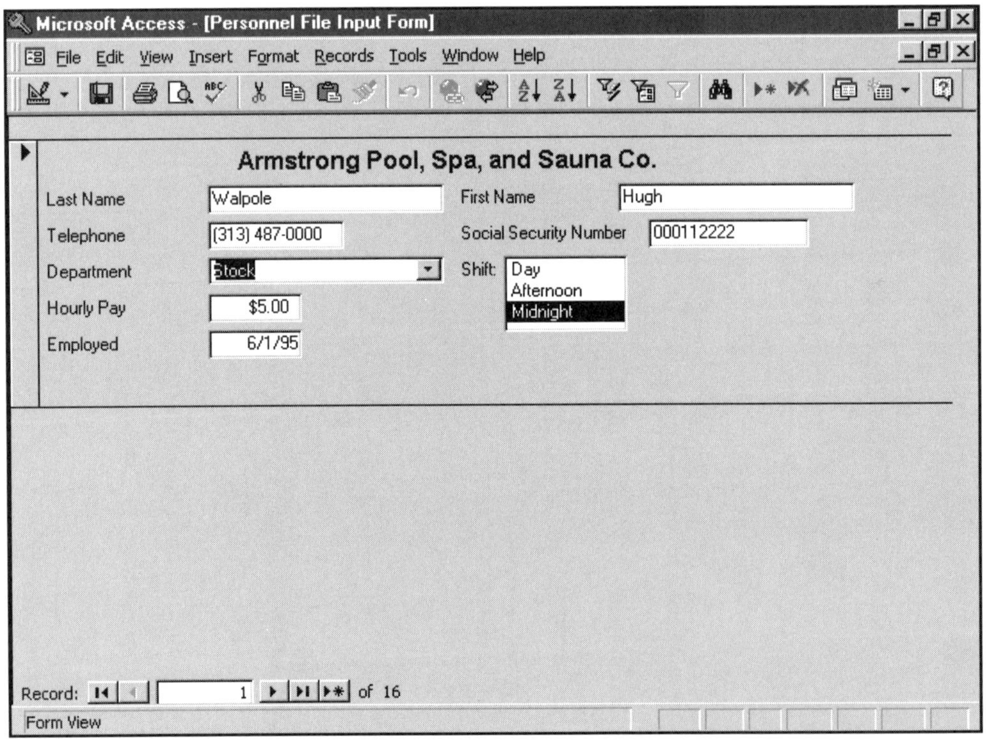


**SLIDE 3.1**

**SLIDE 3.2**

**Tip for Instructors**
Students may require a brief overview of Windows 95 and Windows Explorer. An explanation is provided in the preface of this text.

**Task Time**
**90 minutes**

# Task 1

## Changing the Data Type of a Field

> **Tip for Instructors**
> The Learn on Demand Module/Lesson "Changing the Data Type of a Field" applies to this task.

### Why would I do this?

If you plan your database carefully, you should not have to change a field data type very often. If you create enough databases, however, you will eventually need to modify the data type.

In this task, you learn how to change a number field to a text field so you can add an input mask later. In Lesson 1, the database created by the Database Wizard used input masks to help format phone numbers and zip codes. As you will recall, an input mask applies special field structures to help the user enter data. Input masks are primarily used in Text and Date/Time fields but can be manually applied to number or currency fields. To make it easier, you will change the data type to text so the Input Mask Wizard can be used to apply an input mask in Task 2.

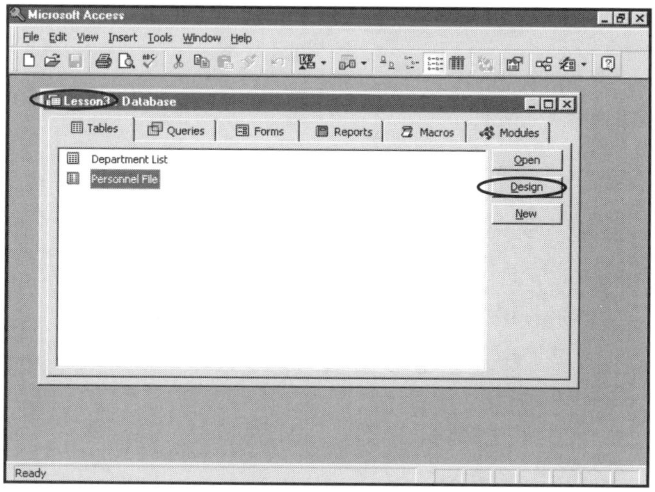


**1** Using Windows Explorer, copy **Less0301** and rename the file **Lesson3**. (Follow your instructor's directions for the location to copy and rename the file.) Launch Microsoft **Access**. Choose **Open an Existing Database**, find the file **Lesson3**, and open the file. This is a slightly expanded version of the file you worked on in Lesson 2.

> **Tip for Instructors**
> It might be easier to copy and rename the file by right-clicking the filename in the Open dialog box and choosing **Copy**, **Rename**.

**2** Select the **Personnel File** table and click the **Design** button to switch to **Design View**.

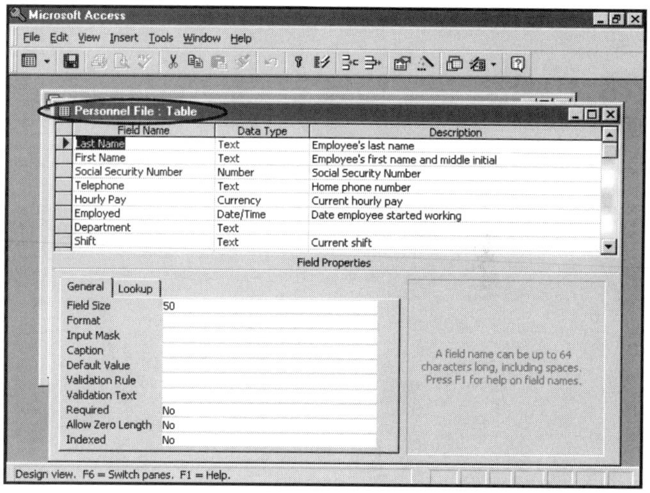


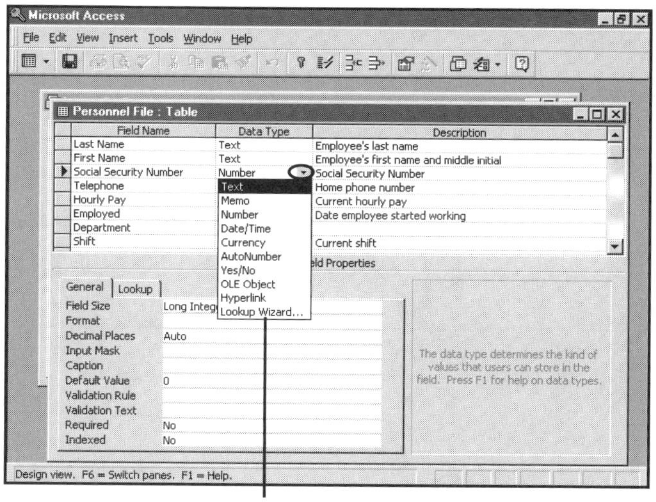


Data Type drop-down menu

> **Tip for Students**
> To open the Explorer, you do not have to close Access. Simply click the **Start** button and open the Explorer. To switch between the programs, click the application name on the taskbar.

**3** Place the cursor in the **Data Type** column of the **Social Security Number** row. Click the arrow to activate the drop-down menu.

**4** Choose the **Text** option from the **Data Type** drop-down menu.

> **Tip for Students** !
>
> The Text data type can contain any character; the Number data type can contain only numbers.

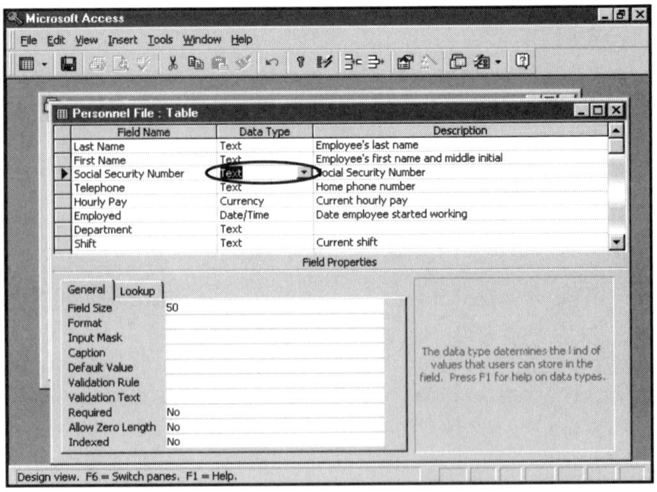


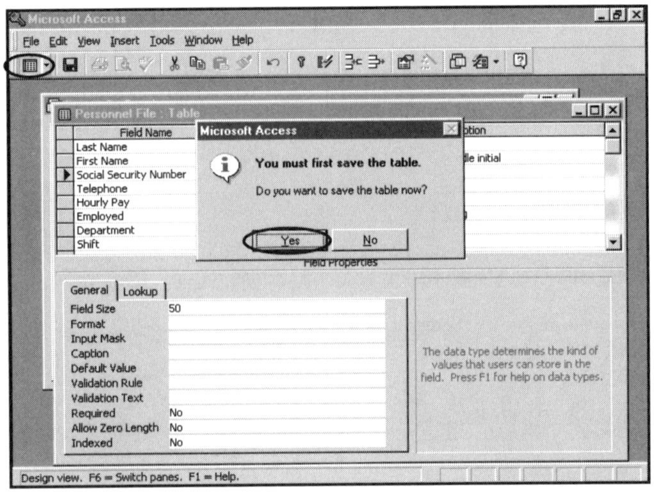


**5** Click the **View** button to switch to **Datasheet View**. Click **Yes** when prompted to save your table.

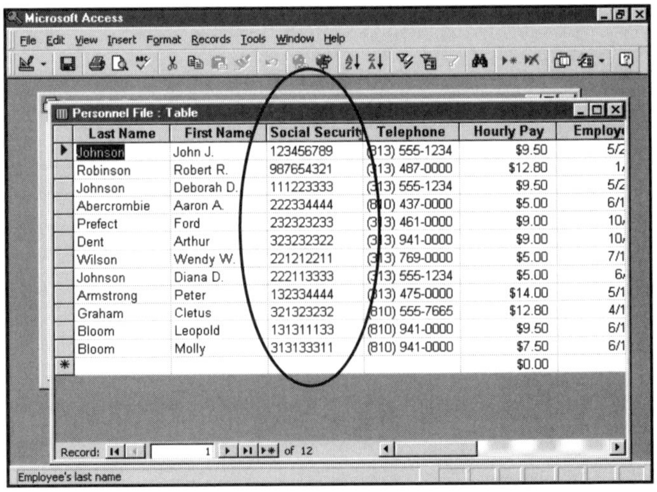


> **Q & A** ?
>
> *Question:* Why did you change the data type of the **Social Security Number** field to **Text**? *Answer:* So you could add an input mask.

**6** Notice that the numbers in the **Social Security Number** field are left-aligned, now that you have designated them as a text data type.

# Task 2

> **Tip for Instructors**
> The Learn on Demand Module/Lesson "Adding Input Masks to Aid Data Entry" applies to this task.

## Adding Input Masks to Aid Data Entry

### Why would I do this?

Many types of information, such as telephone numbers, Social Security numbers, and dates include dashes and parentheses as part of their structure. In Lesson 1, you entered data in some fields that used a pre-formatted structure, while in Lesson 2, the table you designed did not contain that same formatting. Entering data is much easier when the format needed has already been applied to the field structure in the table.

In this task, you learn how to use the Input Mask Wizard to create a formatting structure for the Social Security Number field.

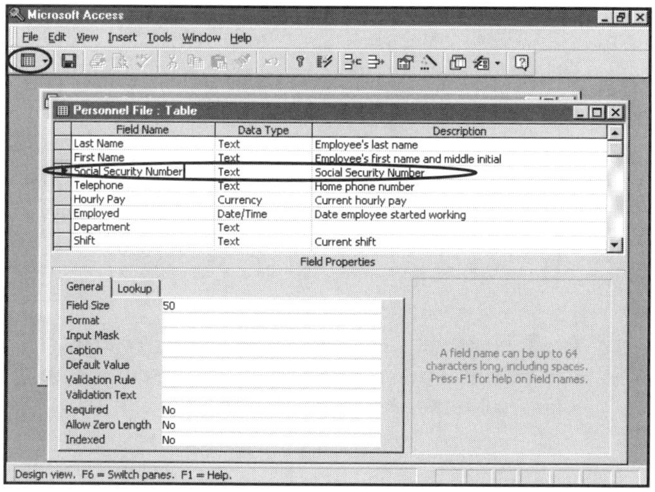


**1** Click the **View** button to change to **Design View**. Click anywhere in the **Social Security Number** field.

> **On Your Mark**
> Some data entry types have a particular formatting. What are some data types that you know always have the same format, even on paper?

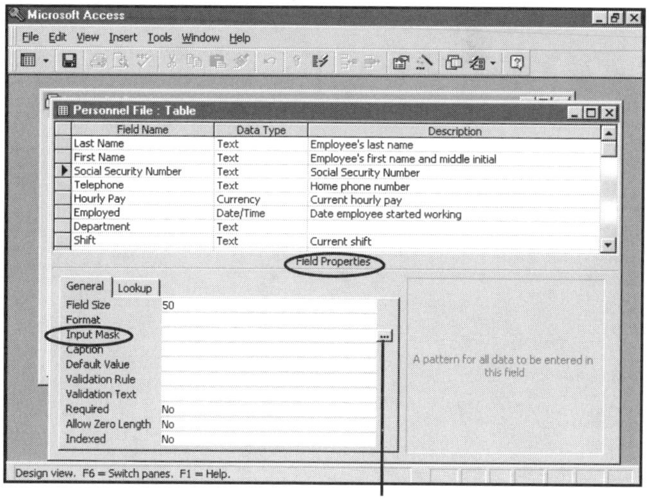


Build button

> **Quicksand**
> A customized installation of Access is necessary to use the Input Mask Wizard because it is part of the Advanced Wizard Package. If this feature cannot be installed, the input mask will need to be typed in manually.

**2** In the **Field Properties** section click in the **Input Mask** box. A **Build** button is displayed on the right edge of the box.

**3** Click the **Build** button. The first **Input Mask Wizard** dialog box opens. Select the **Social Security Number** option.

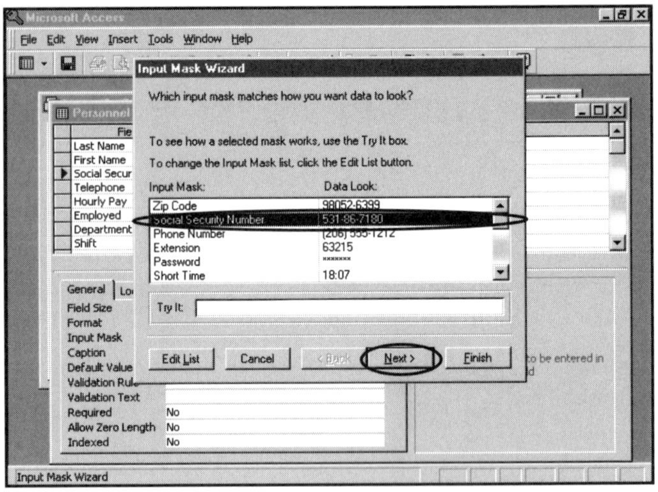


**Pothole:** If your system was set up with a standard installation, you will get a warning that this feature is not installed. This feature is part of the Advanced Wizard package that can be installed as part of a custom installation. Consult with your instructor for further direction. If you are unable to install the Wizard, continue reading this task and you can manually enter the necessary coding. See the In Depth note following Step 6 for assistance.

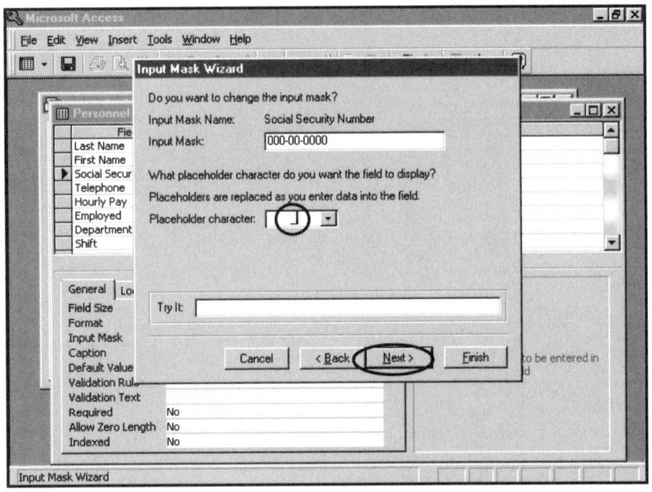


**Tip for Instructors**

Take the time to cover each screen closely. The Input Mask Wizard will be used time and again.

**4** Click Next. The second **Input Mask Wizard** dialog box opens. Accept the underscore as the placeholder.

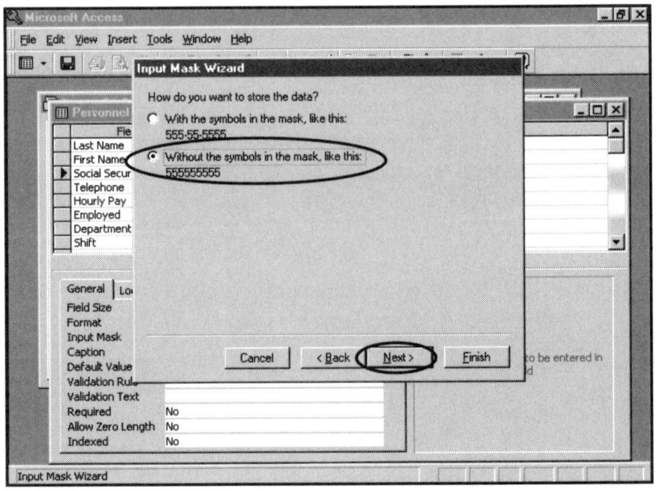


**5** Click Next. The third **Input Mask Wizard** dialog box opens. Choose to store the data without the dashes. This will take less storage space, but the dashes will still be displayed.

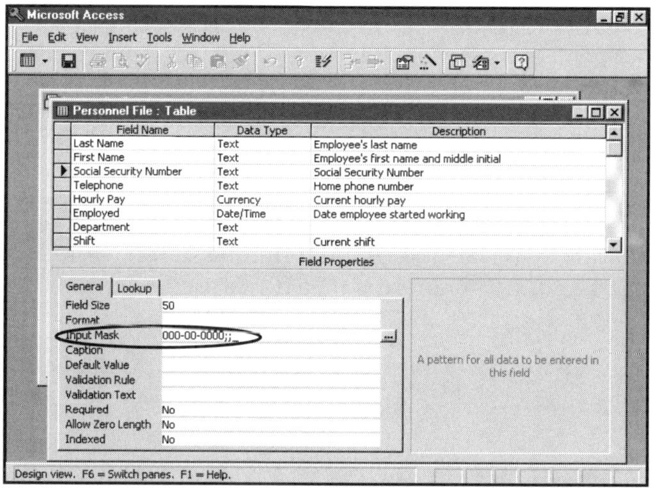


**SLIDE 3.3**

**6** Click **Next**. The last **Input Mask Wizard** dialog box opens. It requires no input. Click **Finish** to close the **Input Mask Wizard**. The input mask is shown in the **Input Mask** box.

**In Depth:** You can manually enter an input mask if you know the proper coding. If you were unable to use the Input Mask Wizard, enter the coding you see in the figure on the Input Mask line for the Social Security Number field.

**Speedy Class**

Use the Office Assistant to investigate more about input masks. Look at the samples available. Try to use some of these.

**7** Click the **View** button to move to **Datasheet View**. Save changes when prompted. Notice that all of the Social Security numbers have dashes in the proper locations.

**Q & A**

*Question:* What is the purpose of an input mask? *Answer:* To format a field entry.

**Pothole:** When you add an input mask to a field in a table that is already used as the basis for a form or record, the input mask will not affect the appearance of the field in either the form or report. You will need to add an input mask to each object.

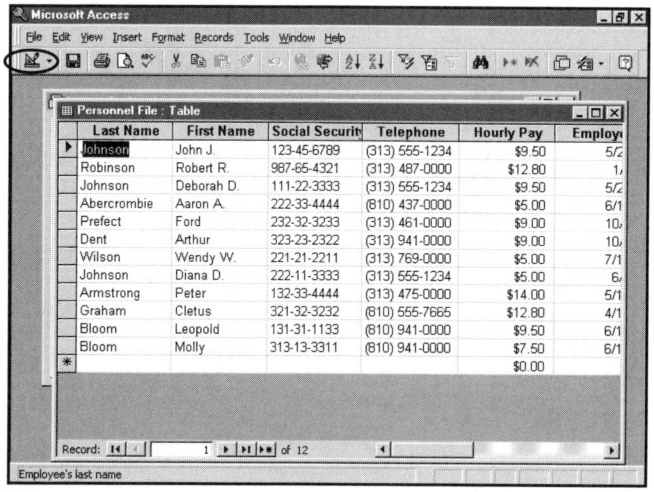


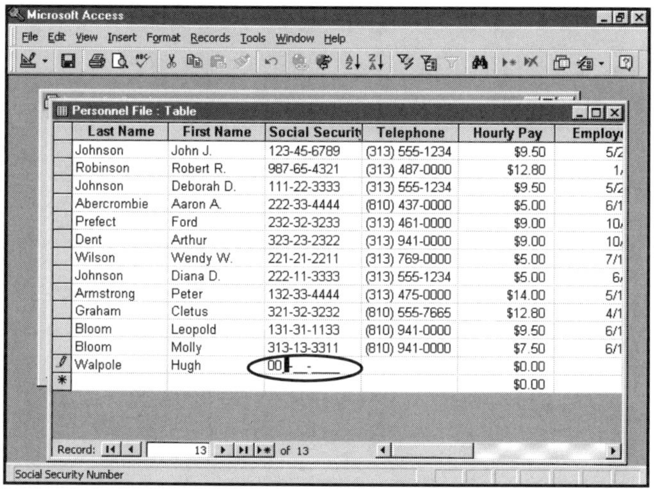


**Quicksand**

Do not type the dashes.

**Tip for Students**

The **Social Security Number** field requires all nine digits because zeros were used in the input mask.

**8** Add another record with the following data: **<u>Walpole</u>**; **<u>Hugh</u>**; **<u>000112222</u>**; **<u>(313) 487-0000</u>**; **<u>5</u>**; **<u>6/1/95</u>**; **<u>Stock</u>**; **<u>Midnight</u>**. Watch how the structure of the Social Security number is displayed as you enter the number.

# Task 3

## Setting Default Values

### Why would I do this?

> **Tip for Instructors**
> The Learn on Demand Module/Lesson "Setting Default Values" applies to this task.

> **On Your Mark**
> Sometimes, a field in a database has a common entry. What fields might have a common entry?

*Default values* are values that are entered into a field as soon as you start editing a record. For example, if most of your employees hire in at $5.00 an hour, you can have the program automatically put that number in the Hourly Pay field every time a new employee record is created. This can save time in entering data if it is used when there will be few exceptions. It also ensures that a field is not left blank.

In this task, you learn how to add the current date to the Employed field, since the only new records you will be adding will be for new employees.

**1** Click the **View** button to move to **Design View**. Click anywhere in the **Employed** field.

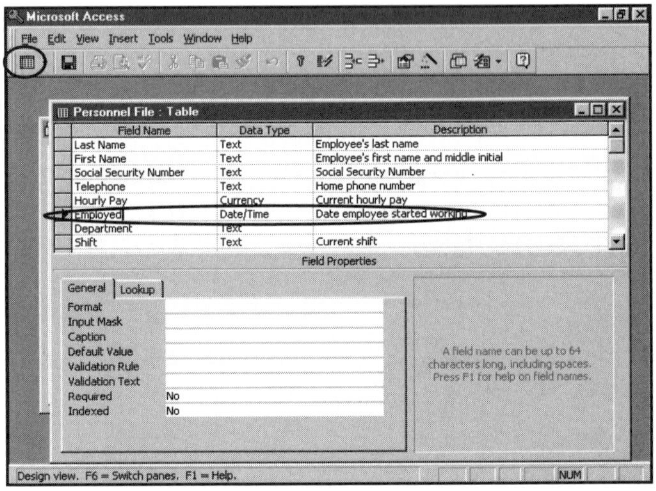


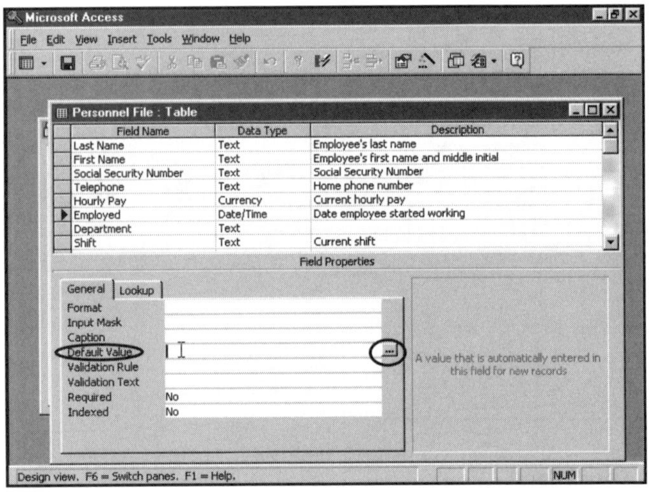


**2** In the **Field Properties** section click in the **Default Value** box. A **Build** button is displayed on the right edge of the box.

**SLIDE 3.4**

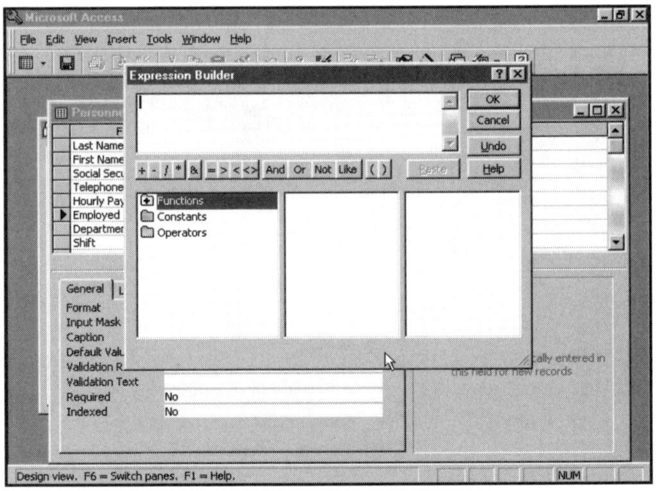


> **Tip for Instructors**
> The **Expression Builder** will cause some students problems. Cover this section slowly and explain each step thoroughly.

**3** Click the **Build** button. The **Expression Builder** dialog box opens.

**4** Double-click the **Functions** option. A subdirectory called **Built-In Functions** is displayed.

> **Concept**
> A *function* is a predefined mathematical equation. Each function has a particular name that represents the equation.

> **Concept**
> A *subdirectory* is the same as a *subfolder*.

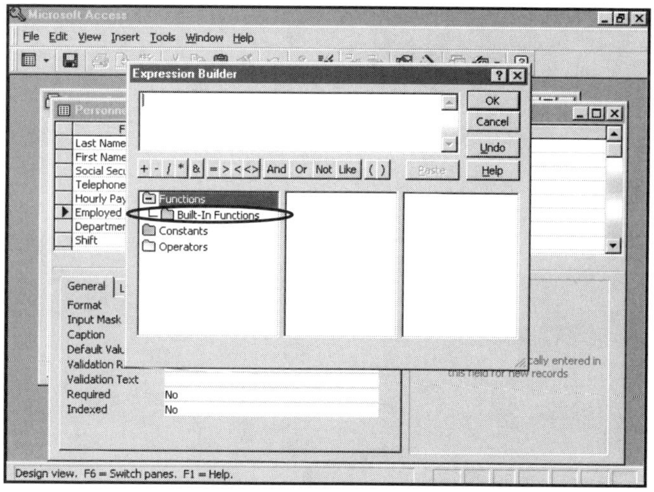


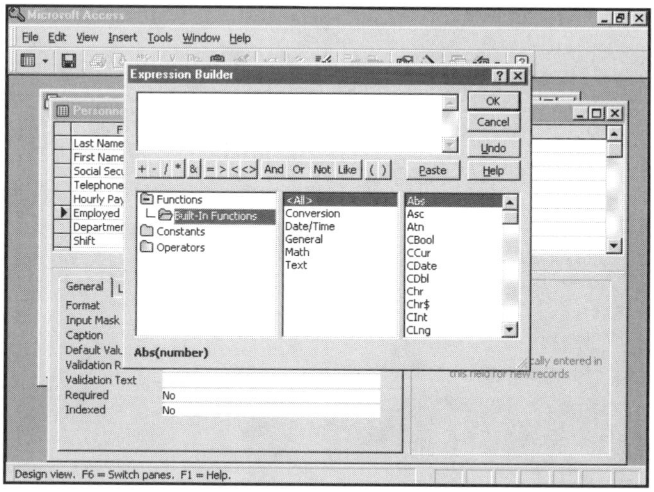


**5** Click the **Built-In Functions** subdirectory. Two new options columns are displayed.

**6** Select **Date/Time** from the middle column. A group of date and time options are displayed in the third column.

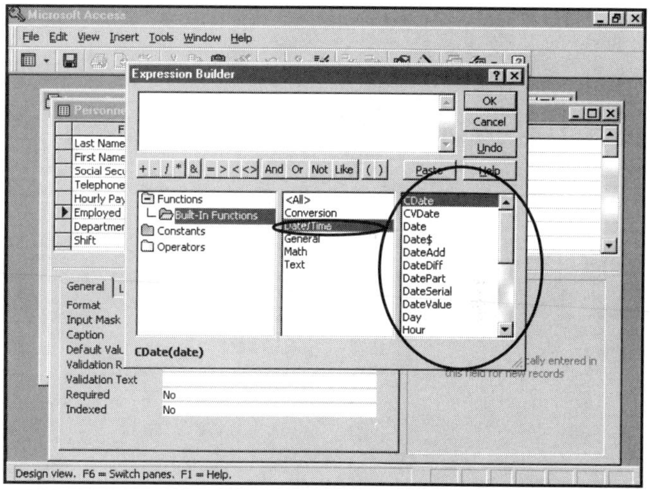


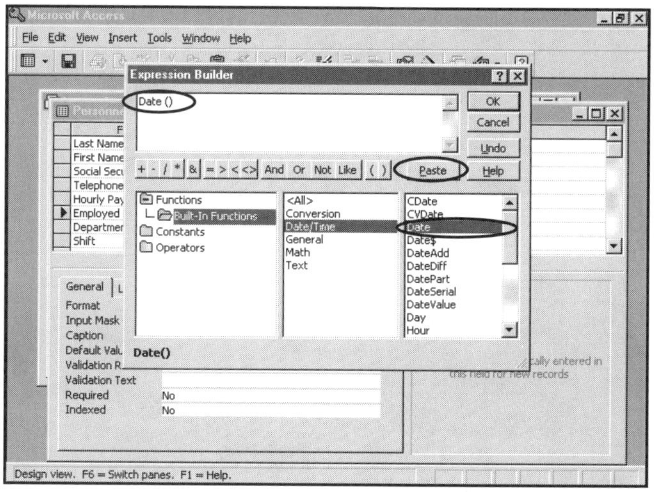


**7** Select **Date** from the third column and click the **Paste** button. The **Date()** option is pasted into the **Expression Builder** work area. This function automatically enters the current date into the Employed field.

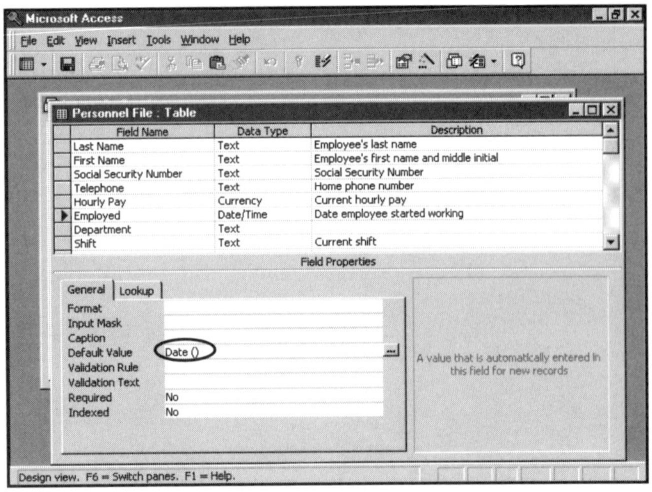


**8** Click **OK**. The **Date()** function is now displayed in the **Default Value** box for the **Employed field**.

> **Q & A** **?**
>
> *Question:* To overwrite a default value when entering records, what do you do? *Answer:* Just select the field and type.

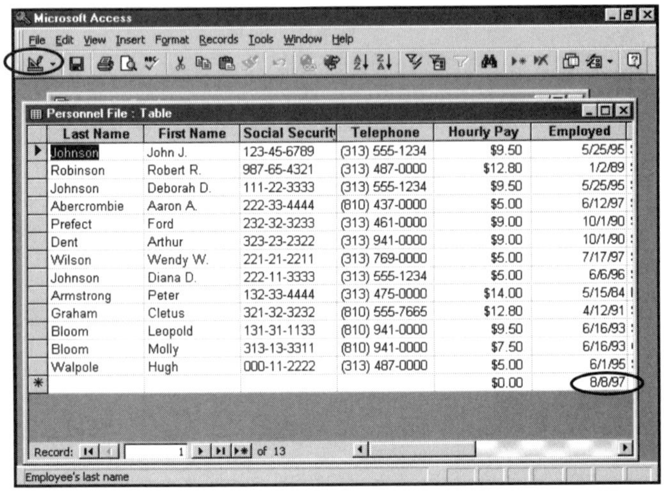


**9** Click the **View** button to move to **Datasheet View**. Save changes when prompted. Notice that the default date already appears in the **Employed** field of the empty record at the bottom of the table.

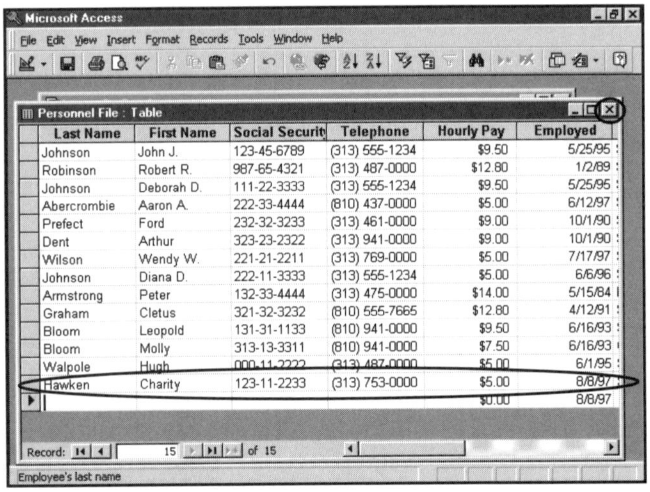


**10** Add another record with the following data as shown: <u>**Hawken**</u>; <u>**Charity**</u>; <u>**123112233**</u>; <u>**(313) 753-0000**</u>; <u>**5**</u>; (accept the current date); <u>**Stock**</u>; <u>**Day**</u>.

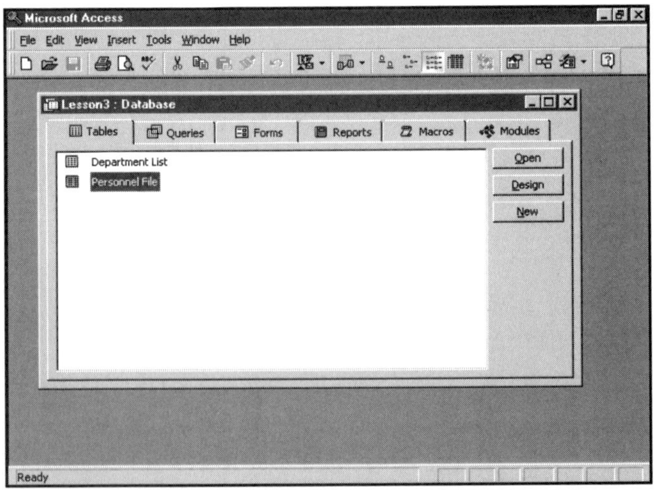


**11** Click the **Close** button to return to the Database window.

# Task 4

## Assigning a Primary Key Field

### Why would I do this?

> **On Your Mark**
> In our society, it is important to have unique identifiers for persons, products, and goods. What are some examples of unique identifiers?

> **Tip for Instructors**
> The Learn on Demand Module/Lesson "Assigning a Primary Key Field" applies to this task.

*Primary key fields* are fields that are used to speed up sorting and finding data in a large table and to link tables together. A primary key field must contain unique data for each record; that is, there can be no duplication in that field from one record to the next. Some tables use sequential numbers, known as counters, as primary keys. Others use fields that are naturally unique, such as Social Security numbers or employee identification numbers.

In this task, you learn how to designate the Social Security Number field as your primary key field.

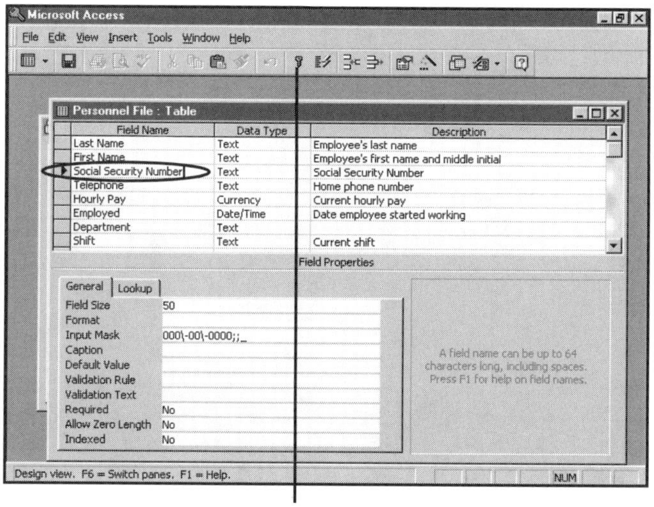


Primary Key button

**1** With the **Personnel File** table still selected, click the **Design** button to move to **Design View**. Click anywhere in the **Social Security Number** field.

> **Q & A**
> *Question:* How do you make a field the Primary Key field? *Answer.* Click the row selector for the field and click the **Primary Key** button.

> **Tip for Students**
> A primary key is not essential in a table unless relationships are necessary between tables. However, it helps with sorting large tables and is recommended.

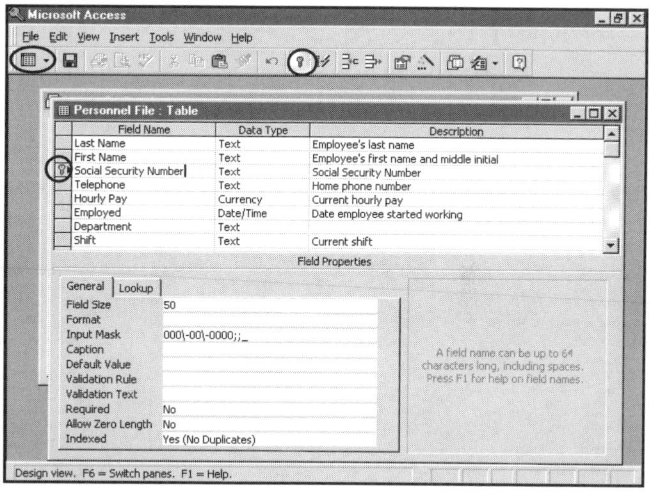


**2** Click the **Primary Key** button in the Table Design toolbar. A key symbol is placed in the row selector column to the left of the field name.

> **Tip for Students**
> The primary key is removed in the same manner as it is added.

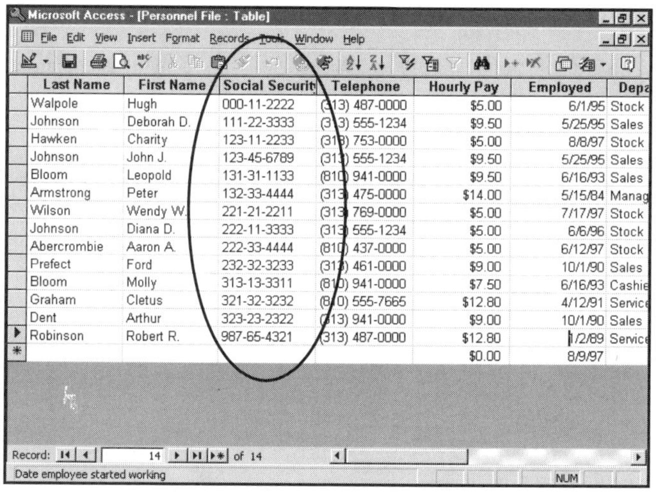


> **Tip for Students**
> If a primary key is assigned to a field that does not contain unique data, an error message appears when the table is saved. If duplicate data is typed in after the key is set, Access will not let you save that record.

**3** Click the **View** button to move to **Datasheet View**. Save changes when prompted. Notice that the table is now sorted in order of Social Security number.

# Task 5

## Adjusting Table Column Widths

> **Tip for Instructors**
> The Learn on Demand Module/Lesson "Adjusting Table Column Widths" applies to this task.

### Why would I do this?

In some small tables you will be using the Datasheet View of the table to enter information. Even with bigger tables, you will still often use Datasheet View to browse through your data. The default column widths in a table are seldom the right width, allowing far too much room for some fields, and cutting off the view of longer fields. There is an easy way to adjust the column widths. In this task, you learn how to adjust the column widths and save the changes to your layout.

> **On Your Mark**
> What might help make a table easier to read?

**1** Click the **Maximize** button to maximize the size of the Datasheet window. Notice that several of the columns are too wide, and not all of the columns are shown on the screen.

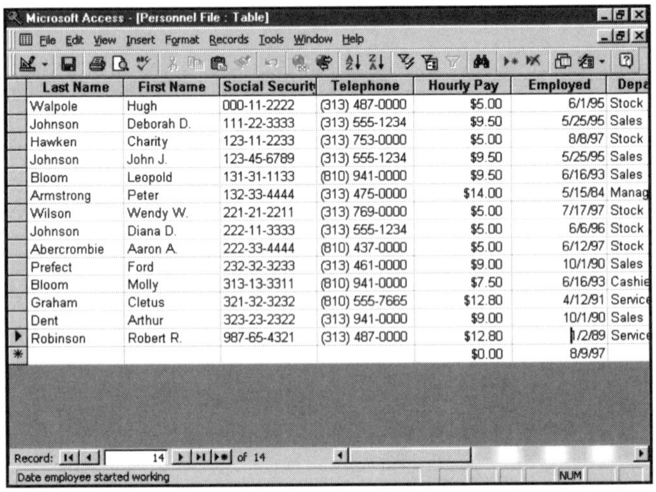


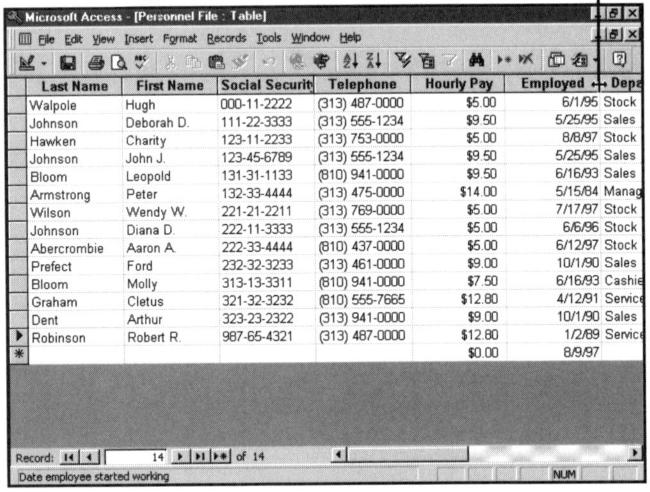


> **Tip for Instructors**
> Changing column width in an Access table is the same as changing column width in an Excel worksheet.

**2** Move the pointer to the right edge of the *field selector* for the **Employed** field. The pointer changes to a two-sided arrow.

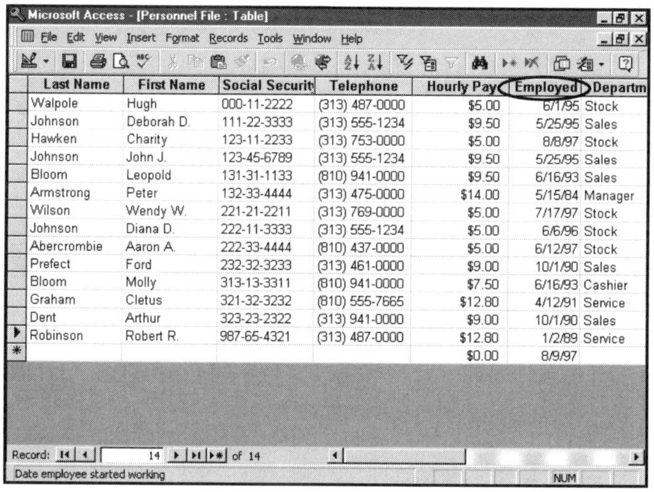


**3** Click and drag the right edge of the **field selector** until the column width is just large enough to show the **Employed** label. It may take more than one try.

**Tip for Instructors**

It is possible that the **Employed** field is already large enough. If it is, change the column width for the **Social Security Number** field.

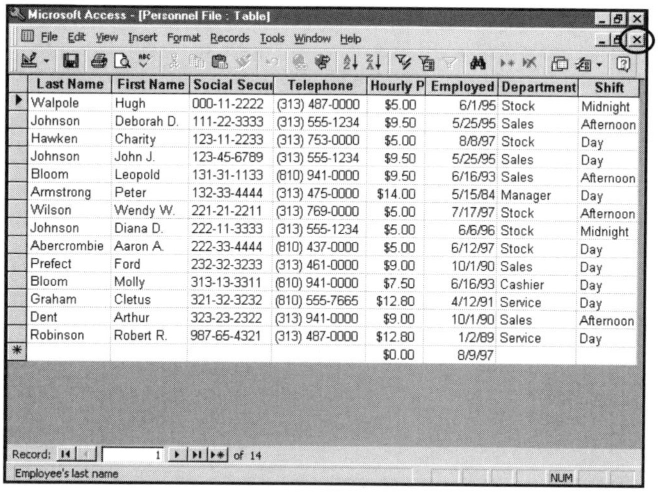


**4** Change the column widths of the other columns as shown in the figure. In some cases, part of the field name in the **field selector** will be hidden. That's ok. The objective is to view all of the record data, without scrolling.

**Quick Tip**: You can automatically adjust a column width by double-clicking on the right edge of the field selector. You can also adjust more than one field at a time by clicking in the middle of a field selector and dragging to the right or left to select multiple columns. You can double-click on the right edge of any one of the selected columns to automatically adjust all of them at once.

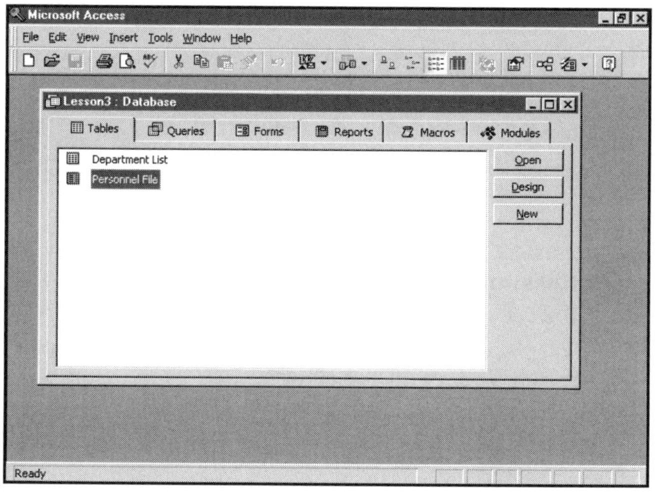


**5** Click the **Close Window** button. Save changes when prompted.

# Task 6

## Adding a List Box to a Form

> **Tip for Instructors**
> The Learn on Demand Module/Lesson "Adding a List Box to a Form" applies to this task.

### Why would I do this?

When there are only a few possible values for a field, a *list box* makes it easy to select the correct entry. By clicking on one of the items in a list box, you also assure that the entry will be spelled correctly. List boxes have certain restrictions. The entries shown in the box are the only possible entries; nothing else can be entered in that field. Also, the list box remains on the screen at all times.

In this task, you learn how to add a list box to the Shift field, which has only three possible values.

**1** Click the **Forms** tab and select the **Personnel File Input Form**.

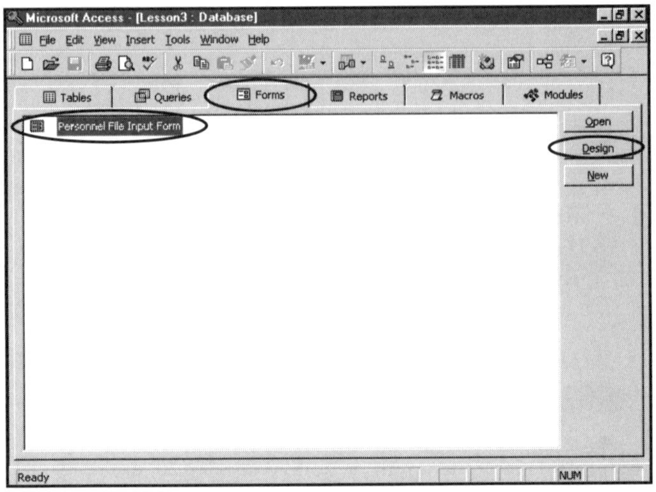


> **On Your Mark**
> Sometimes, only select lists of items provide an appropriate entry in a field. A list can be created to assist in that field. What advantages do you think this would provide?

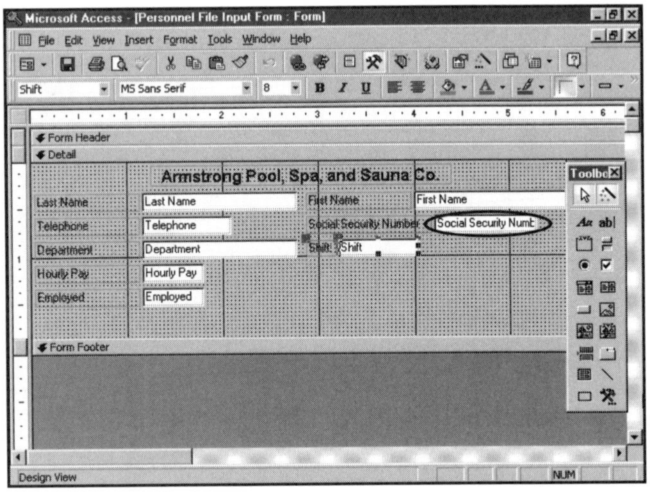


> **Quicksand**
> The text box is the label on the right. Be certain that students do not choose the label instead.

**2** Click the **Design** button to switch to **Design View**. If necessary, move the **Toolbox** so it doesn't interfere with any of the fields. Click the **text box** in the **Shift** field to select it.

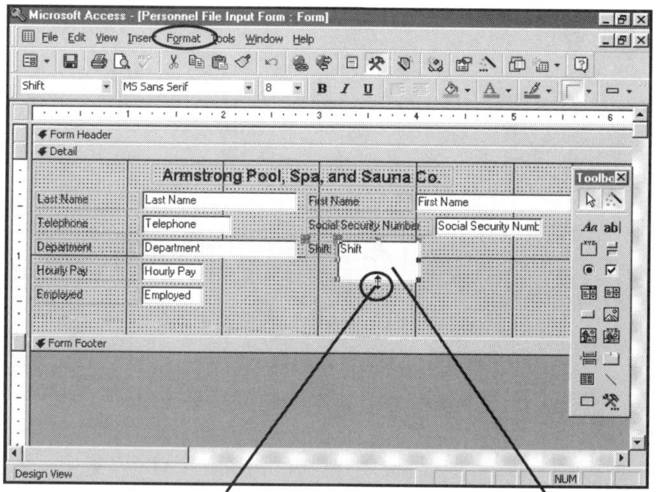


Two-headed arrow used to change the size of the list box

List box

3 Choose **F**o**rmat**, **Change To**, **List Box**. A box opens to the right of the **Shift** label. Grab the bottom handle on the box and resize it as shown in the figure so three lines of text will fit.

**Pothole:** If the **List Box** option is not available from the menu, it means you selected the **label** instead of the **text box** for the **Shift** field. Click the Shift field text box and try again.

4 Click the **Properties** button on the Form Design toolbar. The **List Box**: **Shift** properties dialog box is displayed.

**Pothole:** It is important that the properties dialog box is titled **List Box: Shift**. This indicates that the property box opened is for the list box you just created for the Shift field. If the box has any other title, it means that you clicked the mouse in another part of your screen before clicking the **Properties** button. If this happens, click the title bar of the properties box and drag the box to another part of the screen until you can see the list box. Then click the Shift list box and the properties box will change to the properties box for the selected field.

### Speedy Class

You can right-click the text box, choose **Change To**, and then complete steps 7 and 8 as shown.

Properties button

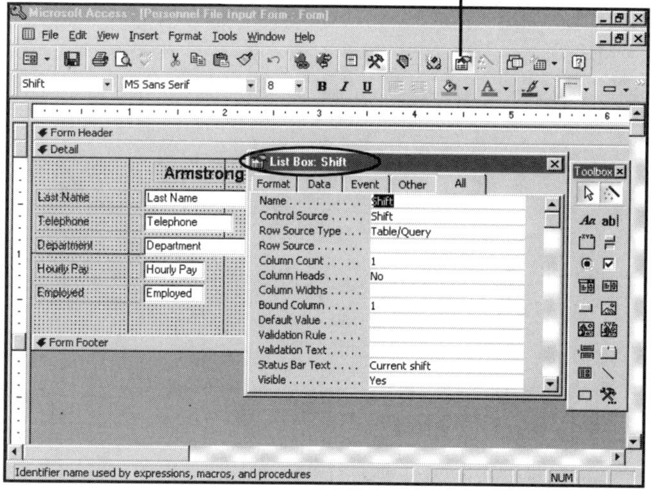


**SLIDE 3.5**

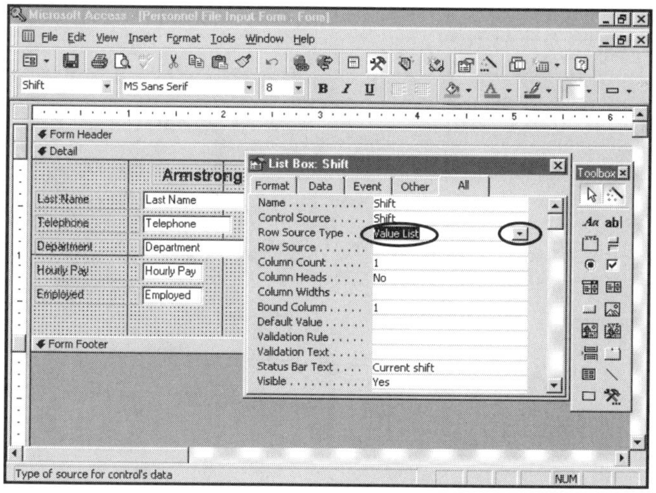


### Concept

The *Value List* option enables you to type in the values needed rather than linking them to another field or table.

5 Click in the **Row Source Type** box. Click the drop-down arrow at the right of the box, and choose **Value List**.

**6** Click in the **Row Source** box. Type the three possible entries exactly as shown: **Day; Afternoon; Midnight**. Make sure you include the semicolons between each item. These three items will appear in the **list box**.

**Quicksand**

If the semicolons are not included, all the data appears as one option.

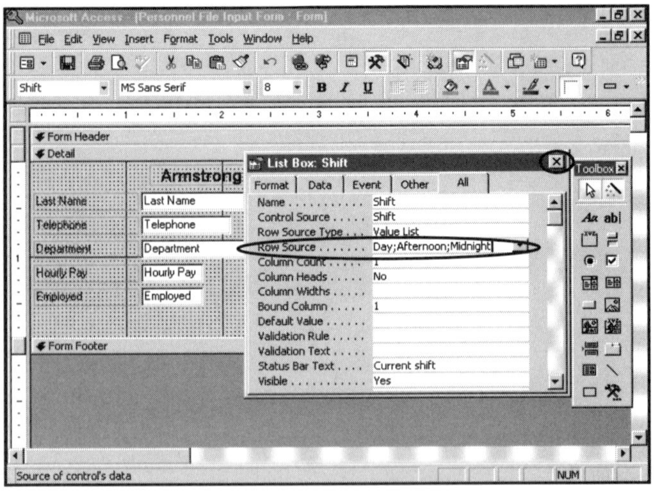


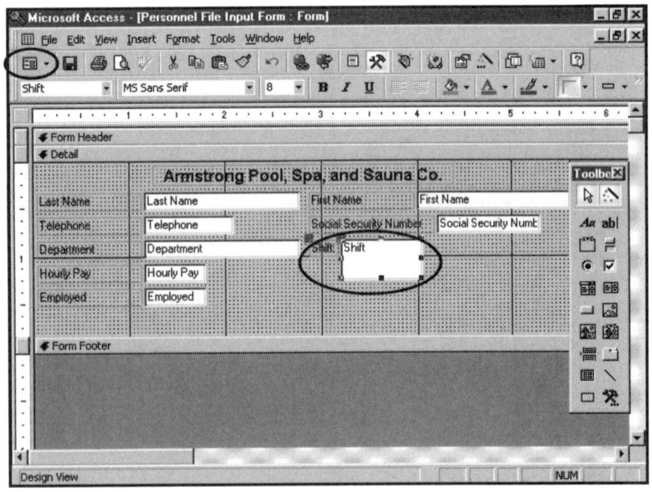


**7** Click the **Close** button to close the **List Box: Shift** properties dialog box. The list box does not show the individual items in Design View.

**Q & A**

*Question:* When would you want to use a **List Box** field in a form?
*Answer:* When the choices for that field are limited to certain entries.

**8** Click the **View** button to switch to **Form View**. You should be able to see all three items in the **list box**.

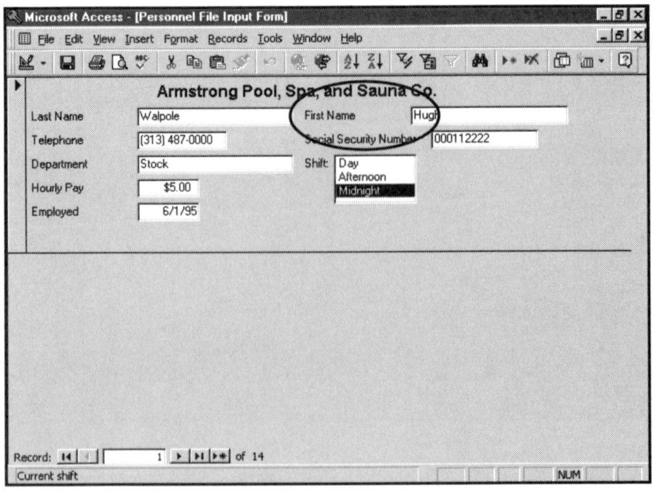


**Pothole:** If the list box has a scroll bar on the right and does not show all of the items, it means that you made the box too small. Return to **Design View**, select the **list box**, and resize it using the middle handle on the bottom edge of the box.

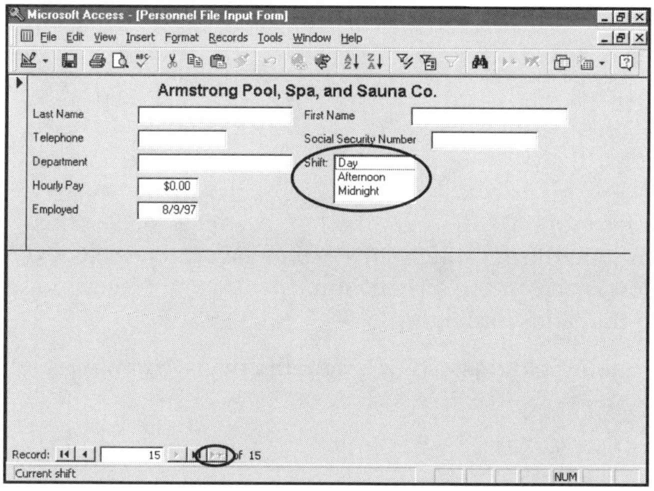


**9** Click the **New Record** button to add a new record. Notice that none of the items in the **list box** are selected.

**Tip for Students**

When in the list box, you can use the arrow keys to move to and select the desired option, and then tab to the next field. Alternatively, you can press the key for the first letter of that option to select it.

**Speedy Class**

Add the input mask to the **Social Security Number** field in this form.

**10** Enter the information for the new record as shown. When you reach the **Shift** field, click **Day** to select the Day shift.

**In Depth:** Notice that today's date shows automatically in the employed date field because of the default property that was set for this field. The Social Security number is not formatted in the form, however, because the input mask was added to the table after the form had been created, and you have not added the input mask formatting to the form.

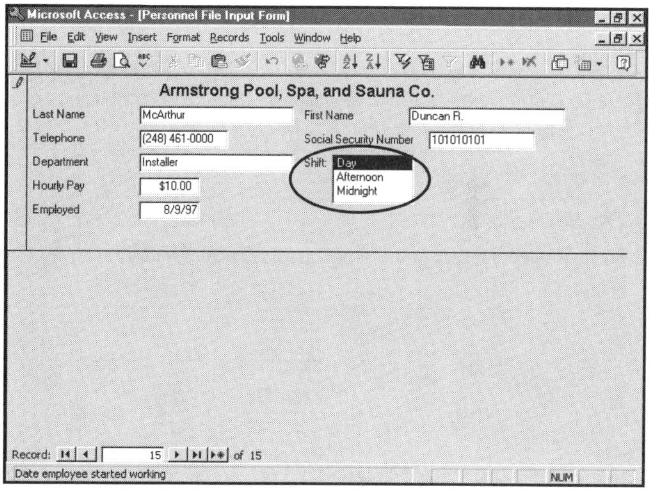


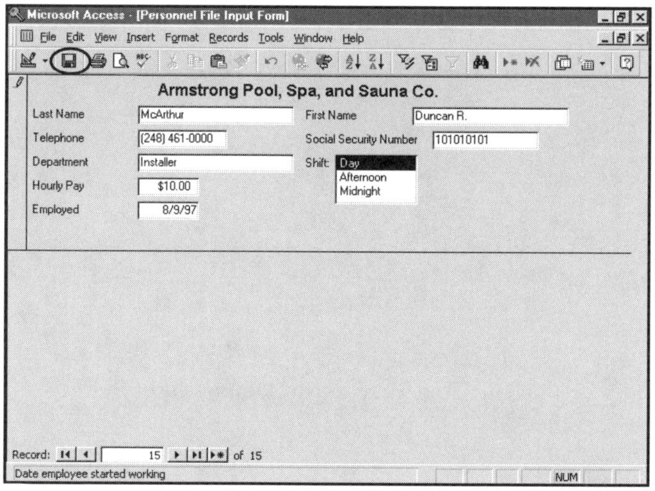


**11** Click the **Save** button to save the changes made to the form.

# Task 7

## Adding a Combo Box to a Form

### Why would I do this?

A list box is handy in some cases, but in others, a *combo box* is far more useful. A combo box is similar to a list box because it helps in the data-entry process. A list of items is presented from which the correct data can be selected. A combo box, however, uses a drop-down list, so it takes up less space on the screen. You can also enter items not found in the data source, whereas the list box restricts you to the items in the list.

In this task, you learn how to add a combo box to the Department field. Instead of typing the items, you will use another table as the data source.

**1** Click the **View** button to switch to **Design View** of the **Personnel File Input Form**.

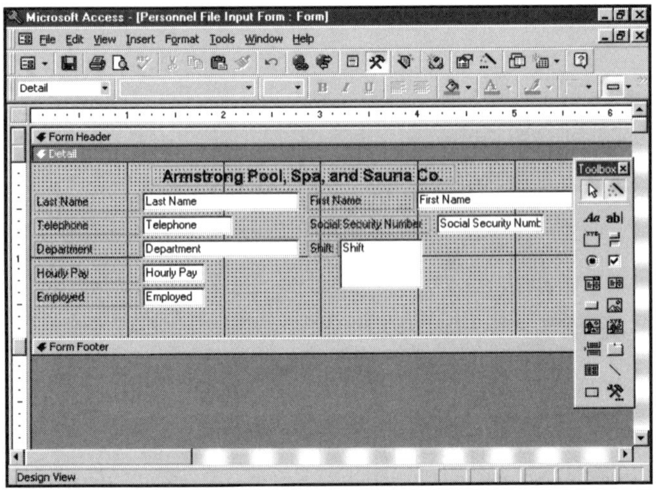

**Tip for Instructors**

The Learn on Demand Module/Lesson "Adding a Combo Box to a Form" applies to this task.

**On Your Mark**

Sometimes a **list box** is too lengthy. What would help that situation?

**Concept**

A *combo box* is a drop-down list box that enables you to either choose from the list or input an item not on the list.

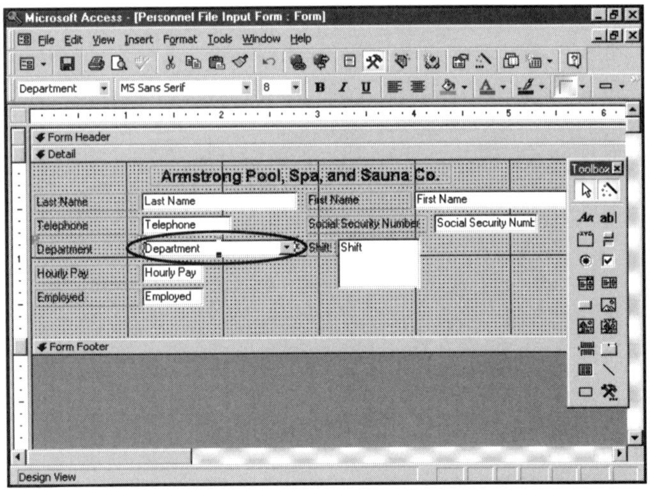

**2** Click the **Text Box** of the **Department** field to select it.

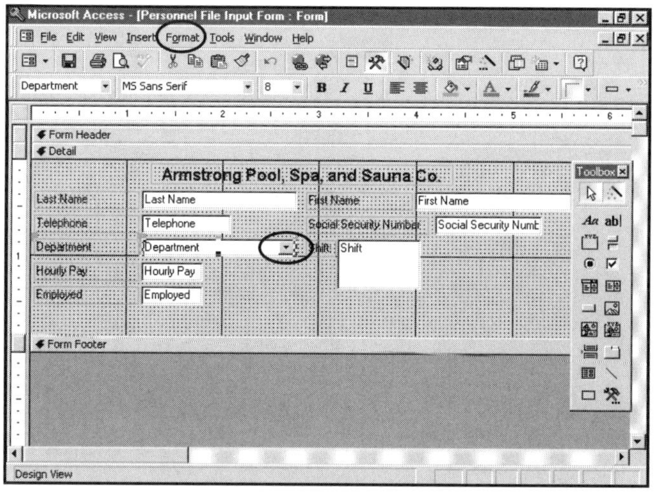


**3** Choose **Format**, **Change To**, **Combo Box**. A drop-down arrow is displayed on the right side of the **text box**.

**Pothole:** If the **Combo Box** option is not available from the menu, it means you selected the **label** instead of the **text box** for the **Department** field. Click the Department field text box and try again.

**Concept**

The *Table/Query* option links the choices in the combo box to a separate table or query.

**4** Click the **Properties** button. The **Combo Box: Department** properties dialog box is displayed. **Table/Query** is the default choice for the **Row Source Type**.

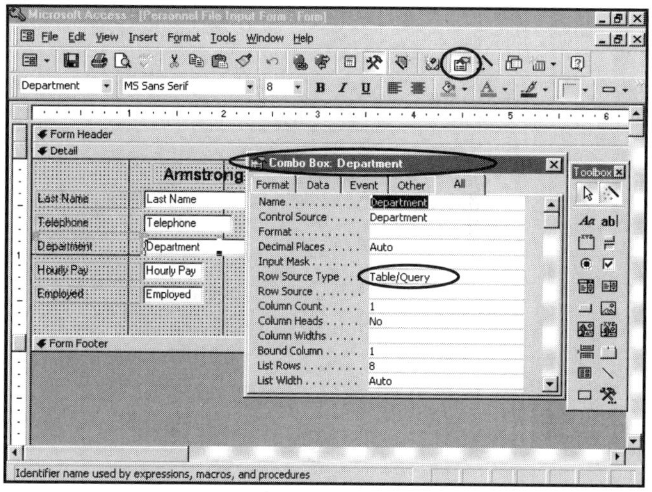


**In Depth:** When you created the list box in the previous task, you selected the option **Value List** in the **Row Source Type** box. This allowed you to type a list of values. In this case, you will accept the default choice to use the **Table/Query** option in the **Row Source Type** box, because you are using a table as the source of the list for the combo box. You could, however, use one of the other options for the Row Source Type with a combo box.

**Tip for Students**

In order to use the **Table/Query Source** feature, the database must already have a table or query resident to pull from.

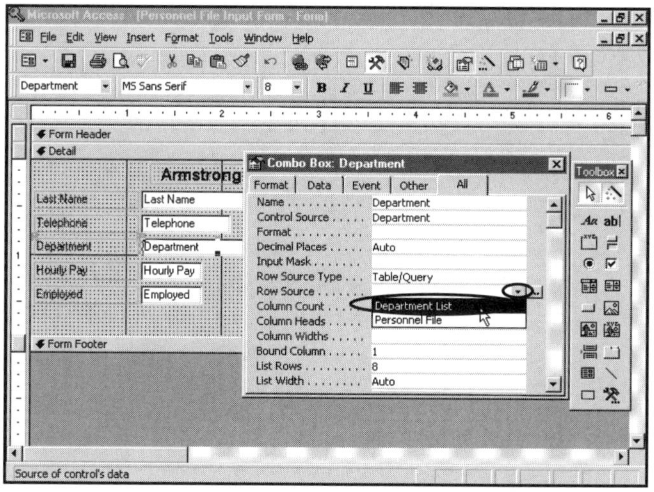


**5** Click in the **Row Source** box. Click the drop-down arrow to display the tables and queries available as data sources. Select **Department List**.

**In Depth:** The Department List is a table that has just one field. This field lists all five of the current departments in the company. You will see the departments listed when you move to Form View to test the combo box.

**6** Click the **Close** button to close the **Combo Box: Department** properties dialog box. The combo box does not show the department list in Design View.

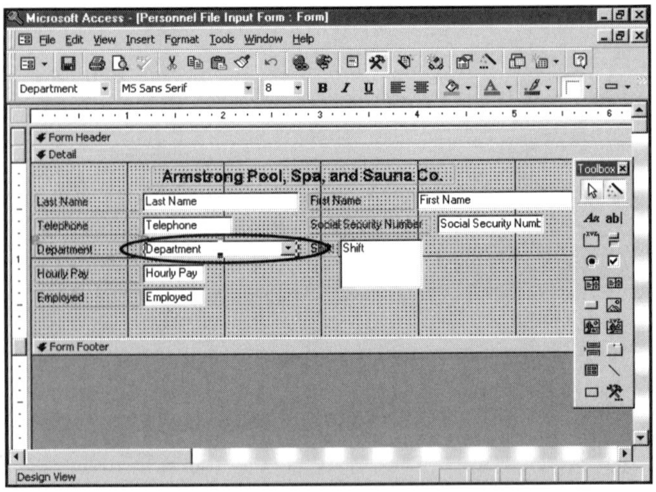


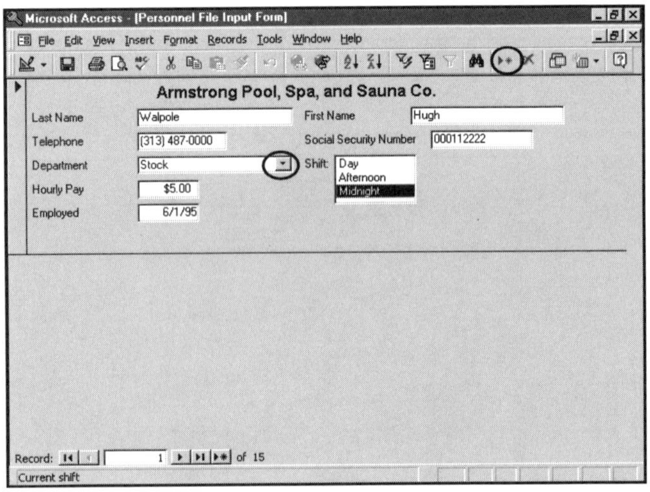


## Q & A

*Question:* What is the difference between a **list box** and a **combo box** in a form? *Answer:* A **combo box** is a drop-down **list box**.

**7** Click the **View** button to move to **Form View**. Notice that the **Department** field has a drop-down arrow on the right side of the **text box**.

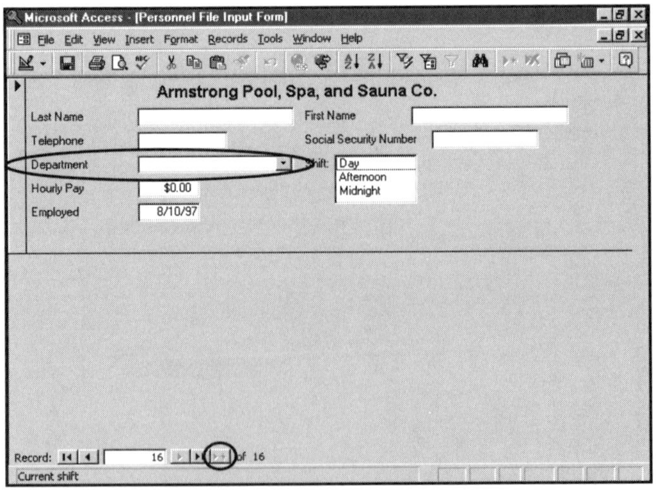


**8** Click the **New Record** button to add a new record. Notice that none of the items in the **combo box** are selected.

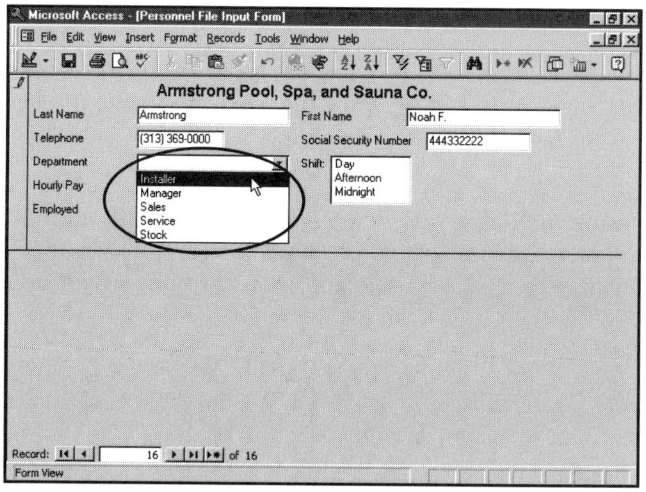


**9** Enter the information for the new record as shown. When you get to the **Department** field, click the drop-down arrow to view the available items.

**Tip for Students**

If you know which entry you desire, you can press the first letter of that entry and it fills in automatically.

**10** Select **Installer** from the **combo box**, then finish filling in the record as shown.

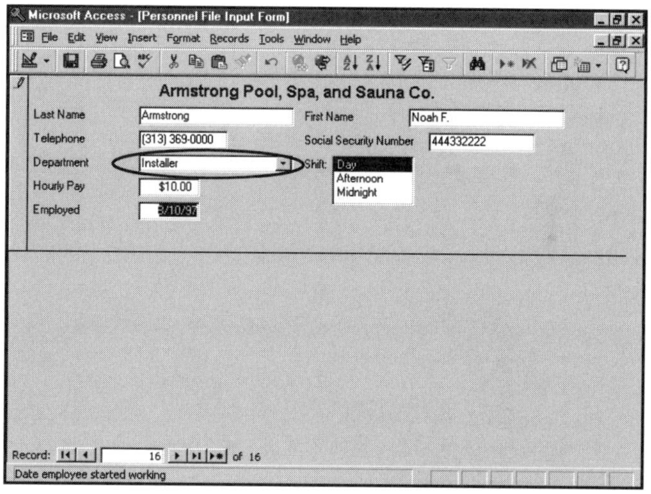


**Quick Tip:** A quick way to select items from a combo box or a list box is to type the first letter of the option you want. The program will choose the option based on the first letters that are typed. When you see your choice in the field text box you can press Enter to select it and move to the next field.

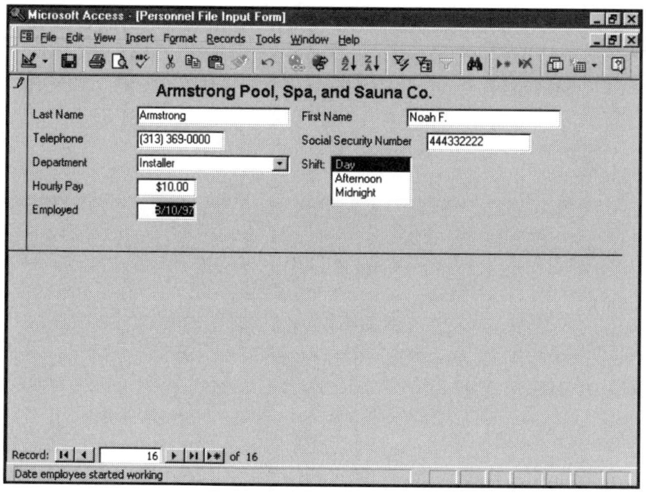


**11** Click the **Save** button to save the changes made to the form.

# Task 8

**Tip for Instructors**

The Learn on Demand Module/Lesson "Adding Headers, Footers, and Page Breaks" applies to this task.

## Adding Headers, Footers, and Page Breaks to a Form

### Why would I do this?

When you created the Personnel File by Department report using the Report Wizard, Access automatically added headers and footers to the report. A *Page Header* or *Page Footer* gives added information to the person reading the report. Since it is often useful to print out a form to view individual records, headers and footers can be useful on forms, too.

In this task, you learn how to add a header and footer and insert a page break so you can print one form per page. This would be useful if you wanted to print individual records for distribution or for filing in each person's personnel file.

**1** Click the **View** button to switch to **Design View**. Notice that there are **Form Header** and **Form Footer** sections available.

**On Your Mark**

What additions might be helpful in a form?

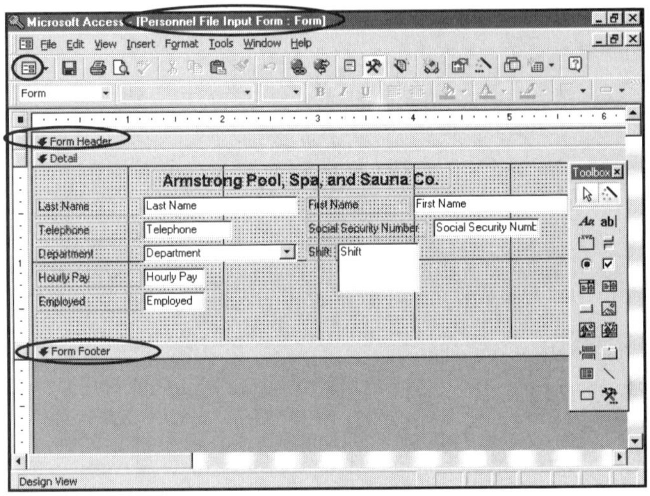


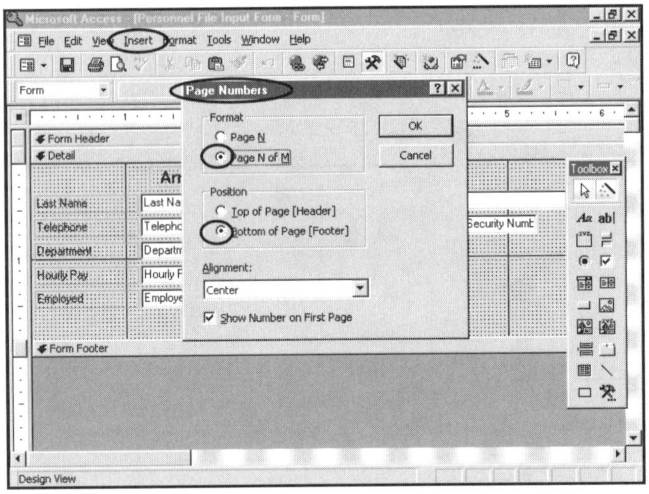


**2** Choose **Insert**, **Page Numbers**. The **Page Numbers** dialog box opens. Click the **Page N of M** option button and the **Bottom of the Page [Footer]** option button. Leave the other options as shown.

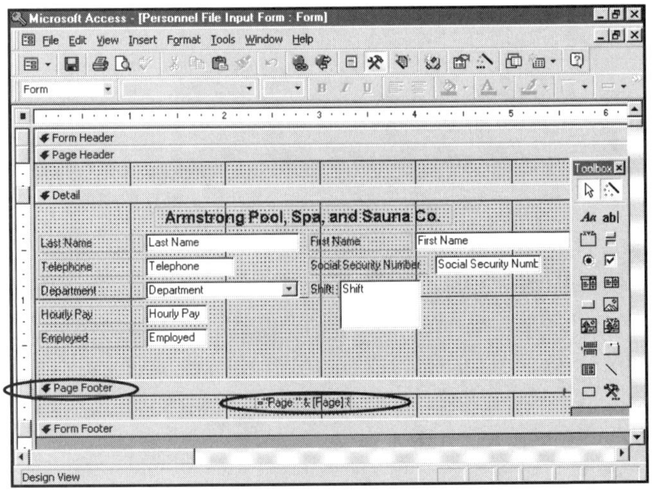


**Quicksand**

The data added is a code and should not be modified in structure.

**3** Click **OK**. The page number is placed in the **Page Footer**. This means that the page number will appear at the bottom of each page.

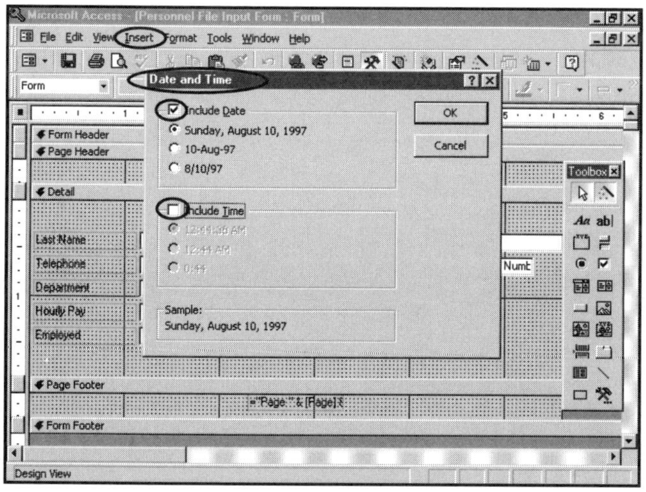


4 Choose **Insert**, **Date and Time**. The **Date and Time** dialog box opens. Accept the long date option from the **Include Date** area as shown, but turn off the **Include Time** option by clicking the check box.

## Concept

The *Form Header* and *Form Footer* appear only on the first and last page, respectively. The *Page Header* and *Page Footer* appear on each page.

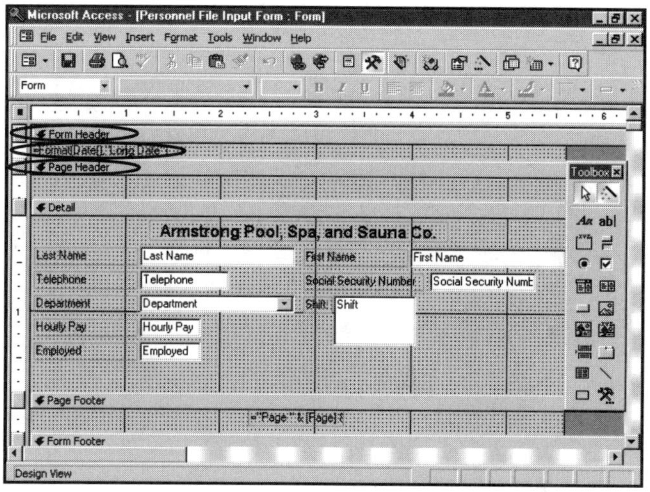


5 Click **OK**. The date is placed in the **Form Header** area, which means it will appear only on the first page. A **Page Header** is also displayed.

## Tip for Students

If the **Page Header** section does not show any space, move the mouse to the top of the **Detail** divider and drag down when the mouse changes to a double-headed arrow.

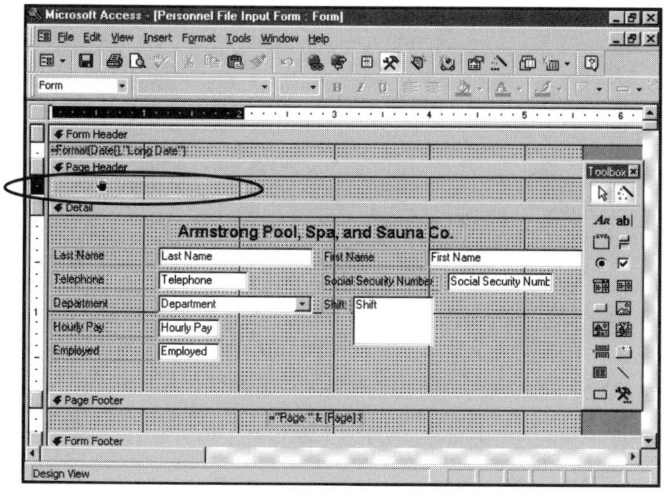


6 Click the date and hold down the mouse button. The pointer changes to a hand. Move the date down to the **Page Header** area as shown.

**7** Release the mouse button to place the date in the **Page Header** area.

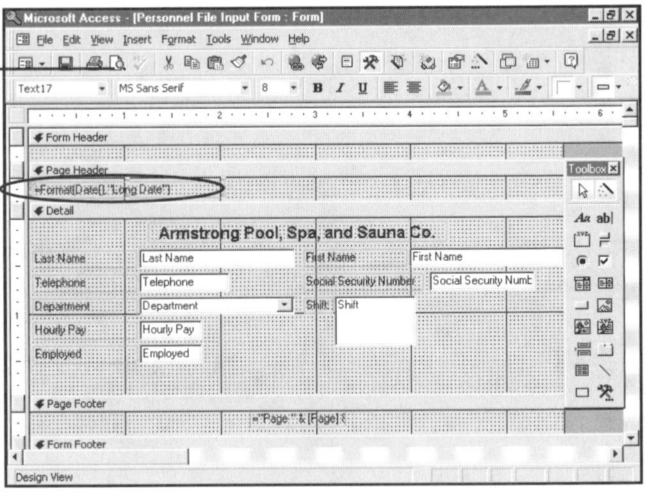


Print Preview button

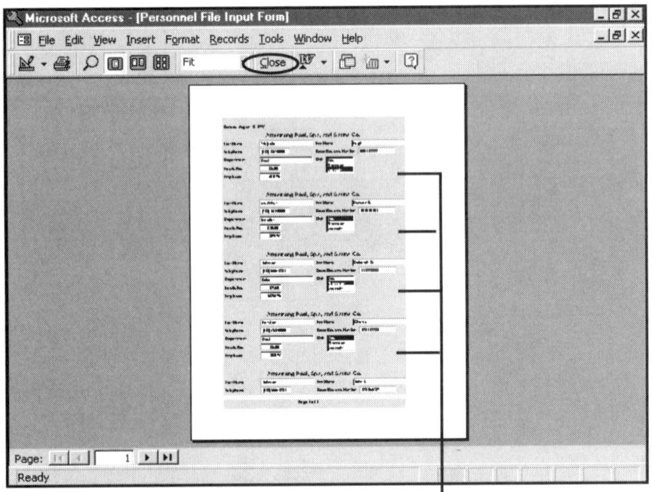


Multiple forms on a page

> **Tip for Instructors**
> Sometimes the forms also split between pages.

**8** Click the **Print Preview** button to see what the printed form will look like. Notice that there are four forms printed on a page.

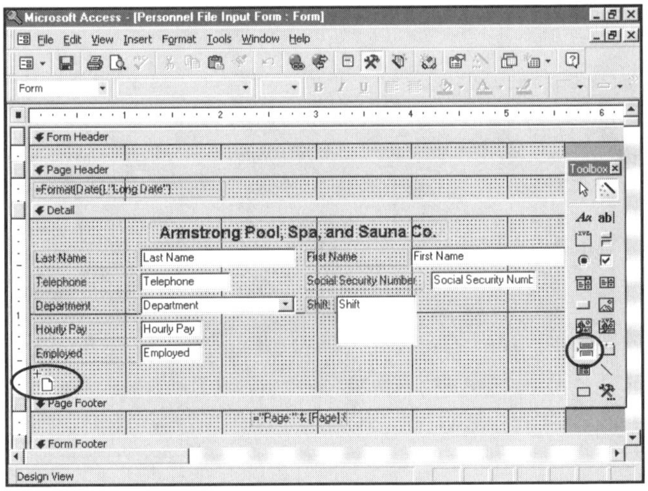


> **Quicksand**
> Be sure students do not drag from the **Page Break** button.

**9** Click **Close** to close the **Print Preview** window. Click the **Page Break** button on the **Toolbox** (do not hold down the mouse button), then move the pointer to the left side of the screen as shown in the figure. The pointer turns into a crosshair with a page attached.

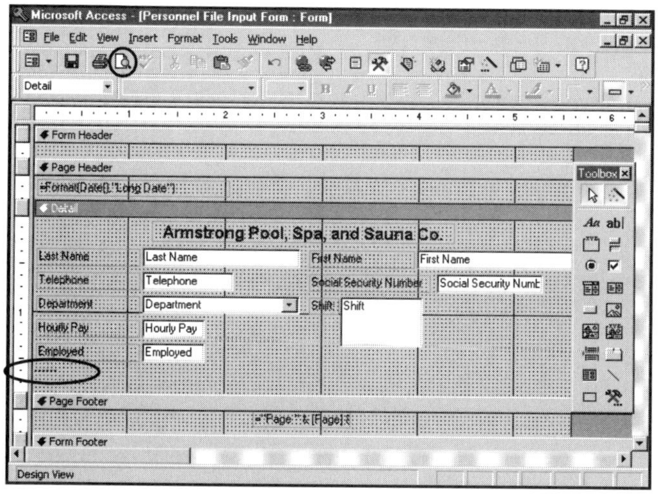


10 Click the pointer just below the **Employed** label to insert a page break. Three dots are inserted to designate a page break after the employed field.

> **Tip for Students** !
> To delete the page break, click it to select it, and then press Del.

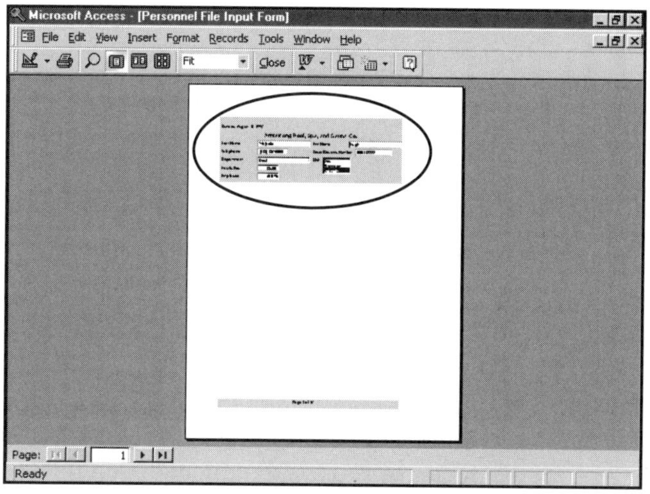


11 Click the **Print Preview** button. Notice that there is only one form per page.

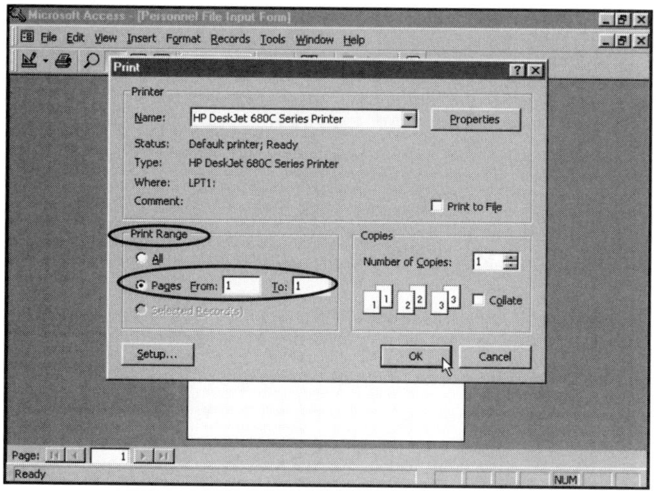


12 Choose **File**, **Print**. In the **Print Range** area, select the **Pages From** option and type **1** in the **From** and **To** boxes.

**13** Click the **OK** button to print the first page of the forms. Click the **Close** button to close the **Print Preview** window, then click the **Close Window** button to close the **Form Design** window. Save changes when prompted. Close the database.

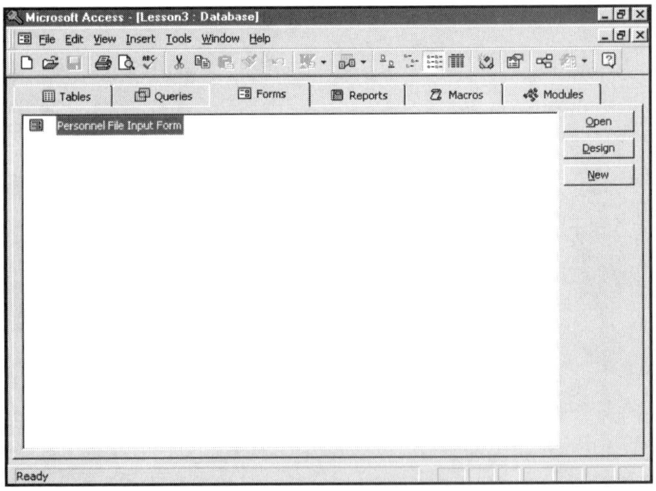


# Student Exercises

## True-False

Circle either T or F.

(T) F **1.** Input masks are used to apply specific formats to text fields.

T (F) **2.** Default values work only with fields that have a Number data type.

T (F) **3.** An input mask added to a field in a table will also appear in previously created forms or reports that include that field.

(T) F **4.** Assigning a primary key can help speed up searching or sorting.

(T) F **5.** You can automatically adjust a column width in Datasheet View by double-clicking the right edge of the field selector.

T F **6.** If the entry you are looking for is not in the List Box you can always type in a new item.

T (F) **7.** A Combo Box gives you a list to choose from and also allows you to type a new entry.

(T) F **8.** You can insert page numbers in either the Page Header or the Page Footer.

(T) F **9.** The Page Break button is found on the Toolbox toolbar.

(T) F **10.** There can be no duplicate entries in a Primary Key field.

# Identifying Parts of the Access Screens

Refer to the figures and identify the numbered parts of the screen. Write the letter of the correct label in the space next to the number.

1. K
2. I
3. H
4. C
5. D
6. L
7. N
8. A
9. F
10. J

**A.** Primary Key button
**B.** Build button
**C.** Properties button
**D.** Page Break button
**E.** Primary Key indicator
**F.** Input Mask field property
**G.** Default Value field property
**H.** Page number
**I.** Date
**J.** List box

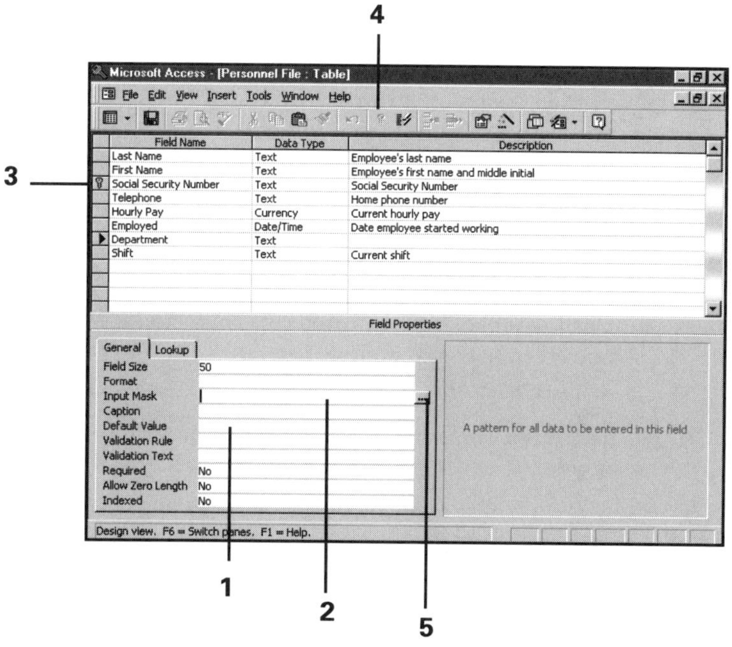


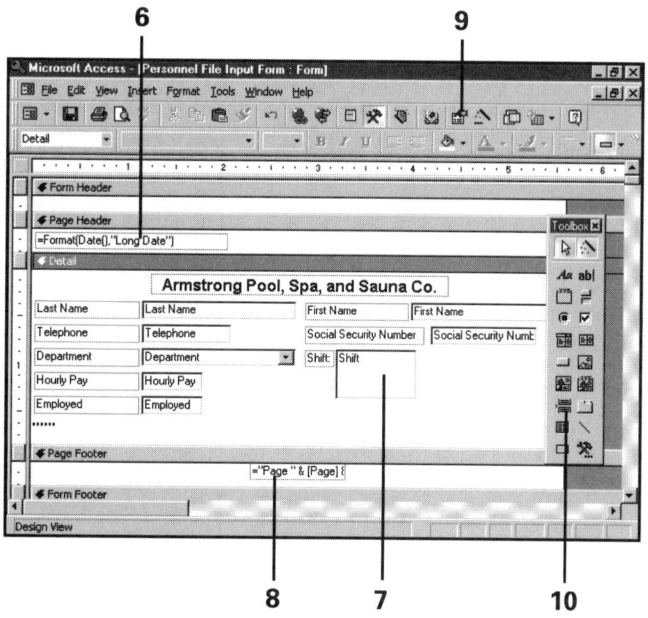

## Matching

Match the statements below to the word or phrase that is the best match from the list. Write the letter of the matching word or phrase in the space provided next to the number.

1. _E_ Where the items for a list box or combo box come from
2. _G_ Button on the Toolbox toolbar which allows printing of one form per page
3. _K_ Prints only on the top of the first page
4. _F_ Applies special field structure for phone numbers, zip codes, etc.
5. _H_ Displays the current date
6. _A_ A field containing unique values
7. _D_ Prints on the bottom of every page
8. _B_ Used to select built-in functions that can be placed on a form, such as dates or page numbers
9. _C_ The label area at the top of the column in a table
10. _I_ In a form, creates a drop-down list of possible data for a field

**A.** Primary key
**B.** Expression Builder
**C.** Field selector
**D.** Page Footer
**E.** Row Source
**F.** Input mask
**G.** Page break
**H.** Date()
**I.** Combo box
**J.** Form Footer
**K.** Form Header

# Application Exercises

## Exercise 1 – Adding Input Masks and Defaults to a Table

1. Using Windows Explorer, make a copy of **Ex0301** and rename the copy of the file **Exercise3**. Launch Microsoft Access. Choose **Open an Existing Database**, find the file **Exercise3**, and open the file. This is a slightly expanded version of the exercises you worked on in Lesson 2.
2. Use the skills that you have learned in this lesson to create **input masks** for the Phone and Zip fields and a **Default Value** for the State field as shown in the figure. See the steps below for more detail. (Note: The widths of the columns in this table have been resized to show all of the fields you will be working on.)
3. Make sure the **Table** tab is selected.

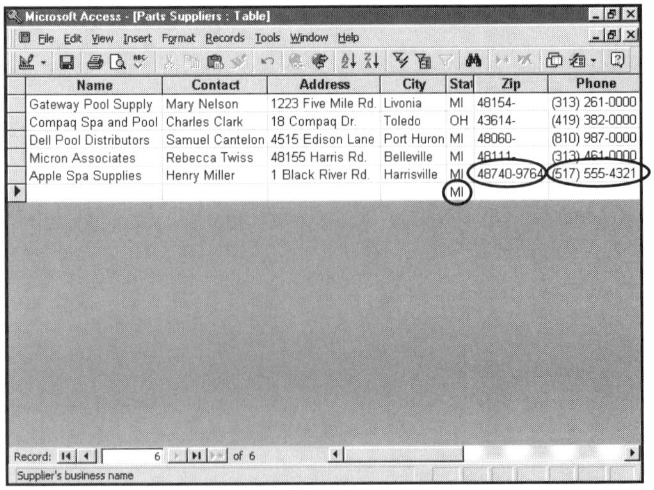

4. Select the **Design View** option for the **Parts Suppliers** table.
5. Select the **Zip** field. Click in the **Input Mask** box in the **Field Properties** area.
6. Click the **Build** button and choose the pre-set **Zip Code** option. Store the **Zip** field information without the dash.
7. Select the **Phone** field (save the table when prompted). Click in the **Input Mask** box in the **Field Properties** area.
8. Click the **Build** button and choose the pre-set **Phone Number** option. Store the **Phone** field information without the symbols.
9. Select the **State** field. Click in the **Default Value** box and type **MI**, since most of the suppliers will be from Michigan.
10. Switch to **Datasheet View** and save your changes when prompted. Enter the following new record, using the input masks and default value you just created: **Apple Spa Supplies**; **Henry Miller**; **1 Black River Rd**.; **Harrisville**; **MI**; **487409764**; **5175554321**; **60 Day**.
11. Adjust the column widths to show all of the data. Choose **File**, **Print** and print a copy of the table in **Landscape** orientation. (In the print dialog box, click the Properties button, click the Paper tab and select Landscape orientation.) Close the table.

## Exercise 2 – Assigning a Primary Key and Adjusting Column Widths

1. Switch to **Design View** of the **Pool Parts Inventory** table.
2. Use the skills that you have learned in this lesson to enter the data into the table as shown. See the steps below for more detail.
3. Click anywhere in the **Part Number** field. (Note: This field will be used as a primary key because each part number is unique.)
4. Click the **Primary Key** button.
5. Move to **Datasheet View**. Save your changes when prompted.
6. Resize the columns as shown.
7. Print a copy of the table in Landscape orientation, then close it. Save your changes when prompted.

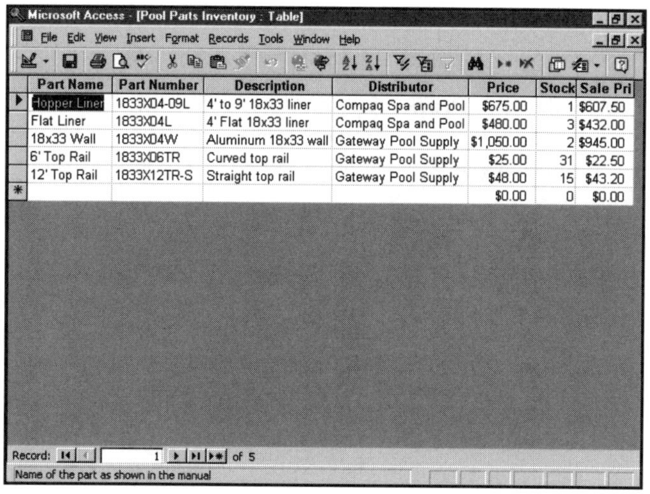


| Part Name | Part Number | Description | Distributor | Price | Stock | Sale Pri |
|---|---|---|---|---|---|---|
| Hopper Liner | 1833X04-09L | 4' to 9' 18x33 liner | Compaq Spa and Pool | $675.00 | 1 | $607.50 |
| Flat Liner | 1833X04L | 4' Flat 18x33 liner | Compaq Spa and Pool | $480.00 | 3 | $432.00 |
| 18x33 Wall | 1833X04W | Aluminum 18x33 wall | Gateway Pool Supply | $1,050.00 | 2 | $945.00 |
| 6' Top Rail | 1833X06TR | Curved top rail | Gateway Pool Supply | $25.00 | 31 | $22.50 |
| 12' Top Rail | 1833X12TR-S | Straight top rail | Gateway Pool Supply | $48.00 | 15 | $43.20 |
| | | | | $0.00 | 0 | $0.00 |

# Exercise 3 – Adding a List Box to a Form

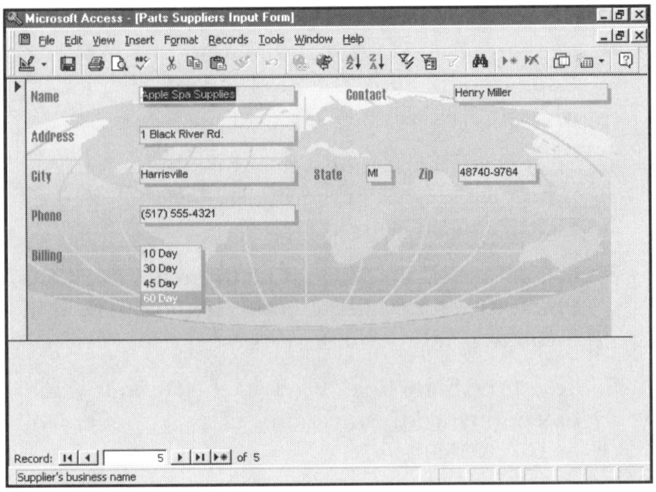


1. Click the **Forms** tab. Open the **Parts Suppliers Input Form** in **Design View**.
2. Use the skills that you have learned in this lesson to add a **list box** to the **Billing** field.
3. Click the **text box** of the **Billing** field.
4. Choose **Format**, **Change To**, **List Box**.
5. Click the **Properties** button on the Form Design toolbar. Choose **Value List** from the **Row Source Type** drop-down menu.
6. In the **Row Source** box type the following entries exactly as shown: **10 Day**; **30 Day**; **45 Day**; **60 Day**.
7. Close the **List Box**: **Billing** properties dialog box and move to **Form View**.
8. Switch back to **Form View** and resize the **list box** as necessary.
9. Move to record 5 if necessary. Choose **File**, **Print**, and click the **Selected Record(s)** option button to print only the current record. Close the form and save your changes when prompted.

# Exercise 4 – Adding a Combo Box to a Form

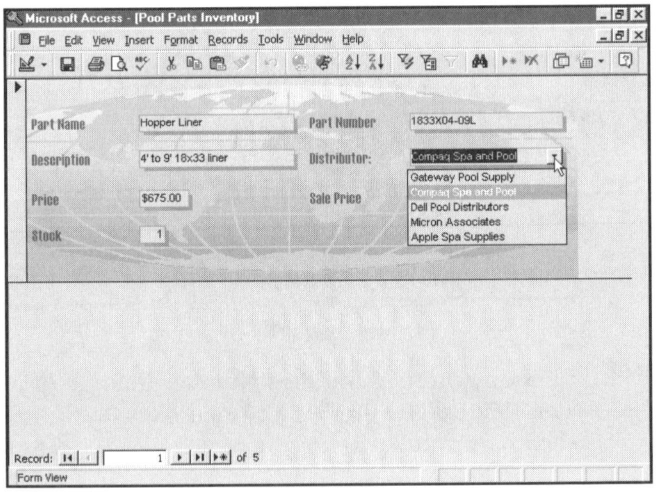


1. Open the **Pool Parts Inventory Input Form** in **Design View**.
2. Use the skills that you have learned in this lesson to add a **combo box** to the **Distributor** field.
3. Click the **text box** of the **Distributor** field.
4. Choose **Format**, **Change To**, **Combo Box**.
5. Click the **Properties** button on the Form Design toolbar. Choose **Table/Query** from the **Row Source Type** drop-down menu.
6. In the **Row Source** box select the **Parts Suppliers** table. The **combo box** will read the information in the first field in that table.
7. Close the **Combo Box: Distributor** properties dialog box and switch to **Form View**.
8. Switch back to **Design View** and resize the **combo box**, if necessary.

9. Choose **<u>F</u>ile**, **<u>P</u>rint** and click the **Selected <u>R</u>ecord(s)** option button to print only the current record. Close the form and save your changes when prompted.

## Exercise 5 – Adding a Header and Footer to a Form

1. Open the **Parts Suppliers Input Form** in **Design View**.
2. Use the skills that you have learned in this lesson to add information to the header and footer areas of the form.
3. Choose **<u>I</u>nsert**, **Page N<u>u</u>mbers**. Place a simple page number on the right-hand side of the **Page Footer**.
4. Choose **<u>I</u>nsert**, **Date and <u>T</u>ime**. Insert the full date and time as shown on the figure.
5. Move the date and time box from the **Form Header** to the right side of the **Page Header**.
6. Click the **Label** button in the Toolbox. Draw a label box in the left side of the Page Header area. Type the company name: **<u>Armstrong Pool, Spa, and Sauna Co.</u>**
7. Change the font size of the company name to 14 point. (See Task 6 of Lesson 2 to review how to do this, if needed.)
8. Adjust the size of the label box as necessary.
9. Use the **Page Break** button to place a page break just under the **Billing** list box.
10. Switch to **FormView**. Choose **<u>F</u>ile**, **<u>P</u>rint** and click the **Selected <u>R</u>ecord(s)** option button to print only the current record. Close the form and save your changes when prompted.

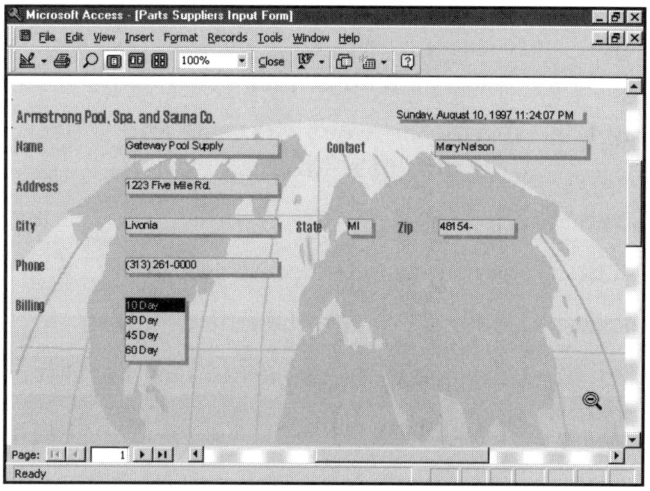

# Lesson 4
## Extracting Useful Information from Large Databases

**Task 1** Opening a Database

**Task 2** Moving between Records and Columns of a Table

**Task 3** Finding Records

**Task 4** Sorting and Indexing Records

**Task 5** Using a Form to Define a Filter

**Task 6** Using Select Queries to Display Data

**Task 7** Calculating Values for a New Column of Data

**Task 8** Creating Queries that Allow the User to Change Criteria Each Time the Query is Used

**Lesson Time**
**90 minutes**

# Introduction

Extracting information from databases is crucial in running many businesses, and is the basis for many types of research. In this lesson, you learn how to work with a database that contains data of all tornadoes occurring in the United States from 1950 through 1995. This database has over 38,000 records, but with the skills you learn in this lesson, you will be able to find the answers to questions such as "How many people have been killed or injured in my county?" "Which states have the most tornadoes?" "Where have the biggest tornadoes occurred?" This is an example of how scientists conduct such research. Because you are dealing with real data, you have the opportunity to ask new questions, discover new relationships, and experience the excitement of doing real research!

In this lesson, you learn how to use form filters and how to create queries.

> **Tip for Instructors**
> The Learn on Demand Module that applies to Lesson 4 is found in the Extracting Useful Information from Large Databases subfolder of Learn Access 97.

# Visual Summary

When you have completed Task 8, you will have created several filters and saved a query that looks like this:

Path Width

| Year | Killed | Injured | Path Width (ft) |
|---|---|---|---|
| 95 | 5 | 60 | 2110 |
| 95 | 3 | 32 | 3000 |
| 95 | 3 | 24 | 900 |
| 95 | 3 | 6 | 2100 |
| 95 | 3 | 5 | 750 |
| 95 | 2 | 11 | 2640 |
| 95 | 2 | 1 | 300 |
| 95 | 1 | 70 | 2110 |
| 95 | 1 | 55 | 3900 |
| 95 | 1 | 20 | 1320 |
| 95 | 1 | 12 | 600 |
| 95 | 1 | 3 | 450 |
| 95 | 1 | 3 | 510 |
| 95 | 1 | 1 | 150 |
| 95 | 1 | 0 | 60 |
| 95 | 1 | 0 | 90 |
| 95 | 0 | 122 | 120 |
| 95 | 0 | 45 | 2640 |
| 95 | 0 | 36 | 450 |
| 95 | 0 | 28 | 220 |
| 95 | 0 | 23 | 2640 |
| 95 | 0 | 22 | 150 |
| 95 | 0 | 22 | 600 |
| 95 | 0 | 20 | 300 |

| Year | Killed | Injured | Path Width (ft) |
|---|---|---|---|
| 95 | 0 | 17 | 360 |
| 95 | 0 | 13 | 220 |
| 95 | 0 | 12 | 1500 |
| 95 | 0 | 12 | 1500 |
| 95 | 0 | 11 | 60 |
| 95 | 0 | 10 | 60 |
| 95 | 0 | 9 | 1200 |
| 95 | 0 | 8 | 210 |
| 95 | 0 | 8 | 300 |
| 95 | 0 | 8 | 300 |
| 95 | 0 | 8 | 600 |
| 95 | 0 | 8 | 90 |
| 95 | 0 | 7 | 600 |
| 95 | 0 | 6 | 980 |
| 95 | 0 | 6 | 2640 |
| 95 | 0 | 6 | 240 |
| 90 | 0 | 5 | 90 |
| 95 | 0 | 5 | 1050 |
| 95 | 0 | 5 | 30 |
| 95 | 0 | 5 | 900 |
| 95 | 0 | 5 | 750 |
| 95 | 0 | 5 | 220 |
| 95 | 0 | 4 | 900 |

Page 1

**SLIDE 4–1**

**SLIDE 4–2**

# Task 1

## Opening a Database

> **Tip for Instructors**
> The Learn on Demand Module/Lesson "Opening a Database" applies to this task.

### Why would I do this?

In the first three lessons you learned how to create and modify a database. Once a database has been created, you need to find and open it in order to use it again. The value of a database is derived from using it to find answers to questions and to extract data that meets certain conditions.

In this task, you learn how to open an existing database.

**1** Find the **Less0401** file that was supplied with your book. Use **Windows Explorer** to make a copy of the file and rename the copy **Lesson4**. (Follow your instructor's directions for the location to use when copying and renaming the file.)

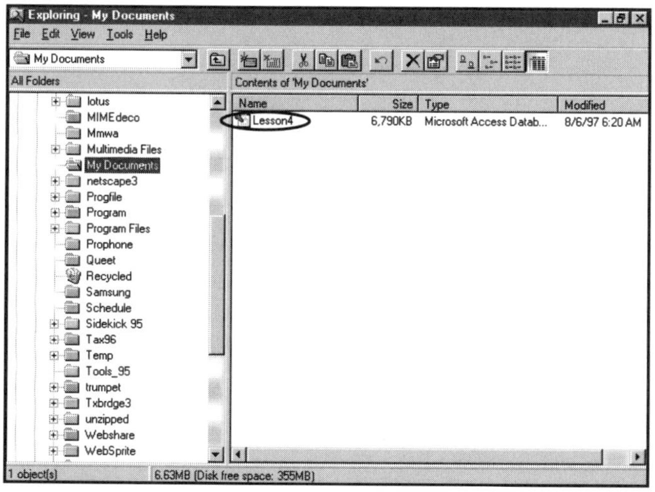


> **On Your Mark**
> Many databases contain an extreme amount of data and the capability to manipulate this data is the strength of the database. Suppose that you have a database with 2,000 agencies that are in five states. Your data includes various officers, the address information, phone information, and employee numbers. What types of information might you need to extract from this data? What types of reports might be needed?

> **Tip for Instructors**
> There are two files for this lesson. Decide which file your lab can hold and provide only one of these files (**Less0401** or **Less0402**) to avoid confusion.

**2** Launch **Microsoft Access 97**. A dialog box opens that provides two choices for creating a new database and an option for opening an existing database.

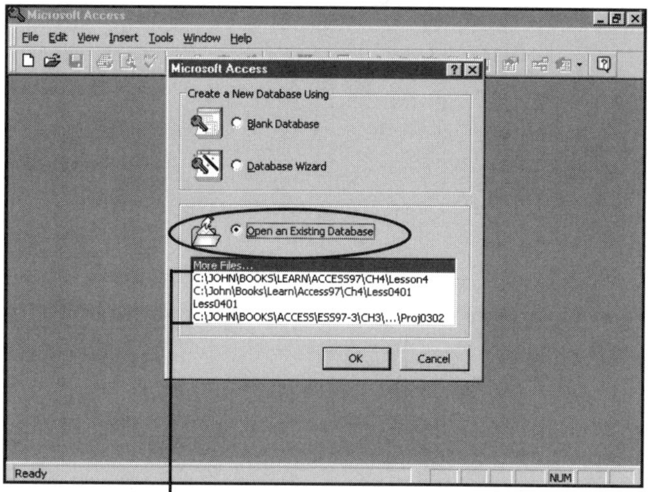


Recently used databases

> **Pothole:** If you are using a computer in a laboratory, you might not have enough room for the 6 megabyte Less0401 file, which covers 45 years. If this is the case, use the 1.4 megabyte **Less0402**, which has ten years' data (1986-1995). Follow all of the other directions in step 1.

**3** Make sure that the **Open an Existing Database** option is selected and click **OK**. The **Open** dialog box is displayed.

> **Quicksand**
> Choosing the file location might be troublesome to those students who are not solidly grounded in file organization through Windows 95.

> **Tip for Instructors**
> Specify again the folder in which the file is located.

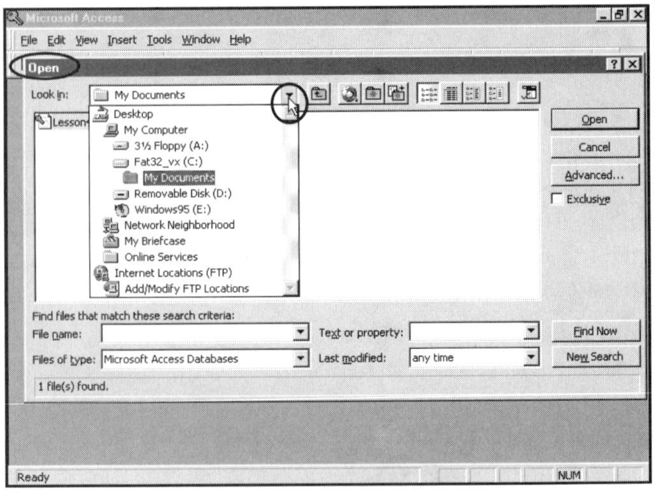


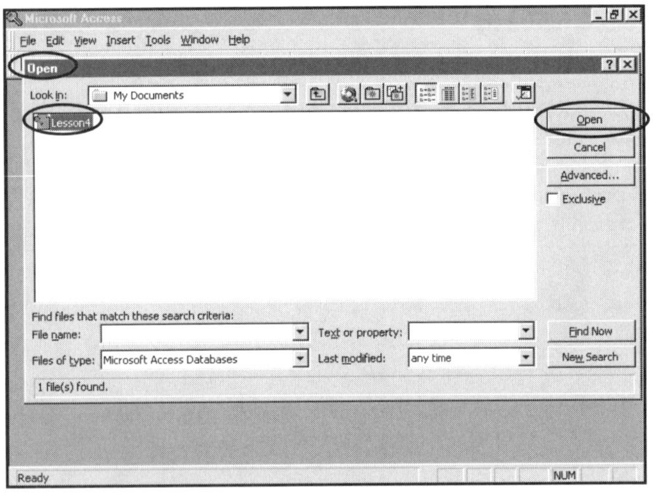


**4** Click the arrow at the right of the **Look in** list and locate the **Lesson4** file that you copied and renamed.

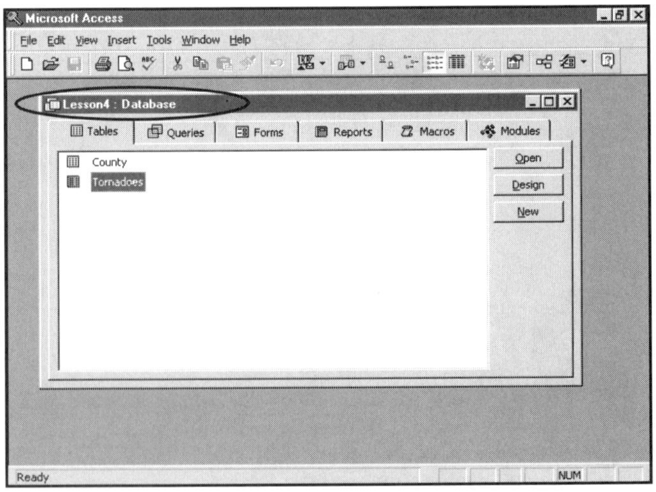


**5** Click the **Lesson4** file and then **Open**. Access opens the **Database window**. The name of the database is shown in the title bar.

# Task 2

## Moving between Records and Columns of a Table

### Why would I do this?

When you are dealing with a large database, it is important to know how to navigate the records. Simply scrolling through 38,000 records looking for what you want will not work well. It is also important to examine the data to understand the kind of information contained in each field. There are some techniques that can be used to move quickly from the beginning to the end of data, and to have columns shift to appear next to each other for easy comparison.

In this task, you learn how to freeze selected columns and how to move to the last record and then the first record in the table.

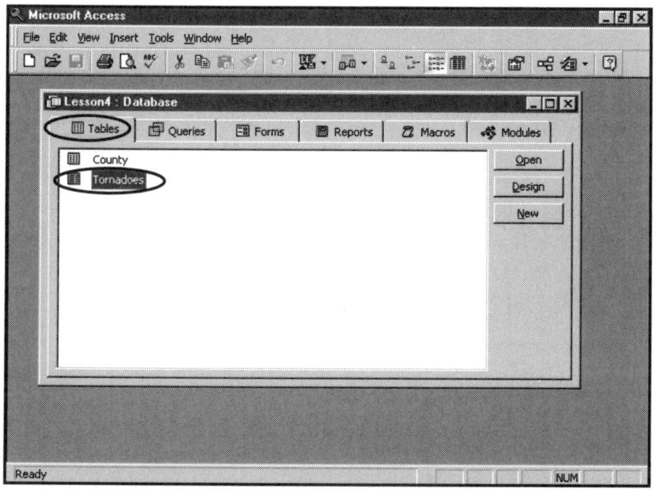


**1** Click the **Tables** tab, if necessary, and select **Tornadoes**.

**Tip for Instructors**

The Learn on Demand Module/Lesson, "Moving between Records and Columns of a Table" applies to this task.

**On Your Mark**

In a large database, what types of problems do you expect when you are looking at the records in a table?

**2** Click the **Open** button. The **Tornadoes** file opens and displays the records. The first column is a sequential number that is used as the key field and the second column indicates the year of the tornado.

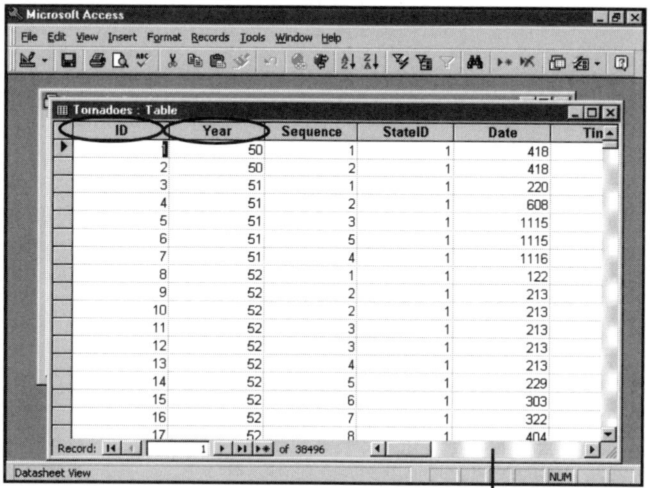


horizontal scroll bar

**Pothole:** The records you see on the screen will not match the ones shown if you are using the smaller version of the database (Less0402). This will occur several times in lessons 4 and 5, but will not affect the outcomes of the tasks.

**3** Use the horizontal scroll bar to scroll the view all the way to the right. The last column contains a code that identifies the county. The first two digits in the code are the state code and the last three digits are the county code.

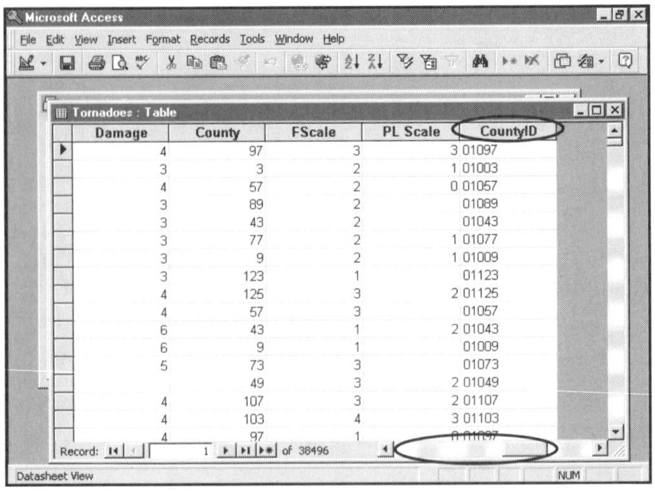


### Tip for Instructors

Many times, students will not choose the header. Remind them to click the gray header to select a column.

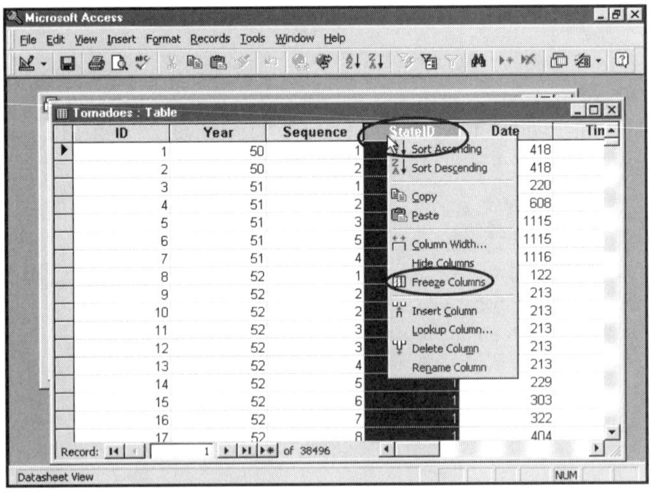


**4** Scroll all the way back to the left. Right-click the **StateID** header to select this column and bring up a shortcut menu.

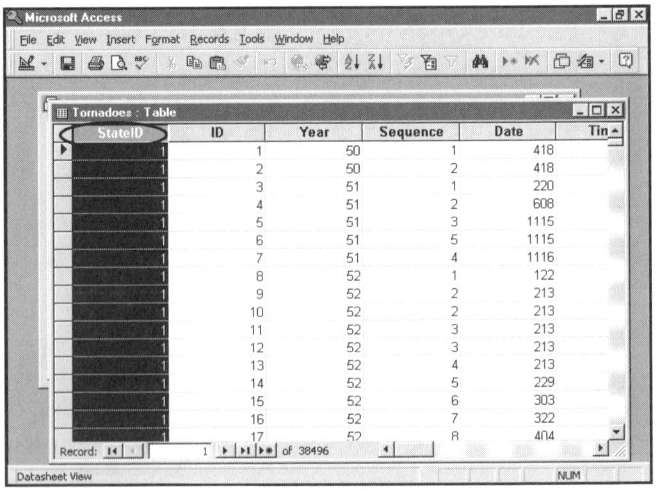


### Concept

Freezing columns locks them on the screen while other data shift over as you move.

**5** Click **Freeze Columns**. Notice that the column is automatically moved to the far left.

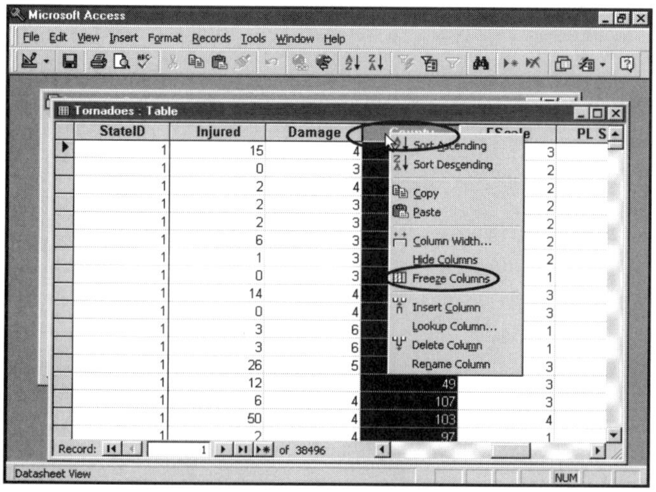


**6** Scroll to the right. Right-click the **County** header to select this column and to bring up the shortcut menu.

**7** Click **Freeze Columns**. The **County** column moves and is now the second column next to the **StateID** column.

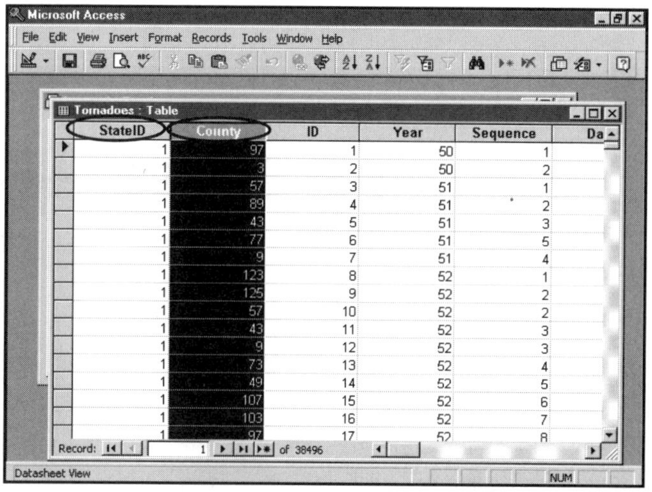


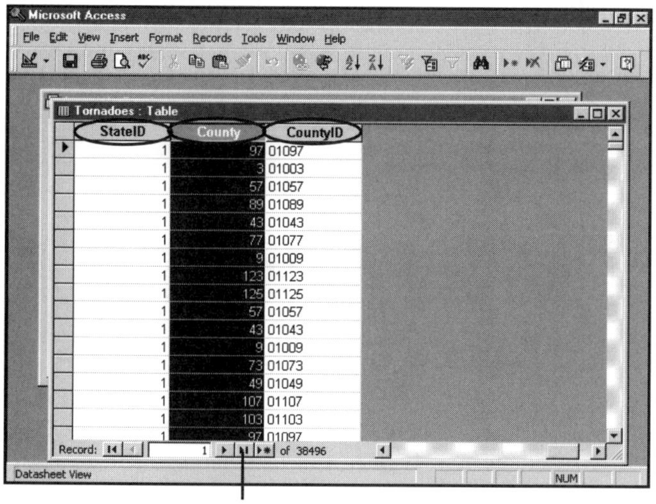


Last Record button

**8** Scroll to the right until there are only three columns displayed: **StateID**, **County**, and **CountyID**. Notice how much easier it is to compare the three columns using the Freeze Columns feature. You can now verify that the **CountyID** field is a combination of the **StateId** and **County** numbers.

> **Tip for Students** !
>
> You can still see the other columns if you need to without unfreezing the columns. Just scroll back or press the arrow keys.

**9** Click the **Last Record** button. Notice that the **StateID** code is 56. The codes used in this database skip some numbers and include some U.S. territories.

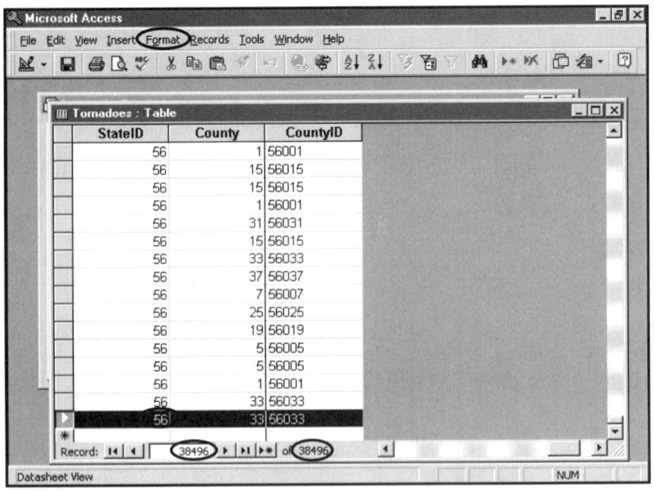


> **Tip for Instructors**
> Note the In Depth box. The information is valuable and may save some confusion.

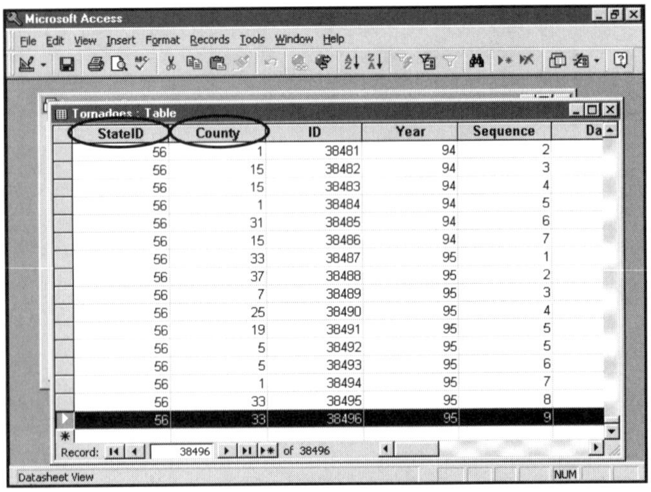


**10** Choose **Format** and **Unfreeze All Columns** to remove the freeze. Notice that the StateID and County columns are still located at the left.

> **In Depth:** The effect of freezing the StateID and County fields is that the columns have been temporarily moved to the left. The **Unfreeze All Columns** action removes the freeze but does not immediately move the columns back to their original position. If you close the table without saving these changes to the layout, the columns will appear in their original location the next time you open the table. However, you can save these changes to the layout for the next time the table is opened. Saving the changes to the layout does not affect the original organization of the fields in the table design.

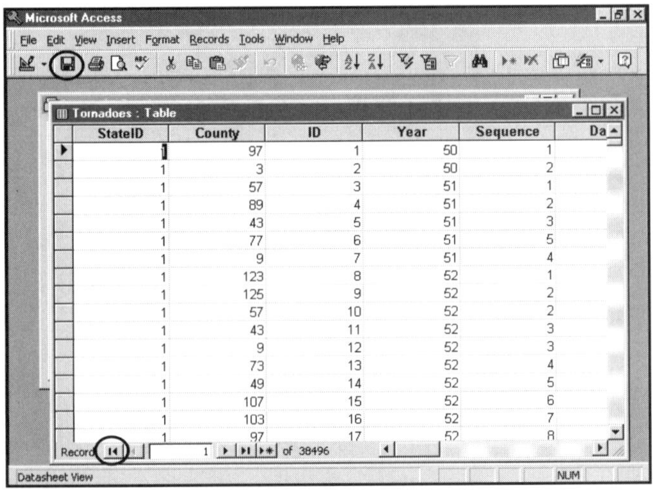


**11** Click the **First Record** button to move to the beginning of the table. Click the **Save** button to save the changes in layout.

# Task 3

## Finding Records

> **Tip for Instructors**
> The Learn on Demand Module/Lesson, "Finding Records" applies to this task.

### Why would I do this?

Sometimes it is not necessary to use a filter or write a query to find the information you need. You may need to locate a particular record to change some information. For instance, in a personnel database you may need to change an employee's address, marital status, or pay rate. In this case, you want to find one record and make the necessary changes. Other times you may want to find a particular record or do a quick search to see if the database contains a record. When you are looking for one particular record, often the quickest way to find it is to use the Find feature.

In this task, you learn how to use the Find feature to determine how many tornadoes have occurred on New Year's Day.

Find button

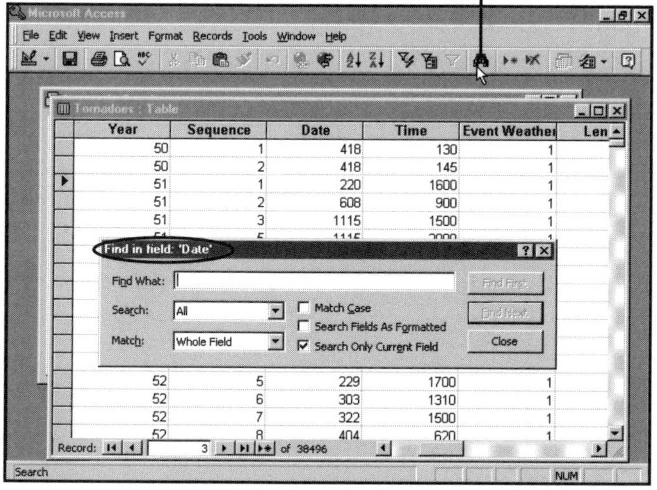


**1** Click anywhere in the **Date** column and then click the **Find** button on the **Table Datasheet** toolbar. The **Find in field:'Date'** dialog box opens.

> **On Your Mark**
> In a large database, what problems might you have finding a specific record?

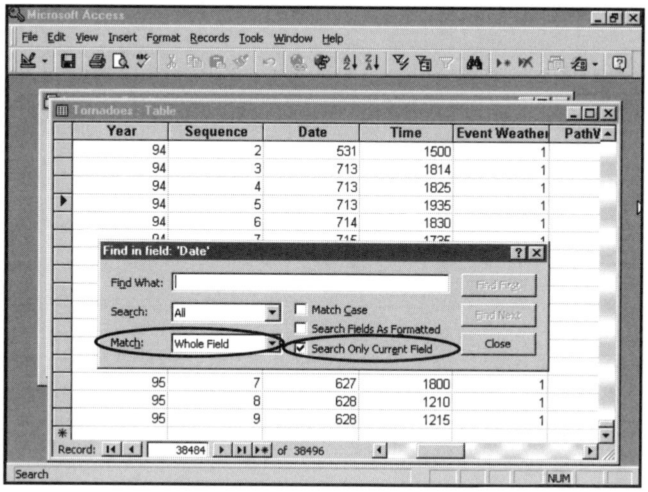


**2** Make sure that the **Search Only Current Field** box is checked and the **Match** box displays **Whole Field**.

**SLIDE 4–3**

**3** Click the **Find What** box and type **101**.

**Tip for Students**

When finding a record using this method, you can use an asterisk as part of the **Find What** field.

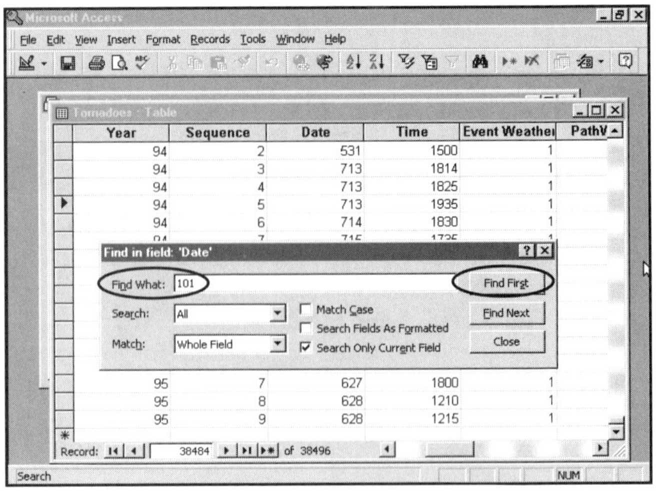


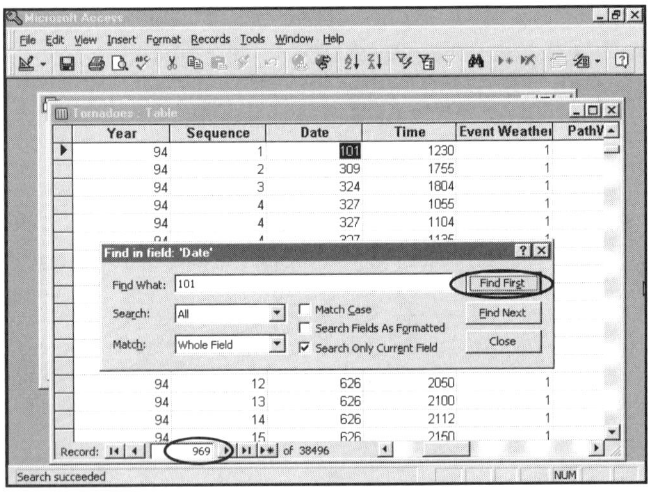


**Tip for Students**

The default is to search all fields. You can specify to search in only the selected field.

**4** Click **Find First**. The first record in the table that has a date of 101 is number 969.

**5** Click **Find Next**. Notice how quickly the program scans the records to find the next occurrence in record number 4773.

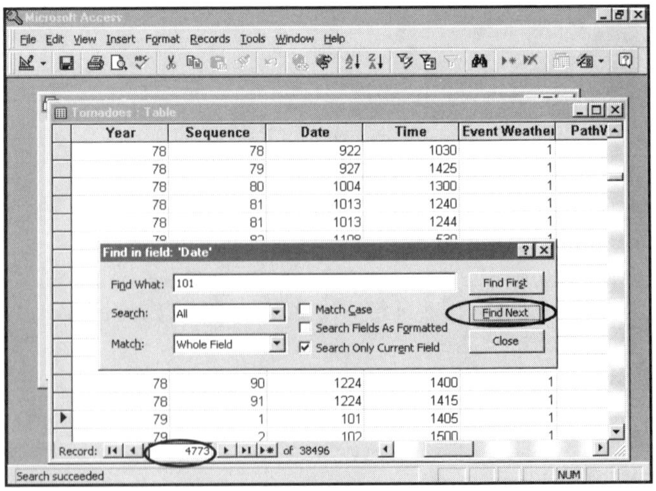


**Speedy Class**

You can also specify that a search string be only part of a field (define something to search for).

**Pothole** If you are using the smaller version of the database (Less0402) there will be only one tornado that occurred on New Year's Day.

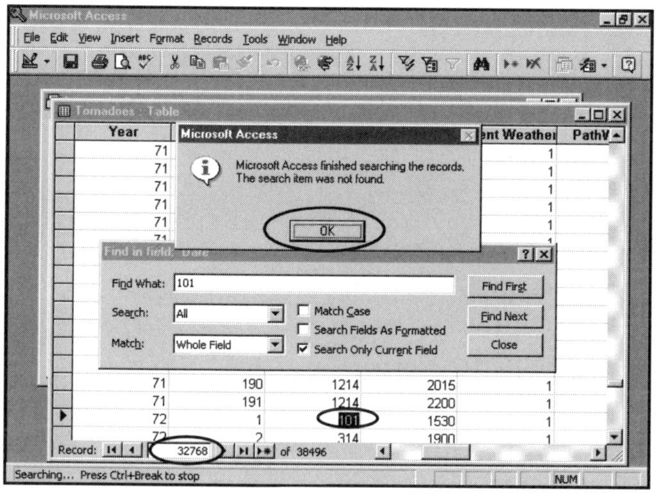


**6** Click **Find Next** twice. Access will find one more occurrence (record 32768). Then, you will see a message stating that Access is finished searching. There are no more records to find. You have determined that there have been only three tornadoes on New Year's Day in the United States from 1950 to 1995.

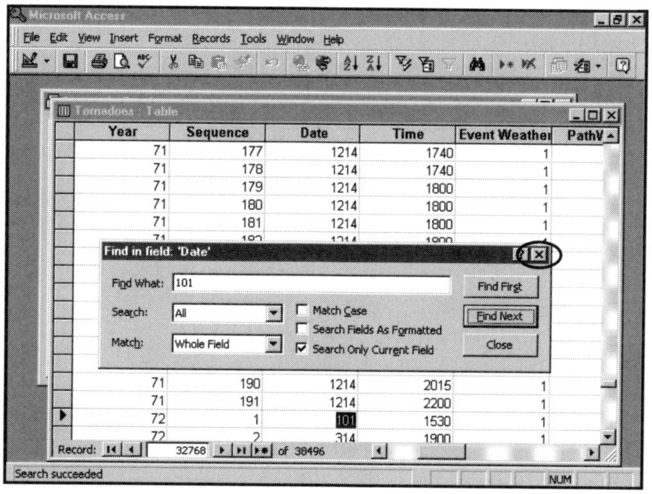


**7** Click **OK** to close the message box.

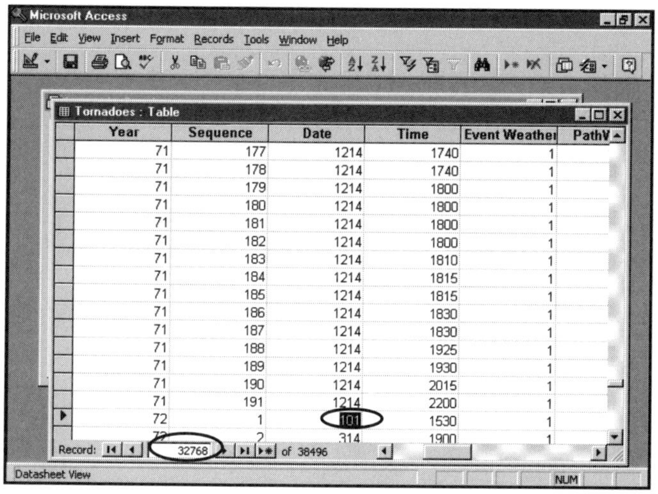


**8** Click the **Close** button on the **Find** dialog box. The table remains open at the last record that was found.

# Task 4

## Sorting and Indexing Records

**Tip for Instructors**
The Learn on Demand Module/Lesson, "Sorting and Indexing Records" applies to this task.

### Why would I do this?

In this table, the records are arranged by date of occurrence, but you have the option of sorting the records by any of the other fields as well. Sorting tools are available that can be used to sort a database on one particular field. Sometimes, however, it is helpful to first index a database before it is sorted. An index can speed up the sorting process on very large databases.

In this task, you learn how to sort the records by the FScale field in descending order. The numbers in this field indicate the intensity of the tornado, where higher numbers indicate stronger tornadoes. You also learn how to index a field to increase sorting speed.

**On Your Mark**
Referring to the first database example (discussed at the beginning of Lesson 4): what are some different ways you might need the data organized?

**Concept**
*Sorting* is the order in which records are displayed. If no sort is applied, the primary key is the sort field. After a sort has been added, it becomes part of the object unless it is removed.

**Concept**
An *indexed field* is a field that Access builds a location guide for. Indexing speeds up sorting and searching on a field.

**1** Scroll to the right and click anywhere in the **FScale** column.

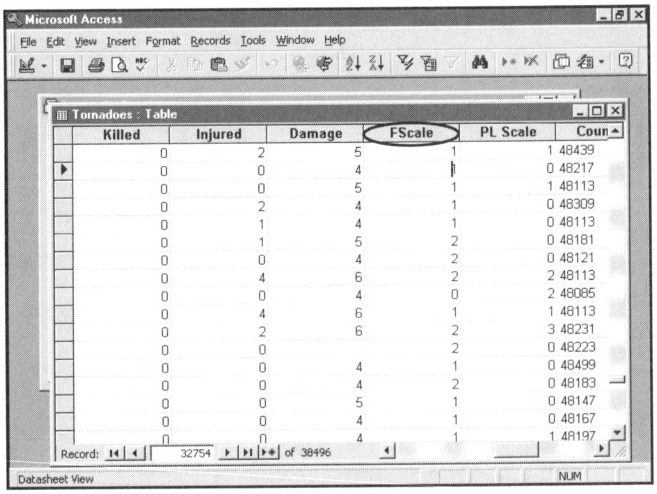


Sort Descending button

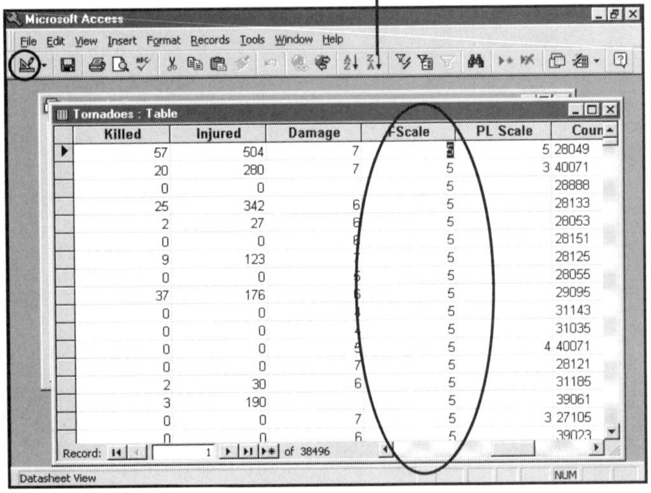


**2** Click the **Sort Descending** button. After a few seconds, the records are reorganized and displayed in descending order according to the contents of the **FScale** field.

**Concept**
When sorting in a database, each record stays intact. In other programs, such as Excel, all data must be selected before sorting. Otherwise, the records are jumbled.

**In Depth:** The time it takes to sort depends on your computer's processor speed. A Pentium processor operating at 133 megahertz takes three or four seconds to sort this table of 38,000 records.

**3** A delay of a few seconds is usually not a problem, but if you have a table with ten or one hundred times as many records, the delay can affect your productivity. Click the **View** button to switch to **Design View**.

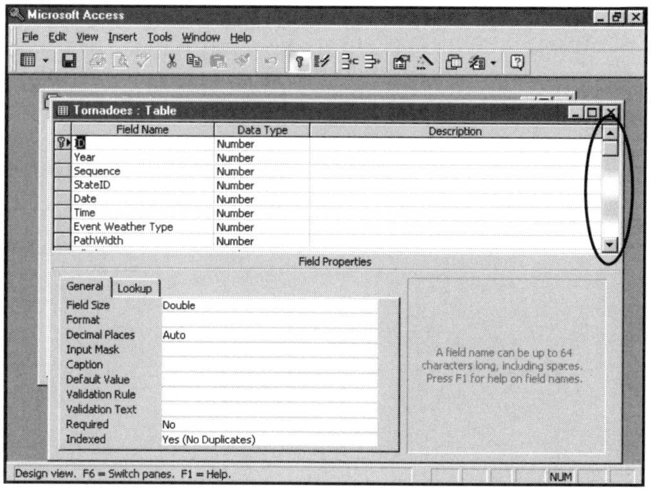


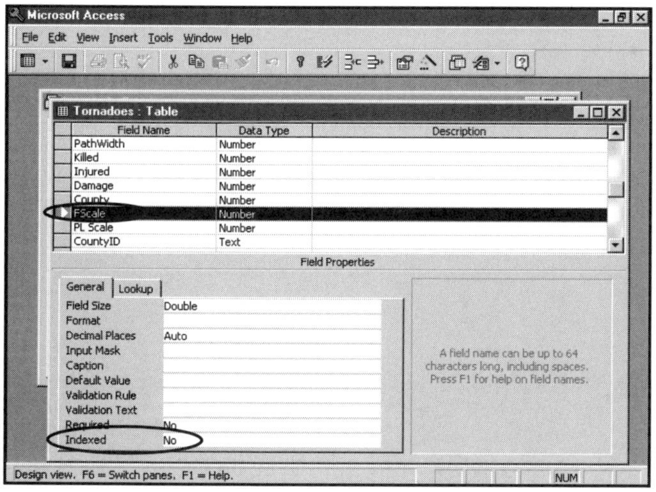


**4** Scroll down the list of fields and click the **Fscale row selector**. The field properties for the **FScale** field are displayed.

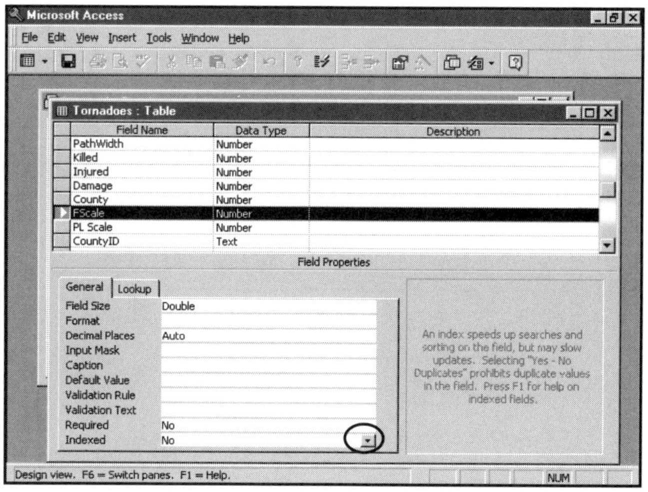


### Tip for Students

When indexing a field, you can choose whether duplicates are allowed. Be sure you select the appropriate choice according to your field.

**5** Click the **Indexed** box. A list arrow appears at the right end of the box.

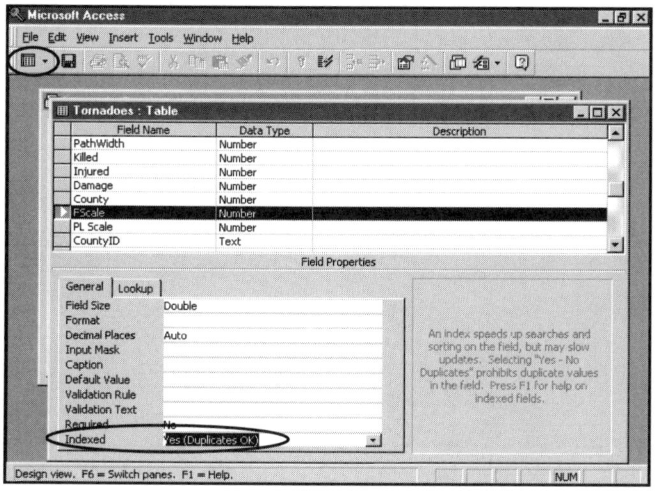


**6** Click the list arrow and click **Yes (Duplicates OK)**.

**In Depth:** The program calculates the order of the records if they are sorted by this field and stores this calculation for later use. If you decide to sort on this field again it will not have to calculate the proper order, so the display will be updated more quickly. The order will have to be recalculated whenever a record is added or deleted, however, so it is better to wait until most of the records have been created before you index the fields.

**7** Click the **View** button and click **Yes** to save the change. The table is displayed in **Datasheet View**.

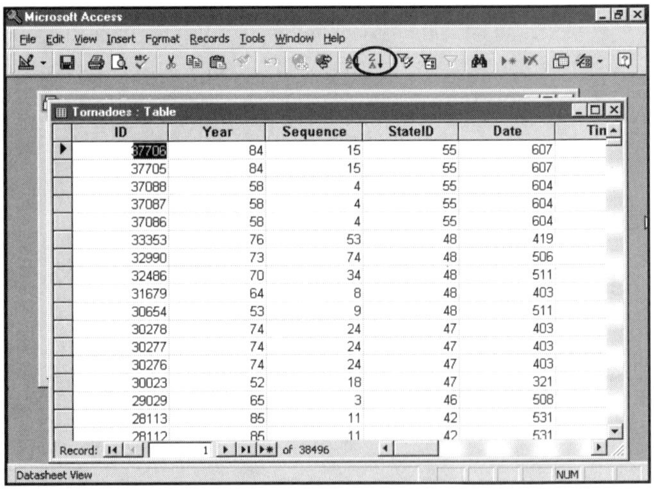


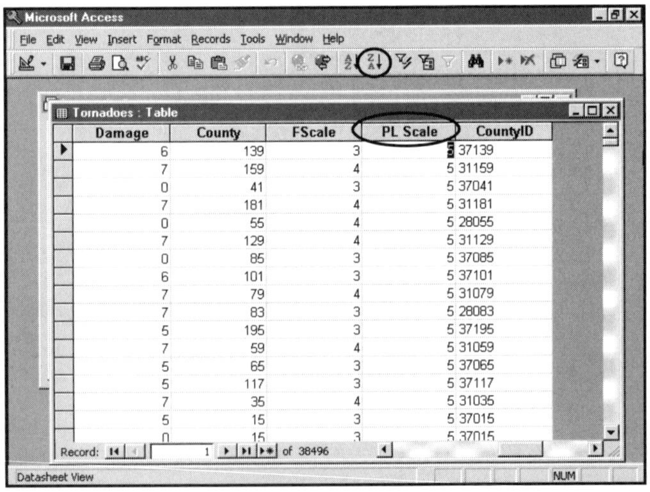


**8** Click anywhere in the **PL Scale** column and click the **Sort Descending** button. Observe how long it takes to sort the table.

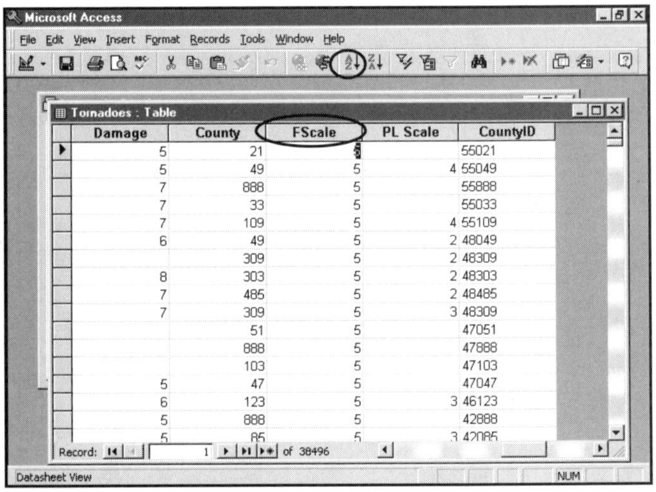


**9** Click anywhere in the **FScale** column and click the **Sort Descending** button. Notice how much faster the sort takes place now that the table is indexed by that field.

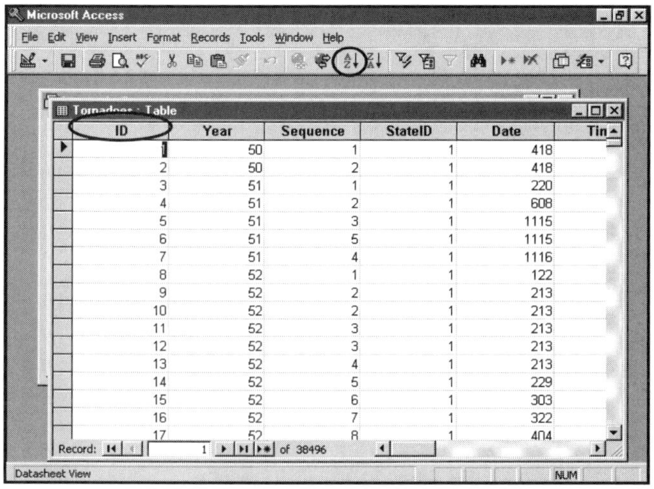


**10** Scroll to the left and click anywhere in the **ID** column. Click the **Sort Ascending** button. This returns the table to its original organization.

# Task 5

## Using a Form to Define a Filter

**Tip for Instructors**

The Learn on Demand Module/Lesson, "Using a Form to Define a Filter" applies to this task.

**Tip for Instructors**

Differentiate between a *filter* and a *query*. A filter is generally used for a temporary, one-time purpose; a query is used so that a filter can be saved and used for a report or form.

### Why would I do this?

There will be times when you want to view only a few of the many records in a database. To show only the records you are interested in viewing, you can create a *filter* that will specify *criteria* which will allow only certain records to be displayed. Using a form filter is a simple way to limit records based on criteria. Generally, if you will want to be able to look at your data with the same filter over and over, you will create a query that can be saved. Form filters are not usually saved, but can provide a quick method for searching your data. Filters also provide a good introduction to some of the concepts you will learn in Task 6 when you create a query. Form filters use the same logical and/or operators, but may seem more intuitive in this format.

In this task, you learn how to use a form to create a filter. You will use it first to restrict the records to those from a particular year. Then you learn how to create more complex filters.

New Object button

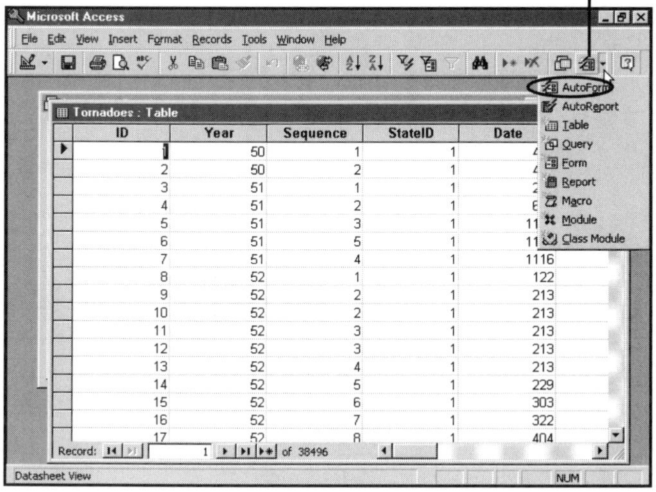


**1** Click the list arrow next to the **New Object** button.

**On Your Mark**

Datasheet View is easy for small sets, but after you begin to assemble masses of information, you might feel overwhelmed and lost. What might you want to create to make viewing the data easier in the table? What if you wanted to view only the records that meet certain criteria?

**Concept**

A *filter* temporarily narrows down the records according to a specified criterion. Much like a strainer holds noodles and lets the water drain out, a filter keeps only certain records that you specify. Unlike a query, it cannot be saved for later use.

**SLIDE 4–4**

**2** Click **AutoForm** and click **Yes** to save the previous changes. The program creates a simple form that displays the fields in the **Tornadoes** table.

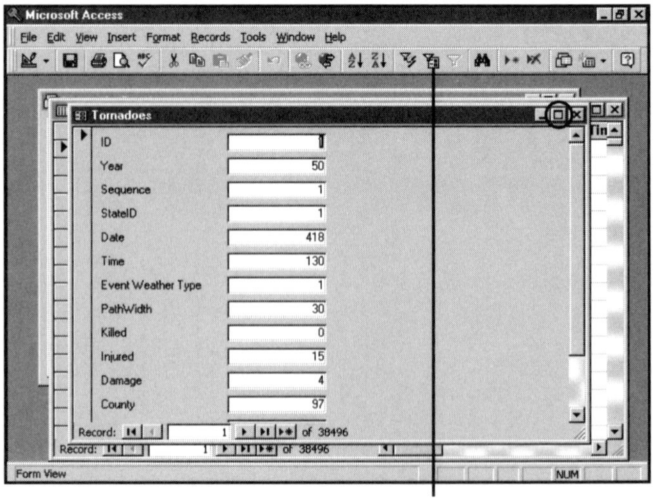


Filter By Form button

**Tip for Instructors**

Although it is not necessary to create an AutoForm to create a filter, it makes it easier to see all of a record at one time.

**Quicksand**

The **Filter by Form** option does not erase or change any records. However, be sure to click the **Filter by Form** button before typing in the filter information. Otherwise, you will overwrite part of the record displayed.

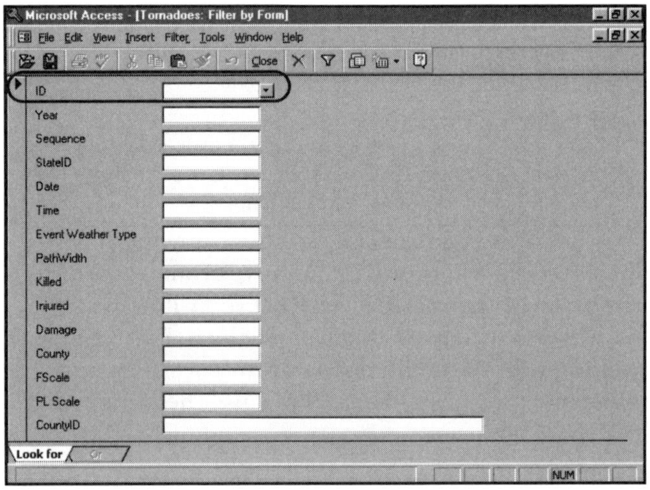


**3** Click the **Maximize** button and then click the **Filter by Form** button. The form is cleared of entries and the ID field is selected.

**In Depth:** Each field box in the form displays a list arrow when the box is selected. This list allows you to select either all the records which have no entry (is null) for the field or all the records that do have an entry (is not null) for the field.

Apply Filter button

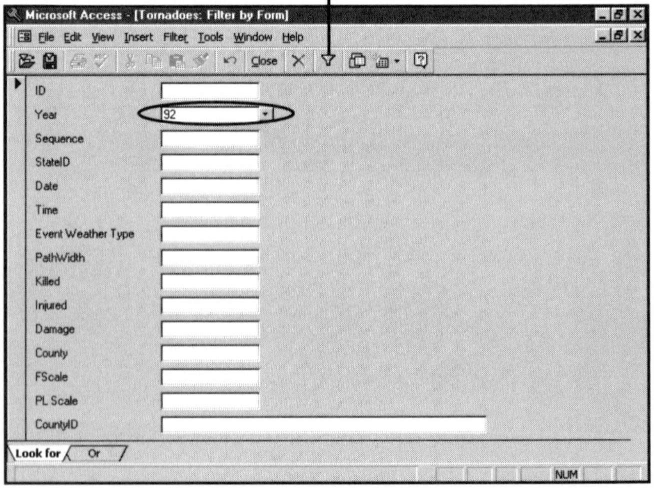


**Tip for Students**

To specify a filter, you can type in the criteria, or you can select from the entries in the drop-down list box of the field.

**4** Click in the **Year** field box and type **92**.

**5** Click the **Apply Filter** button. Notice that there were 1404 tornadoes in 1992.

> **In Depth:** Notice that the screen tip for the **Apply Filter** button now says **Remove Filter.** This is a toggle button that will apply and remove the filter that has been created. Also notice that **FLTR** is highlighted on the status bar which indicates that a filter is currently applied to the data.

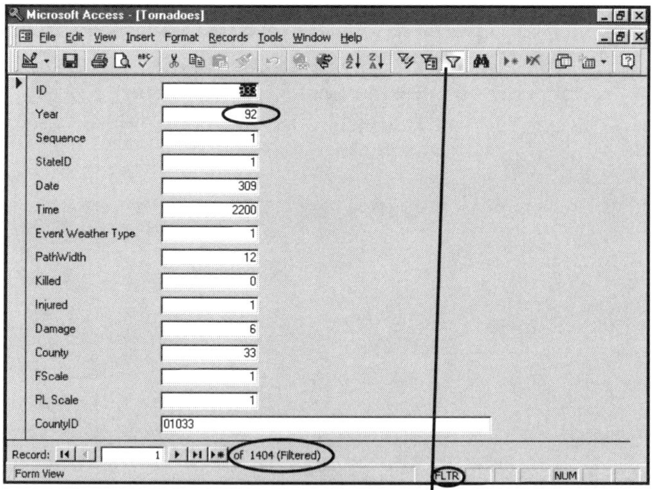


### Tip for Instructors

Point out that the bottom of the screen displays the number of records that have been filtered as well as the one being viewed.

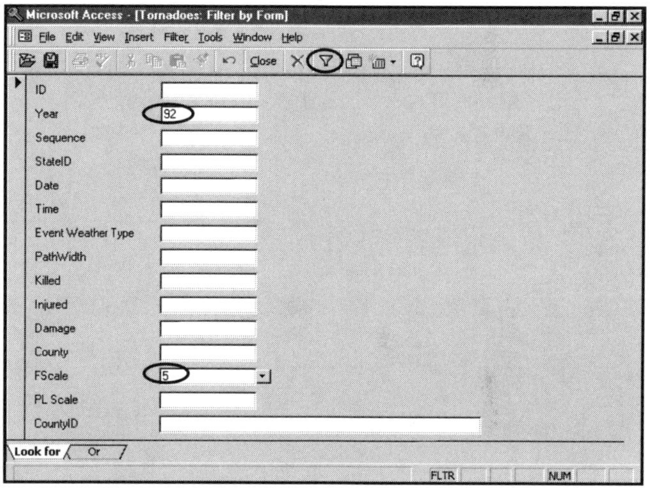


**6** Click the **Filter by Form** button again. Click in the **FScale** field box and type **5**.

### Tip for Students

Each filter must be removed before the next is applied; otherwise, the records will be double-filtered.

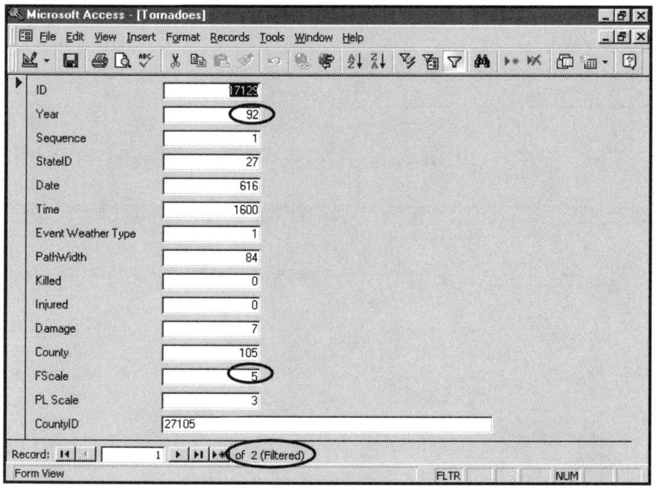


### Tip for Students

When two or more fields are filled in when using the **Filter by Form**, you are creating an And statement. All criteria listed must be met for a record to be displayed.

**7** Click the **Apply Filter** button. Notice that only 2 of the 1404 tornadoes in 1992 were rated a 5.

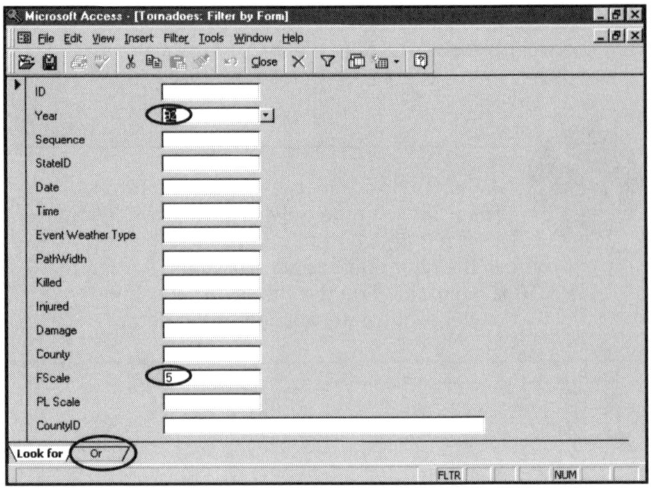


**8** It is also possible to use more than one filter at a time. Click the **Filter by Form** button. Notice that the Year and FScale boxes still contain the previous filter conditions. Also notice the tab at the bottom labeled **Or**.

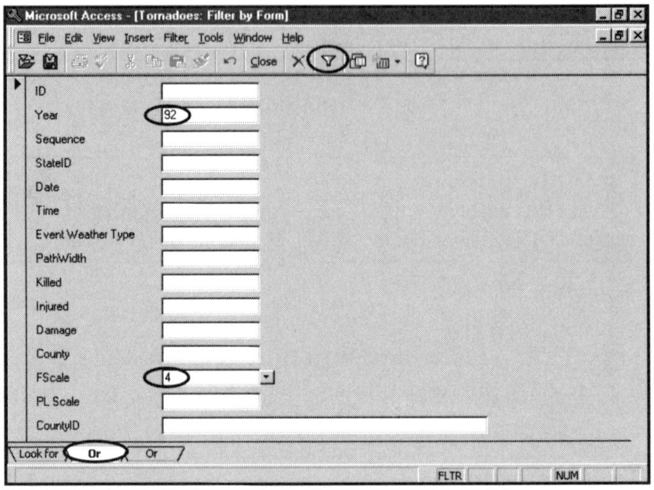


**9** To also look for tornadoes rated 4 in 1992, click the **Or** tab. Type **<u>92</u>** in the Year field box and **<u>4</u>** in the **FScale** field box.

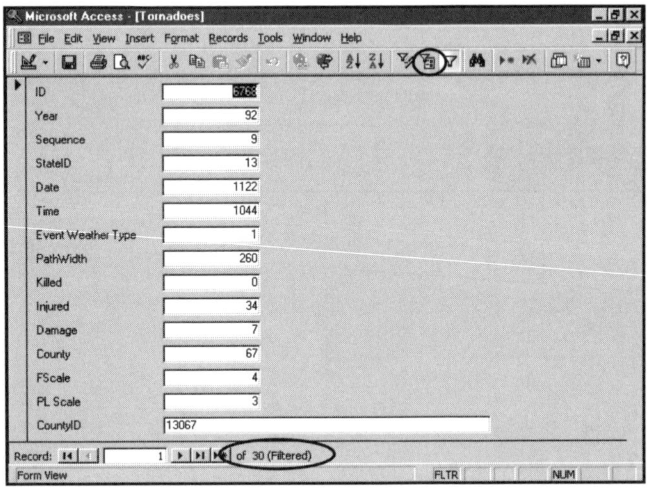


**10** Click the **Apply Filter** button. Notice that there were 30 tornadoes in 1992 rated 4 or 5.

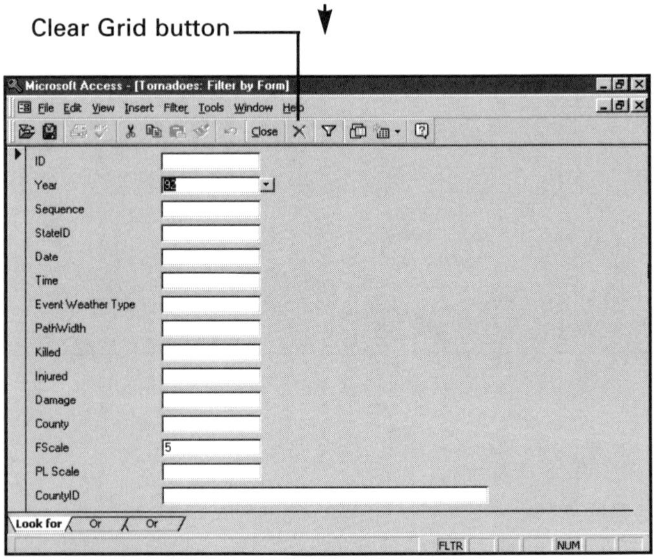


**11** Click the **Filter by Form** button.

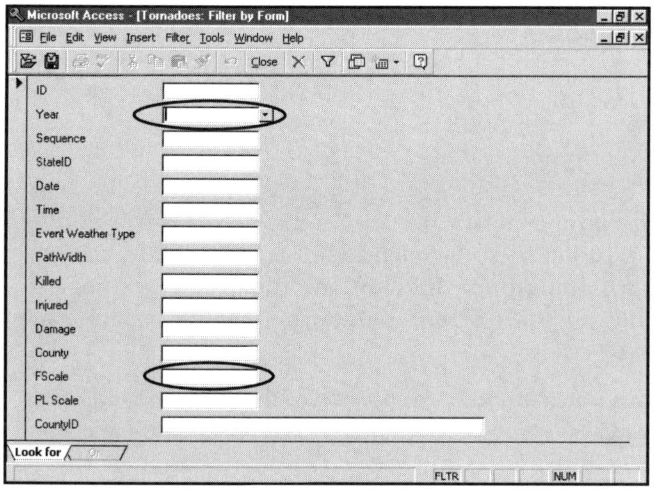


**12** Click the **Clear Grid** button. This removes the values entered for both filters.

**Pothole:** A form can have one filter at a time. The Apply/Remove Filter button does not erase the filter, rather it turns the filter on and off. Once a filter is created, it persists as an invisible part of a table or form. Since you cannot erase a filter, you need to create a new one with no criteria and apply it. Also, any sorting that you do will become the default method of displaying that table or form. Therefore, the last sort you do should be on the primary key field to restore it as the default choice for displaying the records.

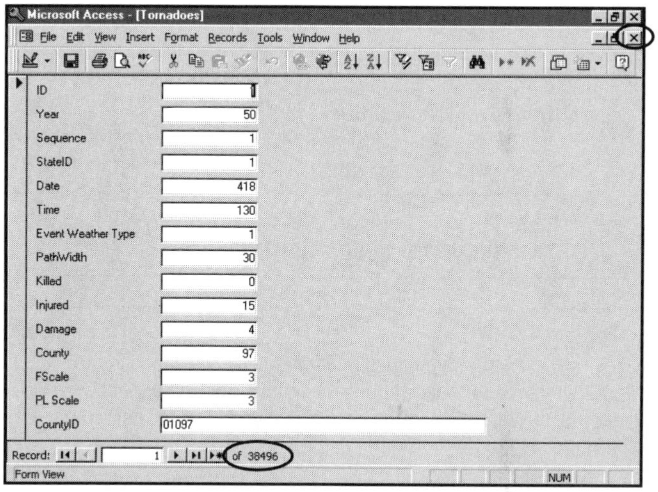


**13** Click the **Apply Filter** button. This replaces the previous filter with a filter that has no conditions.

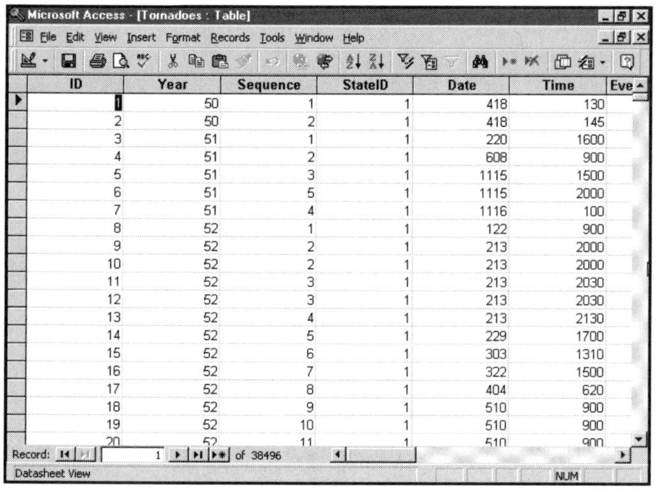


| ID | Year | Sequence | StateID | Date | Time | Eve |
|---|---|---|---|---|---|---|
| 1 | 50 | 1 | 1 | 418 | 130 | |
| 2 | 50 | 2 | 1 | 418 | 145 | |
| 3 | 51 | 1 | 1 | 220 | 1600 | |
| 4 | 51 | 2 | 1 | 608 | 900 | |
| 5 | 51 | 3 | 1 | 1115 | 1500 | |
| 6 | 51 | 5 | 1 | 1115 | 2000 | |
| 7 | 51 | 4 | 1 | 1116 | 100 | |
| 8 | 52 | 1 | 1 | 122 | 900 | |
| 9 | 52 | 2 | 1 | 213 | 2000 | |
| 10 | 52 | 2 | 1 | 213 | 2000 | |
| 11 | 52 | 3 | 1 | 213 | 2030 | |
| 12 | 52 | 3 | 1 | 213 | 2030 | |
| 13 | 52 | 4 | 1 | 213 | 2130 | |
| 14 | 52 | 5 | 1 | 229 | 1700 | |
| 15 | 52 | 6 | 1 | 303 | 1310 | |
| 16 | 52 | 7 | 1 | 322 | 1500 | |
| 17 | 52 | 8 | 1 | 404 | 620 | |
| 18 | 52 | 9 | 1 | 510 | 900 | |
| 19 | 52 | 10 | 1 | 510 | 900 | |
| 20 | 52 | 11 | 1 | 510 | 900 | |



**14** Click the **Close Window** button and click **No** when prompted to save the form. The **Tornadoes** table is displayed.

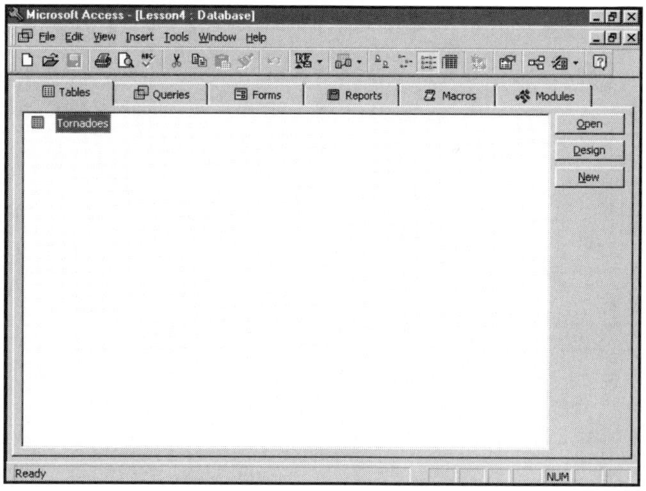


**15** Click the **Close Window** button. The **Database** window is displayed.

# Task 6

> **Tip for Instructors**
> The Learn on Demand Module/Lesson "Using Select Queries to Display Data" applies to this task.

## Using Select Queries to Display the Data

### Why would I do this?

Filters are useful, but they are limited in what they can do. *Queries* are specifically designed to create useable subsets of the data found in large tables. After a query is designed it is run against the current information in the tables. The results of a query are known as a *dynaset*. When you save a query, Access does not save the dynaset, rather it saves the structure of the query so it can be used again. Often reports are based on queries so the information in the reports is limited to the fields and records that are needed.

In this task, you learn how to create a *select query*. Select queries may contain criteria, like a filter, but they can also limit the fields that are displayed and calculate new values based on some of the fields. In this task, you learn how to choose fields in the Tornadoes table to display, enter criteria in the Years and Fscale fields, and calculate the path width of selected tornadoes.

**1** Click the **Queries** tab.

> **Concept**
> A *query* filters the data each time it is used.

> **On Your Mark**
> One of the major advantages of a database is its capability to extract records for special purposes. Think about the databases you might use. What types of records might you want to extract?

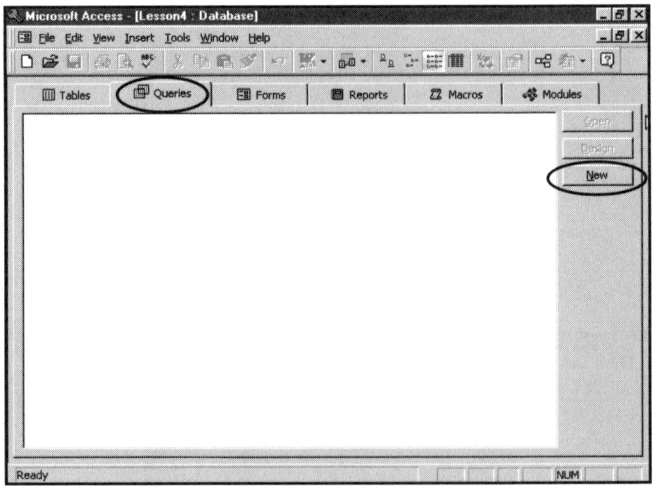


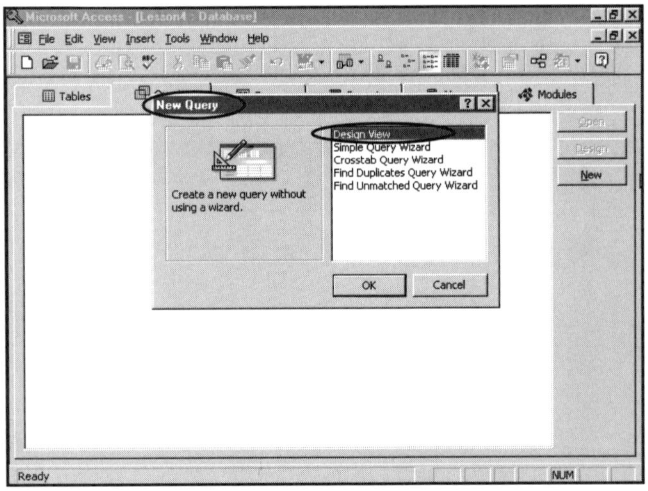


**2** Click the **New** button. The **New Query** dialog box opens.

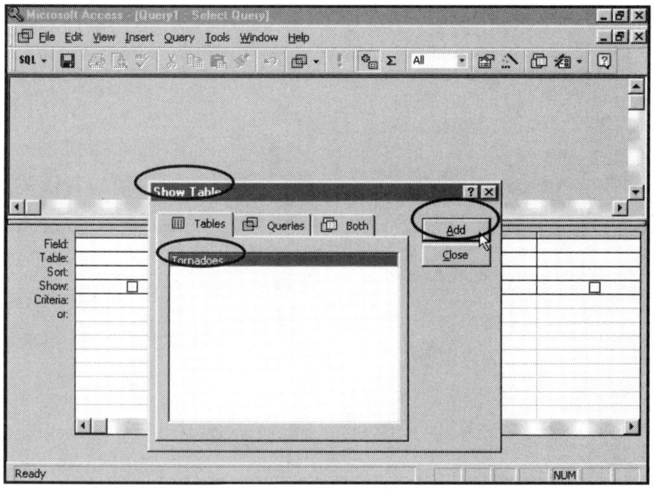


**3** Click **Design View**, if it is not already selected, and then click **OK**. The **Show Table** dialog box opens.

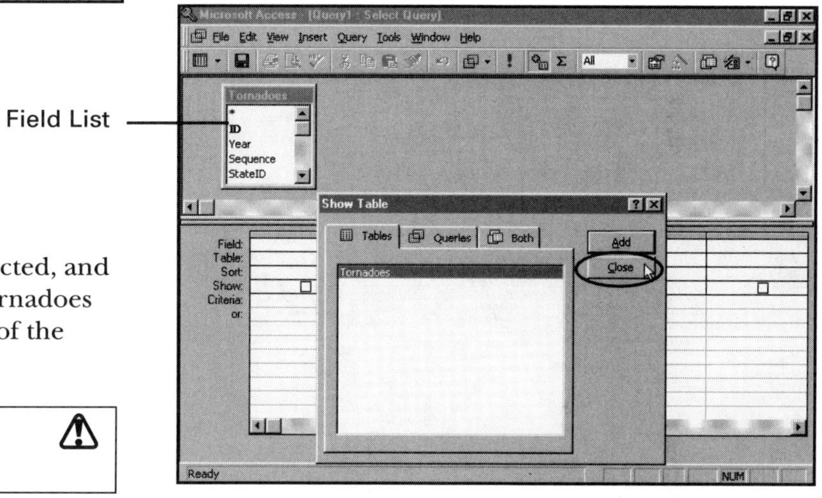


**4** Click **Tornadoes**, if it is not already selected, and then click **Add**. A list of fields in the Tornadoes table is displayed in the upper portion of the window.

**Tip for Instructors**
A query can be based on another query as well.

**SLIDE 4–5**

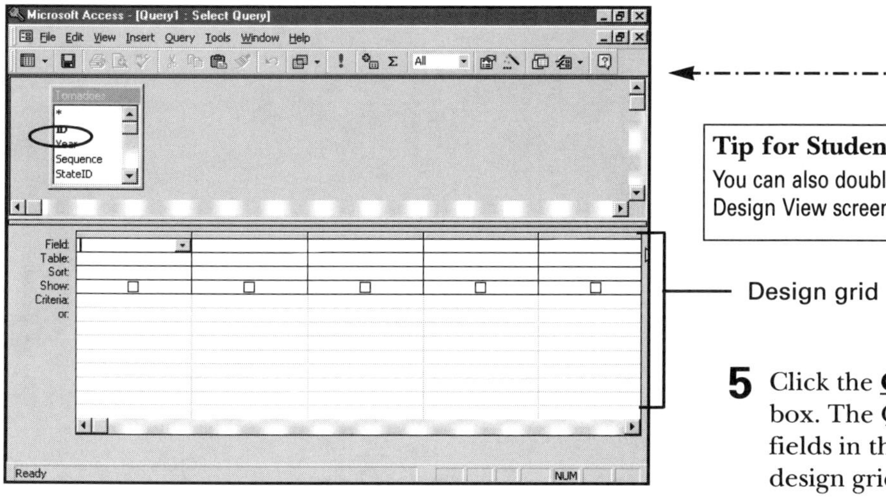


**Tip for Students**
You can also double-click a table/query name to add it to the Query Design View screen.

**5** Click the **Close** button on the Add Table dialog box. The Query Design View shows a list of the fields in the Tornadoes table and an empty design grid.

**6** Double-click the **Year** field. It is placed in the first column of the design grid along with the name of the table from which it comes.

**Tip for Instructors**

A field name can be dragged to the grid as well. If it is dragged onto a space that already has a field name, a new column is added with that field name.

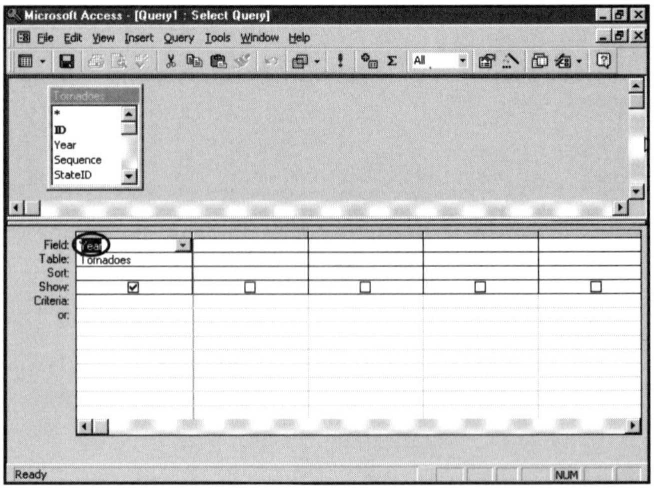

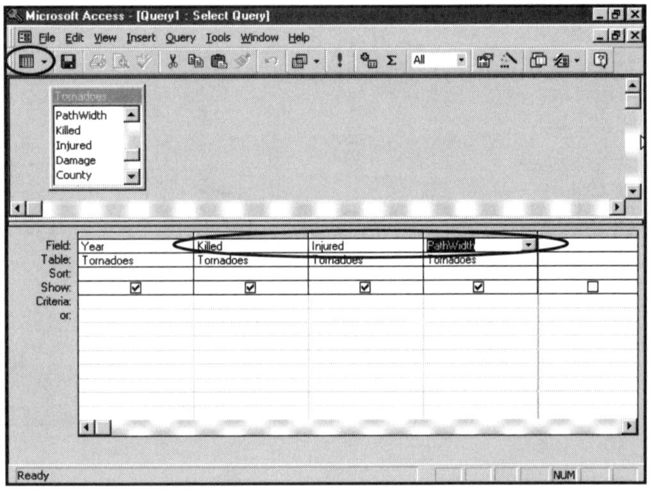

**7** Scroll down the list of fields and double-click the **Killed**, **Injured**, and **PathWidth** fields. They are added to the design grid.

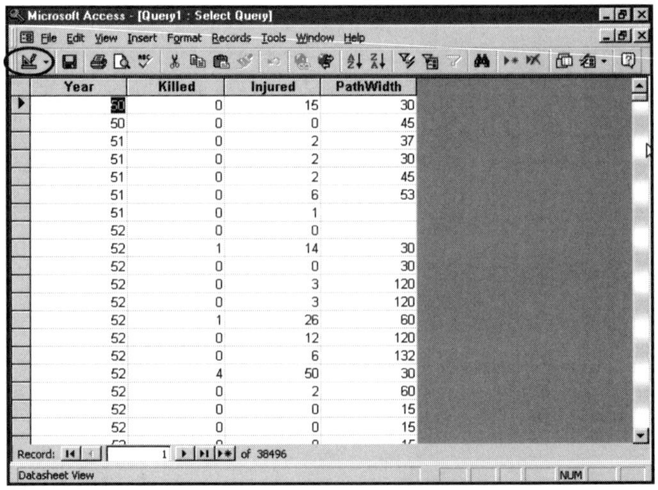

**8** Click the **View** button and switch to **Datasheet View**. All of the records are represented, but only these four fields are displayed.

**9** Click the **View** button to return to **Design View**.

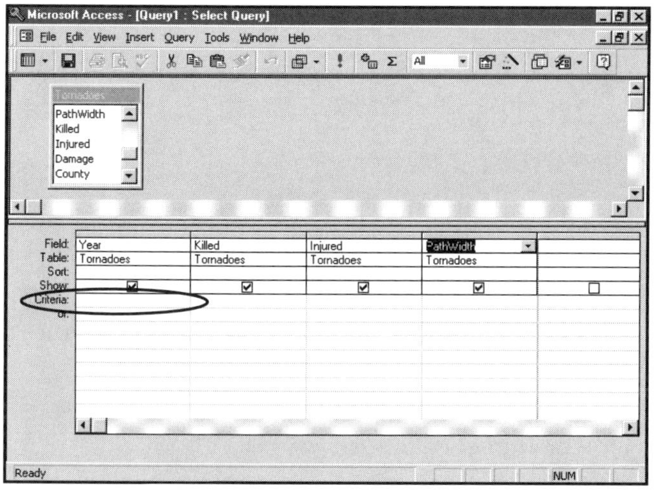


> **Tip for Students** !
> The **Criteria** field is a filter.

**10** Click the **Criteria** box in the first column under Year and type **93**.

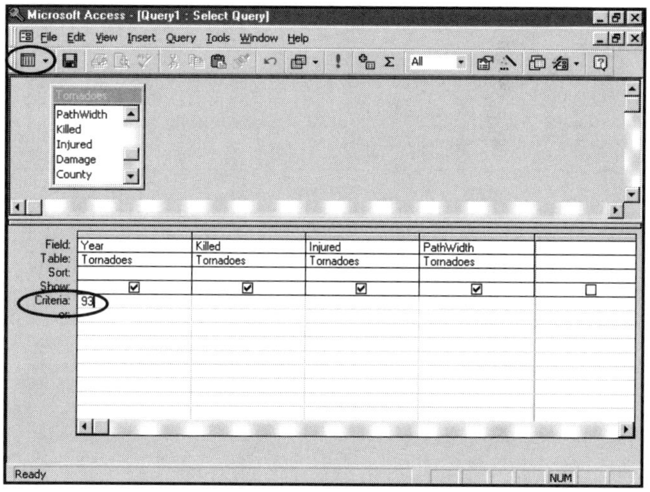


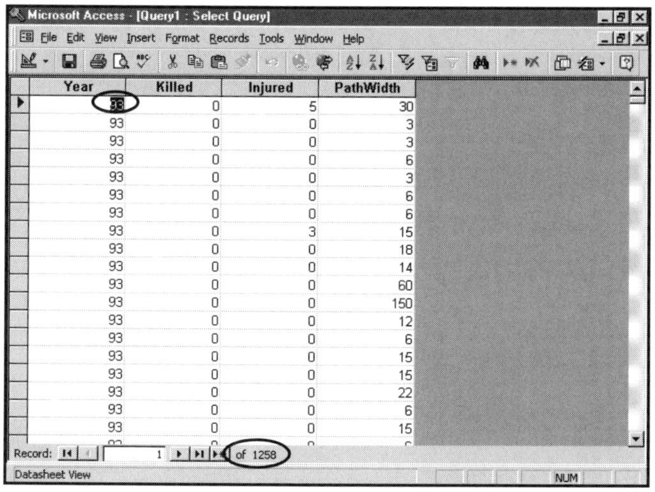


> **Speedy Class**
> The criteria can be used on more than one field with either an Or statement or an And statement. The Or statement will look for either criteria to be met for filtering; the And statement requires that all criteria be met for filtering. For example, Salary>50,000 And Department=Sales finds only the salespersons who made over $50,000 each year. However, Department=Sales Or Department=Accounting finds persons who work for the sales department as well as those who work for the accounting department.

**11** Switch to **Datasheet View**. Only the 1993 tornado records are displayed.

# Task 7

## Calculating Values for a New Column of Data

### Why would I do this?

Sometimes the information you want can be derived from data in the table. For example, in a personnel database, you may need to know an employee's age for various benefits. It is better to store their birth date from which their age can be derived when needed, rather than use valuable storage space for an age field.

In the Tornado database, the tornado's path width was stored in tens of feet in the original table provided by the weather service. This could easily be misunderstood when viewed, so it would be better to display it in feet.

In this lesson, you learn how to create a new column in the table that is calculated from the PathWidth field. You also learn how to create a header for the new column and to hide unwanted columns.

**1** Switch to **Design View**.

**Tip for Instructors**

The Learn on Demand Module/Lesson, "Calculating Values for a New Column of Data" applies to this task.

**On Your Mark**

There are times when two fields can be combined or one field can be calculated to produce another column. What are some specific examples for this type of procedure?

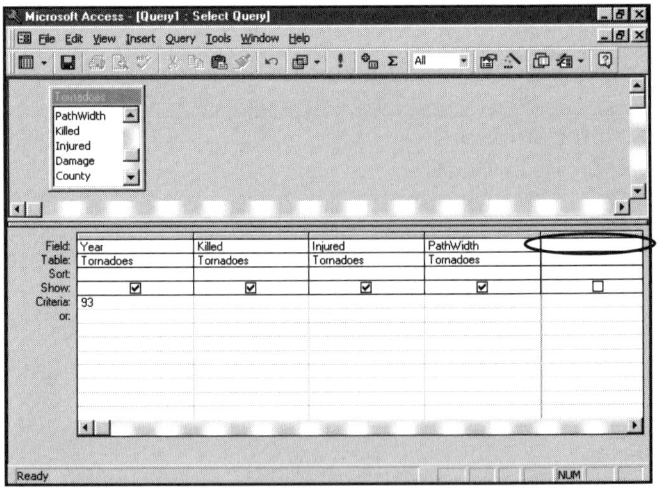

**Quicksand**

Be sure that students have clicked an empty column and in the field row. Otherwise, the criteria will not work as shown in this exercise.

**2** Right-click the **Field** box in the empty column to the right of the **PathWidth** column. A shortcut menu appears.

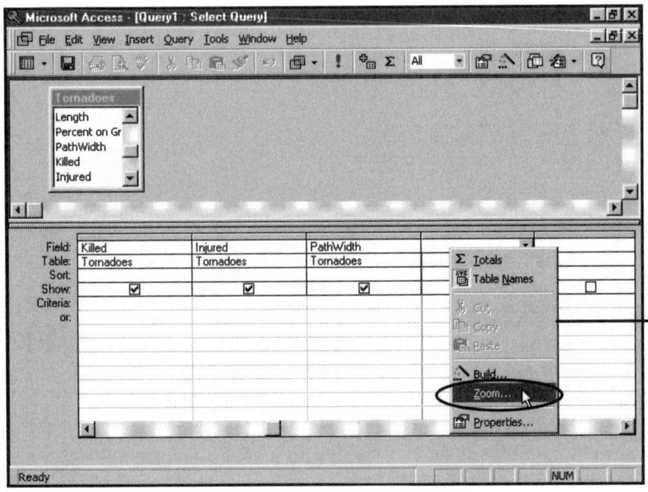

Shortcut menu

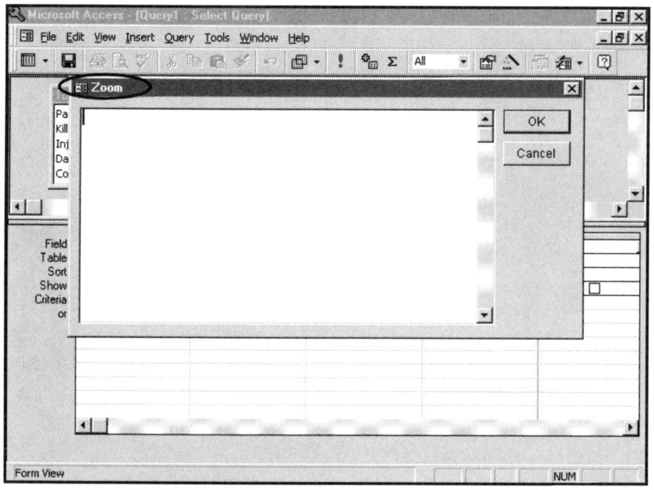


**3** Click the **Zoom** option. The **Zoom** window opens. This window is useful when making longer entries in small boxes.

**Tip for Students** **!**
This step is not necessary but helpful.

**Tip for Students** **!**
This statement tells Access to label a new field with the data to the left of the colon. The data on the right tells Access to multiply the data found in the **Path Width** field by 10.

**4** Type **Path Width (ft): [PathWidth]*10**. Make sure that the first two words are separated by a space but the fieldname is all one word. (The parentheses around **ft** have no special function, they are just used as normal parentheses in this example.)

**Pothole:** A calculated field uses square brackets, [] to enclose the field name, not parentheses, (), or braces, {}. It is easy to get these confused. It is also important that the field name is spelled exactly as it appears in the table field list. If it is misspelled, a parameter box will open asking for more information when you run the query. If this happens, return to the query design and fix the spelling of the field name. You will learn how to create parameter queries in the next task.

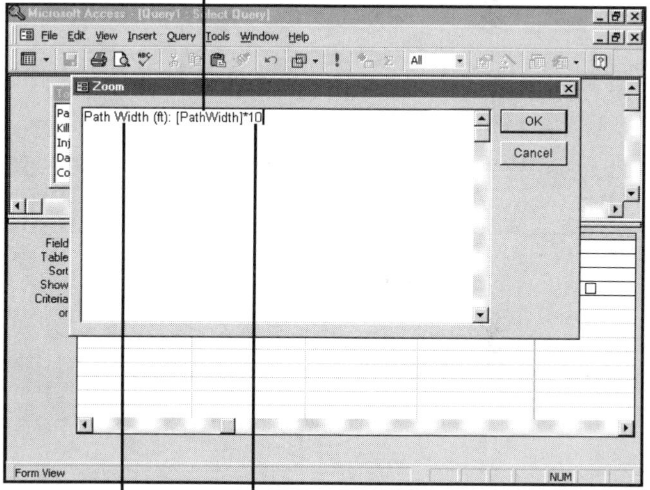


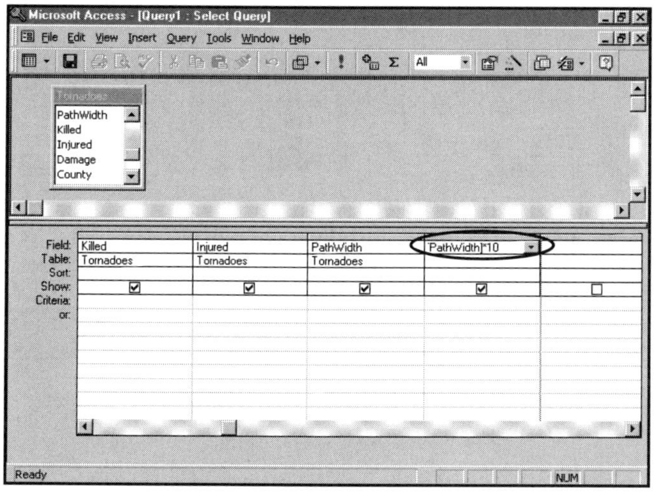


**5** Click **OK**. The statement is placed in the Field box in the new column.

**6** Switch to **Datasheet View**. Notice that the words that were entered to the left of the colon are used as the column header. (Widen the last column if necessary to see the entire header.) Compare the figures in the right two columns to verify the result of the calculation.

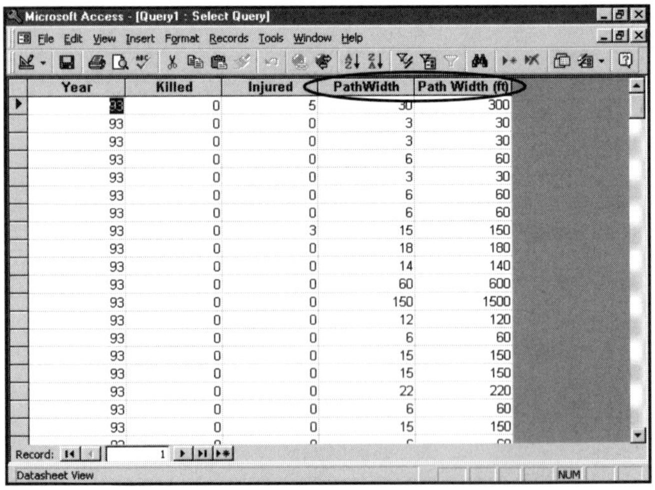


**Quicksand**

If an error message appears regarding a syntax error, the student has entered the expression as criteria rather than as a field.

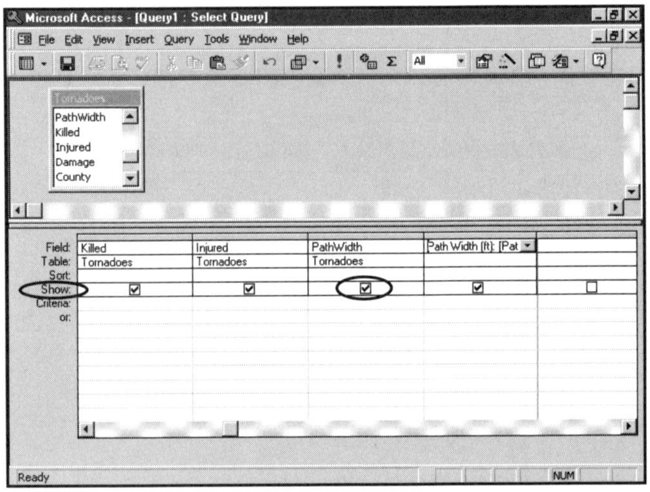


**7** Switch to **Design View**.

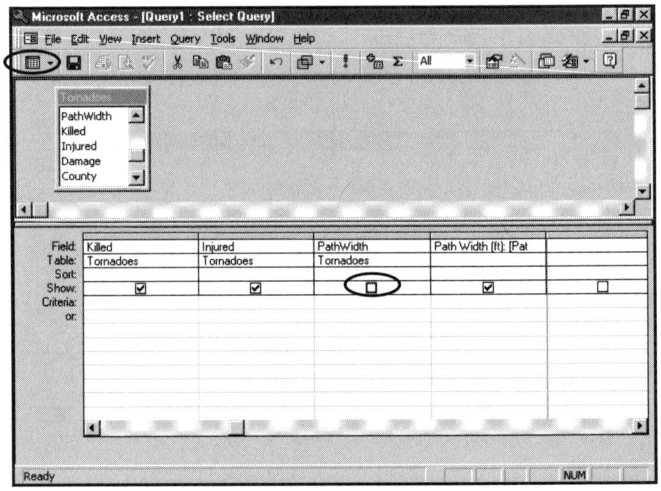


**Tip for Students**

When the Show check box is deselected, that field will not appear in the query dynaset, but it can still be used to set criteria or calculate values in another column.

**8** Click the **Show** check box in the **PathWidth** column to deselect it.

**9** Switch to **Datasheet View**. Notice that the **Path-Width** column does not show.

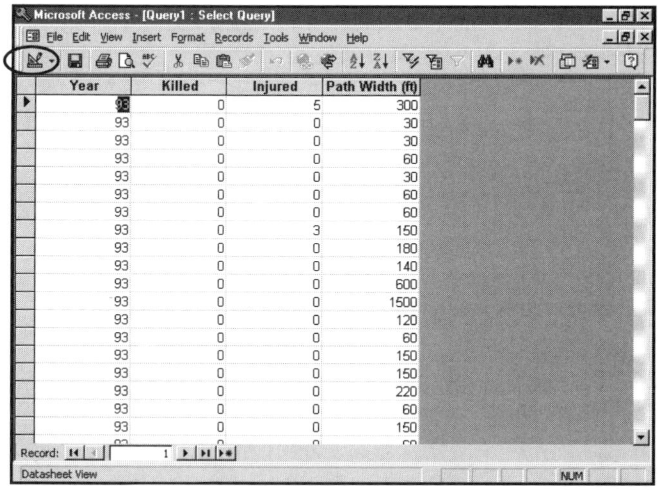


**10** Switch to **Design View**. Click the **Save** button. The **Save As** dialog box opens.

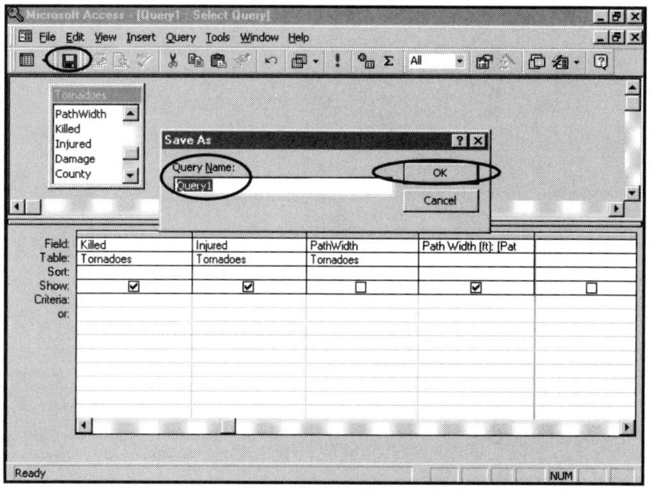


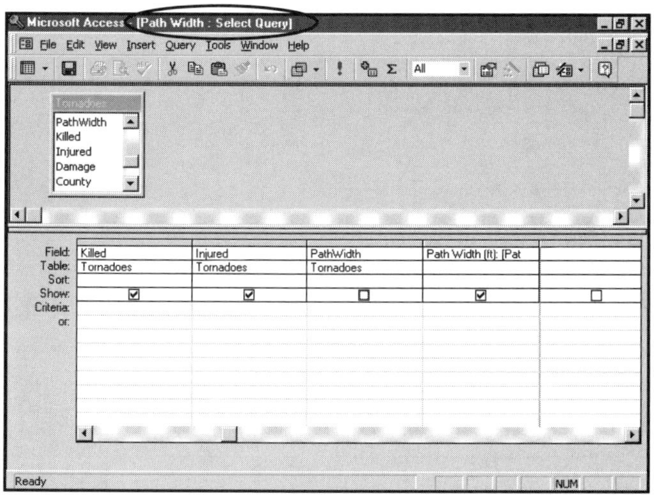


**11** Type <u>**Path Width**</u> in the **Query <u>N</u>ame** box and click **OK**. This saves the query for later use.

# Task 8

**Tip for Instructors**
The Learn on Demand Module/Lesson, "Creating Queries that Allow Criteria Changes" applies to this task.

## Creating Queries that Allow the User to Change Criteria Each Time the Query is Used

### Why would I do this?

The query that you created in Task 6 limits the display to the records for 1993. If you wanted to look at the path width information for several different years, it would be time consuming to change the criteria in the query design each time. Fortunately, there is a way to write the criteria so that a dialog box appears each time you go to Datasheet View which allows you to enter the value for the criteria. Values that define the output are called *parameters* and queries that use this feature are called *parameter queries.*

In this task, you learn how to set up a parameter query so that you can choose the year each time the datasheet is viewed.

**1** Scroll to the left to see the **Year** column of the design grid. Delete the year value that is currently in the criteria box and type **[Enter the Year]**. Notice that square brackets are used to enclose the message.

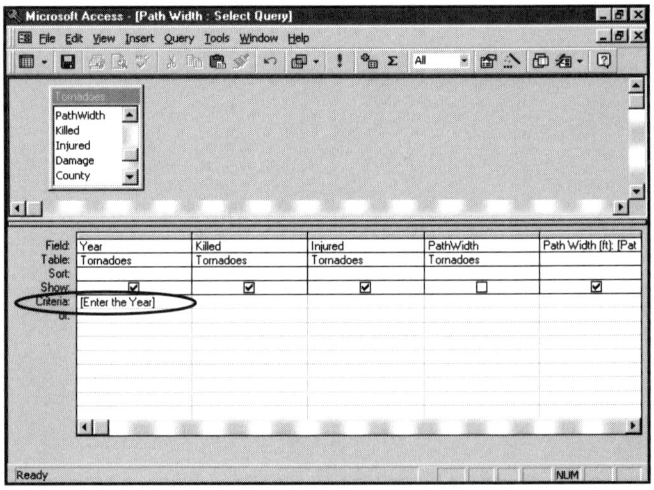


**Pothole:** Square brackets are used to enclose the field names for calculated fields. If the words that are enclosed do not correspond to one of the fields, the program will assume that you intend to enter the values from the keyboard and uses the enclosed words as a prompting message. Two problems can arise from this assumption. If you use a short prompting message that happens to be the name of a field, it will not work as expected. Also, if you misspell a field name or use the name of a field that has been deleted, it will assume that it is a prompting message.

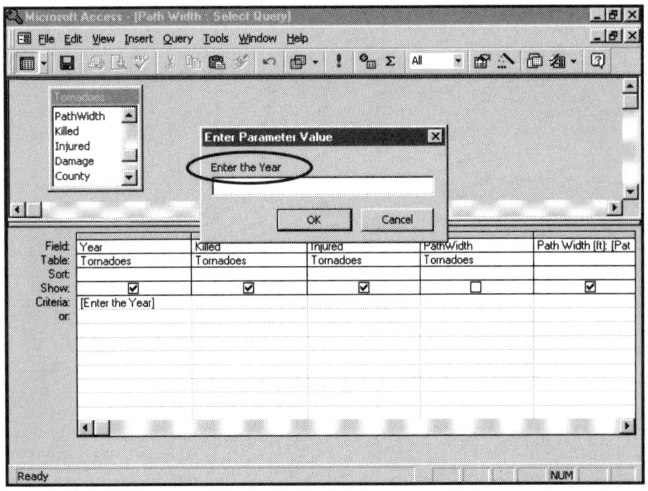


**On Your Mark**
Queries are useful for extracting data, but sometimes the criteria change or different criteria are needed. What tool would be useful in such a query?

**Tip for Instructors**
Cover the Pothole box information. Clarify any misunderstandings.

**2** Switch to **Datasheet View**. A dialog box opens. Notice that the phrase you typed in step 1 between the brackets is used as a prompting message above the box.

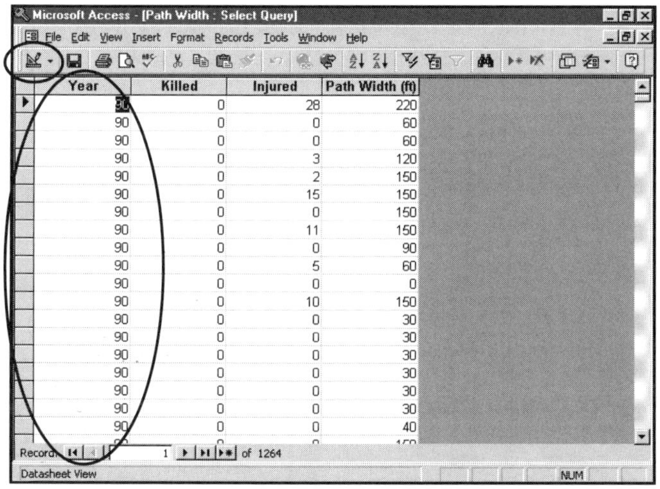


**3** Type <u>**90**</u> and click **OK**. The **Datasheet View** opens and the records shown are limited to those from 1990.

**4** Click the **View** button to switch to **Design View** and click it again to switch to **Datasheet View**. The dialog box reopens.

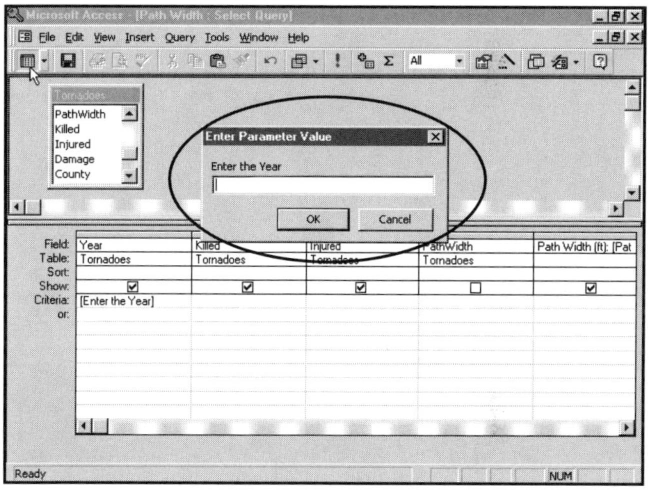


**Quick Tip:** A quick way to bring up the parameter box while still in Datasheet View is to hold down the Shift key and press **F9** on the function row of your keyboard.

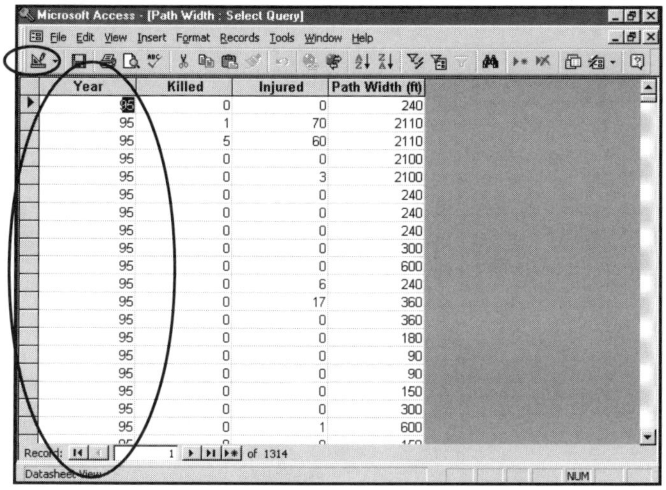


**5** Type <u>**95**</u> and click **OK**. The display is limited to the records for 1995.

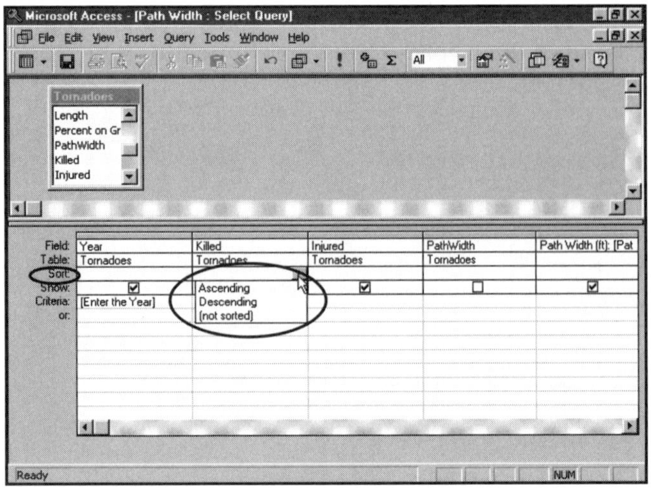


**6** Switch to **Design View**. Click the **Sort** row under the **Killed** field and click the **drop-down arrow**.

**7** Click **Descending** to select it. Do the same for the Injured field.

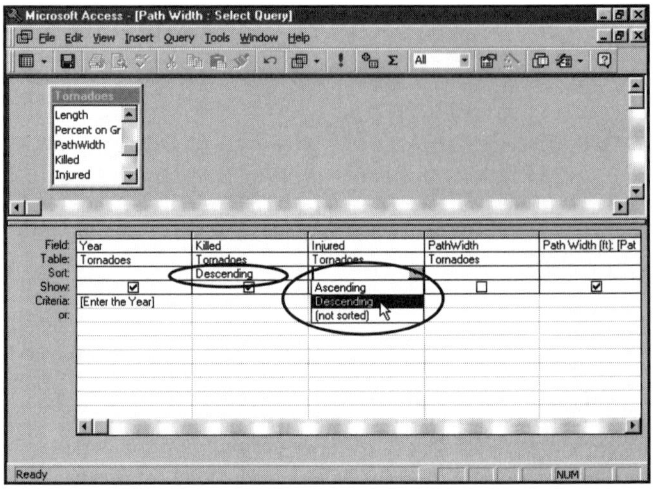


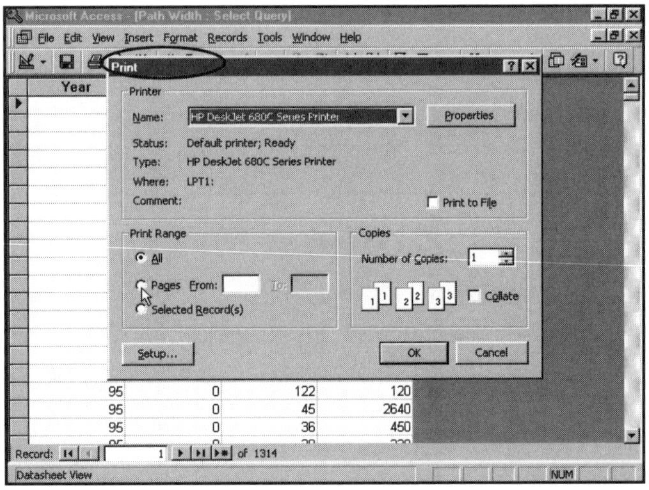


**8** Switch to **Datasheet View**. Type **95** and click **Ok**. Choose **File, Print** to open the **Print** dialog box.

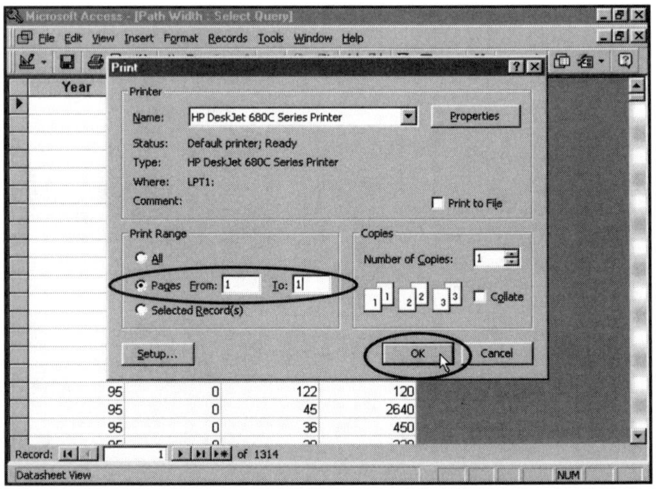


**9** Type 1 in the **Pages From** and **To** boxes.

**Path Width**

| Year | Killed | Injured | Path Width (ft) |
|---|---|---|---|
| 95 | 5 | 60 | 2110 |
| 95 | 3 | 32 | 3000 |
| 95 | 3 | 24 | 900 |
| 95 | 3 | 6 | 2100 |
| 95 | 3 | 5 | 750 |
| 95 | 2 | 11 | 2640 |
| 95 | 2 | 1 | 300 |
| 95 | 1 | 70 | 2110 |
| 95 | 1 | 55 | 3900 |
| 95 | 1 | 20 | 1320 |
| 95 | 1 | 12 | 600 |
| 95 | 1 | 3 | 450 |
| 95 | 1 | 3 | 510 |
| 95 | 1 | 1 | 150 |
| 95 | 1 | 0 | 60 |
| 95 | 1 | 0 | 90 |
| 95 | 0 | 122 | 120 |
| 95 | 0 | 45 | 2640 |
| 95 | 0 | 36 | 450 |
| 95 | 0 | 28 | 220 |
| 95 | 0 | 23 | 2640 |
| 95 | 0 | 22 | 150 |
| 95 | 0 | 22 | 600 |
| 95 | 0 | 20 | 300 |
| 95 | 0 | 17 | 360 |
| 95 | 0 | 13 | 220 |
| 95 | 0 | 12 | 1500 |
| 95 | 0 | 12 | 1500 |
| 95 | 0 | 11 | 60 |
| 95 | 0 | 10 | 60 |
| 95 | 0 | 9 | 1200 |
| 95 | 0 | 8 | 210 |
| 95 | 0 | 8 | 300 |
| 95 | 0 | 8 | 300 |
| 95 | 0 | 8 | 600 |
| 95 | 0 | 8 | 90 |
| 95 | 0 | 7 | 600 |
| 95 | 0 | 6 | 980 |
| 95 | 0 | 6 | 2640 |
| 95 | 0 | 6 | 240 |
| 90 | 0 | 5 | 90 |
| 95 | 0 | 5 | 1050 |
| 95 | 0 | 5 | 30 |
| 95 | 0 | 5 | 900 |
| 95 | 0 | 5 | 750 |
| 95 | 0 | 5 | 220 |
| 95 | 0 | 4 | 900 |

**Page 1**

**10** Click **OK** to print the first page of this query.

**Q & A** **?**
What is the advantage of using a parameter query over a select query? *Answer:* It asks for a specific criterion before creating the report.

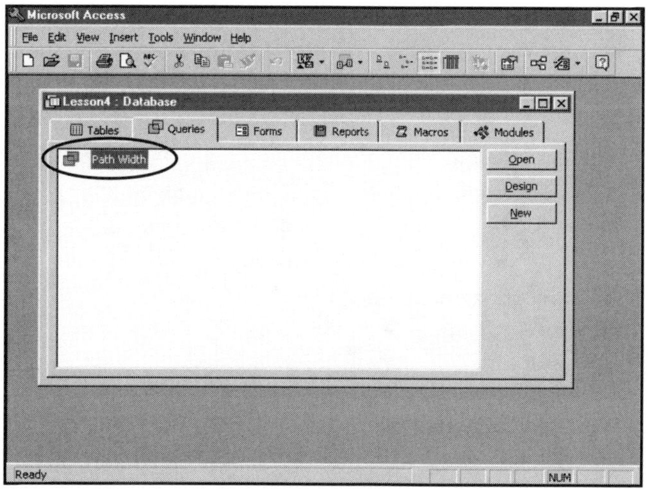


**11** Click the **Close Window** button and then click **Yes** to save the changes. Leave the database open for use in the exercises.

# Student Exercises

## True-False

For each of the following, circle T or F to indicate whether the statement is true or false.

T (F) **1.** Within Access you can save a database file with another name using the Save As command.

(T) F **2.** When you freeze a column, Access automatically moves that column to the far left position in Datasheet View.

(T) F **3.** A calculated field is a field that is derived from other information in the database.

(T) F **4.** One way to find something in a particular field is to select the field and click the Find button. Then type what you're looking for in the Find What box.

T (F) **5.** It is best to create indexes for very large databases before most of the records have been entered.

(T) F **6.** A Form Filter can be used to limit the data to specific records.

T (F) **7.** The Form Filter is limited because you can only apply one filter at a time.

T (F) **8.** To erase a Form Filter, click the Remove Filter button.

(T) F **9.** In a query, you can view selected fields, sort on one or more fields, and set criteria in one or more fields.

(T) F **10.** A parameter query can be used to quickly choose the data you want to look at because it creates a dialog box that prompts you to specify a value.

## Identifying Parts of the Access Screen

Refer to the figure and identify the numbered parts of the screen. Write the letter of the correct label in the space next to the number.

**1.** *D*
**2.** *A*
**3.** *E*
**4.** *B*
**5.** *I*
**6.** *H*
**7.** *C*
**8.** *J*
**9.** *G*
**10.** *F*

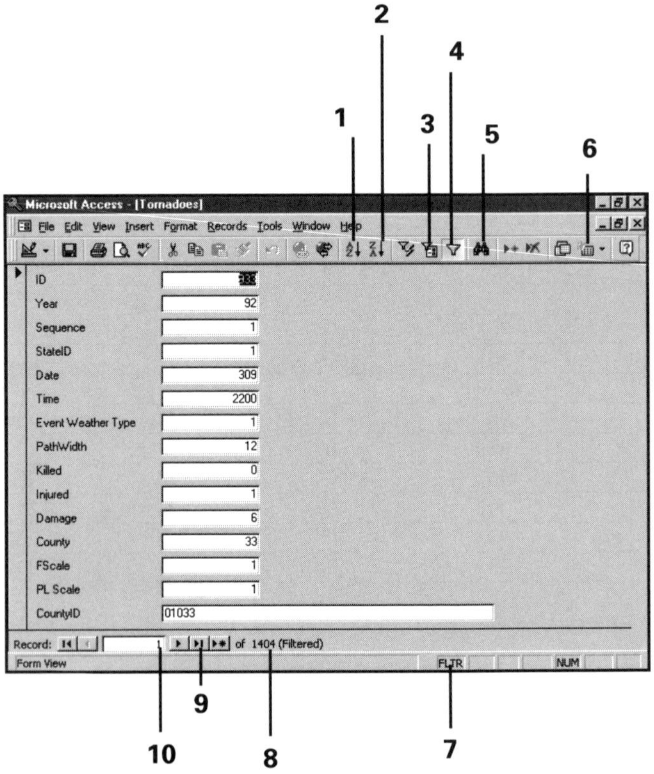


**A.** Sort Descending button
**B.** Apply/Remove Filter button
**C.** Indicates a filter is applied
**D.** Sort Ascending button
**E.** Filter by Form button
**F.** Number of the record that is selected or highlighted
**G.** Last Record button
**H.** New Object button
**I.** Find button
**J.** Number of records filtered

## Matching

Match the statements below to the word or phrase that is the best match from the list. Write the letter of the matching word or phrase in the space provided next to the number.

1. _H_ Name of the button with a picture of binoculars on it
2. _G_ Sort order that sorts in alphabetical order
3. _F_ Used to open the parameter box in Datasheet View of a parameter query
4. _E_ Action that places a field name in the query grid
5. _B_ These are used in a query to surround a field name that is being used in a calculated field
6. _I_ This action brings up a shortcut menu
7. _A_ Used to select fields when adding fields to a query
8. _K_ A type of query that allows the user to enter a value each time the query is run
9. _D_ A command in Datasheet View that moves a column to the far left and keeps it in place as you scroll
10. _C_ A large box used to write expressions so you can see more than what would fit in a small query grid box

**A.** Field List box
**B.** [ ]
**C.** Zoom
**D.** Freeze columns
**E.** Double-click a field name
**F.** Shift+F9
**G.** Ascending
**H.** Find
**I.** Right-click
**J.** Enter
**K.** Parameter query

# Application Exercises

## Exercise 1 – Finding Records

1. Open the **Lesson4** database, if necessary, and open the **Tornadoes** table.
2. Freeze the **Year** column. Scroll to the right until the **FScale** column is next to the **Year** column.
3. These records were grouped together from individual state tables. Even though the Year column looks like it is sorted, if you scroll down you will see that the years start at 50 again (86 if you are using the smaller database) for the next state. Sort the table in **ascending order** on the **Year** column.
4. Click anywhere in the **FScale** column and click the **Find** button.

5. Answer the following questions:
   a. What was the first year in which a tornado occurred that was rated **5** on the FScale? _______
   b. When the scale was created, it defined ratings from zero to 6. How many tornadoes have been rated a 6?

## Exercise 2 – Using a Form to Define a Filter

1. Open the **Tornadoes** table and create an **AutoForm**.
2. Click the **Filter by Form** button. Enter **90** for the Year and 5 for the FScale.
3. Apply the filter and look at the number of records that match the criteria. This is the number of F5 tornadoes in 1990.
4. Use this method to answer the following questions:
   a. How many tornadoes were rated 5 on the FScale in 1990? __________
   b. How many tornadoes were rated 5 on the FScale in 1991? __________
   c. How many tornadoes were rated 5 on the FScale in 1992? _________
5. Clear the grid and use the **Or** feature to determine the number of tornadoes that occurred in 1995 that were rated 3 or 4. ___________
6. Clear the grid. Determine the number of tornadoes that have killed more than 20 people. (Hint: in the **Killed** box, enter **>20**.) _________
7. Close the form. Do not save the form.

## Exercise 3 – Creating a Select Query

1. Create a new query that contains the **Year**, **StateID, Killed**, and **Injured** fields.
2. You are going to determine how many tornadoes killed more people than it injured. Create a calculated field that has the header, **Killed to Injured Ratio,** and divides the number **Killed** by the number **Injured**.
3. Use a criteria of **>0** in the **Killed** and **Injured** fields to eliminate tornadoes where no one was killed or injured. Use a criteria of **>1** in the newly created column to show only those tornadoes where the ratio will be greater than 1, indicating that the number killed was greater than the number injured.

4. Sort in descending order on the new **Killed to Injured Ratio** field.
5. View the datasheet. How many recorded tornadoes killed more people than it injured?

   ________
6. In Datasheet View, resort the query on the **StateID** field. From visual examination, which state ID occurs most frequently? ____ How many times has this state had more people killed than injured from a tornado? ____
7. In the Datasheet View of the query, click the **Print** button to print the results of your query. It should print on one page.
8. Close the query and save it as **More Deaths than Injuries**.

## Exercise 4 – Using a Parameter Query

1. Create a new query based on the **Tornadoes Table** that contains the **Year**, **Killed**, **Injured**, and **FScale** fields.
2. Sort the query in descending order on the **Killed** field.
3. In the criteria box for the **Year** field, enter this prompting message: **[Enter the Year]**.
4. Enter a similar prompting message in the criteria box for the **FScale** field.
5. To limit the records displayed to only those tornadoes that resulted in fatalities, type **>0** in the criteria box for the **Killed** field.
6. Use this parameter query to answer the following questions:
   a. How many F5 tornadoes caused fatalities in 1990? ________
   b. How many F4 tornadoes caused fatalities in 1987?
7. What does the query show when there are no matches? Search for the following:
   a. How many F5 tornadoes caused fatalities in 1973?____ What does the record number show at the bottom? ____
   b. How many F5 tornadoes caused fatalities in 1975?____ What does the record number show at the bottom? ____
8. Close the query and name it **Fatalities by Year**.
9. Close the database and exit Access.

# Lesson 5
## Using Two or More Tables in Combination

**Task 1** Importing or Linking to a Table

**Task 2** Creating a Relationship between Tables

**Task 3** Creating a Union Query that Uses Fields from Both Tables

**Task 4** Using Advanced Parameter Query Methods with a Union Query

**Task 5** Creating a Form that Displays Data from Two or More Tables

**Task 6** Creating a Report that Uses the Union Query

**Lesson Time**
**105 minutes**

# Introduction

There are several techniques that are used to reduce the size of databases. One way is to limit the field size by using two- or three-digit codes for fields that are repeated frequently. For example, if a an entry, such as the name of a state, is repeated many times, it is more efficient to represent that state or county with a number. Then a separate table can be created that contains the number and the corresponding name of the state. When the data is entered, a two-digit number may be entered rather than the full name, thus reducing the overall size of the database. When the data is reported, the name can be recalled from the second table and displayed instead of the number. The two tables are related to each other through a common field such as the state's identifying number. Databases that use related tables are called *relational databases.*

In this lesson, you learn how to import or link a table that contains state names and how to link a table that contains county names to the Tornado data table. You also learn how to create a relationship between the tables and how to create queries, forms, and reports that utilize that relationship.

**Tip for Instructors**
The Learn on Demand Module that applies to Lesson 5 is found in the Using Two or More Tables in Combination subfolder of Learn Access 97.

## Visual Summary

**SLIDE 5–1**

When you have completed Task 6, you will have created a report that looks like this:

**Tornadoes by State**

State Name Oklahoma

County Name Love

| Year | Killed | Injured | FSale |
|---|---|---|---|
| 95 | 3 | 6 | 3 |

County Name Pawnee

| Year | Killed | Injured | FSale |
|---|---|---|---|
| 91 | 1 | 5 | 4 |

County Name Payne

| Year | Killed | Injured | FSale |
|---|---|---|---|
| 90 | 1 | 12 | 3 |

County Name Rogers

| Year | Killed | Injured | FSale |
|---|---|---|---|
| 93 | 7 | 100 | 4 |

County Name Washington

| Year | Killed | Injured | FSale |
|---|---|---|---|
| 91 | 1 | 10 | 2 |

Monday, November 10,1997 Page 1 of 1

**On Your Mark**
One cause for large databases is repetitive data. Suppose that you maintain a database for retraining 1,000 employees. What type of data fields would be necessary? Which of these might contain duplicate entries?

# Task 1

## Importing or Linking to a Table

**Tip for Instructors**

The Learn on Demand Module/Lesson "Importing or Linking to a Table" applies to this task.

### Why would I do this?

In many cases, a large database table is provided by your employer or a government archive. It is unnecessary to recreate the table in every database that uses it. Rather, you can import the table from its original source and use the information in a your own database. In some cases, the company's computer will only allow you to read the data and not to copy or change it. In these instances, it is better to create a link from your database to the database that contains the large table.

In this task, you open a database that contains the names of the counties in the U.S. Then you import a small table of state names into the database that contains the county information. Finally, you learn how to link this database to the large table of tornado data that was used in the previous lesson.

**On Your Mark**

Sometimes, an existing database contains the data we need. What might be useful to save valuable duplication time?

**Concept**

*Importing* a table makes a copy of the original table by placing it in the new database.

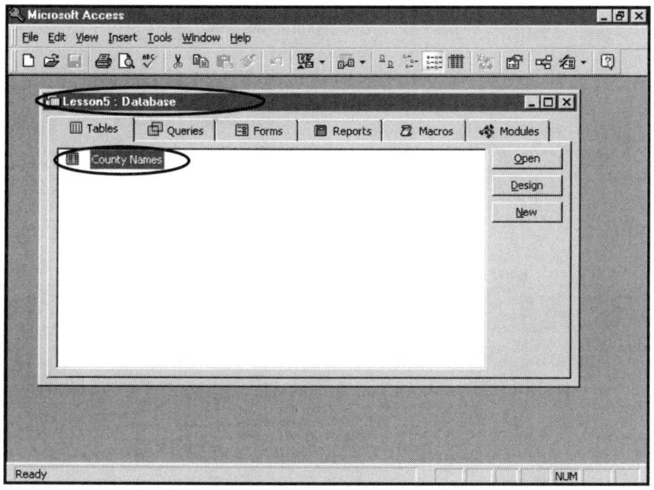


**1** Use Windows Explorer to find the **Less0501** file that was provided with your book and rename it **Lesson5**. Launch Access and open **Lesson5**. Notice that this file contains the table **County Names**.

**2** Choose **File**, **Get External Data**, **Import**. The **Import** dialog box opens.

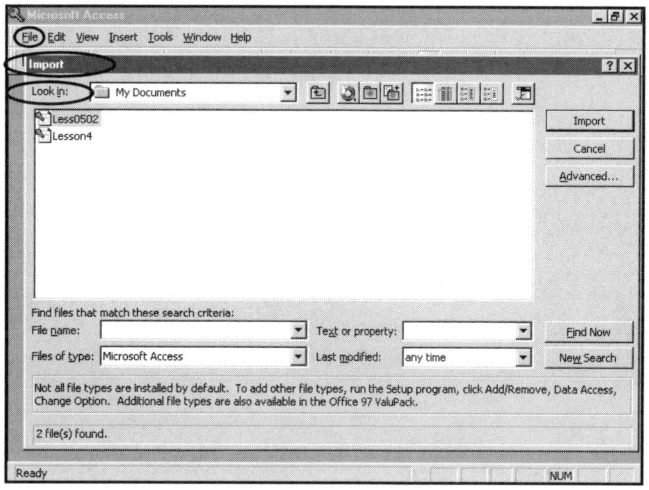


**In Depth:** When you look for files, the list of files in the import dialog box on your screen will be different from those that appear in the figure. Your files may also be located in a different folder on your computer. Click the drop-down arrow at the right end of the **Look-in** box and follow your instructor's direction to locate the correct files.

**3** Find the **Less0502** file that was provided with the book.

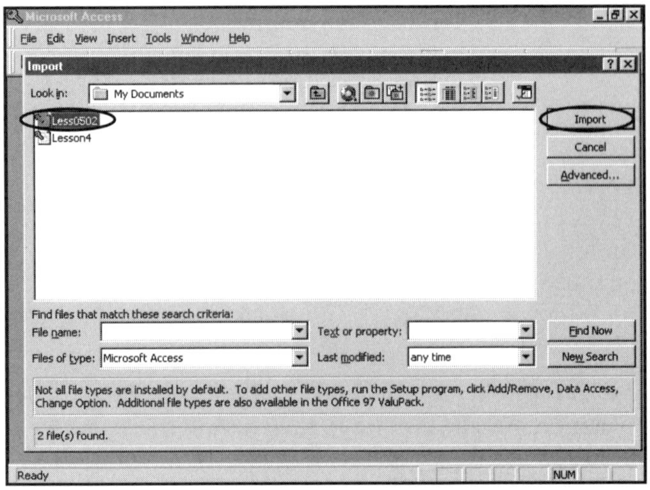


**4** Click the **Import** button. The **Import Objects** dialog box opens. The dialog box resembles the Database window with tabs for the same six database objects.

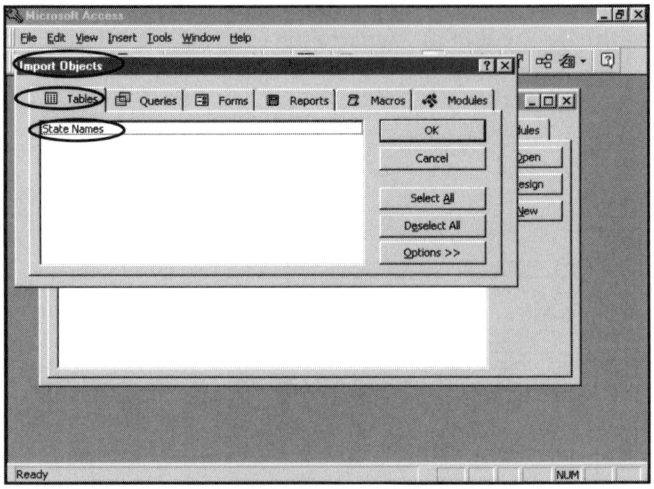


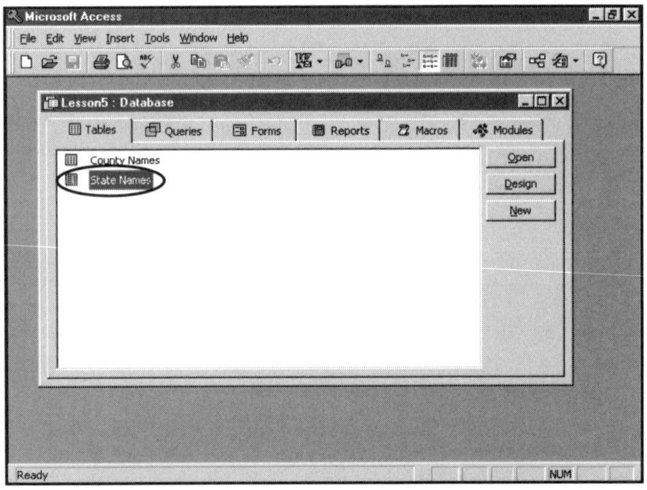


**5** Click the **Tables** tab, if necessary, click **State Names** to select the table of state names, and click **OK**. The table is imported into the Lesson5 database.

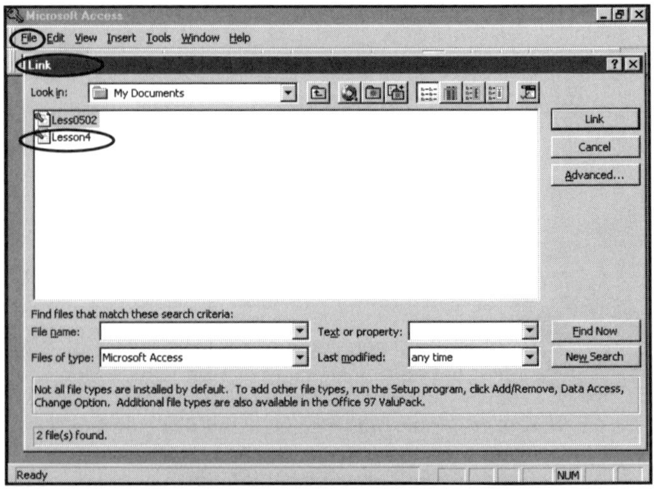


### Tip for Students

By importing a table, you can manipulate the data as you see fit. Any changes you make do not affect the original, or vice-versa.

### Quicksand

Because the **Link** and the **Import Objects** dialog boxes look the same, students should check the title bar before proceeding.

**6** Choose **File**, **Get External Data**, **Link Tables**. The **Link** dialog box opens.

**7** Find the **Lesson4** file that was used in the previous lesson. (If you have not done that lesson, find **Less0401**.)

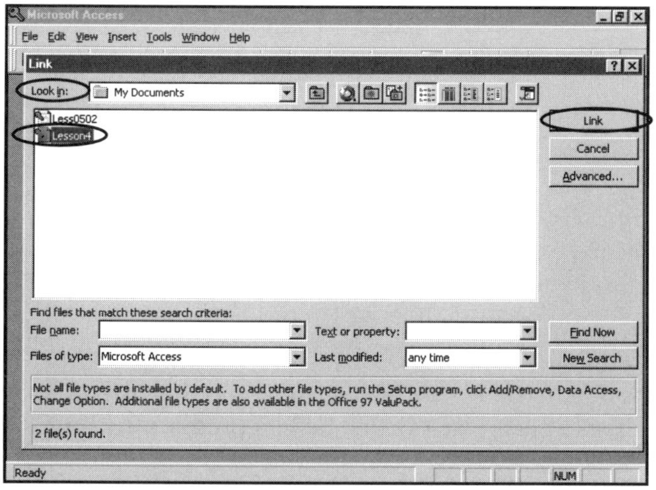


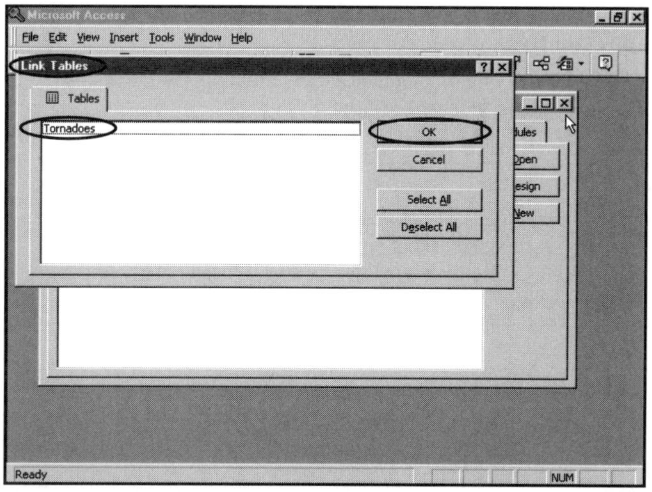


**8** Click **Lesson4** and then click **Link**. The **Link Tables** dialog box opens.

Arrow indicating a linked table

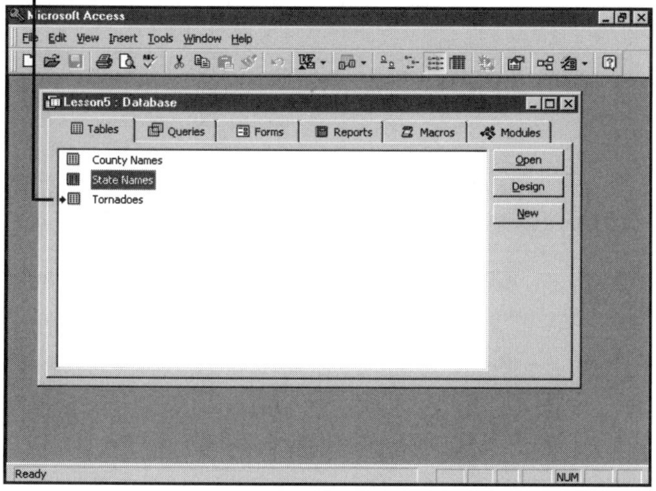


**Q & A**

*Question:* What is the difference between a linked and an imported table? *Answer:* A linked table can only be updated from the original database; an imported table can be manipulated independently of the original database.

**9** Click **Tornadoes** and then click **OK**. The Tornadoes table is linked to the Lesson5 database. Notice the small arrow next to the table's name, indicating a linked table.

**In Depth:** Before you move on to the next task, take a moment to open the tables and examine the fields in each one. Notice that the County Names table contains 3038 records of county names and a corresponding ID number. The State Names table is similarly structured. You worked in Lesson 4 with the Tornadoes table and know that it contains fields for State ID and County ID numbers.

# Task 2

## Creating a Relationship between Tables

### Why would I do this?

The most common way to relate two tables is to connect the primary key field in one table to the same field in another table. In this example, the State Names table has one record for each state and the primary key field is the StateID field. The Tornadoes table also has a field that is used to identify the state in which the tornado occurred. Each state will have numerous tornadoes, so the same state code will occur many times in the Tornadoes table. This type of relationship is called a *one-to-many relationship.*

In this task, you learn how to create one-to-many relationships between the State Names table and the Tornadoes table and between the County Names table and Tornadoes table. In each case the first table represents the "one" side of the one-to-many relationship that will be created.

**Tip for Instructors**

The Learn on Demand Module/Lesson "Creating a Relationship between Tables" applies to this task.

**On Your Mark**

We have arranged our data into various tables to better group and organize our records. What types of projects might we need that incorporates more than one table? Before we can do any of these things, we must first show Access how they relate.

**Concept**

A *relationship* allows two tables to work together, thus preventing duplication of entries. If particular fields require certain data to be unnecessarily repeated, it is best to create more than one table and create relationships. For example, if a database contains company statistics (name, phone, address, and so on), as well as all contact information (date/time, type of contact, and so on), it is unnecessary to key in one company's information for each contact (which may be many).

**1** Choose **<u>T</u>ools**, **<u>R</u>elationships**. The **Relationships** window opens.

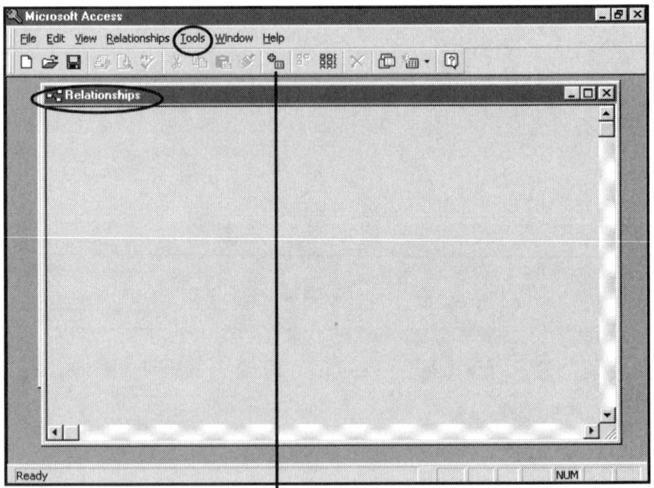


Show Table button

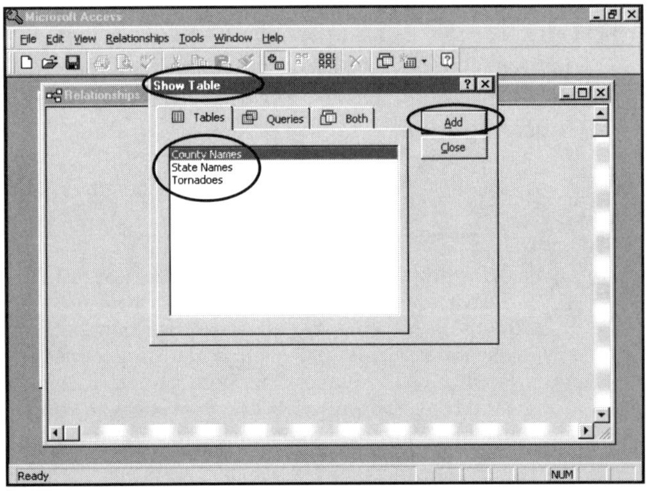


**2** Click the **Show Table** button. The **Show Table** window opens and a list of tables is displayed.

**Concept**

Defining *relationships* tells Access how to bring data together from different tables. A relationship works by matching data in key fields.

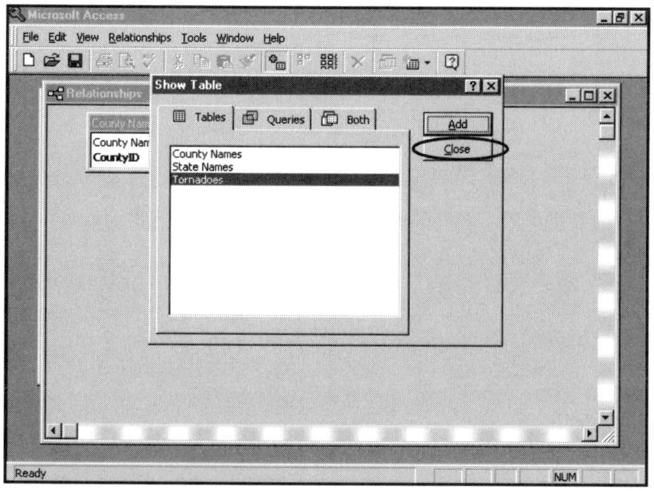


3 Click **Add** to add the **County Names** table. Click **State Names**, click **Add**, click **Tornadoes**, and click **Add** again. All three tables are added to the **Relationships** window.

**Pothole:** You may successfully add a table to the Relationships window, but it could be hidden behind the Show Table window. If you are not sure, move the Show Table window aside. If you have accidentally added a table twice, click on the extra table field list and press Del to remove it.

**Tip for Students**

To move a window, drag its title bar.

Title bar

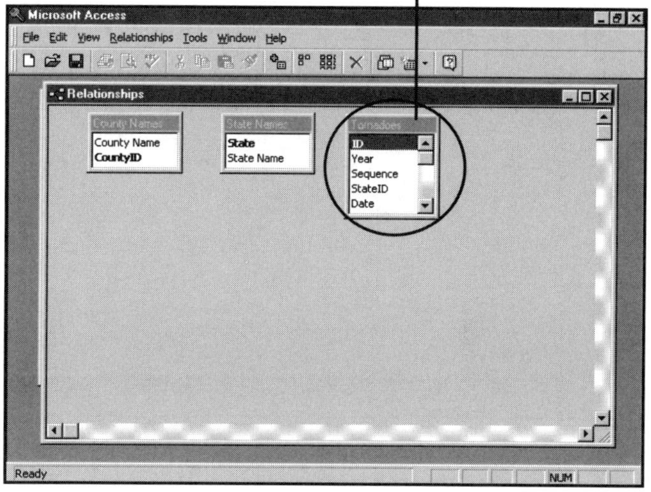


4 Click **Close** to close the **Show Table** window. The three tables are displayed in the **Relationships** window.

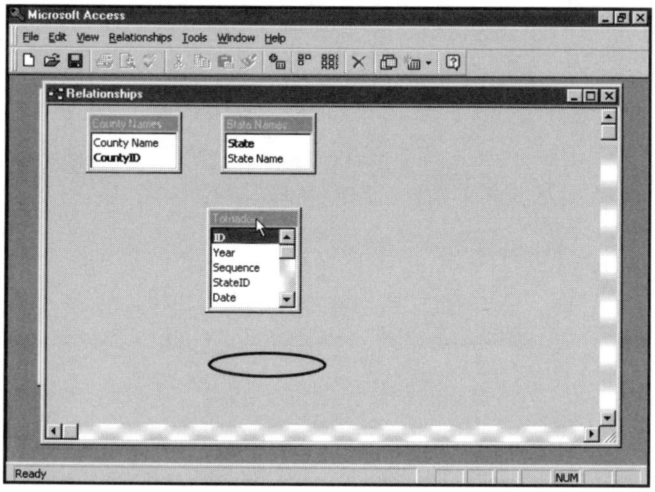


5 The relationship lines will be easier to see if you rearrange the tables so that the **Tornadoes** table is between the other two. Point to the **title** bar of the **Tornadoes** table. Click and drag the table to a spot below the other two tables, as shown in the figure.

**Tip for Instructors**

A one-to-many relationship is created if the first key field used is a primary key or has an index with no duplicates. It is the most common type of relationship. An example of this concept can be found within a sales organization. One salesman may produce many sales and have many customers.

**Quicksand**

Steps 5 and 6 may seem unnecessary; however, their purpose will be exposed as this lesson progresses.

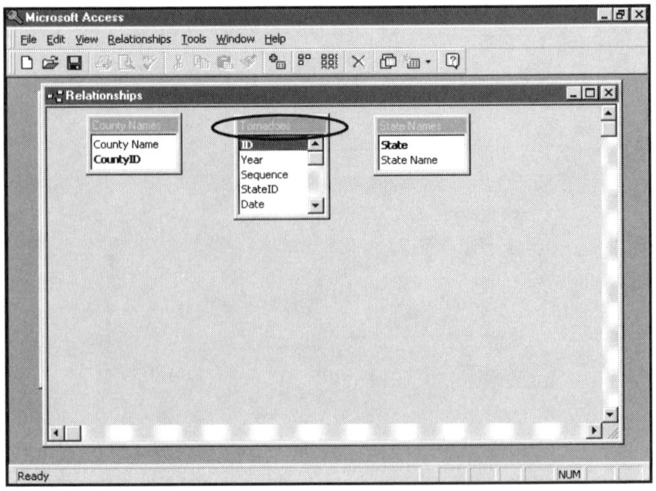


**6** Point to the **title** bar of the **State Names** table. Click and drag the table to the right. Use the same method to move the **Tornadoes** table up between the other two tables, as shown in the figure.

Pointer changes to a two-headed arrow when used to drag the edge.

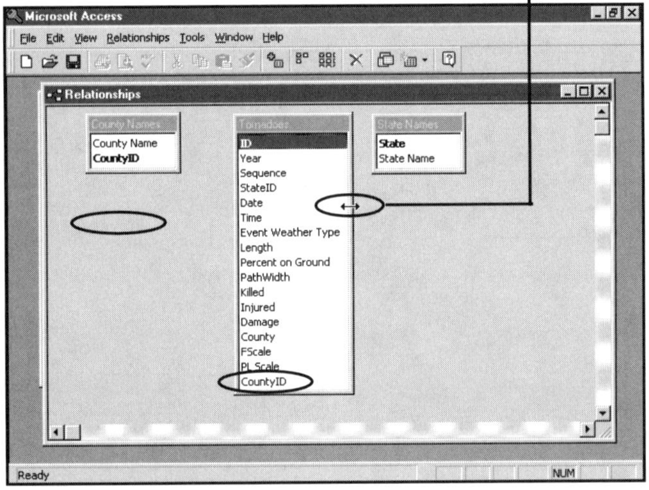


**7** Click and drag the bottom edge of the **Tornadoes** table downward until all of the fields are displayed. Click and drag the right side of the **Tornadoes** table until the full field names are visible.

**Tip for Students**

You might need to maximize the **Relationships** window to display enough space to complete this step.

**In Depth:** It is not necessary to enlarge the table but, if you have room on the screen, it is recommended to reduce the likelihood of mistaking one field for another.

**8** Point at the **CountyID** field in the **County Names** table and hold down the left mouse button. Move the pointer to the **CountyID** field in the **Tornadoes** table and release the mouse. The **Relationships** dialog box opens. Notice the relationship type is one-to-many.

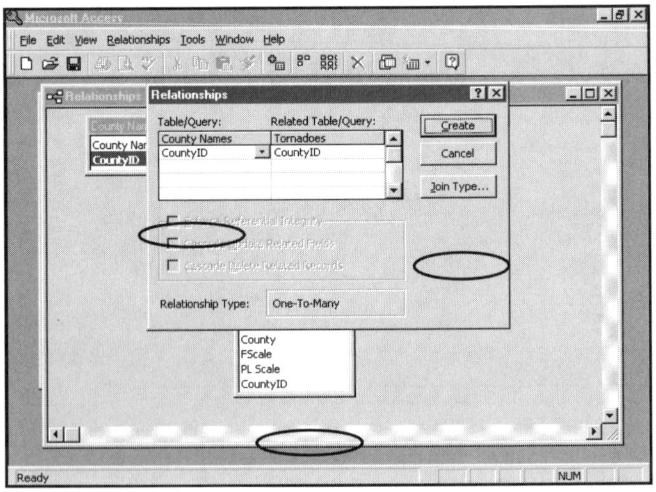


**Tip for Students**

The order in which you create a relationship is important. The field you drag is the "one" field in the relationship, meaning it must be unique. The field that is the destination is the "many" field.

**Tip for Students**

When creating a relationship, the fields selected must be of similar type and properties. Their names do not have to be identical—it's just simpler if they are.

**In Depth:** Notice that the pointer is the shape of a small rectangle while on top of one of the fields in a table. In the open space between the tables, the pointer looks like a universal symbol for "no," or Ø.

**9** Click the **Create** button. A line connects the two fields to indicate that the tables are related.

**In Depth:** The two fields do not have to have the exact same name, but they do have to be the same field type and have the same properties. For example, the CountyID fields in both tables are text fields and the State and StateID fields in both tables are number fields. Also, the field in the "one" side of a one-to-many relationship must be the primary key field.

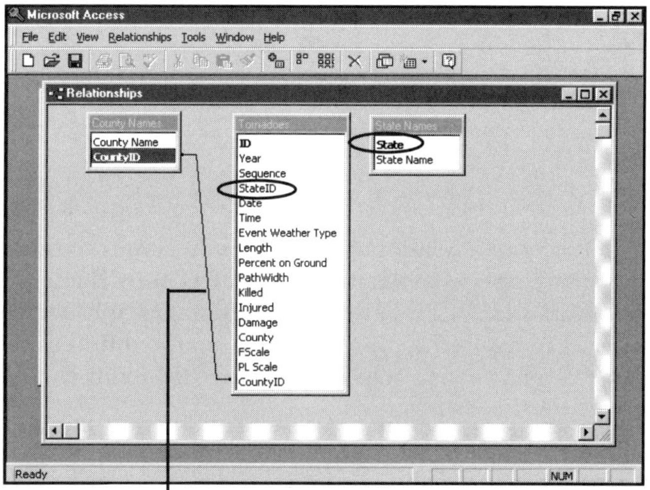


Line indicates related fields

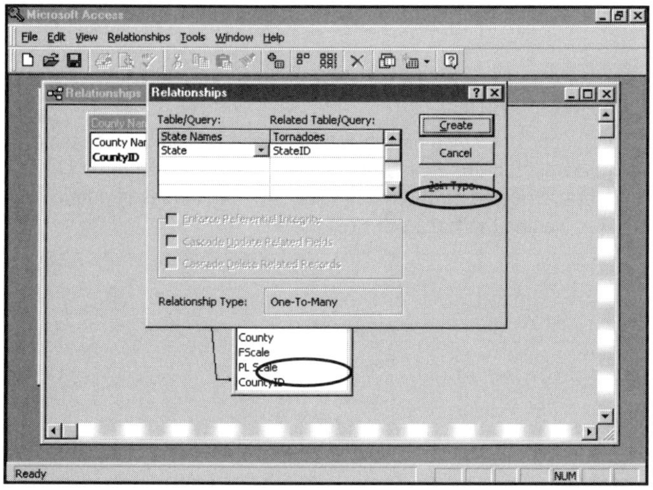


**10** Click and drag from the **State** field in the **State Names** table to the **StateID** field in the **Tornadoes** table. The **Relationships** dialog box opens.

**Tip for Instructors**

Mention to students that the help text has excellent coverage of errors that occur when creating relationships.

Slide 5.3

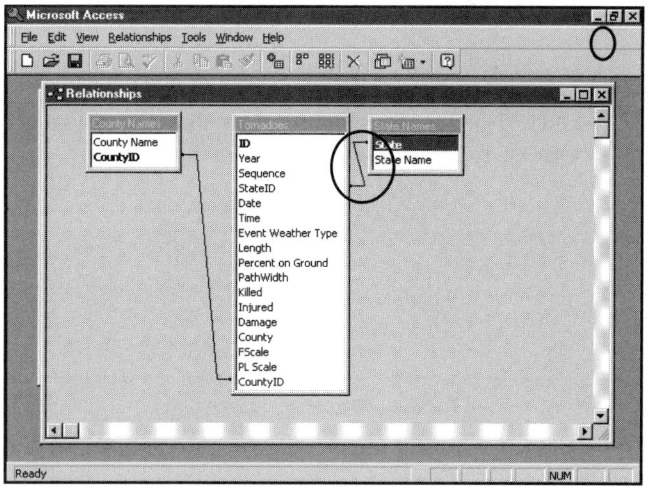


**Q & A**

*Question:* What is the purpose of relationships? *Answer:* To show Access how data in two different tables relate to one another so that queries, reports, and forms can be created from both.

**11** Click **Create**. A second line indicates a relationship between the **State Names** table and the **Tornadoes** table.

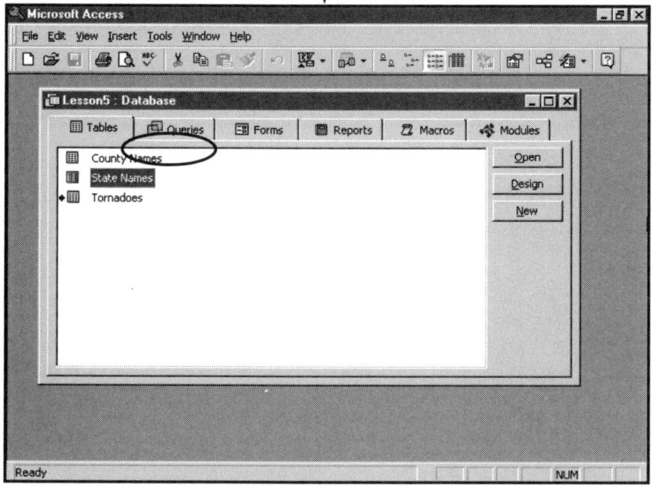


**Concept**

In a one-to-many relationship, *referential integrity* may be used, which verifies that any data keyed into the "many" side of the relationship exists in the "one" table. Referential integrity can be set only if the key field from the primary table is a primary key, the related fields have the same data type, and both tables are in the same database.

**12** Click the **Close Window** button and click **Yes** to save the changes. The **Relationships** window closes and the Database window is displayed.

# Task 3

## Creating a Union Query that Uses Fields from Both Tables

### Why would I do this?

The power of a relational database is the ability to bring together data from a number of different tables. In this lesson, we opened a database with the County Names table, imported the State Names table, and then linked to the Tornadoes table. Then a relationship was established between the tables. Now that the tables are related, a union query can be used so information from the different tables can be included in the query. A *union query* has the same properties as a select query, plus the ability to use fields from more than one table, if the tables are related.

In this task, you use the actual state and county names from the State Names and County Names tables in combination with the fields from the Tornadoes table. You then learn how to add criteria and use parameters to create a powerful tool for analyzing this data.

**Tip for Instructors**

The Learn on Demand Module/Lesson "Creating a Union Query" applies to this task.

**Concept**

After relationships are established, a union query can be created in which more than one table can be used.

**On Your Mark**

Let's suppose that we have a database with two tables: one table with student information and one with class information. The tables are related through a ClassID field. What types of queries might we need to run on this database?

**1** Click the **Queries** tab and click **New**. The **New Query** dialog box opens.

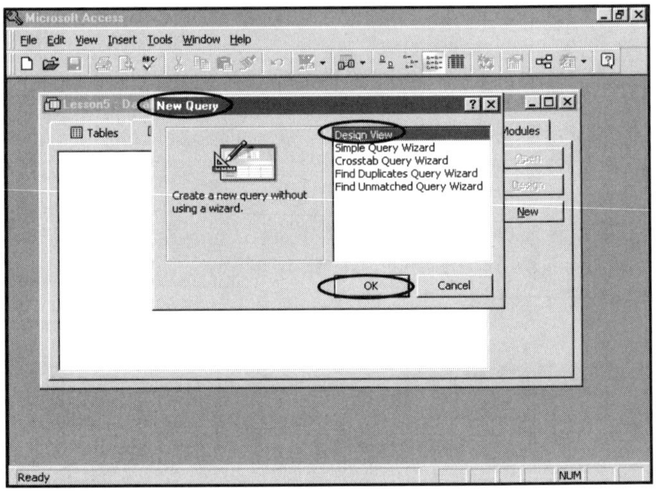


**2** Click **Design View** and click **OK**. The **Show Table** dialog box opens.

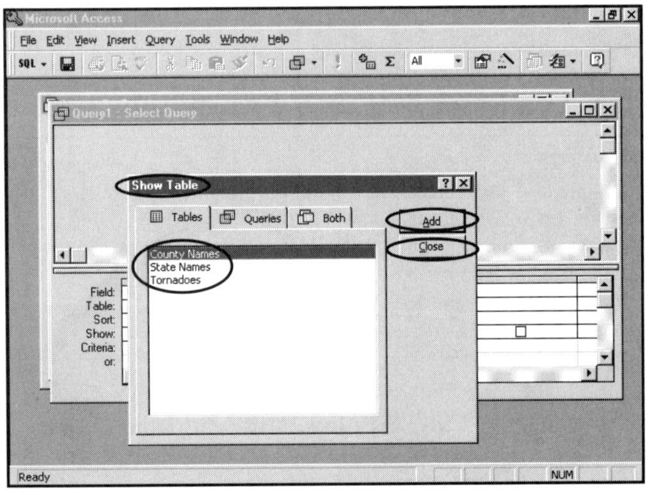

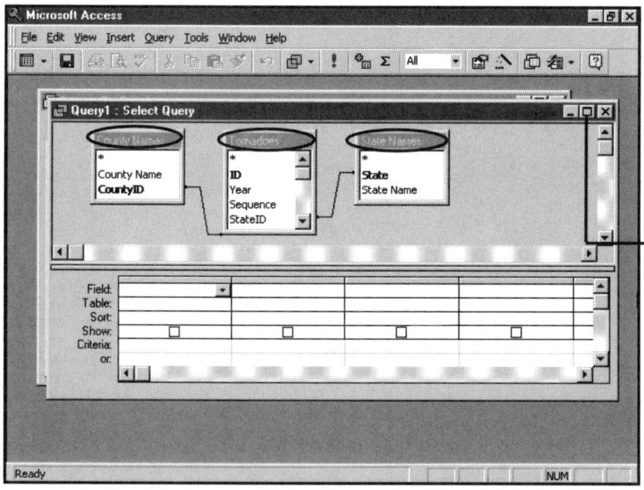


**3** Add the three tables in the order in which they will appear in the query design grid. Add the **County Names**, **Tornadoes**, and **State Names** tables to the design window. Click the **Close** button. The **Query1: Select Query** window opens.

Maximize Window button

**Pothole:** If you add the tables in some other order, simply click the title bar of one of the tables and drag it to its proper position. This is the same technique used when you moved the tables around in the Relationship window. The order the tables appear in the window does not impact the ability to create the query. The suggested order just makes it easier to see the relationship between the tables.

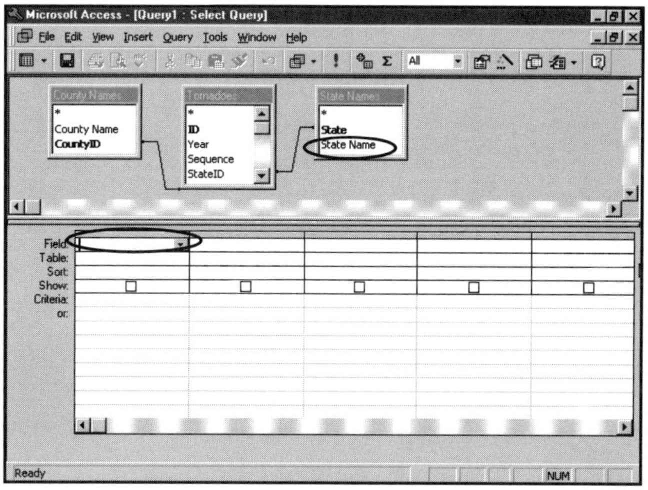


**Tip for Students**

Maximizing the windows gives you more lines for the criteria. This capability is helpful when creating more complex parameters using And and Or statements.

**4** Click the **Maximize Window** button.

Indicates table source

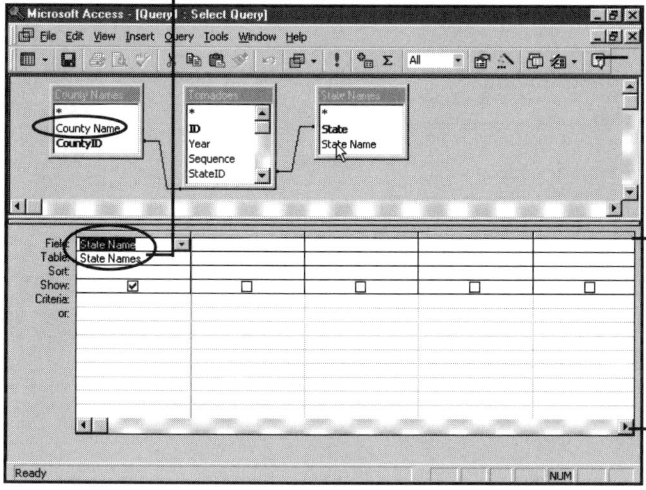


**Tip for Students**

You add the field that is not related in this step. Because of the relationship, Access will use the name of the state in place of the ID when it displays data from the Tornado table.

Query design grid

**5** Double-click **State Name** in the **State Names** table field list box. The State Name field is placed in the first Field text box of the query design grid and the name of the table from which it comes is identified in the Table text box below it.

**6** Double-click **County Name** in the **County Names** table field list box. The County Name field is placed in the second Field text box of the query design grid, along with the name of its table in the Table text box below it.

**SLIDE 5–4**

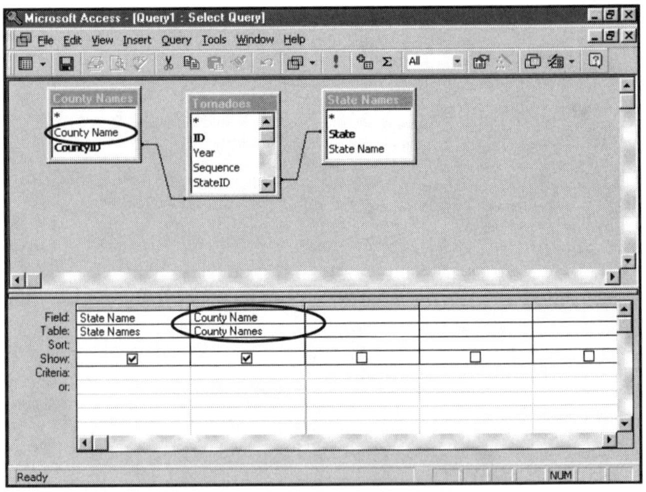


### Tip for Students

You add the field that is not related in this step. Because of the relationship, Access will use the name of the county in place of the ID when it displays data from the **Tornadoes** table.

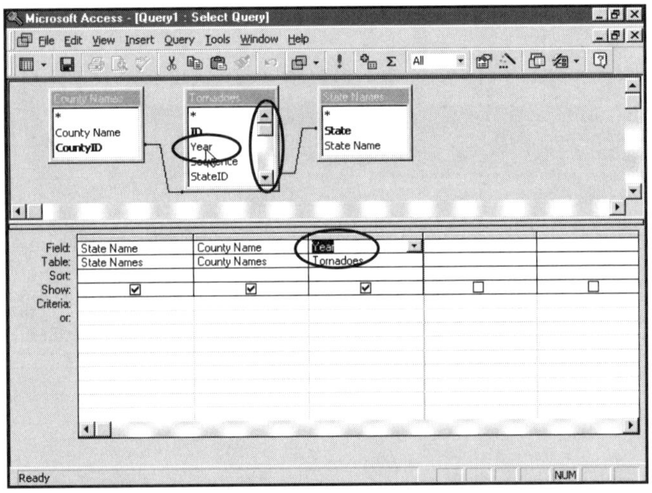


**7** Double-click **Year** in the **Tornadoes** table field list box. Year is added to the query design grid. The source table is Tornadoes.

### Tip for Instructors

Because of the relationships, the county name, not the ID, as well as the state name, not ID, will appear in our query.

**Quick Tip:** You can select several noncontiguous fields from a table at one time by using the Ctrl key on your keyboard. Click the first field to be selected, then hold down the Ctrl key and click each additional field you want to include from that table. When all fields are selected, point to any one of the selected fields and click and drag it to the first open field box in the query design grid. Each of the selected fields will be added to the grid in the same order that they appear in the field list box.

**8** Scroll down the list of fields in the **Tornadoes** table field list box and double click the **Killed**, **Injured**, and **FScale** fields. They are added to the query design grid. (The **FScale** field may be off the screen to the right. Scroll to the right to view the field.) The source table is Tornadoes.

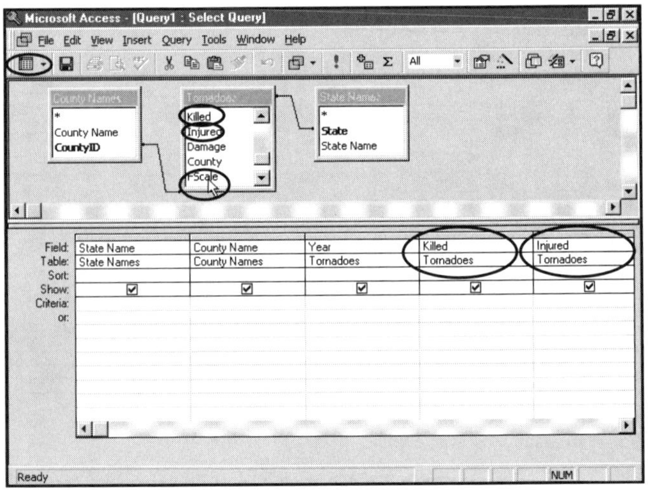

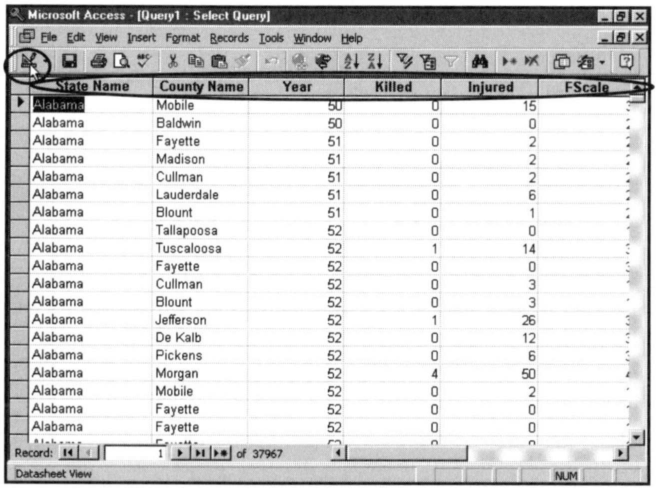


**9** Click the **View** button to switch to **Datasheet View**. The query displays the names of the states and counties instead of just their numbers.

**In Depth:** The number of records shown at the bottom of the screen is less than the total number of records in the Tornadoes table. That is because there are some tornado records that do not have a county name listed or the county code that they have does not match any of the current county names.

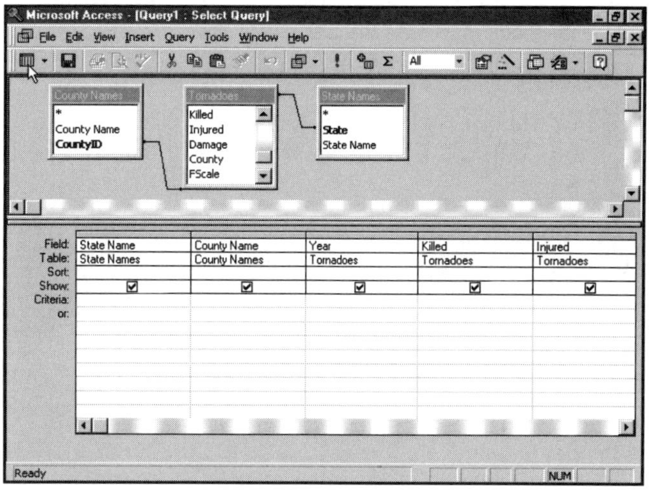


**10** Click the **View** button again to switch to **Design View**.

**Q & A** ?

*Question:* What are some advantages of union queries? *Answer:* Data can be extracted from more than one table.

# Task 4

## Using Advanced Parameter Query Methods with a Union Query

### Why would I do this?

In Lesson 4 you were introduced to parameter queries. As you saw, a parameter query can be used to control the results of a query each time it is run. There are a few extra techniques that can be added to the use of parameters that make them very powerful analysis tools. Parameters can be written in a way that allows you to extract a range of data. For example, in a personnel database you may need to know who will turn 62 in January. You can write a parameter query that allows you to enter a beginning date and an ending date which will give you all of the people who fit the criteria in that range. The use of these techniques makes parameter queries even more flexible, which helps you to create queries that can be tailored to your specific needs each time they are run.

In this task, you learn how to use two different *comparison operators*. These operators, as the name suggests, allow you to compare data in a particular way. The Like operator is used so that the entry made in a parameter box does not have to match all of the letters in the field or so you can see any value in the field. You will also learn how to use the Between . . . And operator to specify a range of dates or numbers.

**Tip for Instructors**

The Learn on Demand Module/Lesson "Using Advanced Parameter Query Methods" applies to this task.

**On Your Mark**

Using our previous example of a class database, our queries can vary in criteria each time we use the queries. What fields might need varying criteria within a query? (ClassID, Quarter/Semester, Year, and so on.)

**1** In the query design grid, click the Criteria text box below the **State Name** field and type **[Enter State]**.

**Tip for Instructors**

Do not let students bog down in the terminology. Explain that a query narrows down the records shown, a parameter query enables the user to make specific requests each time rather than editing, and a union query utilizes more than one table.

**Q & A**

*Question:* What is the purpose of the brackets? *Answer:* To identify parameter criteria or field name.

**Concept**

Using Like in the criteria enables the user to use wildcards.

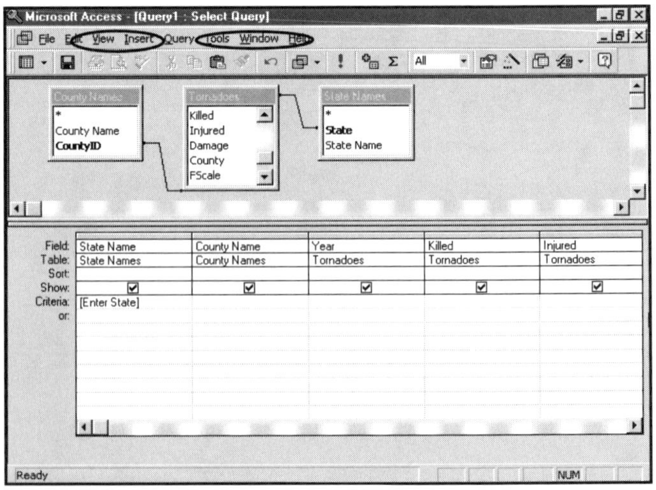


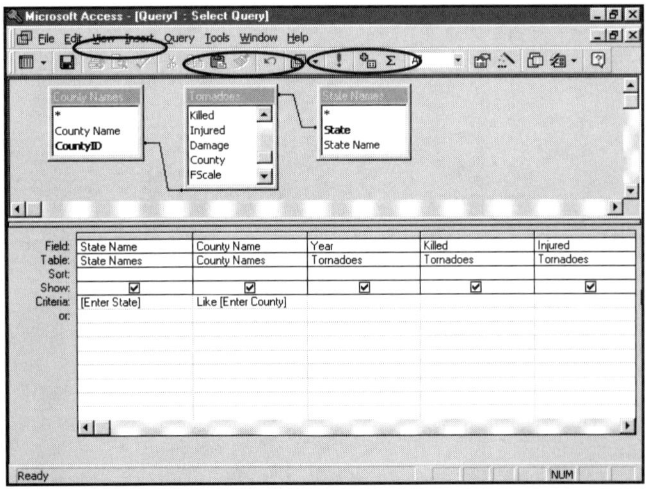


**2** Click the Criteria text box below the **County Name** field and type **Like [Enter County]**. This is a useful variation of the parameter query that allows the use of asterisks to replace all or part of the entry.

**3** Click the Criteria text box below the **Year** field and type **<u>Between [From] And [Through]</u>**. This type of criteria lets you specify a range of years. If you wanted just one year, you would enter the specific year in both the From and Through parameter boxes.

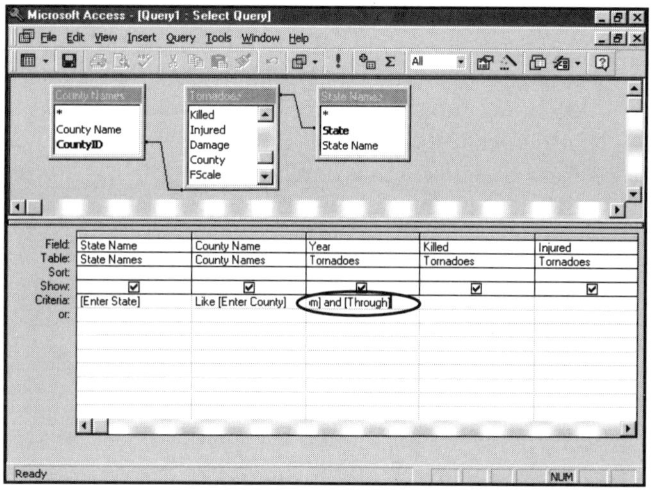


**In Depth:** To see the entire entry for the previous step, right click on it and choose Zoom from the shortcut menu.

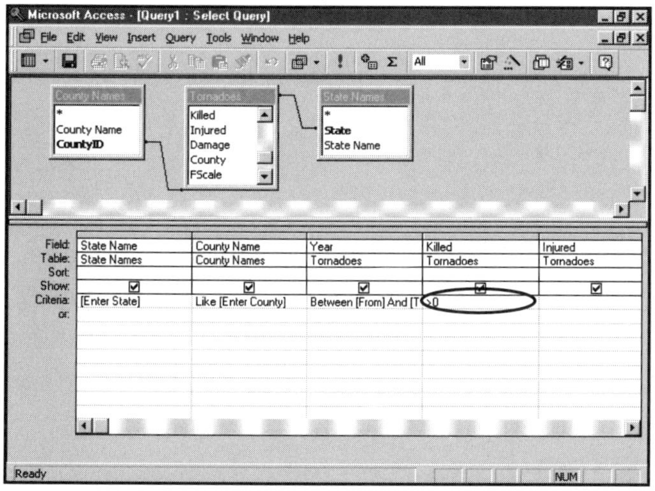


**4** Click the **Criteria** text box below the **Killed** field and type **<u>>0</u>**. This will limit the records to just those tornadoes that caused fatalities.

### Tip for Students

Use logical operators (<, >. =, >=, <=) to create criteria statements. You can also use Is Null for empty fields, Is Not Null for fields with entries, or Like followed by a logical statement for usage of wildcards. If Access needs any additional characters, it will edit your statement.

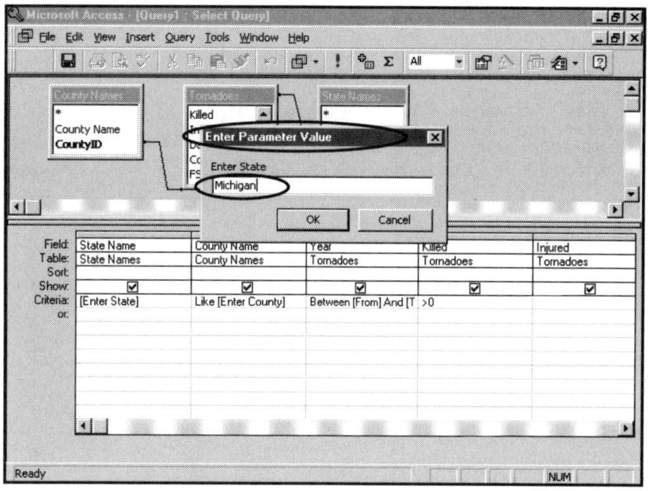


**5** Click the **View** button. The **Enter Parameter Value** dialog box opens. Type **<u>Michigan</u>**.

### Tip for Instructors

Remind students that this criteria is creating an And statement. All data must be met to display any one record. Similar methods can be used for an Or statement.

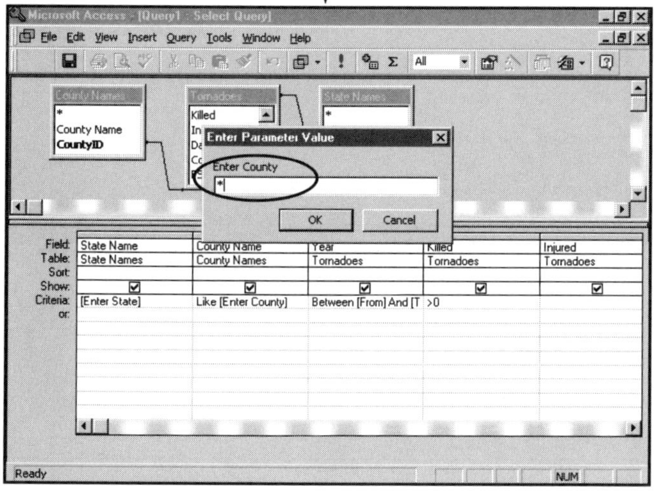


**6** Click **OK**. The **Enter Paramater Value** dialog box for the County opens. Type an asterisk, <u>*</u>, in the box. The use of an asterisk will display all of the county names.

**In Depth:** An asterisk is known as a *wildcard* and can be used to search for any number of characters. It can be used as the first or last character in a string of characters. In this example, the asterisk may be used with part of the county name. For example, if you had typed W*, you would have gotten all of the county names that begin with a W.

**7** Click **OK**. Type **50** in the **Enter Parameter Value** dialog box to indicate 1950 and click **OK**. Type **95** in the next parameter box to indicate 1995 and click **OK** again. The query will display the forty tornadoes that have killed people in Michigan between 1950 and 1995.

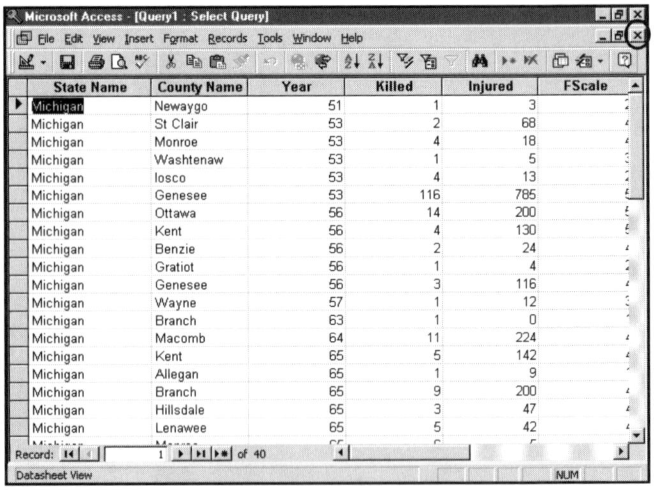


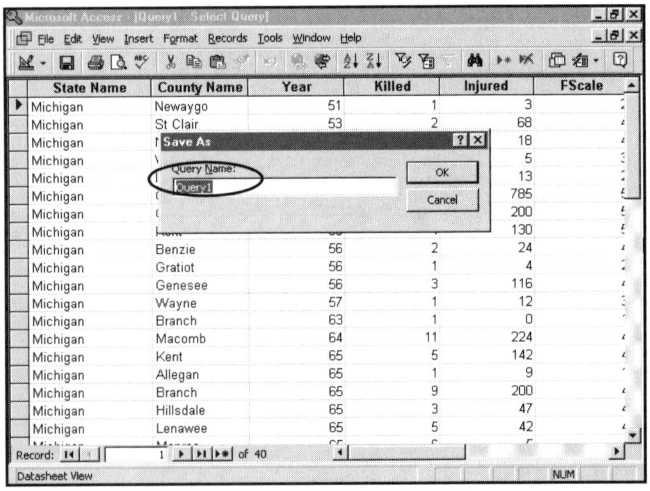


**8** Click the **Close Window** button and click **Yes** to save the query. The **Save As** dialog box opens.

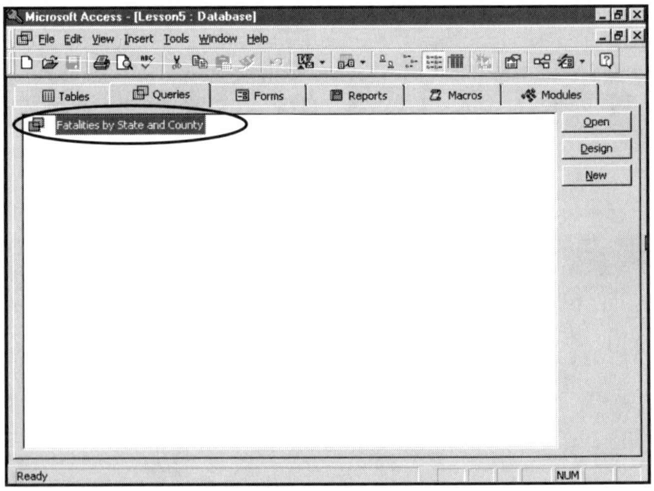


**Q & A** **?**

*Question:* What are the two comparison operators learned in this task? *Answer:* Like, Between And.

**9** Type **Fatalities by State and County** and click **OK**. The query is saved as part of the database for future use.

**Tip for Students** **!**

You can select the table or query from this screen. However, the task does not do this because three tables will be used to create this form.

# Task 5

## Creating a Form that Displays Data from Two or More Tables

### Why would I do this?

Just like a union query is used to include information from more than one table, forms are also capable of showing data from two tables at once, if the tables are related. A special type of form that can be used for this purpose is known as a form with subform. With this type of form you can scroll through records for one table and find the related records from a second table. For example, in a personnel database, you might have one table of departments and another table of personnel information. By using a subform, you can scroll through the department table and see the employees that are assigned to that department. A form with subform is like a form within a form.

In this task, you learn how to create a form that allows you to scroll through the records by state and within that form create a subform that allows you to scroll through the tornadoes that have occurred in that state.

**Concept**

*Subforms* are useful when displaying data from two tables with a one-to-many relationship. The form is created from the "one" side of the relationship; the subform is created from the "many" side of the relationship.

**1** Click the **Forms** tab and click **New**. The **New Form** dialog box opens.

**Tip for Instructors**

The Learn on Demand Module/Lesson "Creating a Form with Data from Two or More Tables" applies to this task.

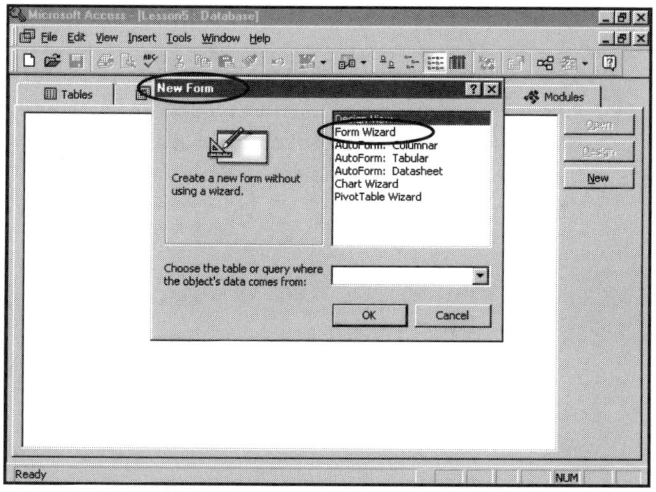


**2** Click **Form Wizard** and click **OK**. The **Form Wizard** dialog box opens.

**On Your Mark**

When viewing data from more than one table, it might be a bit confusing or overwhelming to see relationships in a table or query. What other way of viewing data might be easier to understand?

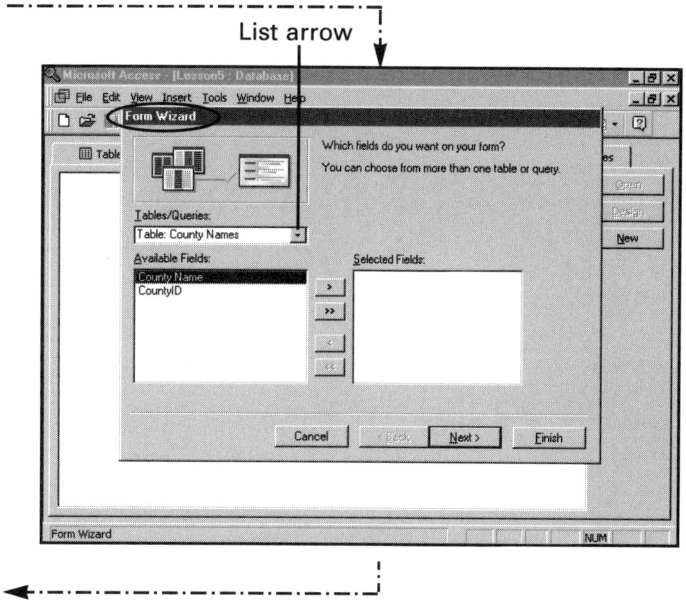


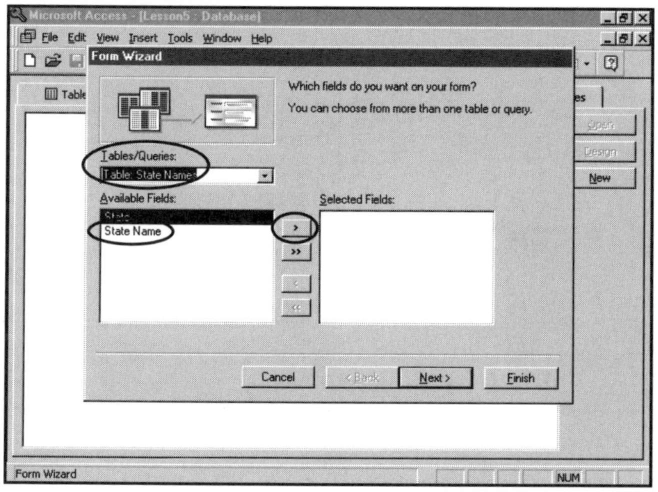


**3** Click the list arrow next to the **Tables/Queries** box and click **Table: State Names**. A list of the fields in that table is displayed in the **Available Fields** box.

**4** Click **State Name** to select it and then click the **Add** button next to the Available Fields box (single arrow pointing to the right). State Name moves to the **Selected Fields** box.

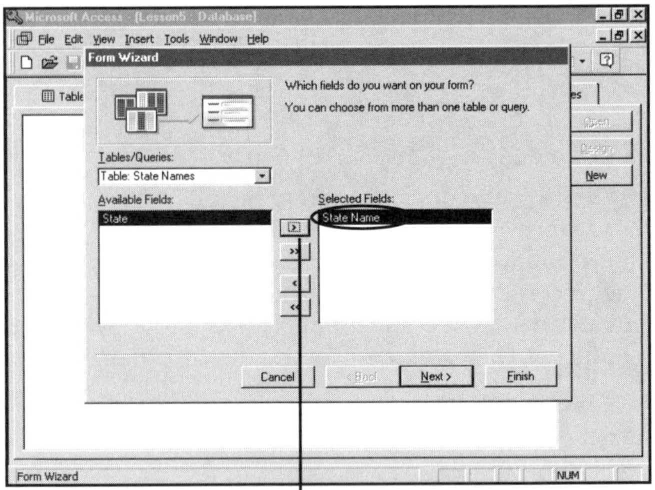


Add button

**Quick Tip:** If you double-click the name of a field in the Available Fields box, it will move to the Selected Fields box automatically. This works faster than selecting a field and clicking the arrow button.

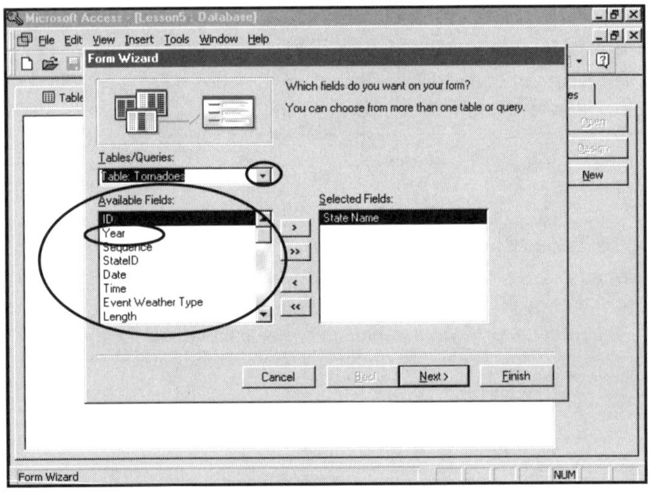


**5** Click the list arrow next to the **Tables/Queries** box and select **Table: Tornadoes**. A list of the fields in the Tornadoes table is displayed in the **Available Fields** box.

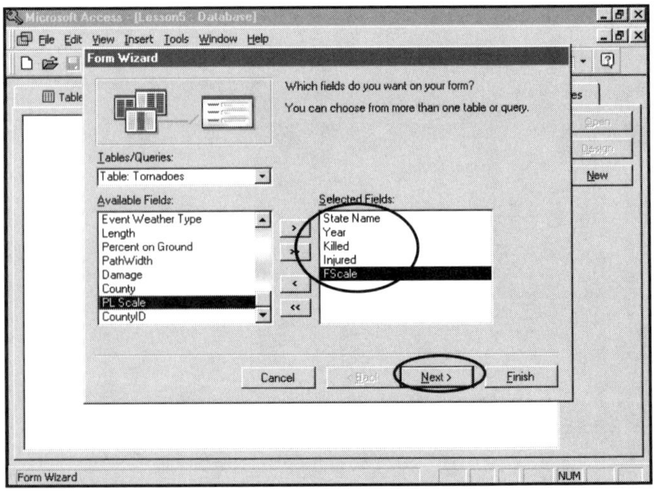


**6** Click **Year** and then the **Add** button to add this field to the Selected Fields box. Scroll down the list and select and add the **Killed**, **Injured**, and **Fscale** fields. The form will use the five fields selected from the two tables.

**7** Click **N**ext. The next **Form Wizard** dialog box opens. This dialog box asks you how you want to view your data. The field selected determines which table is used for the main part of the form. In this case, make sure the State Names table is selected. Also notice that the **Form with subform(s)** option is selected.

### Tip for Instructors

This screen and the next do not appear when only one table/query is used. Be sure to explain carefully.

### Concept

The *subform* can be used without the form, if necessary. A subform is a form within a form. For example, a database that contains student information and course information may have a form with a subform—the form being the student's personal information and the subform being the courses the student has taken.

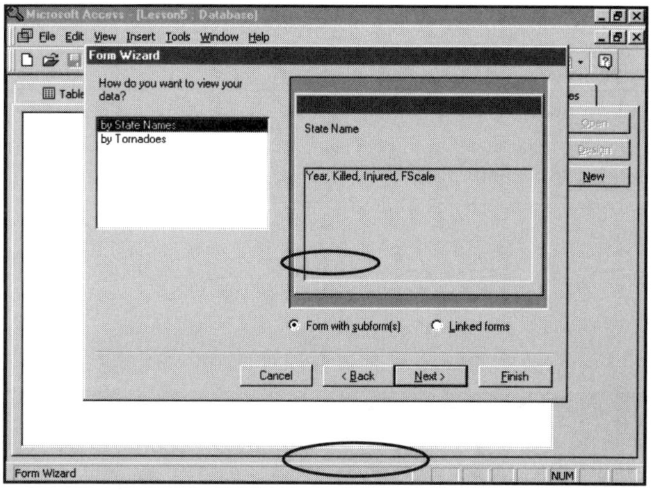


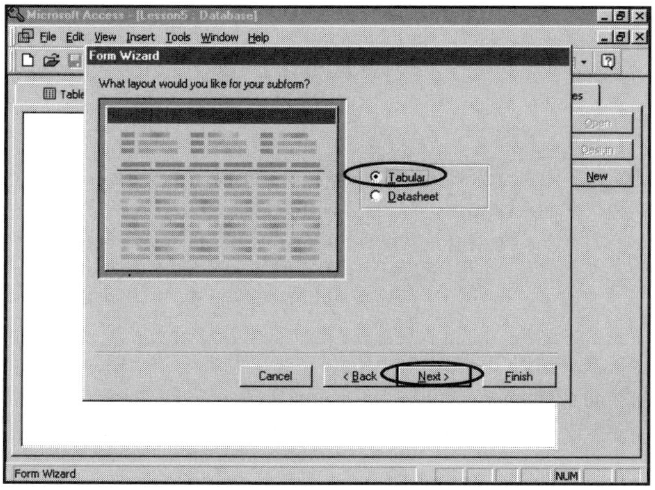


**8** Click **N**ext. Click the **T**abular option button to select a tabular layout for your subform.

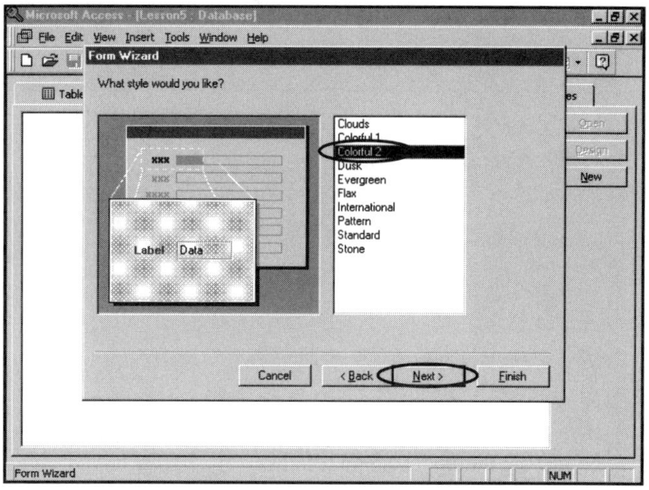


**9** Click **N**ext. Click the different layout options and select one that you like. (The following figures use Colorful 2.)

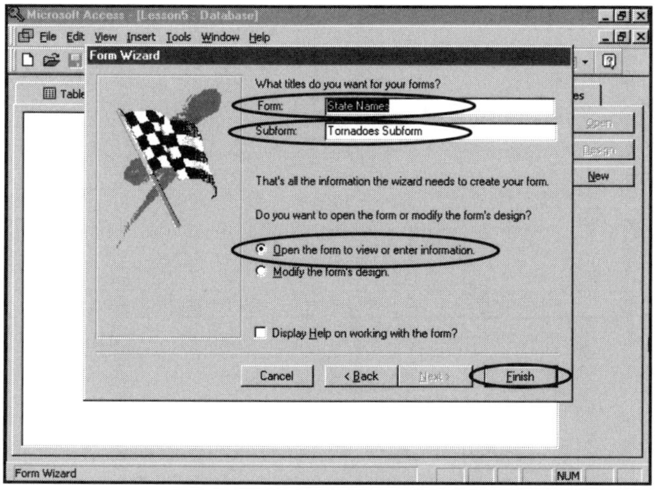


**10** Click **N**ext. Leave the suggested titles for the form and subform based on the table names from which the data is drawn as shown. Make sure the **O**pen the form to view or enter information option is selected.

**11** Click **Finish**. You have designed a main form based on the State Names table and a subform based on the Tornadoes table. The two forms are related so that when you scroll through the state names, the tornado records shown in the subform are just for that state.

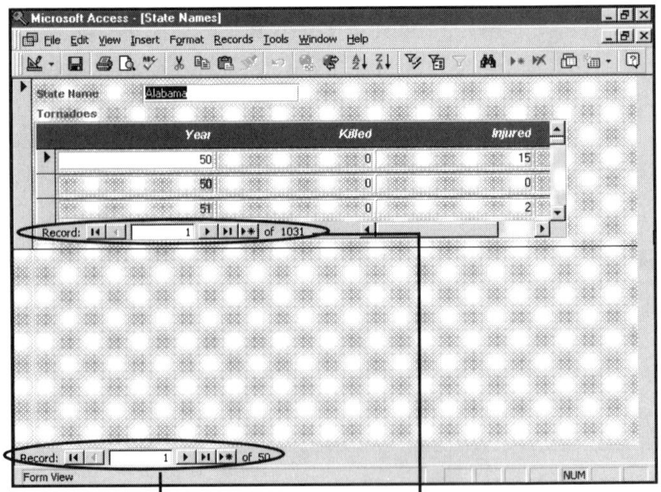


Navigation buttons for the State form

Navigation buttons for the Tornadoes subform

**Concept**

The only records shown in the subform are related to the current record of the form.

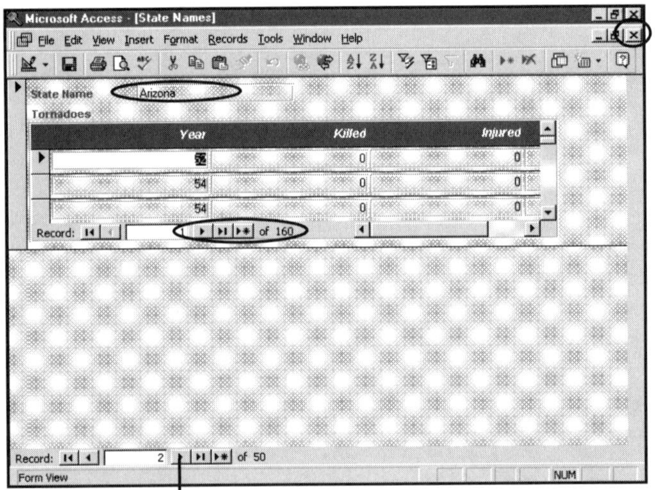


Next record button

**12** Click the **Next Record** navigation button on the **State Names** form. Notice that the name of the state changes from Alabama to Arizona and the related records in the subform change as well.

**Quicksand**

Some students might use the incorrect navigation buttons. The ones at the bottom of the screen are the correct ones.

**Q & A**

*Question:* When do the records of the subform change? *Answer:* When moving through the form records.

**13** Click the **Close Window** button. The form closes and the Database window shows the names of the two forms.

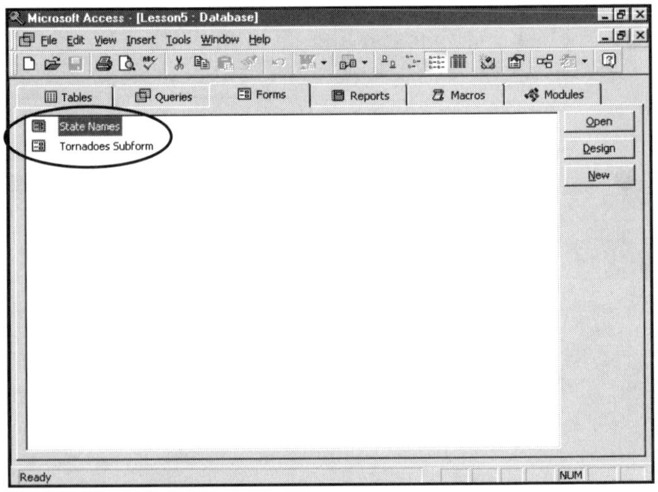

# Task 6

## Creating a Report that Uses the Union Query

### Why would I do this?

Using the Report Wizard, you can produce a report that contains fields from more than one related table. As you have seen with queries and forms, it is useful to be able to include data from more than one table. To limit the records that are included in a report, you create a union query and set criteria to extract the data you need. When dealing with a large database, such as the Tornadoes table, it is helpful to limit the records so the report is smaller and includes only those records that are needed. Reports that are very large often contain too much information, which results in the reports not being used effectively.

In this task, you learn how to use the Report Wizard to create a report based on the Fatalities by State and County query you created in Tasks 3 and 4.

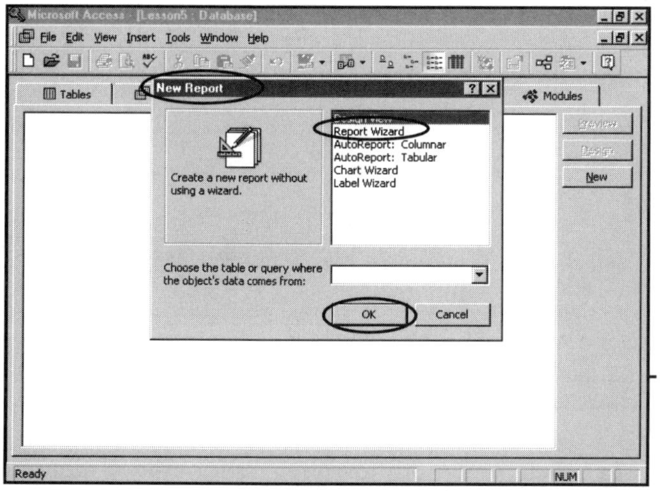


**1** Click the **Reports** tab and click **New**. The **New Report** dialog box opens.

**Tip for Instructors**

The Learn on Demand Module/Lesson "Creating a Report that Uses the Union Query" applies to this task.

**Q & A**

*Question:* What do you suppose is the most common use for a union query? *Answer:* To create a report.

**Concept**

Most reports are created from a query created specifically for a report.

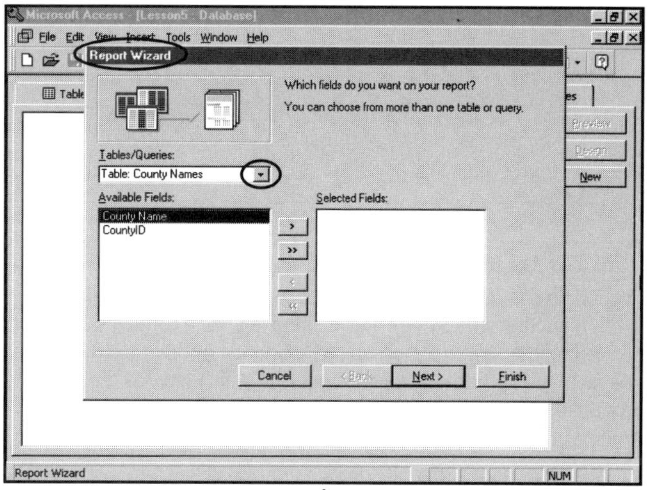


**2** Click **Report Wizard** and click **OK**. The **Report Wizard** dialog box opens.

All button

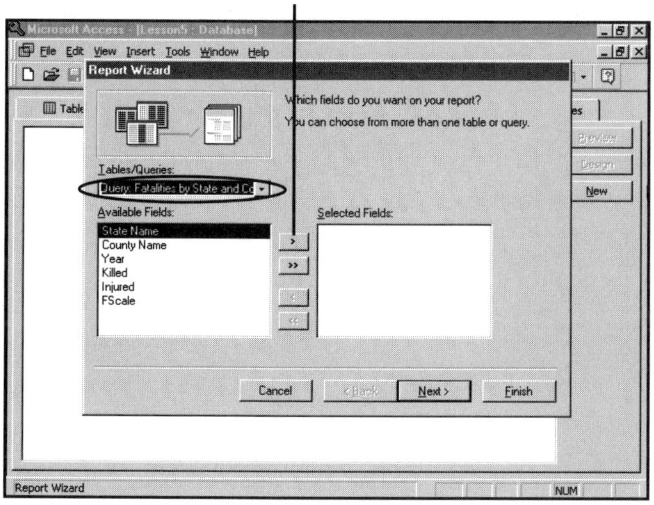


**3** Click the list arrow on the **Tables/Queries** box and click **Query: Fatalities by State and County**.

4 Click the **Add All** button to move all of the fields into the **Selected Fields** box.

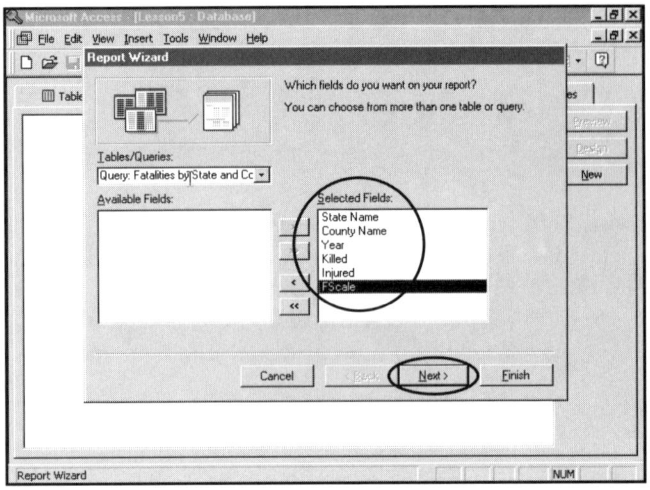


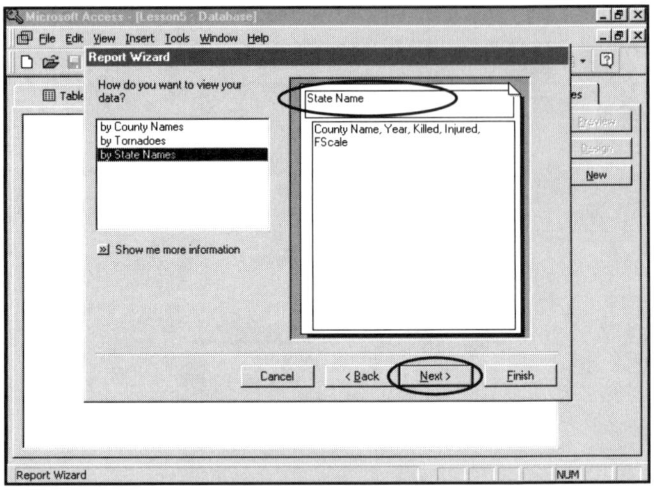


5 Click **Next**. Leave the suggested grouping of records by the State Name field as shown.

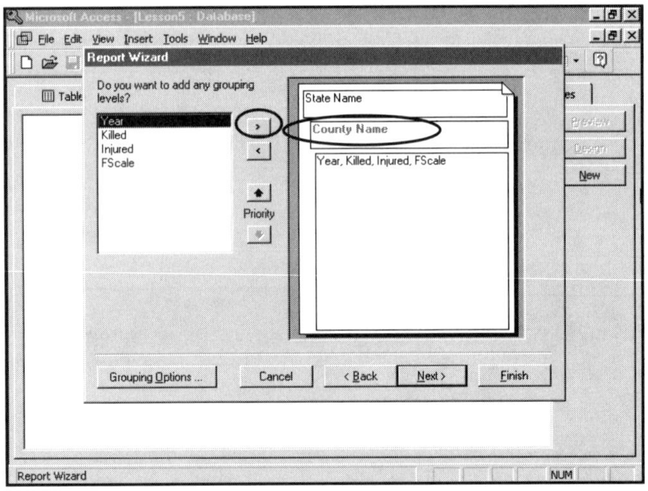


6 Click **Next**. Additional suggestions for grouping the records are provided. In this case, it makes sense to group the records by the County Name field. Click **County Name** in the field list box and then the **Add** button. The example report changes to show how the records are grouped.

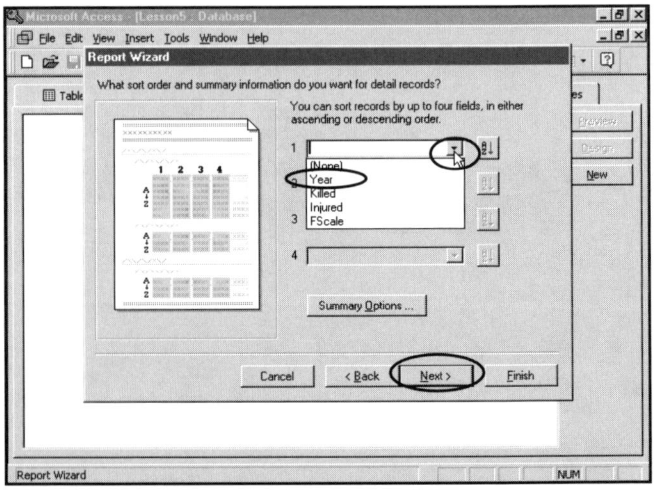


**Tip for Instructors**

Grouping can be done with more than one field, with one grouping within another. The example given here is a main grouping of the State records, with a subgrouping by County. Another example students may appreciate is a phone book, in which records are grouped by cities first and then subgrouped by last name.

7 Click **Next**. You can now sort the records on up to four of the remaining fields. Click the list arrow next to the first sort order text box to display a list of appropriate fields.

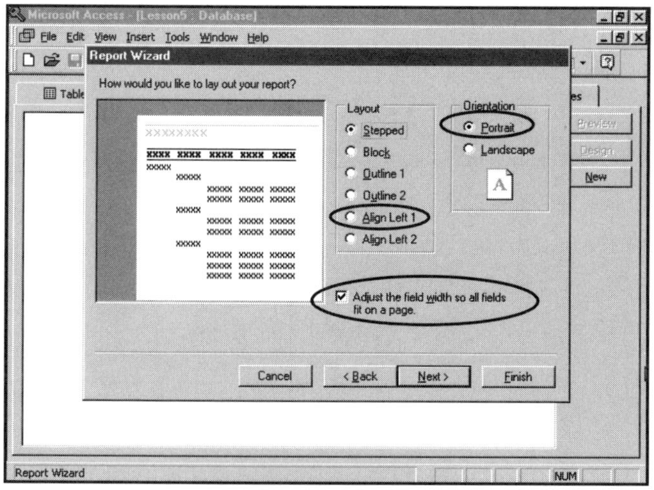


**8** Click **Year**. This is the only field that will be sorted. Click **Next**. Several report layout options are provided.

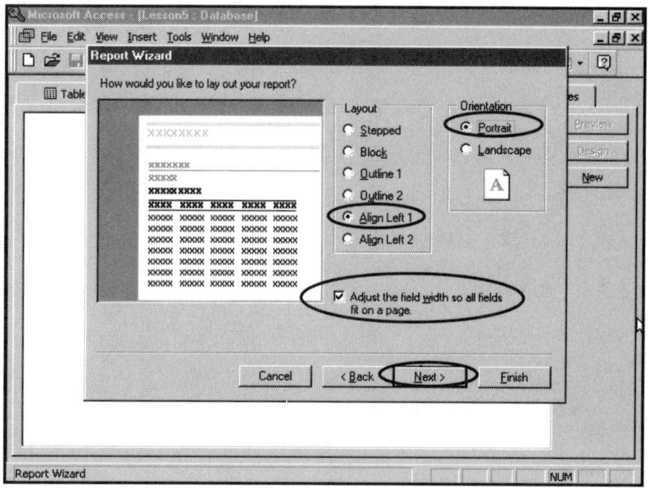


**9** Click the **Align Left 1** and **Portrait** orientation option buttons. If necessary, click the **Adjust the field width so all fields fit on a page** check box to select it.

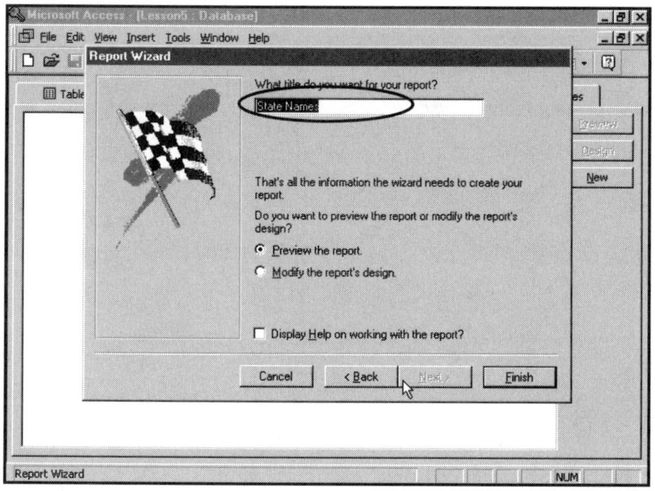


**10** Click **Next**. Several style options are displayed. Choose **Bold** and click **Next**.

**11** Type **<u>Tornadoes by State</u>** as the title for your report.

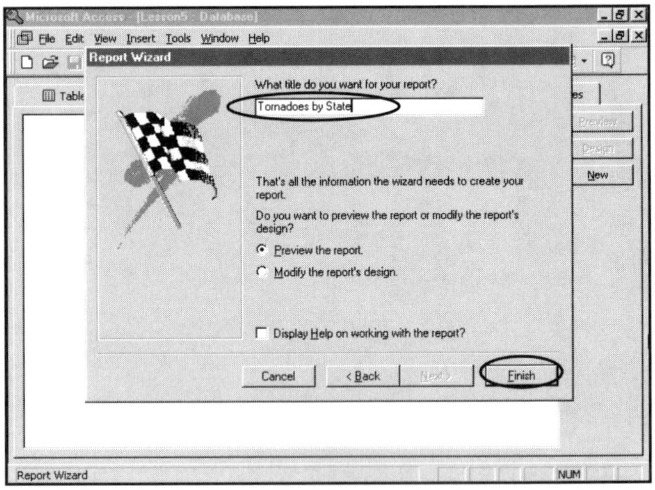


**Concept**

Using a parameter query to create a report makes each report specialized according to the parameters.

**12** Click **<u>F</u>inish**. The **Enter Parameter Value** dialog box opens.

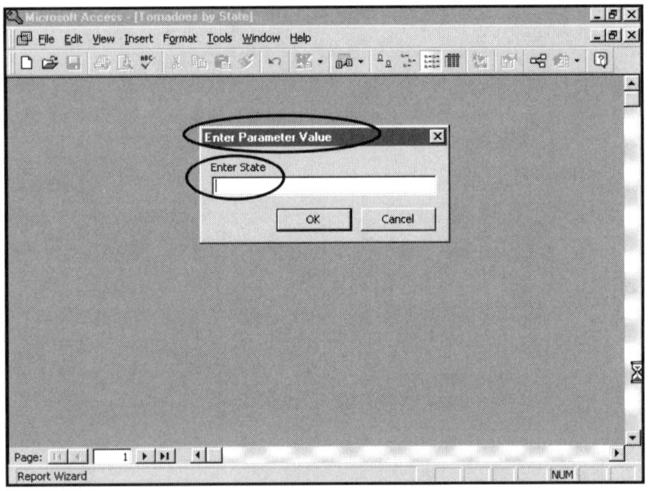


**In Depth:** This report is based on a parameter query. Therefore, before the report will open you need to respond to each of the Enter Parameter Value dialog boxes. This will be true each time the report is printed or opened to preview. This report allows you to control the records that are included in the report based on the parameters that were established in the query.

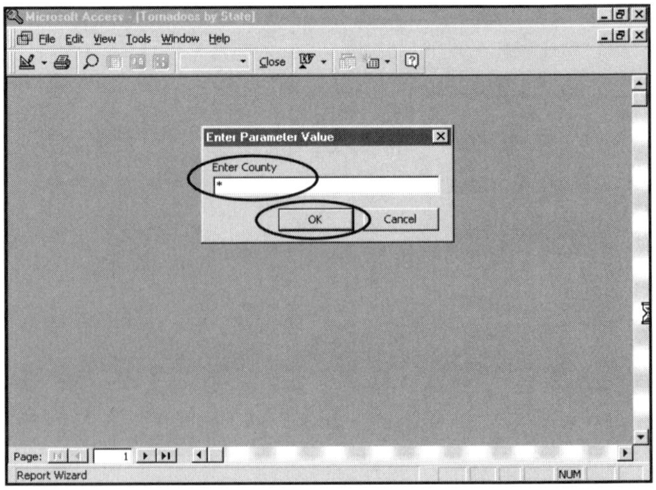


**13** Type **<u>Oklahoma</u>** in the **Enter State** parameter box and click **OK**. In the next dialog box, type <u>*</u>, to indicate all counties.

**14** Click **OK**. Type **90**, click **OK**, type **95**, and click **OK**. This limits the report to all the counties in Oklahoma that had a tornado which killed at least one person between 1990 and 1995. (Remember: the query has a criteria of >0 in the Killed column). A preview of the report is displayed.

**Quicksand**
Before printing, make sure that all of the data labels and fields are completely visible. If not, some revision needs to be made.

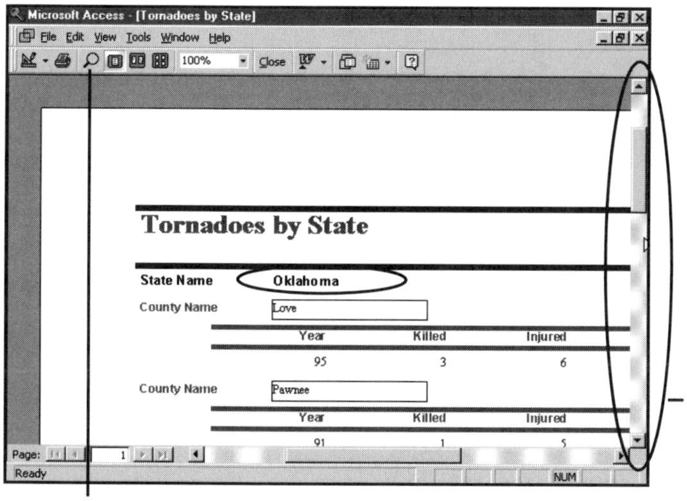


Zoom button

**15** Scroll through the report and use Zoom to get a look at the layout of the report. Notice that the page navigation buttons are dimmed because this report is only one page long. Click the **Print** button to print the report.

**Pothole:** Be careful to check the page length before you print a report that is based on a large table. You can use the navigation buttons to determine how long a report is: Click the Last Record button, ⏭, to move to the last page of the report.

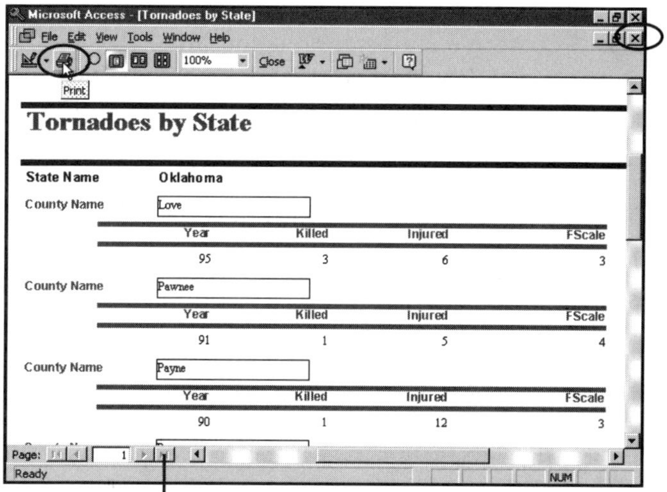


Last Record button

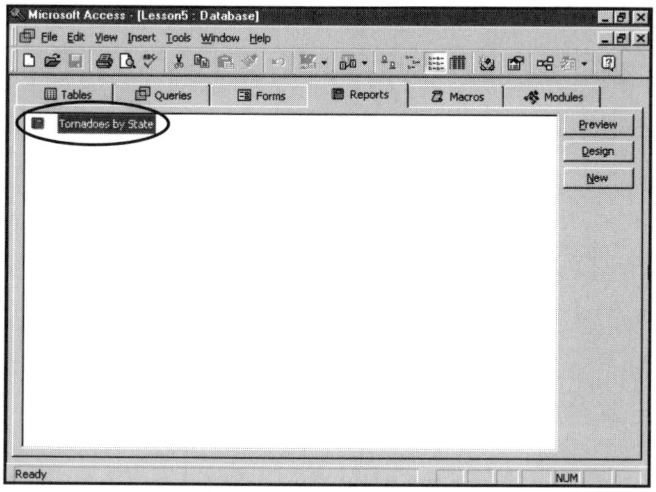


**Q & A**
*Question:* Why do we create reports from a query? *Answer:* To limit the records printed in the report.

**16** Click the **Close Window** button. The report closes and its name is displayed in the **Database** window. Close the database and exit Access.

# Student Exercises

## True-False

For each of the following, circle T or F to indicate whether the statement is true or false.

T (F) **1.** To create a relationship between two tables, both tables must include a field with exactly the same name.

(T) F **2.** The link tables option is best used for large databases or databases that you cannot copy or change.

T (F) **3.** If you use the Form Wizard to create a form, you will be able to view fields from two tables at the same time, even if the tables are not related.

(T) F **4.** A one-to-many relationship occurs when data in the related fields occurs one time in one table and many times in the related table.

(T) F **5.** The most common way to relate two tables is to connect the primary key field in one table to the same field in another table.

T (F) **6.** A union query has different properties than a select query.

(T) F **7.** Using "Like" as part of a parameter query criteria allows the user to use a wildcard when searching the database.

(T) F **8.** In a parameter query, the "Between. . . And" operator allows the user to specify a range of dates or numbers.

T (F) **9.** For large databases, it is best to create a report based on a union query in order to see all of the records in the database displayed in the report.

T (F) **10.** In a report, you can group records on only one field.

## Identifying Parts of the Access Screen

Refer to the figure and identify the numbered parts of the screen. Write the letter of the correct label in the space next to the number.

**1.** *F*
**2.** *G*
**3.** *D*
**4.** *B*
**5.** *C*
**6.** *E*
**7.** *H*
**8.** *A*

**A.** Join line
**B.** Simple parameter criteria
**C.** "Like" parameter criteria
**D.** Field source row
**E.** Parameter criteria that allows a range of data
**F.** View button
**G.** Field list title bar
**H.** Criteria that restricts data to a positive number in this field

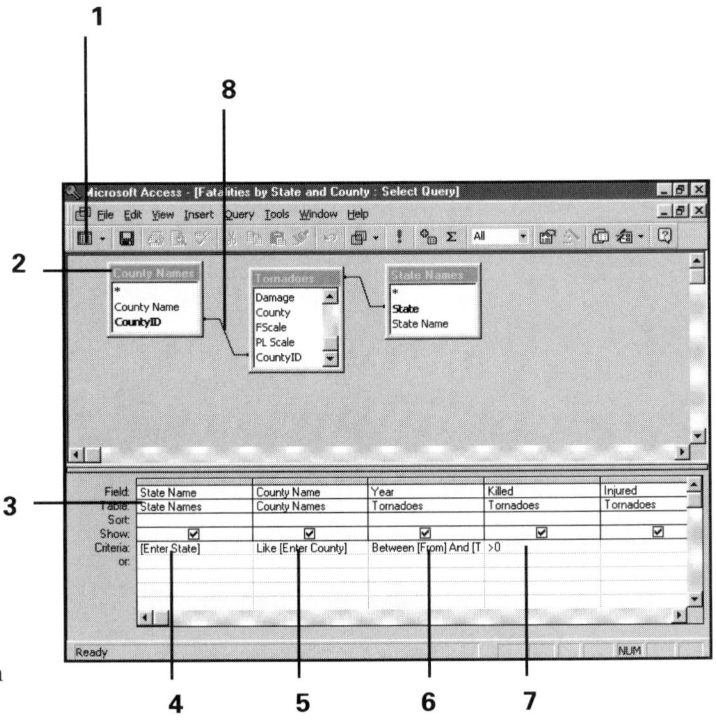

## Matching

Match the statements below to the word or phrase that is the best match from the list. Write the letter of the matching word or phrase in the space provided next to the number.

1. _E_ Button used to establish a relationship between tables in the Relationship dialog box
2. _G_ Indicates a linked table
3. _J_ An example of a wildcard symbol
4. _A_ A type of relationship where data occurs one time in one table and several times in another table
5. _H_ Show Table button
6. _B_ Symbol for the Add button which moves a single field from the Available Fields box to the Selected Fields box in Form Wizard
7. _D_ Moves to the last record in a database form or report
8. _C_ View button
9. _F_ Symbol for the Add All button which moves all fields from the Available Fields box to the Selected Fields box in Form Wizard
10. _K_ A way to use information from another table without having the table reside in your database

**A.** One-to-many relationship

**B.** >

**C.** 

**D.** 

**E.** Create

**F.** >>

**G.** 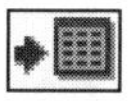

**H.** 

**I.** Relate

**J.** *

**K.** Link

# Application Exercises

The following exercises use the **Lesson5** database. The first three exercises are meant to be done together.

## Exercise 1 – Creating a Table of FScale Descriptions

1. Launch Access and open the **Lesson5** database.
2. Create a new table that has two fields: **FScale** and **Description**. The FScale field is a number field and the Description field is a text field. Make the **FScale** field the primary key field. Name the table **Description of the FScale**.

3. Enter the following data into the table:

| F Scale | Description |
|---|---|
| 0 | Light Damage (40-72 mph) |
| 1 | Moderate Damage (73-112 mph) |
| 2 | Significant Damage (113-157 mph) |
| 3 | Severe Damage (158-206 mph) |
| 4 | Devastating Damage (207-260 mph) |
| 5 | Incredible Damage (261-318 mph) |

## Exercise 2 – Creating a Relationship between the Tornadoes Table and the Description of the FScale Table

1. Choose **Tools** and **Relationships** from the menu to open the **Relationships** window.
2. Click the **Show Table** button and then add the new table.
3. Drag a relationship between the **FScale** field in the **Description of the FScale** table and the **FScale** field in the **Tornadoes** table.
4. Close the **Relationships** window and save the changes.

## Exercise 3 – Creating a Union Query that Uses the Description of the FScale

1. Create a new query and add the **Tornadoes**, **State Names**, and **Description of the FScale** tables.
2. Double-click the **State Name** field in the **State Names** table, the **Year** and the **FScale** fields in the **Tornadoes** table, and the **Description** field in the **Description of the FScale** table to add them to the query design grid.
3. Click the **Save** button to save the query and name it **Exercise Three**.
4. Type 89 in the Criteria box below the the Year field and type >2 in the Criteria box below the FScale field.
5. Click the **View** button to switch to **Datasheet View** to view the results. There were 36 tornadoes with an FScale rating greater than 2 in 1989.

6. Click the **Print Preview** button to preview the query and then print the query. (Hint: Adjust the column widths as needed to print the full FScale description.) Write your name on the printout to hand in.
7. Close the query and save the changes.

## Exercise 4 – Creating a Report Based on a Query

1. Create a report, using Report Wizard, based on the **Exercise Three** query.
2. Include in the report all of the fields that are in the query. View by **State Name**. Do not use any grouping levels. Sort on **Year**. Choose **Align Left 2** and **Portrait** orientation. Choose any style. Title the report **Exercise Four**.
3. If needed, adjust the **Description** text box size so the entire description shows in the report.
4. **Print** the report. Write your name on it.

## Exercise 5 – Creating a Form with Subform Based on Related Tables

1. Use the Form Wizard to create a new form based on the **Tornadoes** table, **State Names** table, and the **Description of the FScale** table.
2. Use the **Year** and **FScale** fields from the **Tornadoes** table, the **State Name** field from the **State Names** table, and the **Description** field from the **Description of the FScale** table.
3. View the data by **Description of the FScale**. This selection will determine the main form and will change the option in the Form Wizard from Single Form to Form with Subform.
4. Finish the form. Scroll the main form to show the tornadoes with a rating of **4**.
5. Look at the navigation bar on the subform. How many tornadoes were rated a 4? _______

# Exercise 6 – Adding a Table to Describe the Event Weather Type

1. Create a new table named **Weather Type** in the **Lesson5** database to hold the following data. The **Event** field is a number field. Designate it as the primary key field. The **Description** field is a memo field.

| Event | Description |
|---|---|
| 1 | Tornado |
| 2 | Funnel cloud |
| 3 | Water spout |
| 4 | Water spout moving ashore |
| 5 | Tornado moving over large body of water |
| 6 | Hail, average size of hailstones are greater than 3/4 inches in diameter |
| 7 | Non-tornadic winds greater than 50 knots (57+ miles per hour) |
| 8 | Hail aloft, average size of hailstones are greater than 3/4 inches in diameter |
| 9 | Extreme turbulence |

2. Create a relationship between the **Weather Type** table and the **Tornadoes** table using the **Event** and **Event Weather Type** fields.
3. Create a union query that contains the **State Name** field in the **State Names** table, the **Year** and the **Event Weather Type** fields in the **Tornadoes** table, and the **Description** field in the **Weather Type** table.
4. In the **Criteria** box below the **Event Weather Type** field, type **[Enter Weather Type code 1-9]**.
5. Save the query and name it **Type of Weather**.
6. View the query and adjust the columns as needed so all of the information prints on one page. **Print** a list of tornadoes that were seen moving over a large body of water (event 5).
7. Close the database and exit Access.

# Lesson 6

SLIDE 6–1

# Using Queries and Reports to Analyze Data



**Lesson Time**
**105 minutes**

# Introduction

Databases traditionally have been used to store large lists of related information so that information can be extracted as needed. Data analysis was often done by sending the database information to a spreadsheet. Access has a number of features that allow you to perform data analysis right in the database. These include various ways to count, add, summarize, and group information. There are data analysis features included in the table, query, form, and report functions of Access.

In previous lessons you used business and scientific databases as examples. In this lesson you will use a social science database, a transcription of the Alcona County Michigan 1900 Federal Census. You will learn how to analyze a large amount of historical census data to gain an understanding about what life was like in a rural county in Michigan at the turn of the century.

**On Your Mark**

Perhaps the most logical purpose for a database is data analysis. Of the databases you have practiced with, what are some examples of analysis you could use?

## Visual Summary

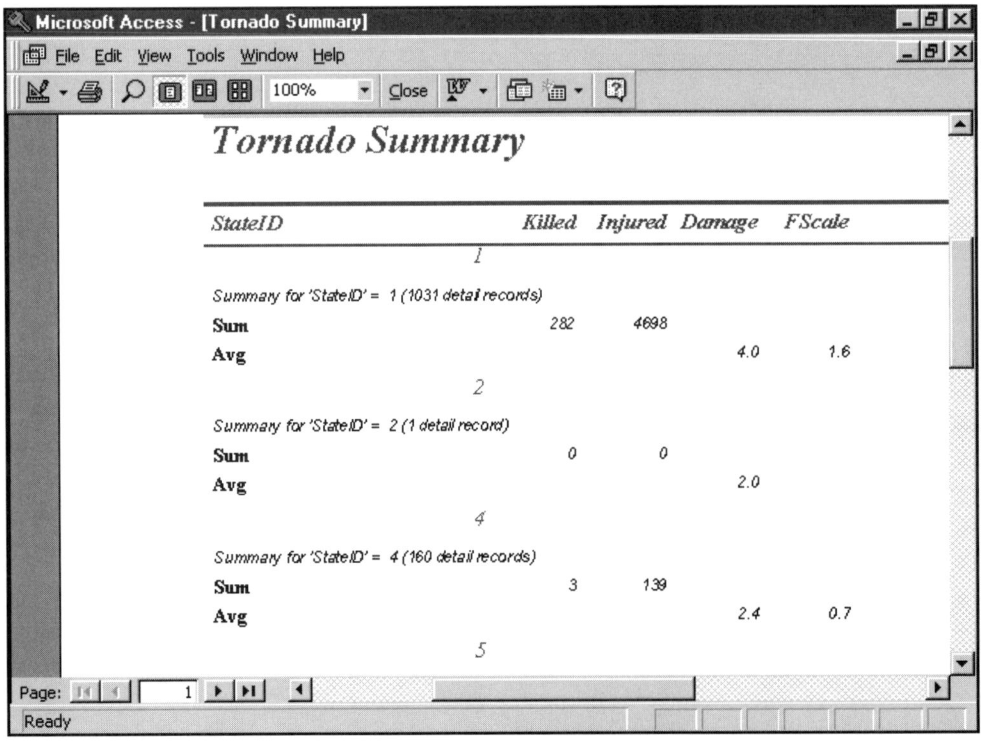


When you have completed this lesson, you will have created several data summaries, one of which will look like this:

SLIDE 6–2

**Tip for Instructors**

The Learn on Demand Module that applies to Lesson 6 is found in the Using Queries and Reports to Analyze Data subfolder of Learn Access 97.

# Task 1

## Creating a Simple Crosstab Query

### Why would I do this?

Creating a *crosstab query* is particularly useful when you need to see the relationship among several categories of numeric data. A crosstab query displays summarized values (sums, counts, and averages) from one field in a table and groups them based on at least two other fields. It displays data in a spreadsheet format with data from one field displayed on the vertical axis in the left column and data from another field displayed on the horizontal axis across the top. The intersection of the two fields is used for the summary data of a third numeric field. For example, a crosstab query might display school districts names on the vertical axis down the left column, and the students' gender across the top, and with average SAT scores in the data area. Crosstab queries help group and summarize several fields at a time.

In this task, you learn how to use a crosstab query to display the types of occupations that the men and women of the county had in 1900.

**Tip for Instructors**

The Learn on Demand Module/Lesson "Creating a Simple Crosstab Query" applies to this task.

**Tip for Instructors**

An example for a crosstab query is a sales organization. Different salespersons sell the same type of products. A crosstab query can calculate the total products sold by each salesperson as well as by the product.

**Concept**

Some queries do not display data clearly. A *crosstab query* can clarify this data. A crosstab query can calculate a total for data that is grouped both horizontally and vertically so the datasheet is more compact.

**1** Using Windows Explorer, make a copy of **Less0601** and rename the copy **Lesson6**. Launch Microsoft Access. Choose **Open an Existing Database**, find the file **Lesson6**, and open the file.

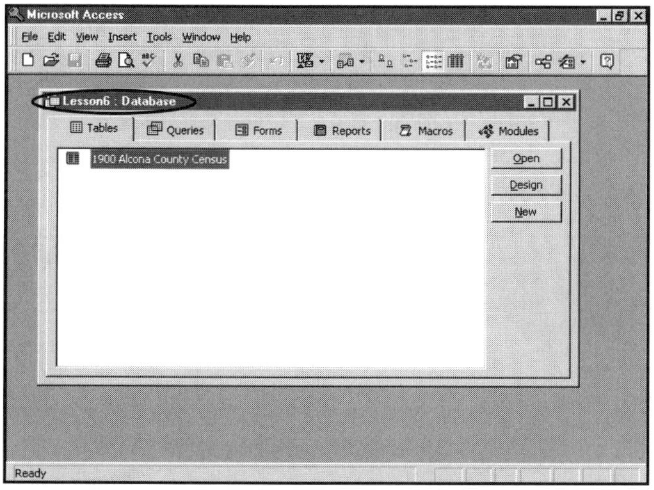


**2** Select the **Queries** tab. Several queries have already been created for this database.

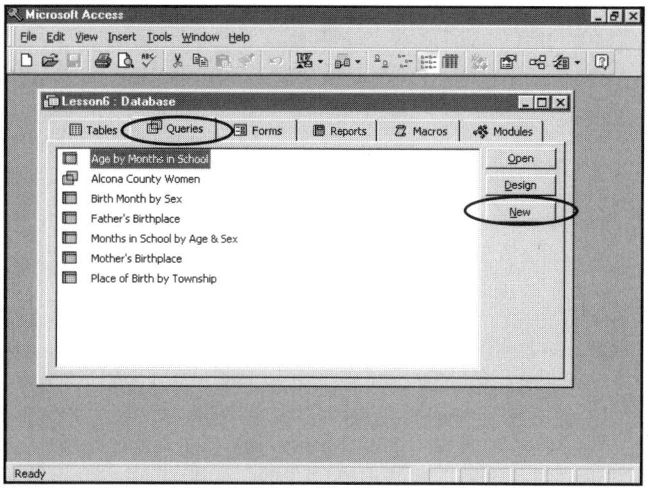


**3** Click the **New** button to create a new query. The **New Query** dialog box opens. Select the **Crosstab Query Wizard** option.

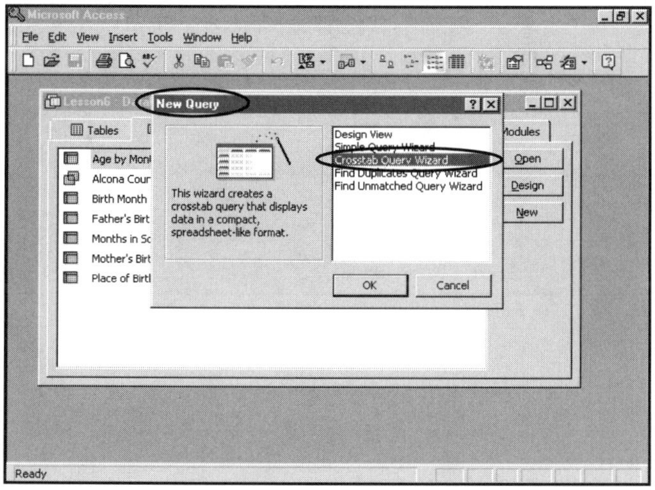

**4** Click **OK**. The first **Crosstab Query Wizard** dialog box opens, asking which table or query should be used as a data source. You will be using information from the **1900 Alcona County Census** table, which is the default selection.

### Tip for Instructors

The **Crosstab Query Wizard** is different from the **Simple Query Wizard**. Take your time to cover each screen thoroughly to avoid confusion. The Help text has a good deal of helpful information for assistance.

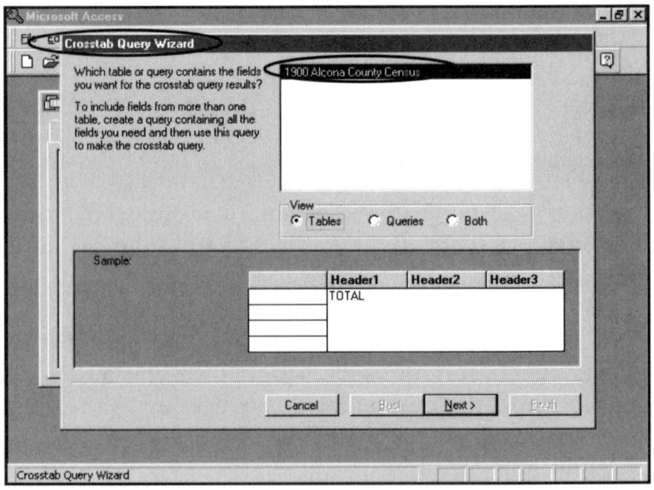


### Tip for Instructors

A crosstab query can be created with more than one table if a select query is created and used to create the crosstab query.

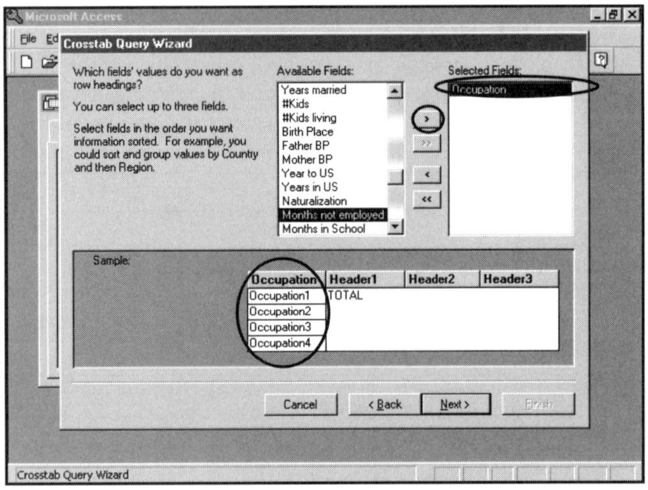


**5** Click **<u>N</u>ext** to move to the second **Crosstab Query Wizard** dialog box, which allows you to select the row heading(s) for the crosstab. Scroll down the field list, select **Occupation**, and click the **Add** button to add the field to the **Selected Fields** box.

### Concept

The column and row headings specify the way the calculations will be grouped. In our salesperson example, the column headings could be products and the row headings could be the salespersons.

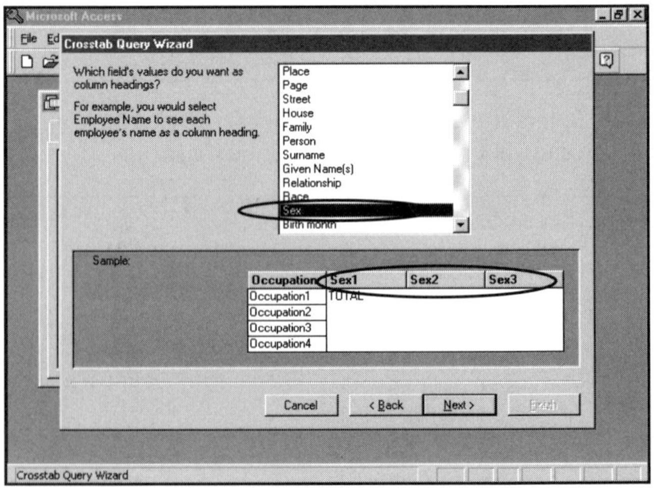


**6** Click **<u>N</u>ext** to move to the third **Crosstab Query Wizard** dialog box, which allows you to select the column heading(s) for the crosstab. Scroll down the field list and highlight **Sex**.

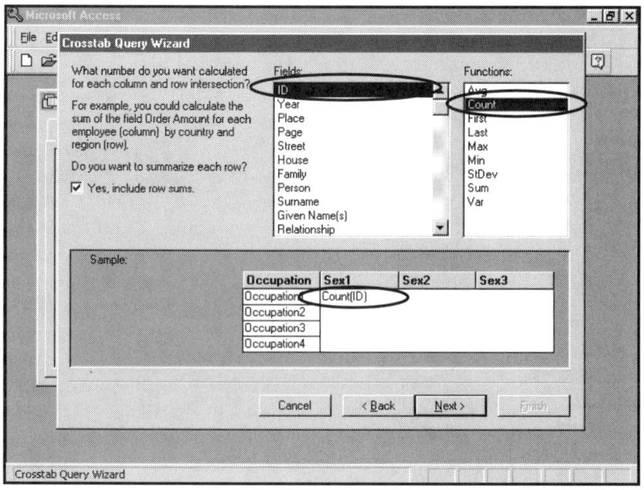


7 Click **Next** to move to the fourth **Crosstab Query Wizard** dialog box, which allows you to choose the method of summarizing your data. Leave **ID** selected in the **Fields** box, then select **Count** from the **Functions** box. This will count the number of men and women in each of the occupational categories.

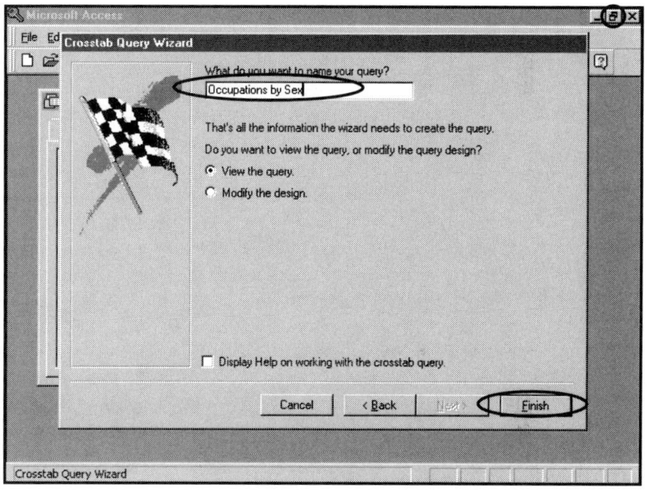


8 Click **Next** to move to the fifth **Crosstab Query Wizard** dialog box. Change the name of the crosstab to **Occupations by Sex**.

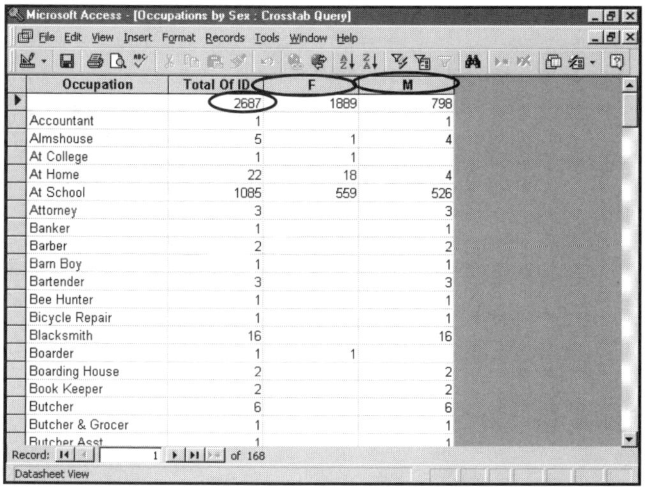


9 Click **Finish**, then click the **Maximize** button to maximize the window. A list of occupations is displayed (note that 2,687 people, mostly women and small children, do not have occupations listed).

**Q & A** **?**

*Question:* How does a crosstab query vary from a union query?
*Answer:* A crosstab query creates summary data between two tables.

**10** Click in the *field selector* area at the top of the **Total of ID** column. The whole column is selected.

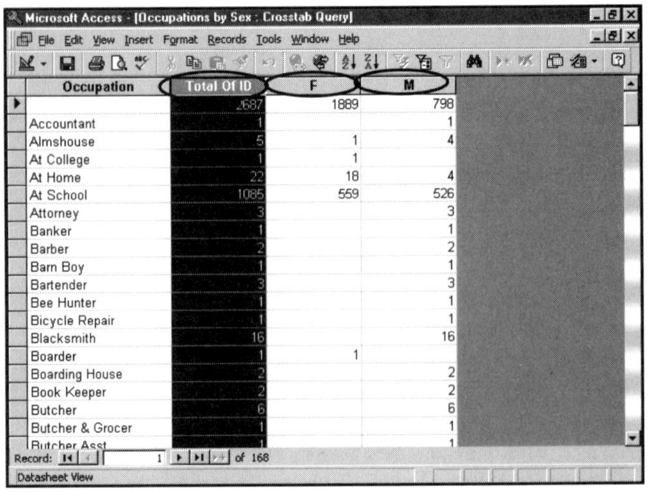


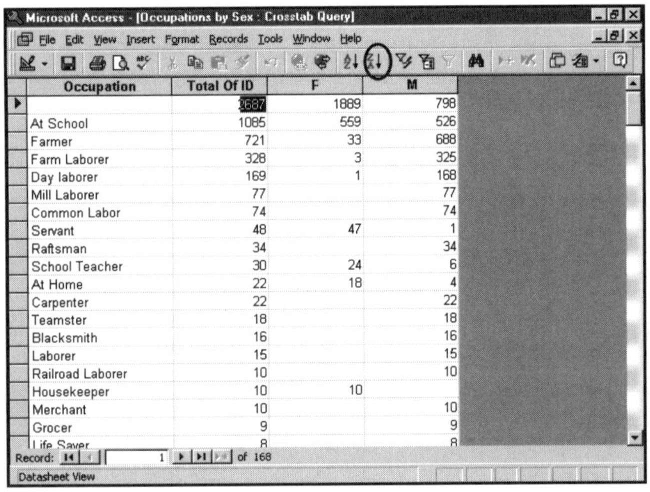


**11** Click the **Sort Descending** button to look at the most common occupations.

> **Quicksand**
> The crosstab query might not look exactly like the screen shot. There might be some extra columns. If so, hide them for this example.

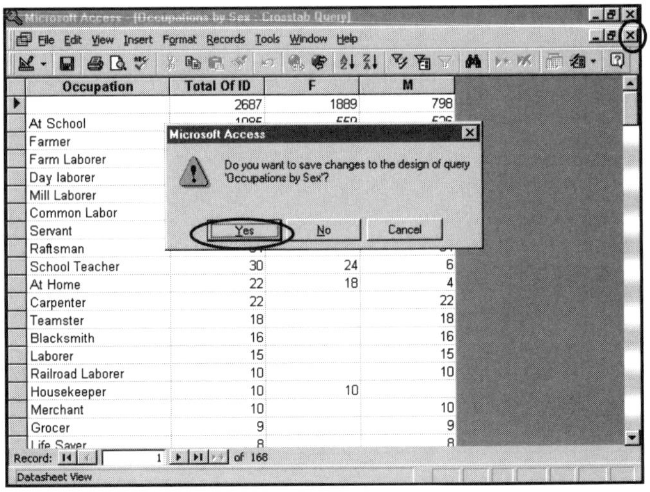


**12** Click the **Close Window** button to close the crosstab query. When prompted to save your changes, click **Yes**.

# Task 2

## Creating a Multilevel Crosstab Query

### Why would I do this?

A simple crosstab creates a tabular display showing how one field is summarized based on two other fields that are used to create the row heading and the column heading. The cells are filled with summary data that relies on those fields. Sometimes you may want to further subdivide the analysis by using more than two fields. A multilevel crosstab can summarize one field based on more than two other fields. The additional fields are added to the row headings, subdividing the row headings, while only one field is used for column headings.

In this task, you learn how to create a crosstab query that counts the number of people according to sex, location, and marital status. The columns will be based on the Marital Status field and the rows will be based on the Place and Sex fields. The resulting crosstab allows the user to see how many people of each sex and marital status lived in each location.

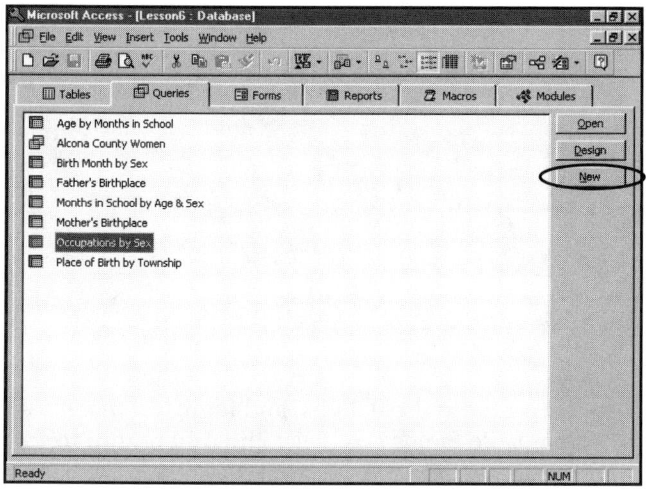


**1** In the **Database Window**, select the **Queries** tab, if necessary.

> **Tip for Instructors**
> The Learn on Demand Module/Lesson "Creating a Multilevel Crosstab Query" applies to this task.

> **On Your Mark**
> A crosstab query is used to compare two fields and display some sort of comparison. When might you need to compare three or more fields?

**2** Click the <u>N</u>ew button to create a new query. The **New Query** dialog box opens. Highlight the **Crosstab Query Wizard** option.

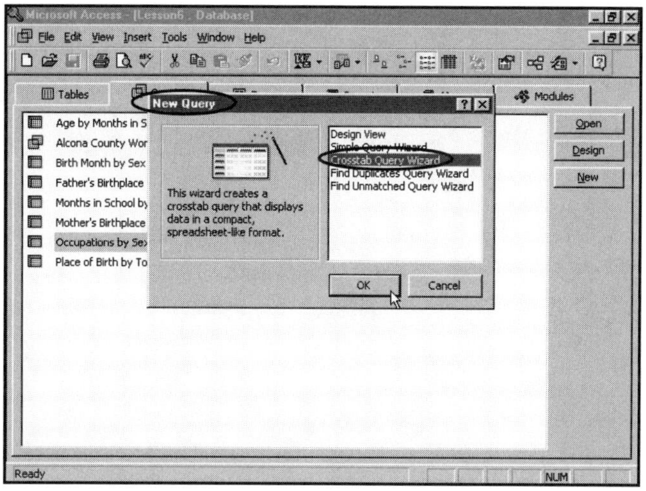


> **Concept**
> A multilevel crosstab query simply adds a second row to the query, thus a second summary of the data. There would be multiple entries for each row of totals, one to match the second row heading.

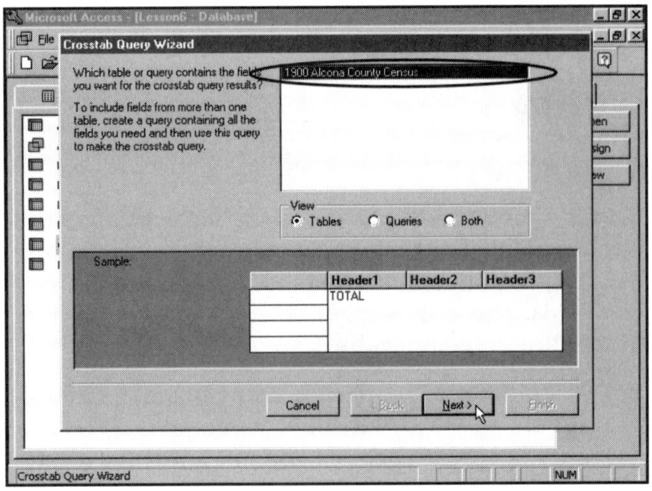


**3** Click **OK**. The first **Crosstab Query Wizard** dialog box opens, asking where you want the data to be taken from. You will be using information from the **1900 Alcona County Census** table, which is the default selection.

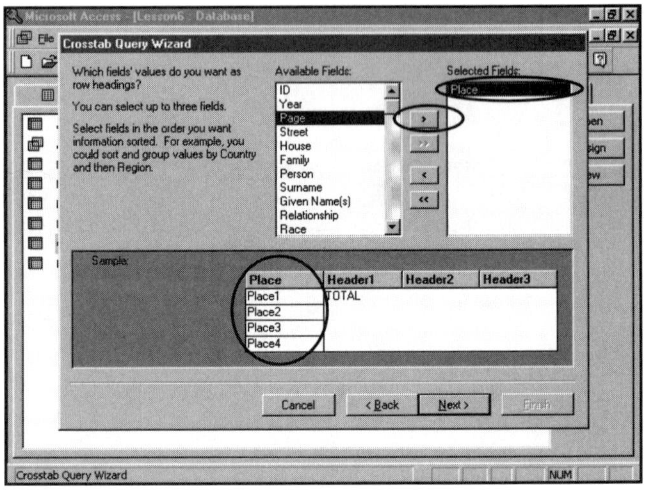


**4** Click **Next** to move to the second **Crosstab Query Wizard** dialog box. Highlight **Place** in the **Available Fields** box and click the **Add** button to move the field into the **Selected Fields** box.

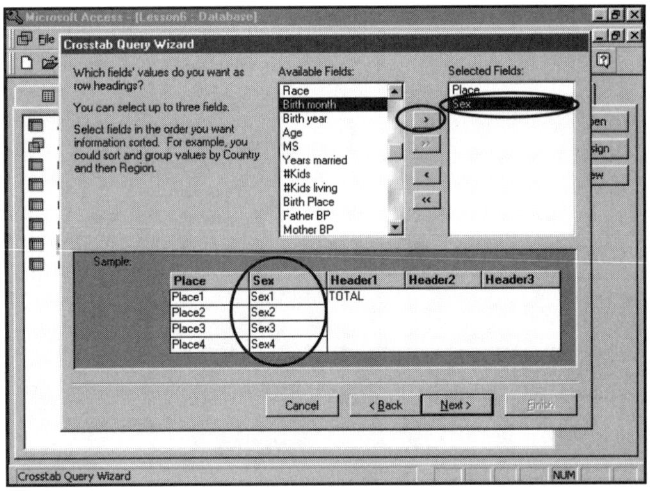


**5** Scroll down the field list and highlight **Sex** in the **Available Fields** box. Click the **Add** button to move the field into the **Selected Fields** box. Notice that a second set of row headings is displayed in the preview area.

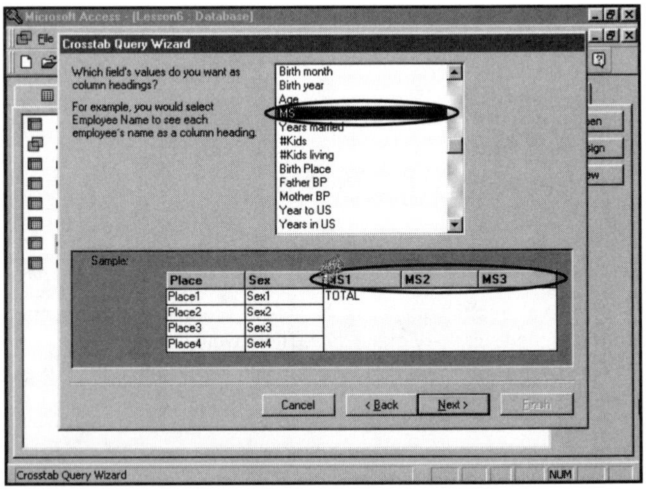


**6** Click **Next** to move to the third **Crosstab Query Wizard** dialog box. Scroll down the field list and highlight the marital status (**MS**) field.

**7** Click **Next** to move to the fourth **Crosstab Query Wizard** dialog box. Leave **ID** selected in the **Fields** box, then select **Count** from the **Functions** box.

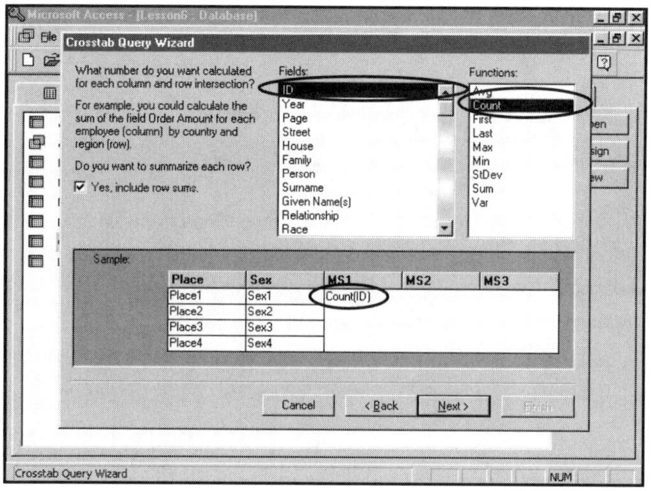


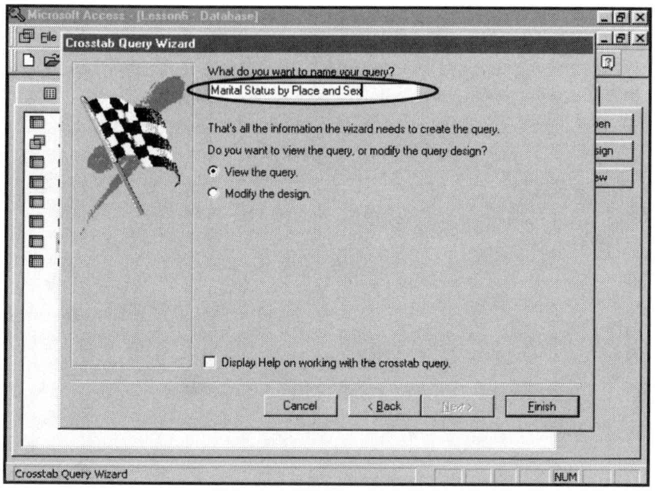


**8** Click **Next** to move to the fifth **Crosstab Query Wizard** dialog box. Change the name of the crosstab to **Marital Status by Place and Sex**.

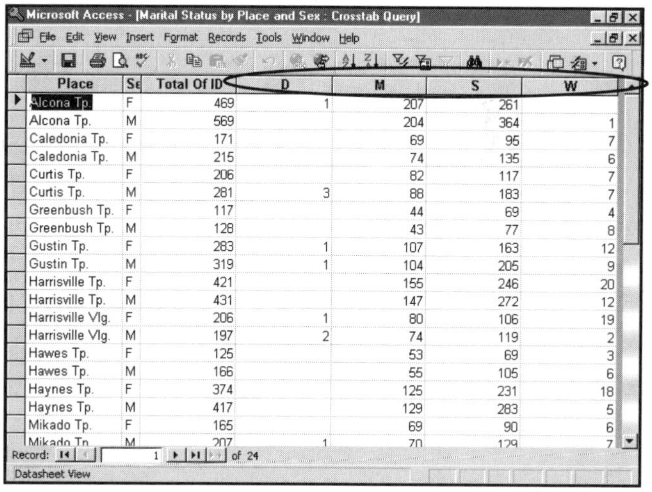


| Place | Se | Total Of ID | D | M | S | W |
|---|---|---|---|---|---|---|
| Alcona Tp. | F | 469 | 1 | 207 | 261 | |
| Alcona Tp. | M | 569 | | 204 | 364 | 1 |
| Caledonia Tp. | F | 171 | | 69 | 95 | 7 |
| Caledonia Tp. | M | 215 | | 74 | 135 | 6 |
| Curtis Tp. | F | 206 | | 82 | 117 | 7 |
| Curtis Tp. | M | 281 | 3 | 88 | 183 | 7 |
| Greenbush Tp. | F | 117 | | 44 | 69 | 4 |
| Greenbush Tp. | M | 128 | | 43 | 77 | 8 |
| Gustin Tp. | F | 283 | 1 | 107 | 163 | 12 |
| Gustin Tp. | M | 319 | 1 | 104 | 205 | 9 |
| Harrisville Tp. | F | 421 | | 155 | 246 | 20 |
| Harrisville Tp. | M | 431 | | 147 | 272 | 12 |
| Harrisville Vlg. | F | 206 | 1 | 80 | 106 | 19 |
| Harrisville Vlg. | M | 197 | 2 | 74 | 119 | 2 |
| Hawes Tp. | F | 125 | | 53 | 69 | 3 |
| Hawes Tp. | M | 166 | | 55 | 105 | 6 |
| Haynes Tp. | F | 374 | | 125 | 231 | 18 |
| Haynes Tp. | M | 417 | | 129 | 283 | 5 |
| Mikado Tp. | F | 165 | | 69 | 90 | 6 |
| Mikado Tp. | M | 207 | 1 | 70 | 129 | 7 |

**9** Click **Finish**. A list of males and females in each place is summarized by the number who are divorced, married, single, and widowed. This crosstab also gives you the total number of males and females in each location. Notice that in most locations there are more males than females.

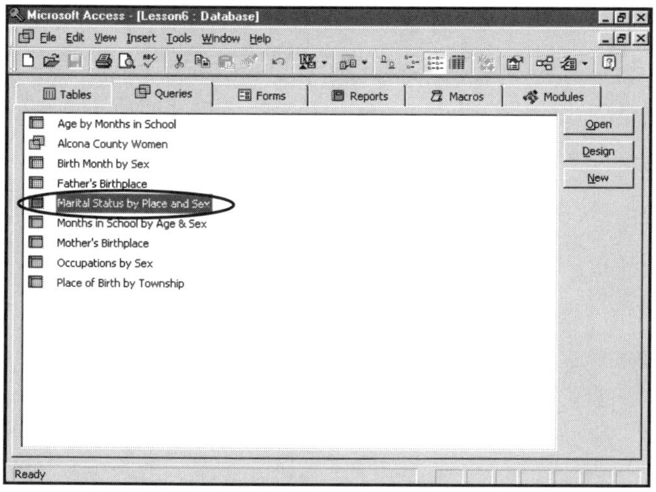


**Quicksand**

The crosstab query might not look exactly like the screen shot. There might be some extra columns. If so, hide them for this example.

**10** Click the **Close Window** button to close the crosstab query. If prompted to save your changes, click **Yes**.

# Task 3

## Editing a Query

### Why would I do this?

When you create a query using the **Crosstab Query Wizard**, you are allowed to choose the fields to be used for the row and column headings, but that is about all. In order to analyze only certain data that meets special conditions, you have two choices—create a separate query that restricts the data and base the new query on the old query, or create a query and edit it in **Design View**.

In this task, you learn how to use Design View to edit a query of all women in Alcona County to show only those women living in Haynes Township who have had children. You will also edit the query to sort the data.

**1** In the **Queries** tab, select the **Alcona County Women** query.

**Tip for Instructors**

The Learn on Demand Module/Lesson "Editing a Query" applies to this task.

**On Your Mark**

After a query has been created, you might need another query with a similar design. How might you save time creating the second query?

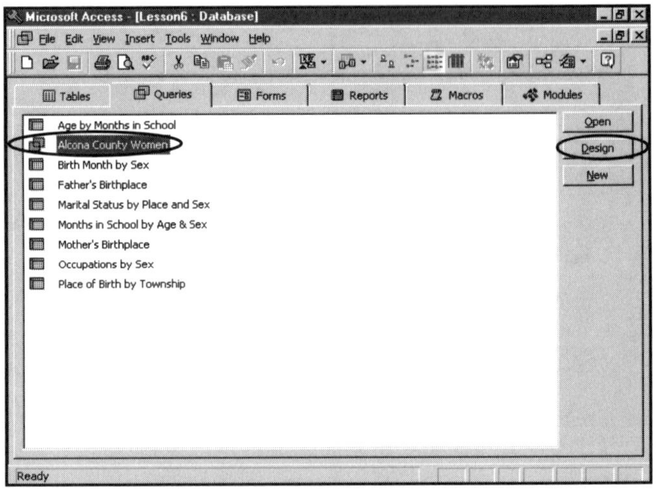


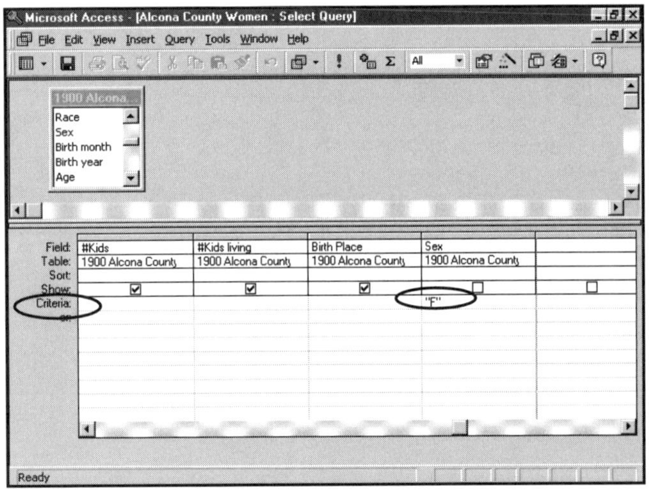


**2** Click the **Design** button. The **Design View** is displayed. Scroll to the right until the last four fields are shown. Notice that the **Criteria** text box for the **Sex** field contains an **"F"**, which restricts the query to only females.

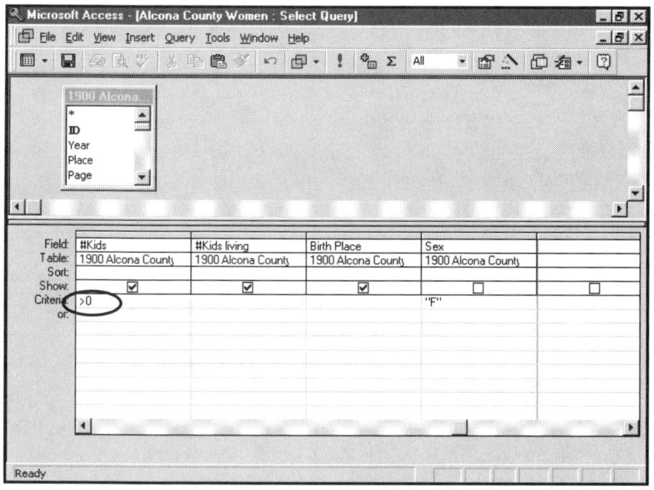


**3** In the **Criteria** text box below the **#Kids** field, type **>0**. This will restrict the output to women who have had at least one child.

**In Depth:** If you place two criteria-on the same row, both criteria must be met for a record to be displayed. This is known as an **And** condition. The row underneath the criteria row is the **Or** criteria row. If criteria is entered on both lines, the second criteria is on the **Or** line, and the record will be displayed if either condition is true. This is known as an **Or** condition.

**Tip for Students**

More than two criteria can be set in a query, either as an And statement or as an Or statement.

**4** Select **Place** from the **Field List** box. Make sure an empty field is available on the right.

**Quicksand**

When creating an And statement with more than two criteria, simply place all criterion on the same row. When creating an Or statement, each criteria must be on a different row. If any two criteria are on the same row, both criteria must be met (which is an And statement).

Empty field

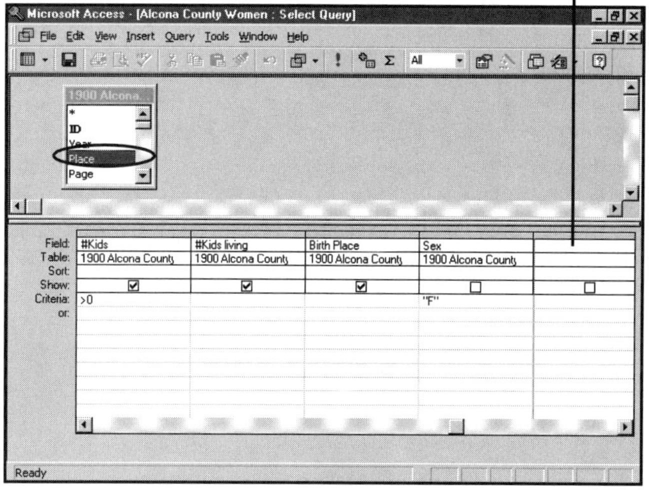


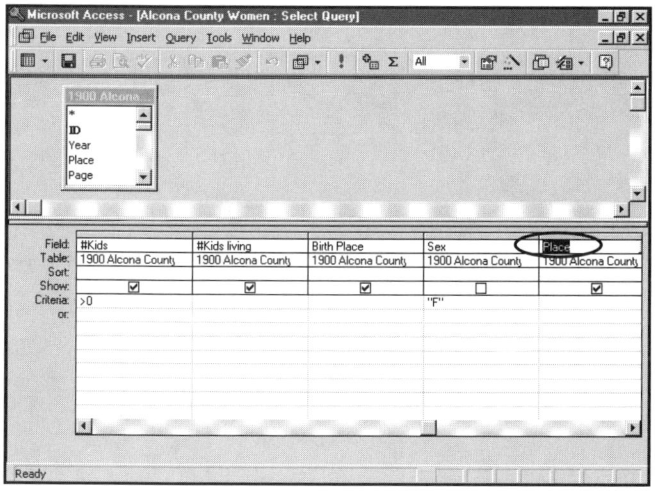


**Quick Tip:** You can also double-click on the **Place** field and it will automatically be placed in the next open field text box.

**5** Click and drag the **Place** field to the **Field** row and drop it in the empty field text box to the right of the **Sex** field text box.

**6** Click the **Show** check box below the **Place** field to keep this field from being displayed when the query is run.

**Pothole:** If the new column was the last empty column showing on your screen, the first time you click anywhere in the column, the program adds another empty column to the right. In this case, the check mark in the show box does not go away, and you have to click it a second time. Make sure the check mark is not showing to ensure that the **Place** field does not show when you run the query.

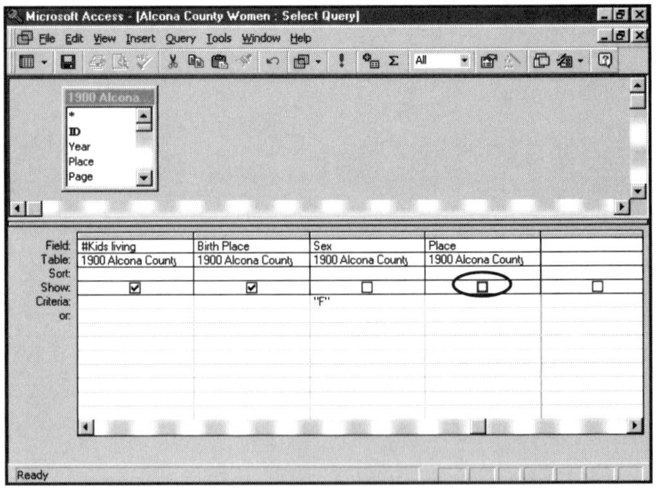


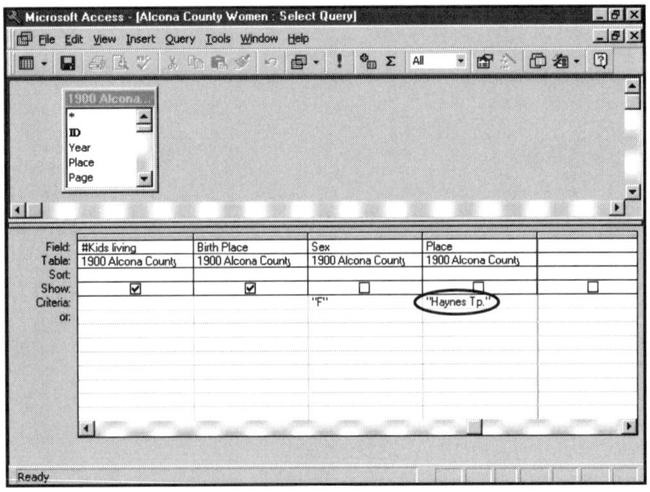


**7** Type **Haynes Tp.** in the **Criteria** text box below the **Place** field. When you click outside the **Criteria** text box, the program puts quotation marks around the text you typed.

**Tip for Students** **!**

Criteria for a Text data type field need quotes around them. If not provided by the user, Access adds them.

**Pothole**: If you run your query and no records are shown, chances are you have typed a criteria incorrectly. In this example, if you leave the period off the end of *Haynes Tp.* the query will find nothing because it needs an exact match.

Run button

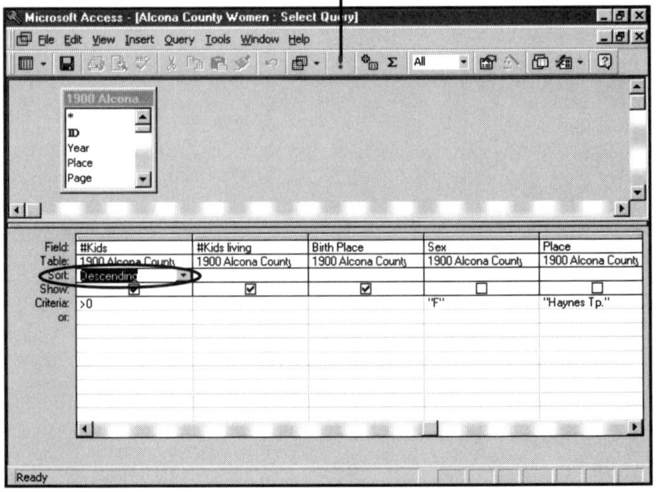


**Tip for Students** **!**

You can use a wildcard if you are uncertain exactly how each field was keyed in.

**8** Scroll back so you can see the **#Kids** field. Click in the **Sort** box and choose **Descending** from the drop-down list. This will set the order of display starting with the woman with the most children.

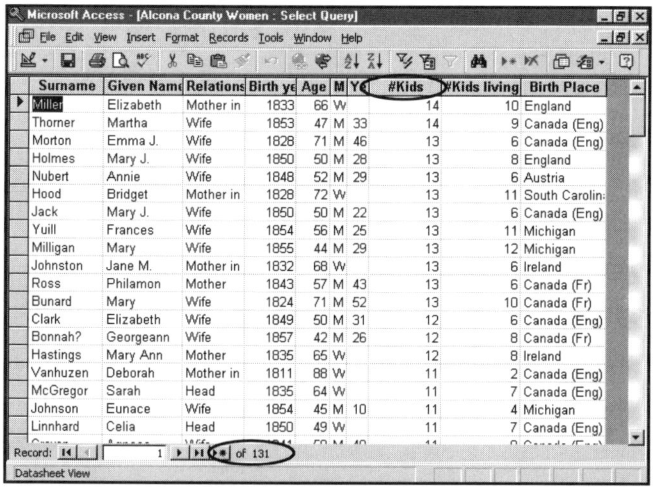


9 Click the **Run** button to see the results of your edits. Notice that **131** women in the township are mothers. Also notice that the records are sorted in descending order by the number of children each woman had.

**In Depth:** The Run button is another way to view the results of a query. You can use either the View button or the Run button. Some special types of queries, known as action queries, require the use of the Run button to run the query against the data to change records or make new tables. This type of query is not covered in this book.

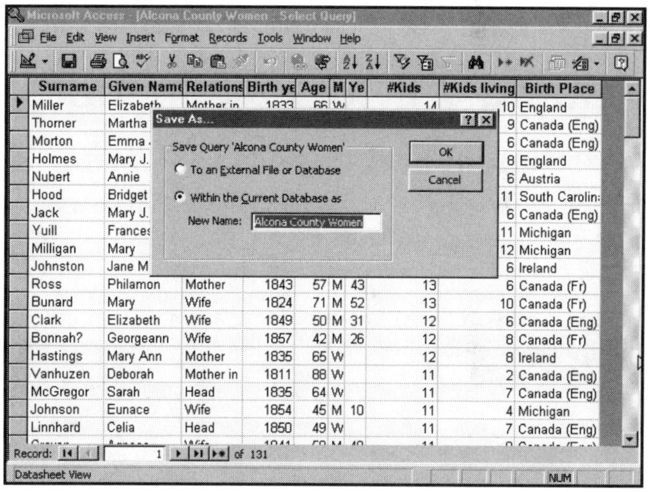


**SLIDE 6–3**

10 To save this version of the query without overwriting the original version, choose **File** and **Save As/Export** from the menu. The **Save As** dialog box opens.

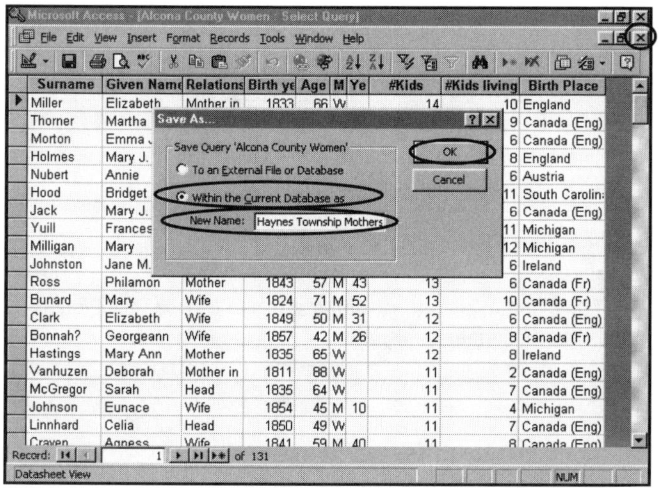


**Q & A** ?

*Question:* How do you save an edited query into a new query?
*Answer:* Use **Save As/Export**.

11 Make sure the **Within the Current Database as** action button is selected, then type **Haynes Township Mothers** in the **New Name** box.

**12** Click **OK**. Click the **Close Window** button to close the query.

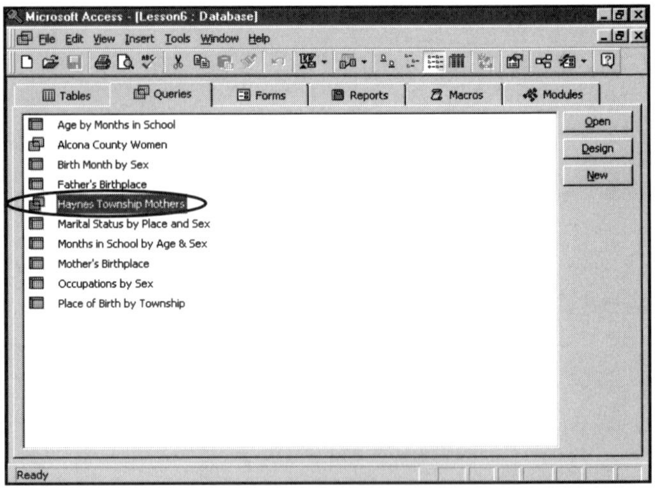


# Task 4

## Adding the Totals Function to a Query

### Why would I do this?

Instead of showing records that match certain conditions, you will sometimes want the query to provide summary data only. Crosstab queries will do that for two or more fields, but you will often want to summarize data for a single field. The **Totals** button in the query **Design View** allows you to do a single field summary.

In this task, you learn how to create a query that counts the number of people born in each place listed in the **Birth Place** field.

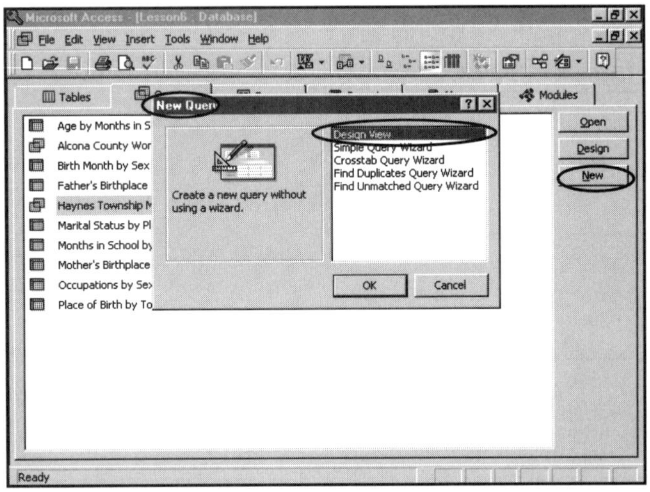


**1** Click the **New** button. The **New Query** dialog box opens. Select **Design View**.

**On Your Mark**

What types of data summary might be useful in a query?

**Tip for Instructors**

The Learn on Demand Module/Lesson "Adding the Totals Function to a Query" applies to this task.

**Concept**

The **Totals** button gives the user the ability to choose select functions to be performed in a query.

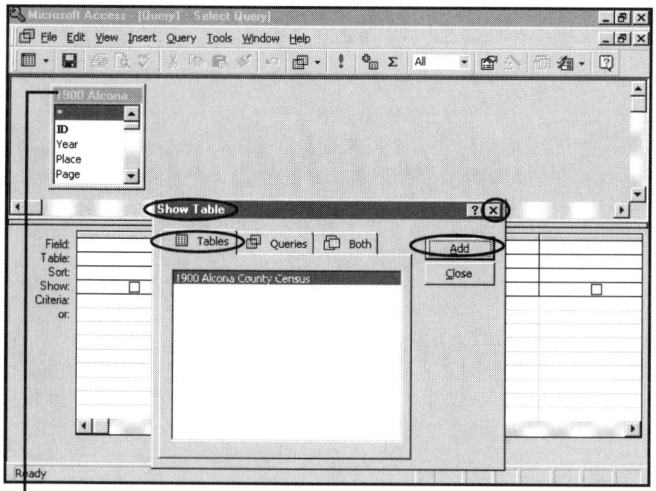


Field List box

2 Click OK. The **Show Table** dialog box opens. Select the **Tables** tab, if necessary. The **1900 Alcona County Census** is highlighted. Click the **Add** button. The table **field list** is added to **Design View**.

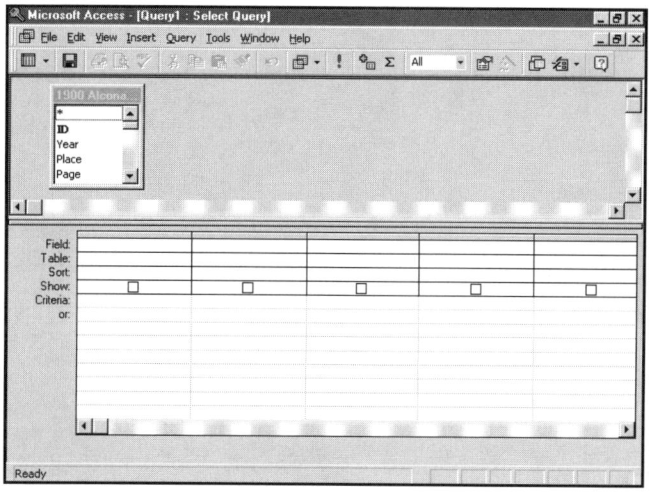


3 Click the **Close** button to close the **Show Table** dialog box. The empty **Design View** is displayed.

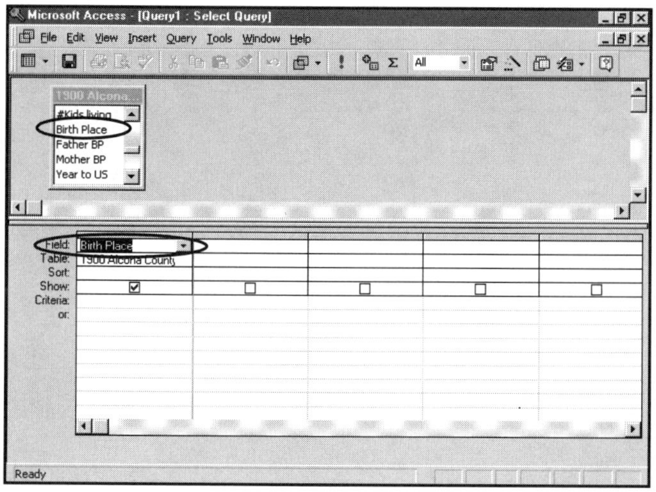


4 Scroll down the **field list** until you see the **Birth Place** field. Double-click to add this field to the first empty Field text box.

**5** Scroll to the top of the **field list**. Select the **ID** field and double-click to add it to the next open Field text box.

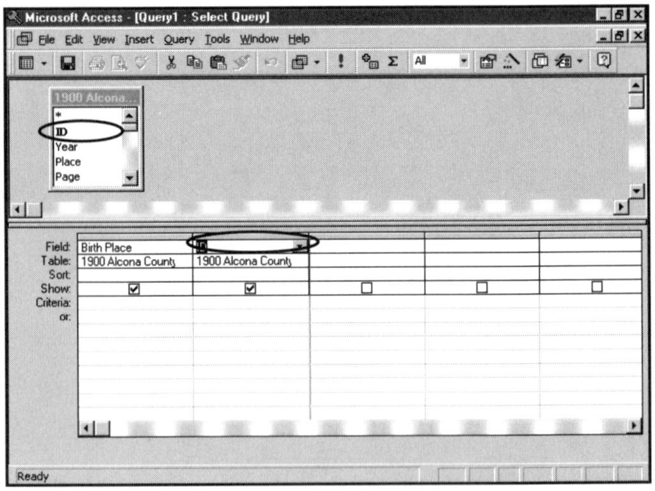

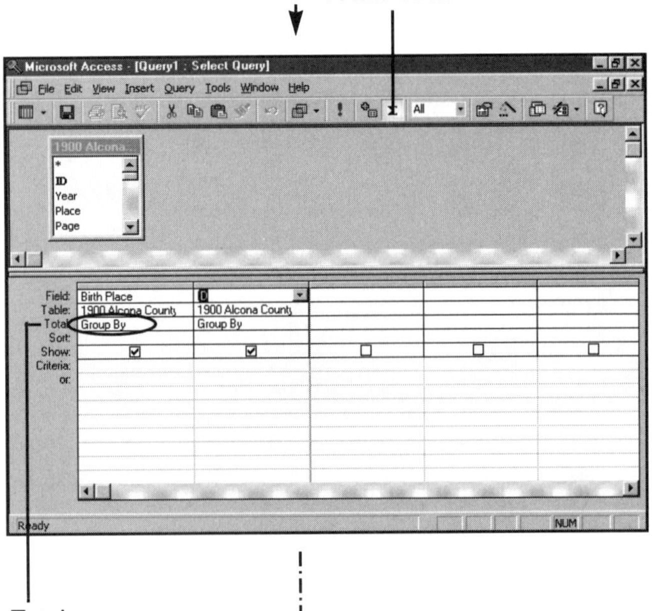


### Tip for Instructors

The **Group By** option simply tells the query to group the data together by this field without performing any calculations on these records. In this example, the query will place all records from one **Birth Place** into one group.

**6** Click the **Totals** button. A new **Total** row is added to the search grid. Notice that the default choice in the Total row is Group By, which is correct for the Birth Place field.

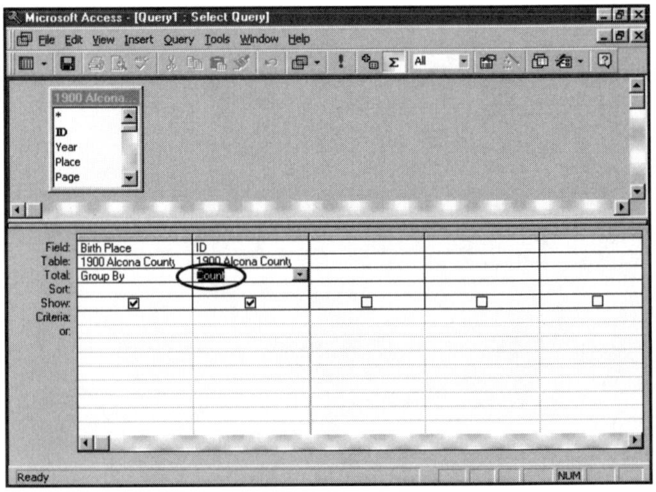

**7** Place the cursor in the **Total** text box below the **ID** field. Click the drop-down arrow and select **Count** from the list. This will give you a count for the grouped birthplaces.

### Tip for Instructors

The **Count** option simply counts the total records for each group. In this example, the query will count each record in each **Birth Place** group. The **ID** field simply makes each record unique so that it can be counted.

**8** Place the cursor in the **Sort** text box below the **ID** field. Click the drop-down arrow and select **Descending** from the list. This shows the most common birthplaces first.

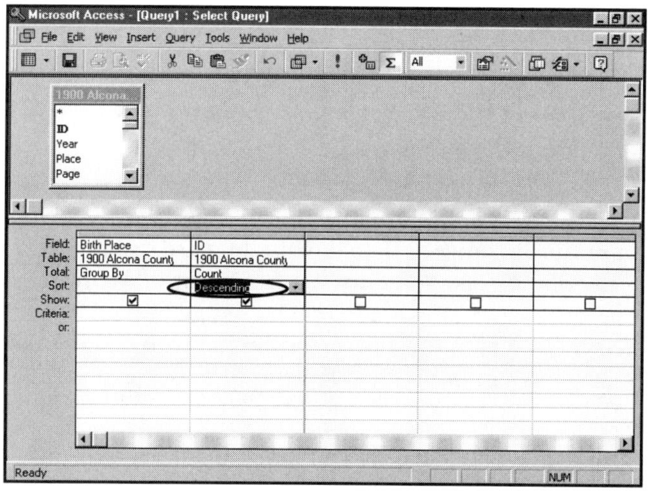


**Tip for Students** !

When using **Totals**, blank fields will not be included in the calculations.

**9** Click the **Run** button. A summary list of birthplaces is shown.

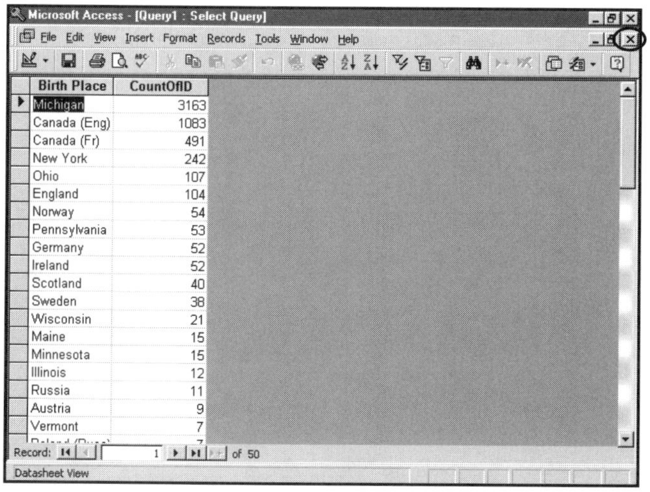


**10** Click the **Close Window** button. When prompted to save changes, click **Yes**. The **Save As** dialog box opens.

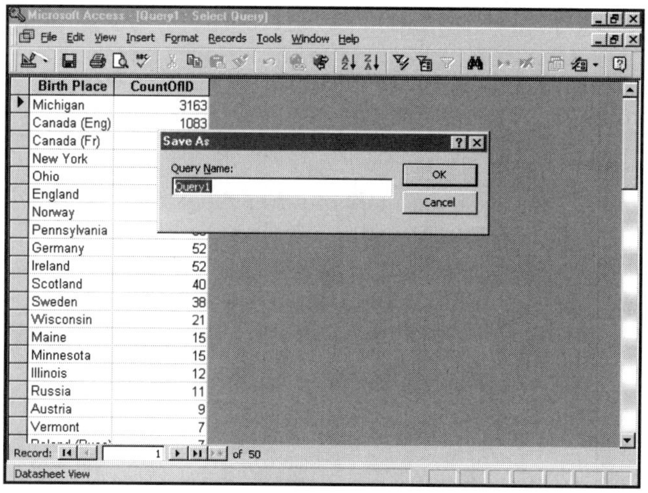


**Q & A** ?

*Question:* What is the purpose of the **Totals** option in a query?
*Answer:* To summarize one field of data.

**11** Type **Summary of Birthplaces** and click **OK** to return to the Database window.

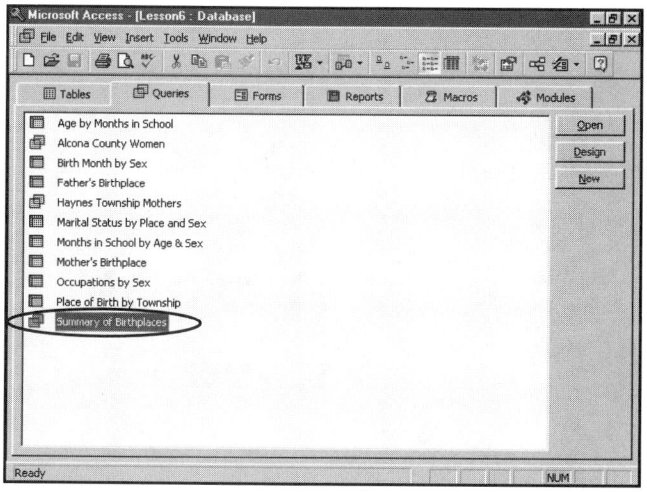

# Task 5

## Creating a Pivot Table in a Form

### Why would I do this?

A *pivot table* is an interactive table that is used to perform calculations, and it is often the best way to analyze large amounts of complex data. Pivot tables are usually associated with an Excel spreadsheet, but pivot tables can be created in Access and edited using Excel tools. In Access, a pivot table is displayed as a form allowing you to print data on a separate page for each change in a selected category. While a pivot table performs much the same as a crosstab query, it offers greater flexibility to analyze data in different ways. Rather than having to create a new query, you can use a Pivot table and rearrange row headings, column headings, and page fields until you achieve the desired results.

In this task, you learn how to quickly calculate the average age of the males and females in each township and village in Alcona County.

**On Your Mark**

Look at the data you have in your County database. What are some of the data summaries you may need? Might these summaries be resummarized, using the same fields only in a different order?

**Tip for Instructors**

You must have Excel installed on the computers to create or use a PivotTable.

**Concept**

PivotTables are interactive and perform calculations based on how the data is arranged. Data can be displayed horizontally or vertically, and the total can be calculated by rows or columns.

**Tip for Instructors**

The Learn on Demand Module/Lesson "Creating a Pivot Table in a Form" applies to this task.

**1** Click the **Forms** tab and then click the **New** button. The **New Form** dialog box opens.

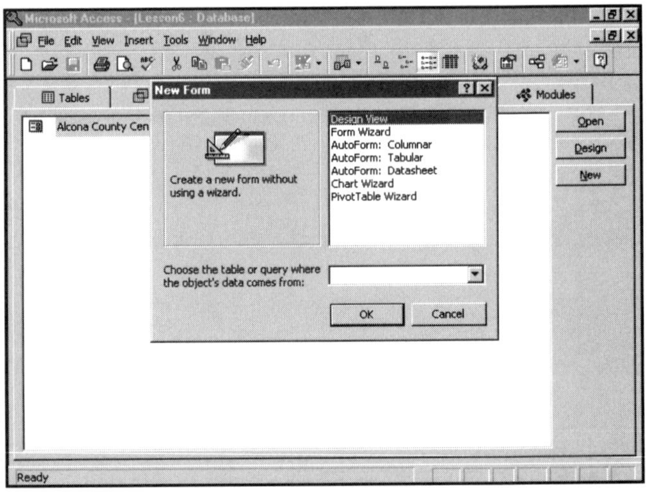


**2** Click the **PivotTable Wizard** and select the **1900 Alcona County Census** from the drop-down list.

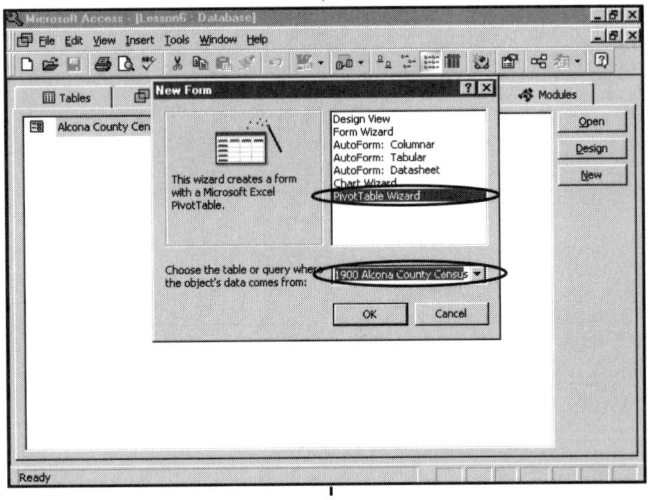


**3** Click **OK**. The first **PivotTable Wizard** dialog box opens. It is an introduction to the PivotTable Wizard.

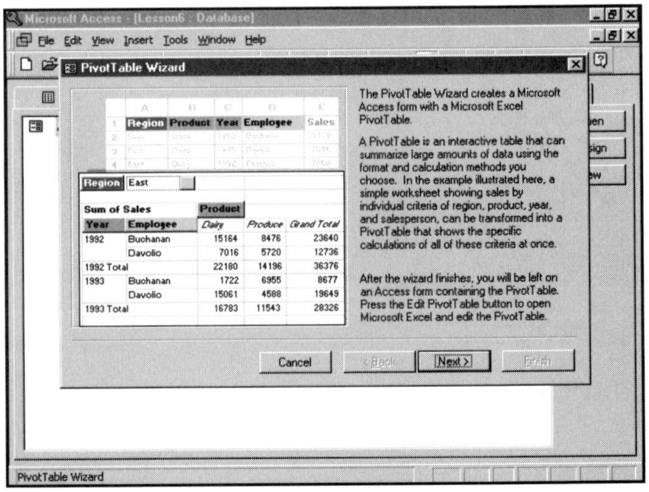

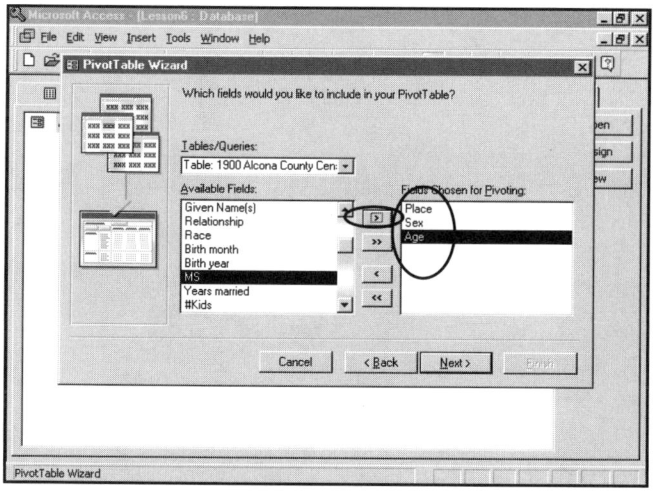


**4** Click **Next**. The second **PivotTable Wizard** dialog box opens. Select the **Place** field and click the **Add** button to add it to **Fields Chosen for Pivoting**. Do the same for the **Sex** and the **Age** fields.

### Tip for Instructors

An example for a PivotTable is an analysis of sales by product for each employee. Employee names could be listed as the column headings with the product categories as the row headings. Sales amounts could then be calculated by product category by each salesperson on each row and column.

**5** Click **Next**. After a minute or so, the third **PivotTable Wizard** dialog box is displayed. Excel was opened in the process and can be seen in the background. The fields you chose are shown on the right side of the dialog box.

### Tip for Instructors

Read each screen thoroughly.

**Pothole:** You must have Excel installed on your computer for this procedure to work. If you get an error message telling you that the program can't find Excel, move to another computer or skip the rest of this task. When Excel opens, the Office Assistant may also open. Click the Close button to close it.

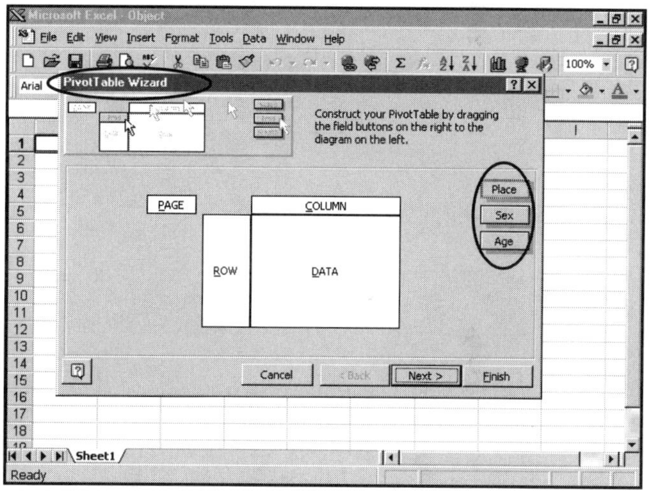


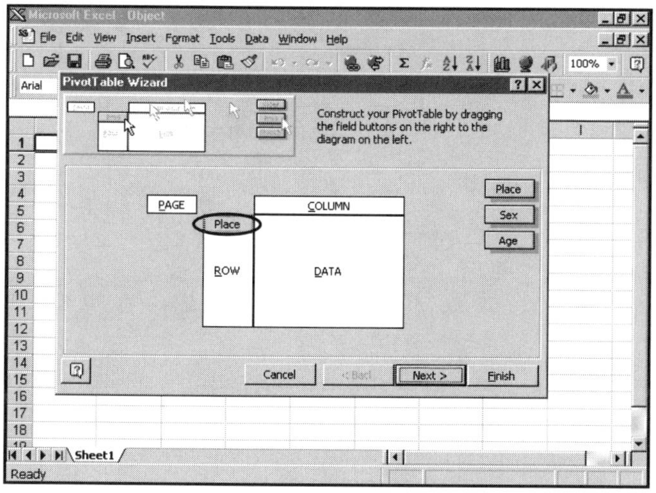


**Pothole:** For Step 6 to work properly, you must drag the field name into the box. If you try to place it outside the box, the place-holder for the field name will not move.

**6** Click and drag the **Place** field into the white box labeled **ROW**. The **Place** field is positioned at the top of the row area.

**7** Click and drag the **Sex** field into the **COLUMN** area and the **Age** field into the **DATA** area, as shown in the figure.

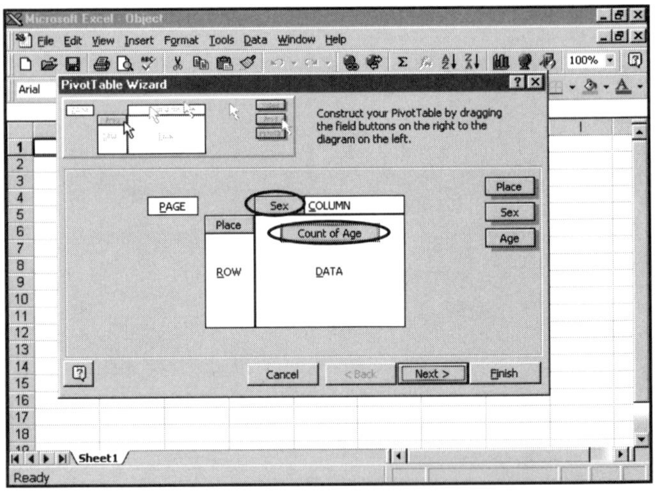


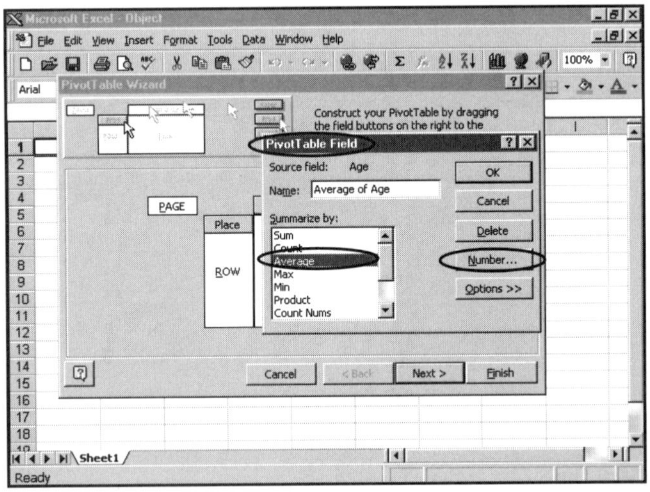


**8** Double-click the **Count of Age** box in the **DATA** area. The **PivotTable Field** dialog box opens. Select **Average** from the list.

**Tip for Students** !

Double-click the function to change it.

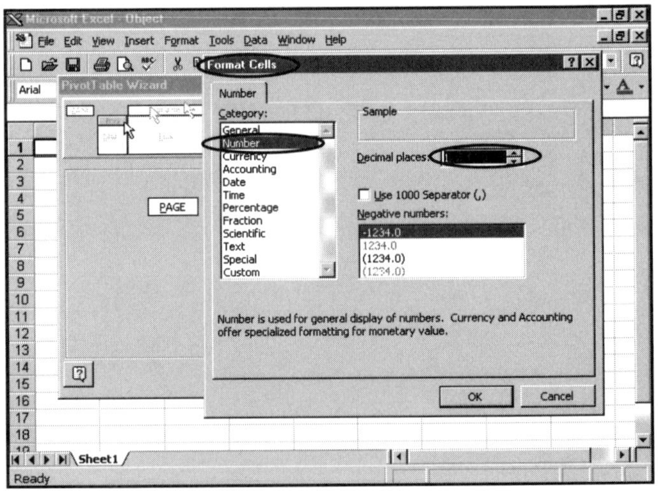


**Tip for Students** !

The numbers in a PivotTable can be formatted, just like the ones in Excel.

**9** Click the **Number** button. The **Format Cells** dialog box opens. Click **Number** in the **Category** box, and select **1** in the **Decimal places** box.

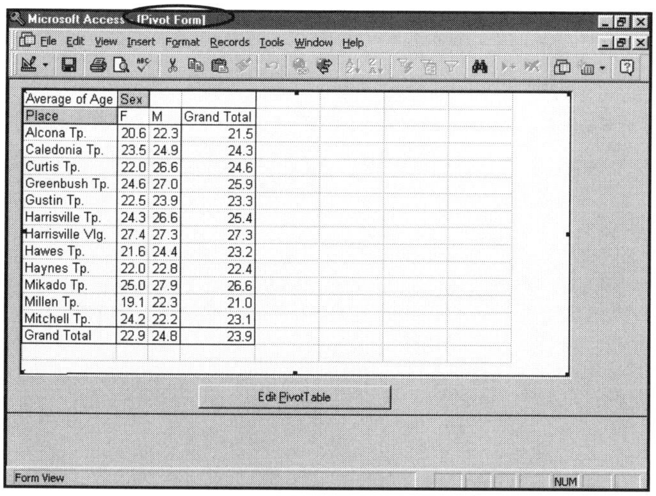


**10** Click **OK** twice, then click **Finish**. Excel is closed, and the pivot table is displayed as a **Pivot Form** in Access.

> **In Depth:** You can only edit the pivot table in Excel. If you click the **Edit PivotTable** button, it will launch Excel and open a toolbar that can be used to edit your pivot table. To return to Access, close the Excel window. It is also best to print the data from Excel.

**SLIDE 6–4**

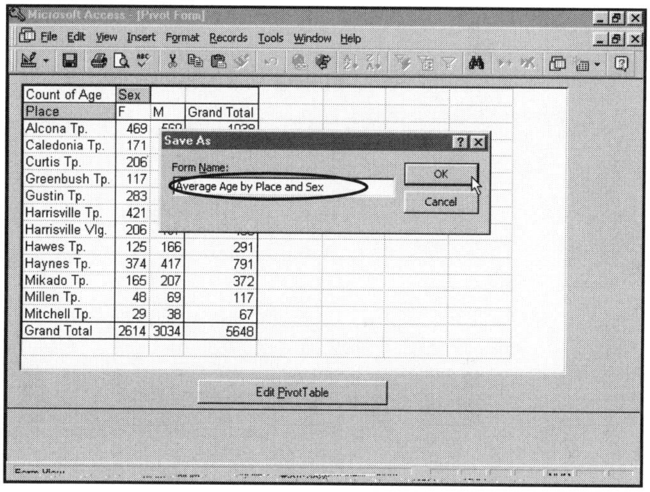


**11** Click the **Close Window** button and choose **Yes** when asked if you want to save your changes. Type **Average Age by Place and Sex** in the **Save As** dialog box.

> **Tip for Students**
>
> The PivotTable is like a linked object. It is placed within Access and can be used in Access; however, it must be edited in Excel.

> **Q & A**
>
> *Question:* Where is a PivotTable created/edited? *Answer:* Excel.

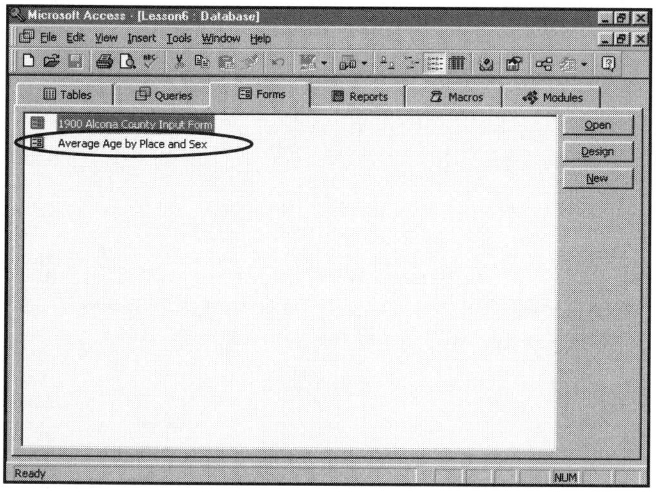


**12** Click **OK** to return to the Database Window.

# Task 6

## Creating a Report that Groups Data and Displays Subtotals and Totals

### Why would I do this?

You have learned how to analyze and specify data using tables (with filters), queries, and forms. There is also a technique for grouping and summarizing data using reports. Reports create a professional-looking layout for your data and are used to distribute information.

In this task, you learn how to look at the average age, number of children, and number of children living for the women in each location.

**On Your Mark**

For what other component might you need summary data?

**Concept**

*Subtotals* display the data in a report by grouping and summarizing the data.

**1** Click the **Reports** tab and click **New**. The **New Report** dialog box opens.

**Tip for Instructors**

The Learn on Demand Module/Lesson "Creating a Report that Displays Subtotals" applies to this task.

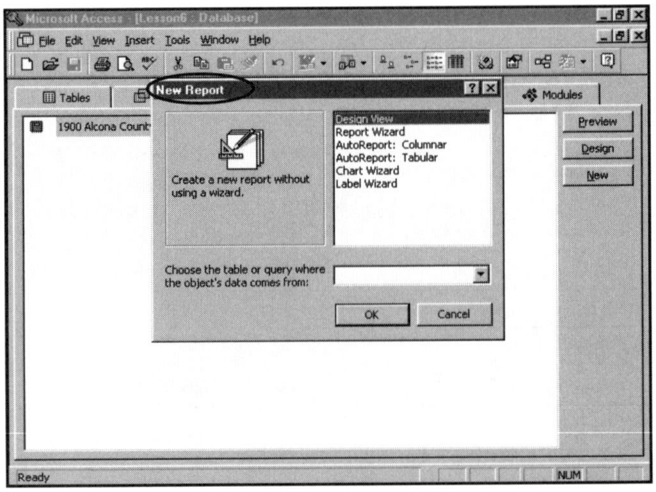


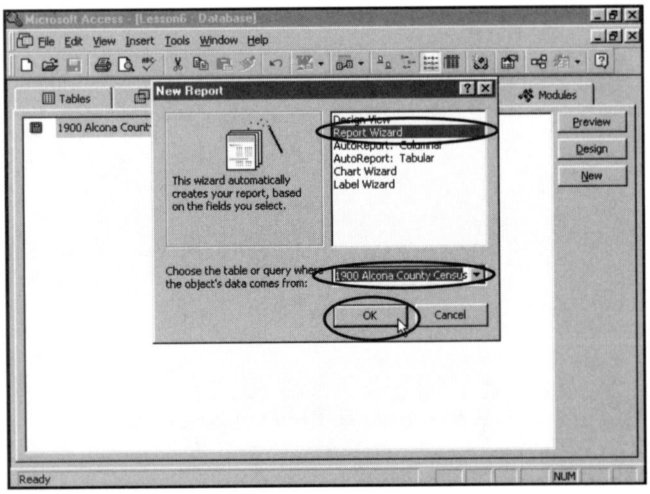


**2** Select the **Report Wizard** and choose the **1900 Alcona County Census** table as a data source, as shown in the figure.

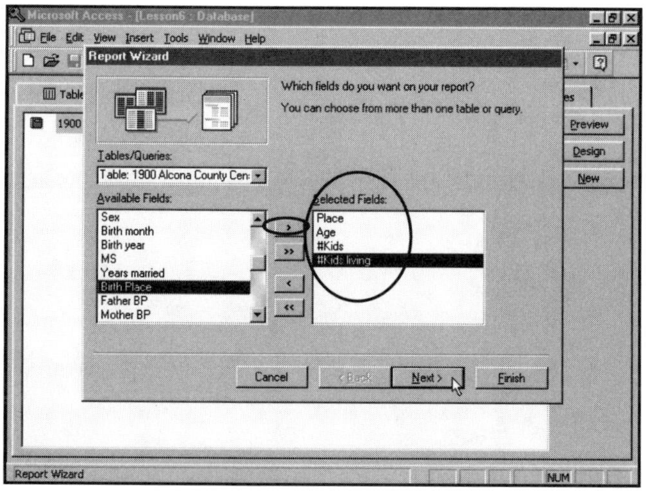


**3** Click **OK**. In the first **Report Wizard** dialog box, highlight the **Place** field and click the **Add** button to add the field to the **Selected Fields** box. Follow the same procedure to select the **Age**, **#Kids**, and **#Kids living** fields.

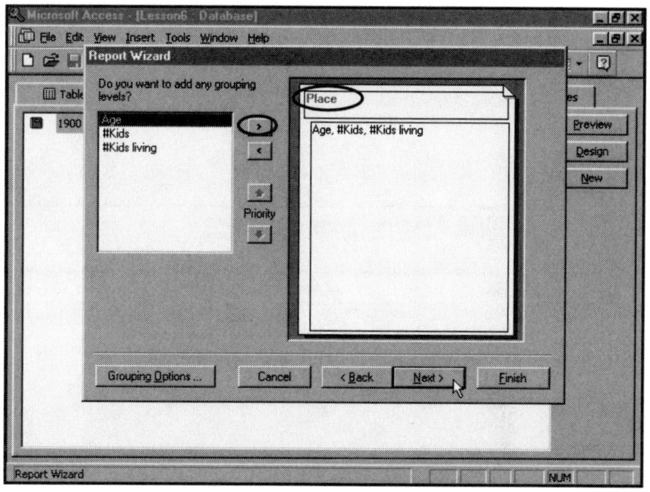


**4** Click **Next**. In the second **Report Wizard** dialog box, highlight the **Place** field and click the **Add** button to add the field to the **preview box.**This will group the report by place.

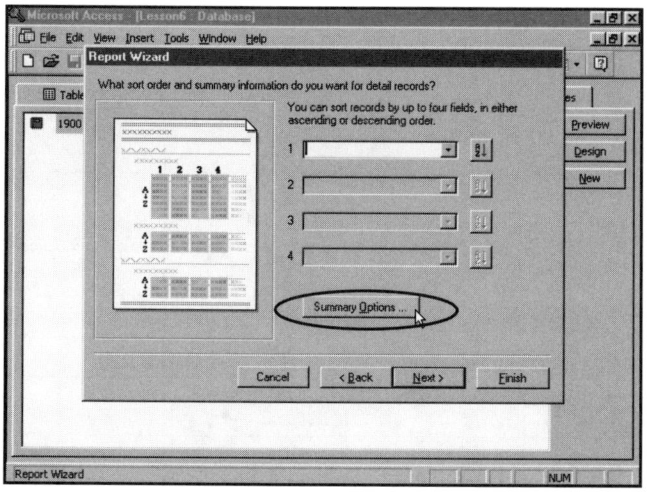


**5** Click **Next**. The third **Report Wizard** dialog box opens. It allows you to sort the data (which is unnecessary in this case) and includes a **Summary Options** button.

**6** Click the **Summary Options** button. The **Summary Options** dialog box opens. Select **Avg** for all three fields. In the **Show** box, select **Summary Only**.

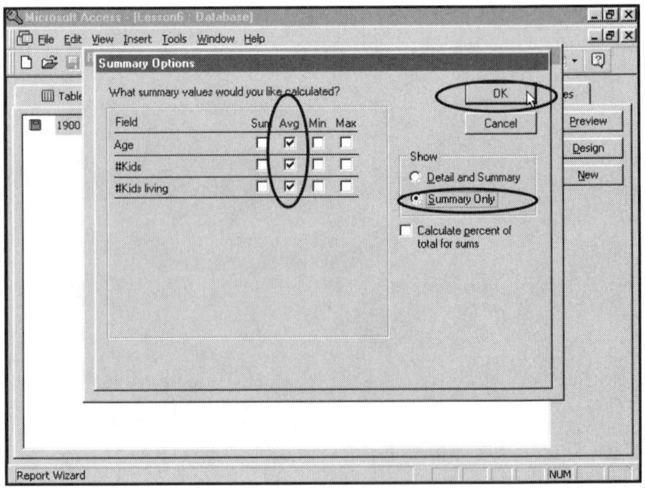


> **Tip for Students**
>
> The only fields that will allow you to use summary options are those that are numeric.

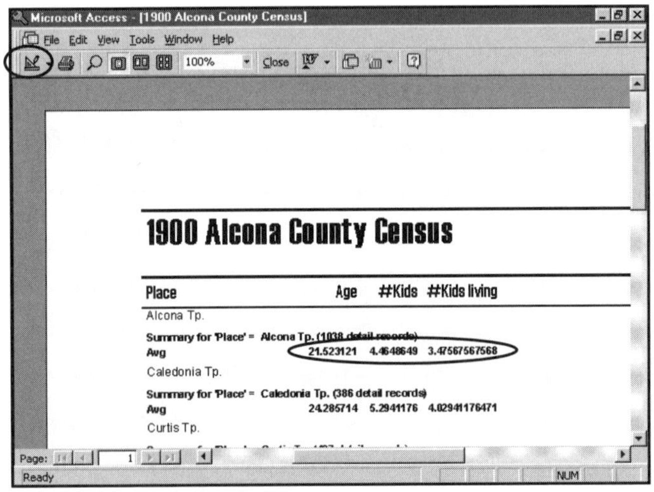


**7** Click **OK** to return to the third **Report Wizard** dialog box, then click **Finish** to accept the default layout and design options. A preview of the report is displayed. Notice that the averages show more than one decimal place.

> **In Depth:** You can continue through the **Report Wizard** to customize the layout and design of your report if you choose. The layout of your report will look different from the one in the figure if the default settings on your computer are different, or if you go through the rest of the Wizard and select another layout.

**8** Click the **View** button to switch to **Design View**. (If necessary close the Toolbox.) In the **Place Footer** section, click the **=Avg(Age)** box, hold down the Shift key, and click **=Avg(#Kids)** and **=Avg(#Kids living)**. All three fields are currently selected.

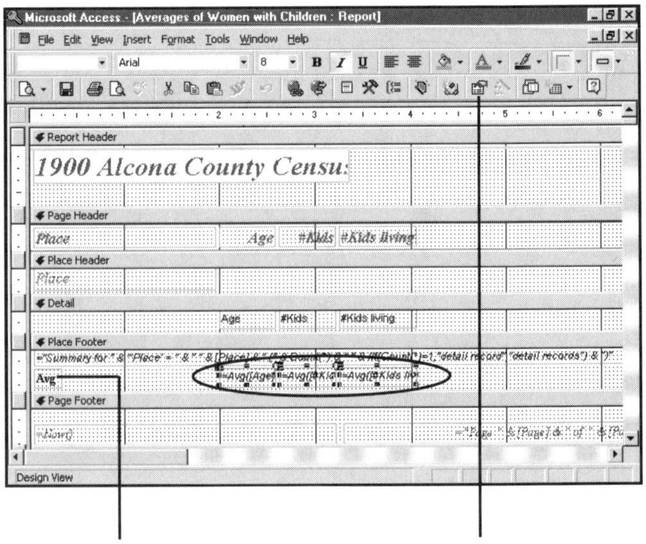


Type of summary

Properties button

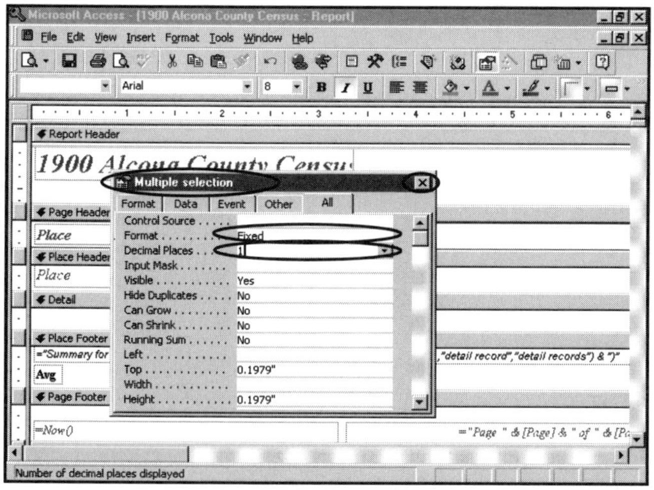


**9** Click the **Properties** button to display the **Multiple selection** properties dialog box. Click in the **Format** box, and click the drop-down arrow. Select **Fixed** for the number type. In the **Decimal Places** box, select **1**, as shown in the figure.

**In Depth:** Each item on a report is known as a control, and can be modified by the use of a Properties box. When you select an item and then click the Properties button, the title bar of the Properties box has the name of the part of the report you have selected. In this case, you selected three controls used to calculate the averages, so the title in the Properties box is *Multiple selection.* If you had selected just one control, the name of that one control would be the title of the Properties box.

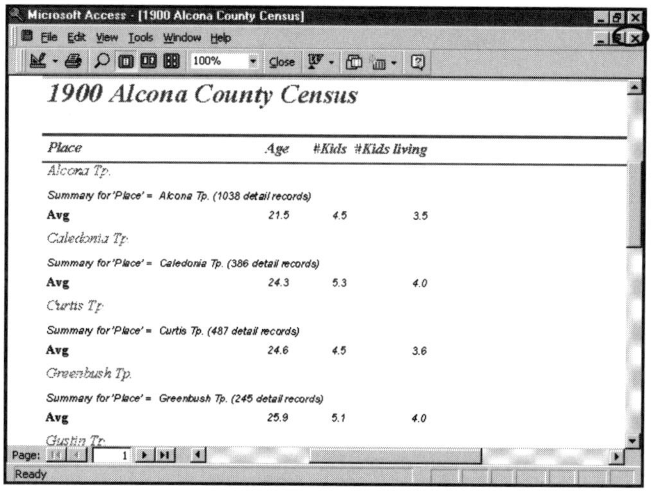


**10** Click the **Close Window** button to return to **Design View**. Click the **Print Preview** button to view your changes. Use the scroll bars to show the maximum information on the screen. Notice that the average woman had five children and lost one. Click the **Print** button to print the report.

**SLIDE 6–5**

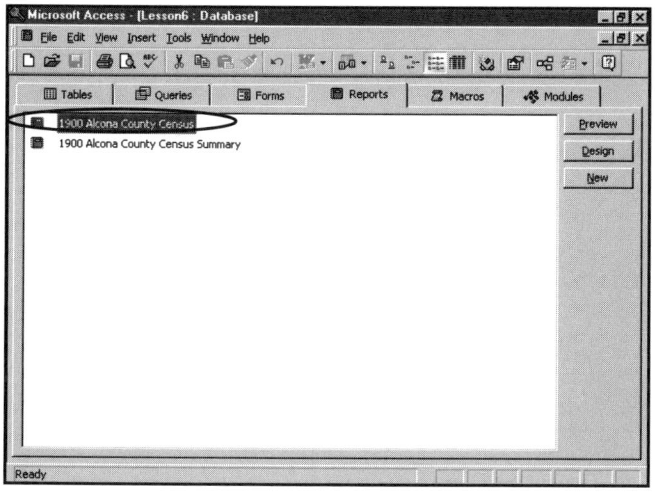


**11** Click the **Close Window** button and choose **Yes** when asked if you want to save your changes.

**12** Select the **1900 Alcona County Census** report that you just created. Choose **Edit**, **Rename**, then type **Averages of Women with Children**. Press Enter to record the name change.

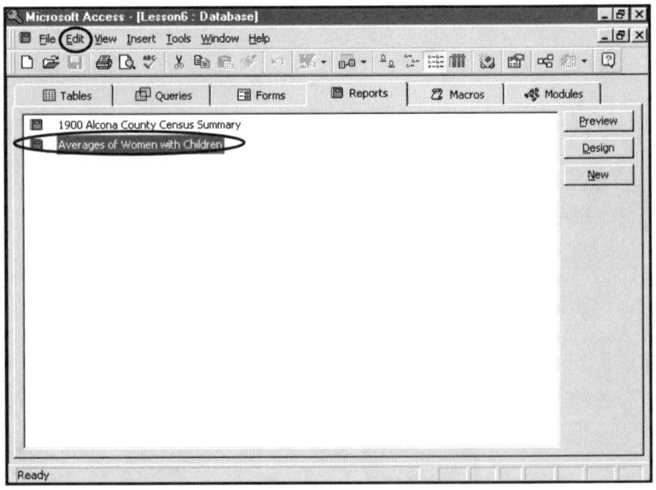


**13** Close your **Lesson 6** database.

# Student Exercises

## True-False

For each of the following, circle T or F to indicate whether the statement is true or false.

(T) F **1.** Data analysis features are included in the tables, queries, forms, and reports functions of Access.

(T) F **2.** The summary data that shows in the intersection of a crosstab query must be numeric

(T) F **3.** A simple crosstab creates a tabular display that shows how one field may be summarized based on two other fields.

T (F) **4.** A multilevel crosstab can summarize one field based on multiple fields as column headings.

T (F) **5.** When editing a query, if you place two criteria in the same Criteria row, a record that meets either criteria is displayed.

(T) F **6.** To determine the average of data in a single field, the Totals button in the query Design View should be used rather than a pivot table.

T (F) **7.** Pivot tables created in Access are edited in Access.

T (F) **8.** When you create a pivot table using the PivotTable Wizard, Access opens Excel at the same time the first dialog box opens.

T (F) **9.** Pivot tables are less flexible to use than crosstab queries.

(T) F **10.** Reports can be used as a data analysis tool because they can group data and display subtotals and totals.

# Identifying Parts of the Access Screens

Refer to the figures and identify the numbered parts of the screen. Write the letter of the correct label in the space next to the number.

1. *D*
2. *E*
3. *C*
4. *B*
5. *A*

**A.** Decimal places
**B.** Number format
**C.** Properties button
**D.** Type of summary
**E.** Field to be summarized

6. *J*
7. *H*
8. *F*
9. *I*
10. *G*

**F.** Field List
**G.** Totals button
**H.** Design grid
**I.** Run button
**J.** Field to be summarized

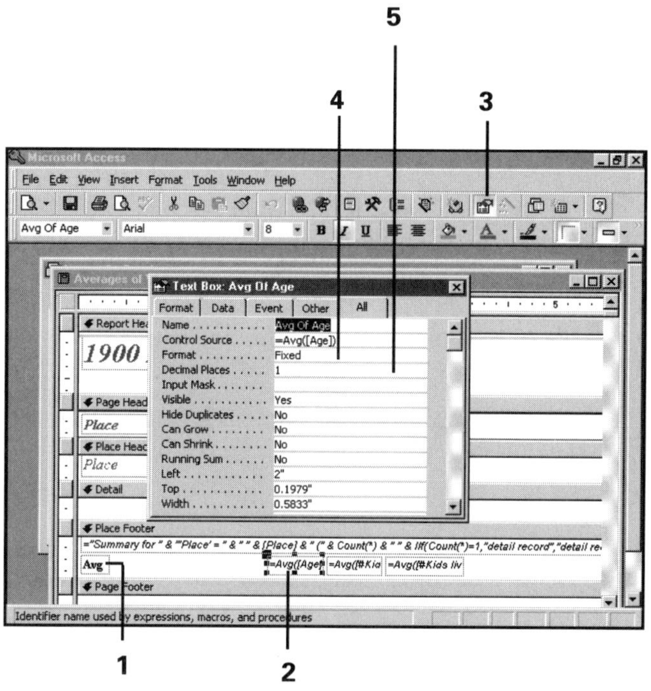


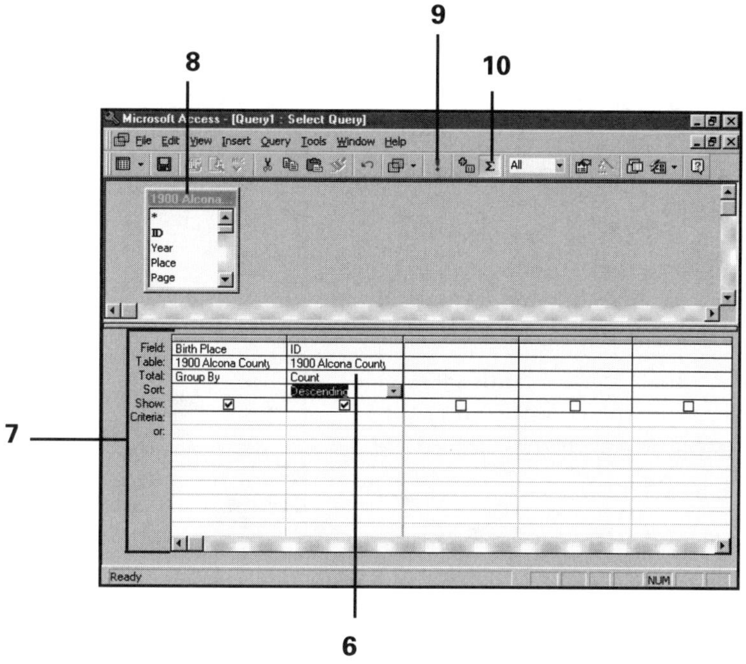

# Matching

Match the statements below to the word or phrase that is the best match from the list. Write the letter of the matching word or phrase in the space provided next to the number.

1. _I_ Where you set number types and decimal places in a report
2. _E_ A query function that groups and summarizes data on multiple fields
3. _A_ Shows the results of a query
4. _J_ Accessed by choosing New from the Forms tab
5. _F_ In the Report Wizard this activates a dialog box to select types of summaries
6. _B_ Determines whether a field is displayed in a query
7. _C_ Must be open when a pivot table is created or edited
8. _H_ Where the crosstab function is found
9. _D_ A type of form that summarizes complex data and performs calculations
10. _K_ Allows you to summarize a single field

**A.** Run button
**B.** Show check box
**C.** Excel spreadsheet
**D.** Pivot table
**E.** Crosstab
**F.** Summary Options button
**G.** Maximize button
**H.** Query tab
**I.** Properties box
**J.** PivotTable Wizard
**K.** Totals button

# Application Exercises

## Exercise 1 – Creating a Simple Crosstab Query

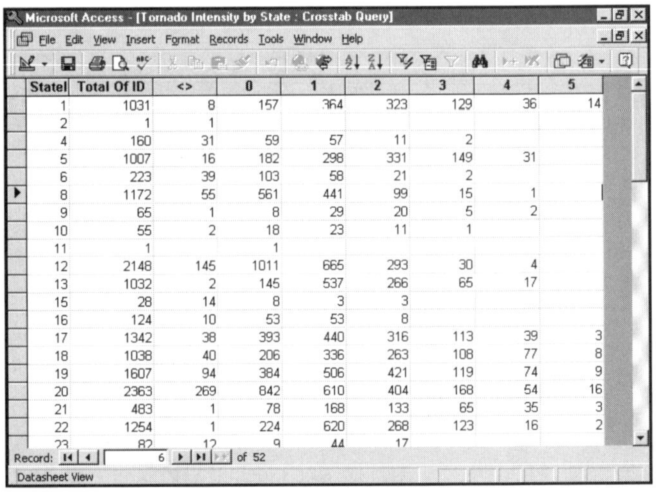


| StateI | Total Of ID | <> | 0 | 1 | 2 | 3 | 4 | 5 |
|---|---|---|---|---|---|---|---|---|
| 1 | 1031 | 8 | 157 | 364 | 323 | 129 | 36 | 14 |
| 2 | 1 | 1 | | | | | | |
| 4 | 160 | 31 | 59 | 57 | 11 | 2 | | |
| 5 | 1007 | 16 | 182 | 298 | 331 | 149 | 31 | |
| 6 | 223 | 39 | 103 | 58 | 21 | 2 | | |
| 8 | 1172 | 55 | 561 | 441 | 99 | 15 | 1 | |
| 9 | 65 | 1 | 8 | 29 | 20 | 5 | 2 | |
| 10 | 55 | 2 | 18 | 23 | 11 | 1 | | |
| 11 | 1 | | 1 | | | | | |
| 12 | 2148 | 145 | 1011 | 665 | 293 | 30 | 4 | |
| 13 | 1032 | 2 | 145 | 537 | 266 | 65 | 17 | |
| 15 | 28 | 14 | 8 | 3 | 3 | | | |
| 16 | 124 | 10 | 53 | 53 | 8 | | | |
| 17 | 1342 | 38 | 393 | 440 | 316 | 113 | 39 | 3 |
| 18 | 1038 | 40 | 206 | 336 | 263 | 108 | 77 | 8 |
| 19 | 1607 | 94 | 384 | 506 | 421 | 119 | 74 | 9 |
| 20 | 2363 | 269 | 842 | 610 | 404 | 168 | 54 | 16 |
| 21 | 483 | 1 | 78 | 168 | 133 | 65 | 35 | 3 |
| 22 | 1254 | 1 | 224 | 620 | 268 | 123 | 16 | 2 |
| 23 | 82 | 12 | 9 | 44 | 17 | | | |

1. Using Windows Explorer, make a copy of **Ex0601** and rename it **Exercise6**. Launch Microsoft Access. Choose **Open an Existing Database**, find the file **Exercise6**, and open the file. This is a smaller version of the tornado database you used in Lesson 4.
2. Use the skills that you have learned in this lesson to create a simple crosstab query as shown in the figure. See the steps below for more detail.
3. Click the **Queries** tab to select it.
4. Click the **New** button and select **Crosstab Query Wizard**.
5. Select the **Tornadoes** table.
6. Select the **StateID** field for the row heading.

7. Select the **FScale** (the measure of a tornado's intensity) field as the column heading.
8. Select the **Count** function to count the **ID** field.
9. Name the query Tornado Intensity by State.
10. View the query. Adjust the columns widths so you can view all of the columns on screen. (Check StateID 48 to make sure the data has not changed to scientific notation. Readjust the column width if necessary to show the full number.) The results in the column labeled <> represent tornadoes that were not rated. This a notation for not equal.
11. Choose **File, Print.** Close the query, saving your changes when prompted.

## Exercise 2 – Creating a Multilevel Crosstab Query

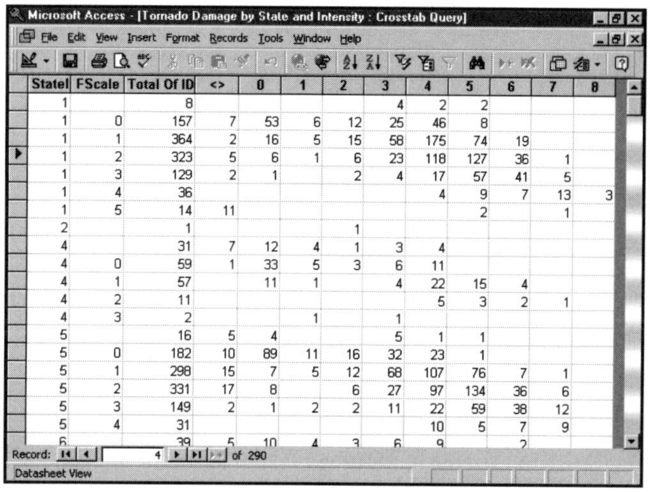


| StateI | FScale | Total Of ID | <> | 0 | 1 | 2 | 3 | 4 | 5 | 6 | 7 | 8 |
|---|---|---|---|---|---|---|---|---|---|---|---|---|
| 1 | | 8 | | | | | 4 | 2 | 2 | | | |
| 1 | 0 | 157 | 7 | 53 | 6 | 12 | 25 | 46 | 8 | | | |
| 1 | 1 | 364 | 2 | 16 | 5 | 15 | 58 | 175 | 74 | 19 | | |
| 1 | 2 | 323 | 5 | 6 | 1 | 6 | 23 | 118 | 127 | 36 | 1 | |
| 1 | 3 | 129 | 2 | 1 | | 2 | 4 | 17 | 57 | 41 | 5 | |
| 1 | 4 | 36 | | | | | | 4 | 9 | 7 | 13 | 3 |
| 1 | 5 | 14 | 11 | | | | | | 2 | | 1 | |
| 2 | | 1 | | | | 1 | | | | | | |
| 4 | | 31 | 7 | 12 | 4 | 1 | 3 | 4 | | | | |
| 4 | 0 | 59 | 1 | 33 | 5 | 3 | 6 | 11 | | | | |
| 4 | 1 | 57 | | 11 | 1 | | 4 | 22 | 15 | 4 | | |
| 4 | 2 | 11 | | | | | | 5 | 3 | 2 | 1 | |
| 4 | 3 | 2 | | | 1 | | 1 | | | | | |
| 5 | | 16 | 5 | 4 | | | 5 | 1 | 1 | | | |
| 5 | 0 | 182 | 10 | 89 | 11 | 16 | 32 | 23 | 1 | | | |
| 5 | 1 | 298 | 15 | 7 | 5 | 12 | 68 | 107 | 76 | 7 | 1 | |
| 5 | 2 | 331 | 17 | 8 | | 6 | 27 | 97 | 134 | 36 | 6 | |
| 5 | 3 | 149 | 2 | 1 | 2 | 2 | 11 | 22 | 59 | 38 | 12 | |
| 5 | 4 | 31 | | | | | | 10 | 5 | 7 | 9 | |
| 6 | | 39 | 5 | 10 | 4 | 3 | 6 | 9 | | 2 | | |

1. Use the skills that you have learned in this lesson to create a multilevel Crosstab query as shown in the figure. See the steps below for more detail.
2. Make sure the **Queries** tab is selected.
3. Select the **New** option and select the **Crosstab Query Wizard**.
4. Select the **Tornadoes** table.
5. Select the **StateID** field for the row heading, then select the **FScale** field as the subheading for the StateID field.
6. Select the **Damage** field for the column heading. (The damage ratings go from minor damage at the lower end of the scale to millions of dollars of damage in the 7 and 8 categories.)
7. Select the **Count** function to count the **ID** field.
8. Name the query Tornado Damage by State and Intensity.
9. View the query. For each **StateID** the intensity scale is listed in the second column. Notice that not all states had tornadoes at all levels of intensity. The third column is the total of each category of intensity by state. The data under the columns labeled <> (not equal) through **8** is the number of tornadoes in each range of monetary damage. For example, in State #1 (Alabama), Fscale 4, there were a total of 36 tornadoes, and all of them had a monetary damage rating of 4 or higher.

The amount of monetary damage for each tornado is a code representing a range of damage as follows:

| | |
|---|---|
| 0 | No damage |
| 1 | Less than $50 |
| 2 | $50 to $500 |
| 3 | $500 to $5,000 |
| 4 | $5,000 to $50,000 |
| 5 | $50,000 to $500,000 |
| 6 | $500,000 to $5 million |
| 7 | $5 million to $50 million |
| 8 | $50 million to $500 million |
| 9 | $500 million to $5 billion |

10. Adjust the columns widths so you can view all of the columns on the screen. Scroll through the query to make sure figures have not changed to scientific notation. Readjust the column width as necessary.

11. Choose **File**, **Print**. Print one page of the query. Save the query and leave it open to use in the next exercise.

## Exercise 3 – Editing a Crosstab Query

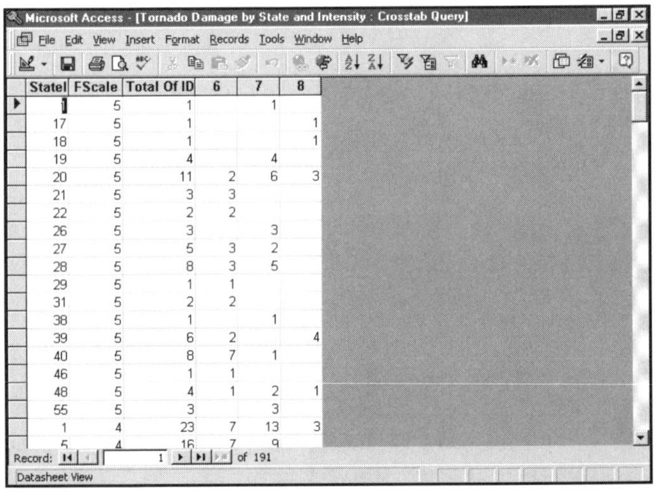


1. Use the skills that you have learned in this lesson to edit a multilevel crosstab query as shown in the figure. See the steps below for more detail.

2. Click the **View** button to change to Design View of the **Tornado Damage by State and Intensity** query.

3. Sort the **FScale** field in **descending** order.

4. Run the crosstab query to view the results of your edits.

5. Choose **File**, **Print**. Print the first page of the query. Close the query, saving your changes when prompted.

## Exercise 4 – Using the Totals Function in a Query

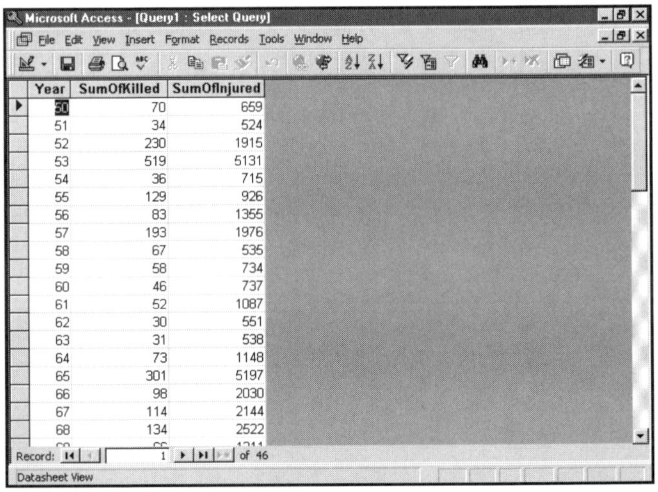


1. Use the skills that you have learned in this lesson to create a query that uses the **Totals** function.

2. If necessary, click the **Queries** tab to select it.

3. Click the **New** button and select **Design View**.

4. **Add** the **Tornadoes** table.

5. Add the **Year**, **Killed**, and **Injured** fields into the design grid.

6. Click the **Totals** button to add a Totals row.
7. Select the **Sum** function in the **Totals** row for the **Killed** and the **Injured** fields.
8. Run the query to see the number of people killed and injured by tornadoes in the U.S. by year.
9. Choose File, Print.
10. Close the query and name it **Tornado Casualties by Year**.

# Exercise 5 – Grouping Data and Displaying Totals in a Report

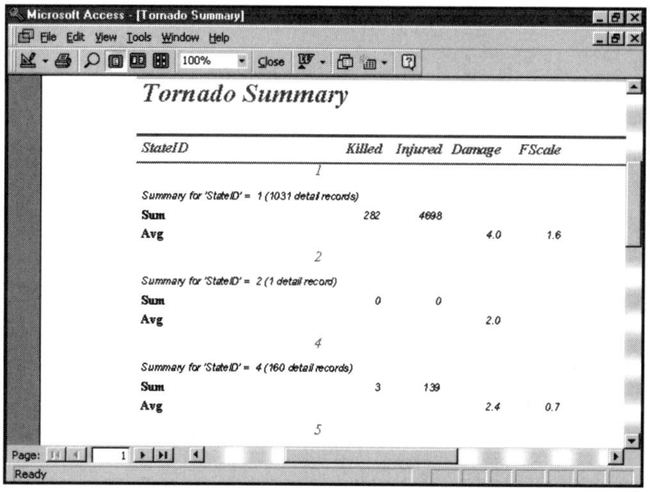


1. Use the skills that you have learned in this lesson to group and summarize data using the report summary.
2. Click the **Reports** tab to select it.
3. Click the **New** button. Choose Report Wizard and select the Tornadoes table as the source of data for this report.
4. Select the **StateID**, **Killed**, **Injured**, **Damage**, and **FScale** fields.
5. Group on the **StateID** field.
6. Click the **Summary Options** button.
7. Select the **Sum** function for the **Killed** and the **Injured** fields.
8. Select the **Avg** function for the **Damage** and the **FScale** fields.
9. Select the **Summary Only** option. Click **OK.** (Sorting is unnecessary.)
10. Accept the default layout, orientation, and style options.
11. Name the report **Tornado Summary** and preview the report.
12. Move to Design View and select both the **=Avg(Damage)** and **=Avg(FScale)** fields.
13. Click the **Properties** button and change the **Format** to a **Fixed** number and the **Decimal Places** to **1**.
14. Preview the report.
15. Choose File, Print. Print the first page of the report.
16. Close the report and save your changes. Exit Access.

# Lesson 7

## Connecting to Other Types of Files and Getting Help

**Task 1** Linking an Access Table to a Word Document

**Task 2** Merging an Access Table with a Word Document

**Task 3** Importing a Table from Excel

**Task 4** Importing Tables from Other Database Programs

**Task 5** Adding Hyperlinks to the Database

**Task 6** Getting Help Using the Office Assistant

**Task 7** Getting Help On the Internet

**Task 8** Finding Reference Books and Self-Help Textbooks

# Introduction

Your database does not exist by itself. As you have seen, the data may come from somewhere else, as in the case of the Tornado database which was obtained over the Internet from the U.S. Weather Bureau. Likewise, the reports, queries, and forms you create may need to be seen by others. In Lesson 5 you saw that you can import other Access tables or link to other Access tables. Access also has several powerful tools that you can use to share your database by importing information from a spreadsheet or document. The files you link to may be on your computer or on a computer anywhere in the world over the Internet. You can also use this ability to connect to other files to get help. There is help available from the files stored in your computer as well as from Microsoft's Internet site.

In this lesson, you learn how to use this connectivity to share the results of your work, and to get help when you need it.

**Tip for Instructors**

The Learn on Demand Module that applies to Lesson 7 is found in the Connecting to Other Types of Files and Getting Help subfolder of Learn Access 97.

**On Your Mark**

Today's world revolves around sharing data. What are some ways you would like to connect your database to other data?

## Visual Summary

When you have completed this lesson, you will have created a document that merges data from a table of addresses, imported a table of data from a non-Access source, and found help on the Internet. The merged document and the imported table look like this:

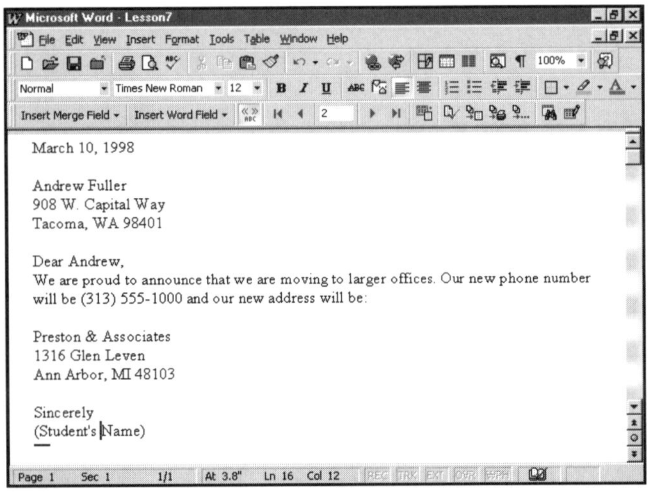


**SLIDE 7–1**

**SLIDE 7–2**

**Lesson Time**
**60 minutes**

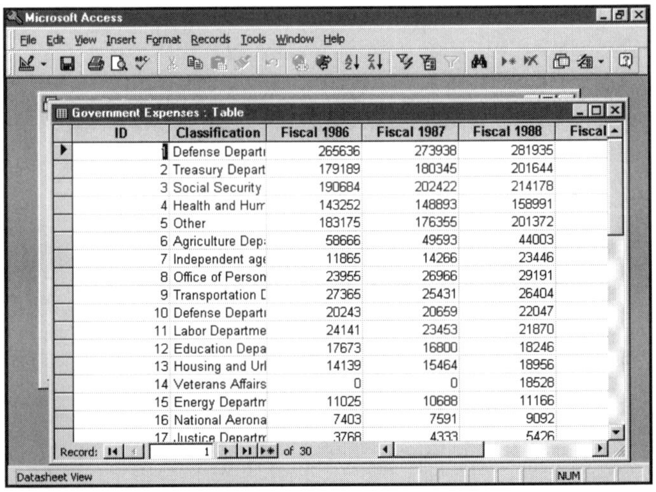

# Task 1

## Linking an Access Table to a Word Document

### Why would I do this?

Databases that contain names and addresses can be merged with Microsoft Word documents to create a series of documents where each document contains data that is unique to that individual. We have all received mail that has a label attached with our names and addresses on it, and most of us have received letters that have our names, birthdays, addresses, or phone numbers imbedded in the text. These are examples of how an organization can communicate with its members. Such mailings are not limited to the postal service; you can also create mailings that use FAX or e-mail.

In this task, you learn how to create a letter to notify your business associates that you are moving and will have a new address and phone number.

**1** Find the **Less0701** database and rename it **Lesson7**. Launch Access and open **Lesson7**. The Addresses database table contains five records and is similar to the table you created in **Lesson 1**.

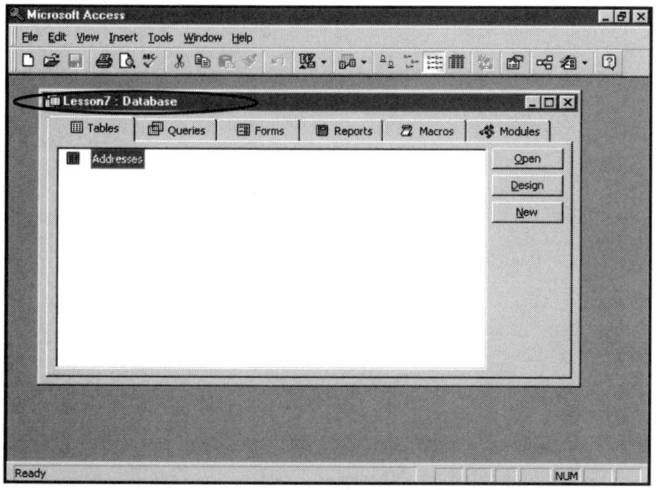


**Tip for Instructors**

The Learn on Demand Module/Lesson "Linking an Access Table to a Word Document" applies to this task.

**On Your Mark**

The first place you may need to share data is within your own computer or LAN. What types of connections would be useful to minimize your workload?

**2** If it is not already highlighted, select the **Addresses** table and click the list arrow to the right of the **Office Links** button on the Standard toolbar.

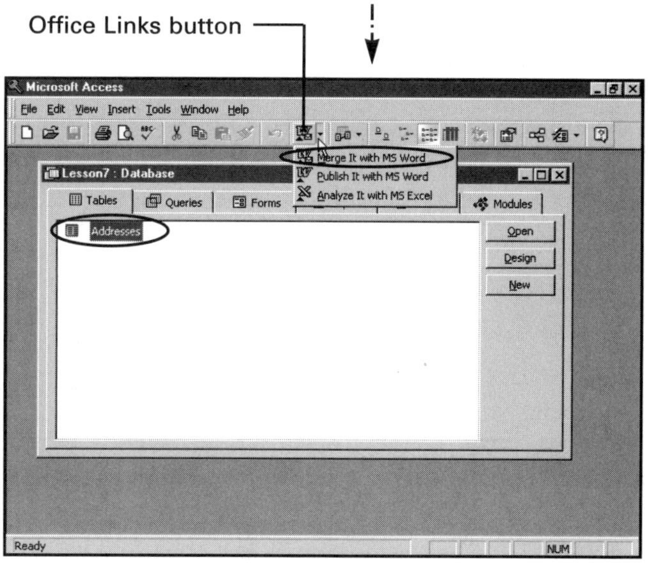


**Tip for Instructors**

A good example of a database used to merge into a word processing document is junk mail. Ask your students how many of them have received a letter that says they, specifically by name, may be the next sweepstake winner. These letters are typed as one letter and then merged into a large database to produce millions of copies.

**3** Click **Merge It with MS Word**. The **Microsoft Word Mail Merge Wizard** window opens.

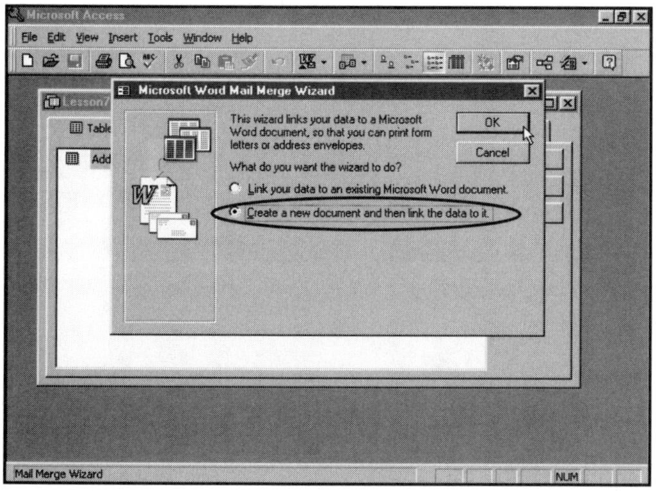

**4** Click **<u>C</u>reate a new document and then link the data to it**. Click **OK**. Microsoft Word launches and a new document opens. Notice that the Mail Merge toolbar is displayed.

**Tip for Students**

You can also perform a merge beginning in Word. Simply use the Mail Merge option. When you get the data source, choose the appropriate database file. You will then be able to choose a table or query to merge with.

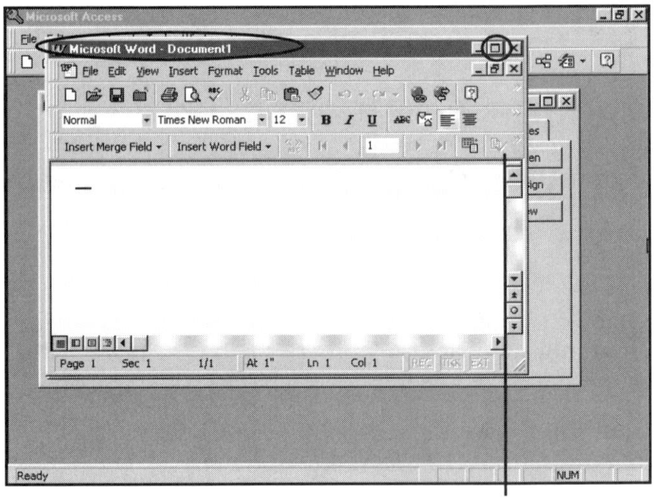

Mail Merge toolbar

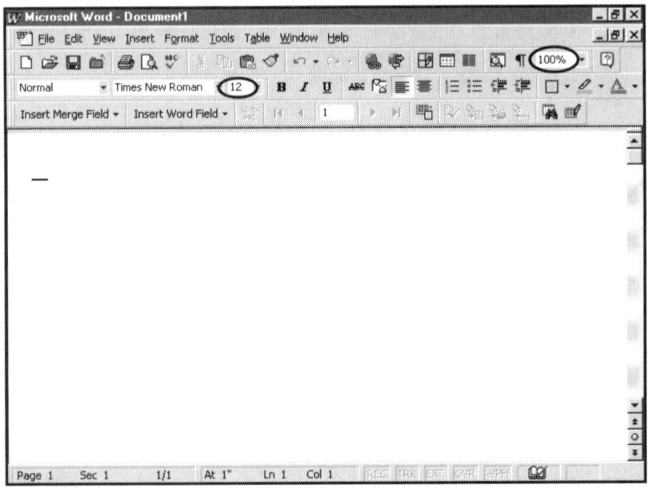

**5** Maximize the **Word** window, change the Zoom to **100%**, and set the Font Size to **12**, as shown.

**Pothole:** The Mail Merge toolbar should open. It may be above or below the Formatting or Standard toolbar. If it does not open, you can open it by choosing **<u>V</u>iew**, **<u>T</u>oolbars** from the menu and then clicking **Mail Merge**.

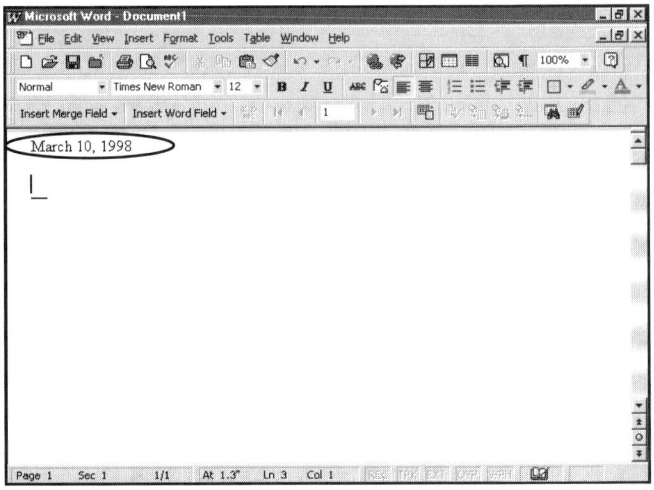

**Quick Tip:** Notice that when you begin typing the date, Word automatically suggests the month, then the date. If you press ↵Enter twice, once to accept the month and the next time to accept the rest of the date, the date will be completed for you.

**6** Type today's date in the first line and press ↵Enter twice.

**7** Click the **Insert Merge Field** button on the **Mail Merge** toolbar. A list of fields from the **Addresses** table in the **Lesson7** database is displayed.

**SLIDE 7–3**

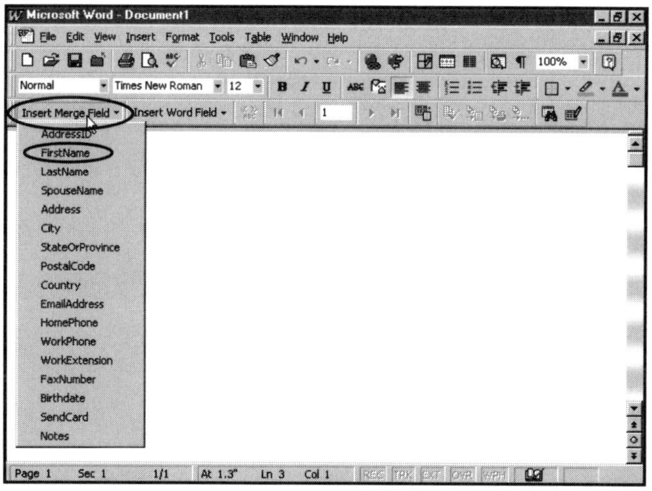


**8** Click **FirstName**. The name of the field is placed in the document.

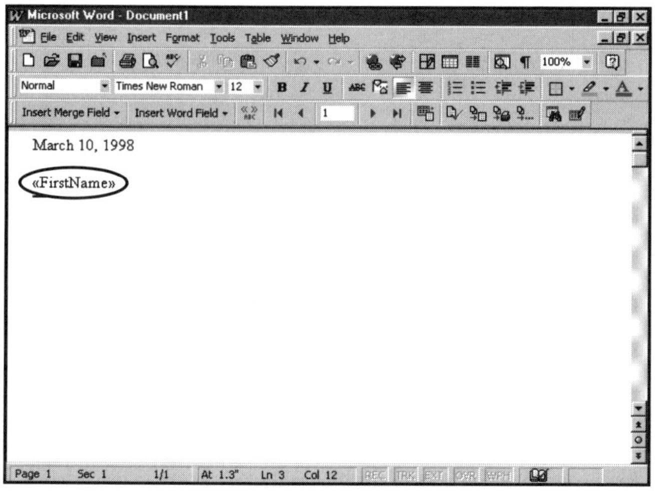


**Quicksand**

Take care to space out the merge codes, just as you would if you were typing the actual data. If you must correct any errors, be careful not to erase any of the code.

**9** Press Spacebar to enter a blank space after the first name. Click the **Insert Merge Field** button again and click **LastName**.

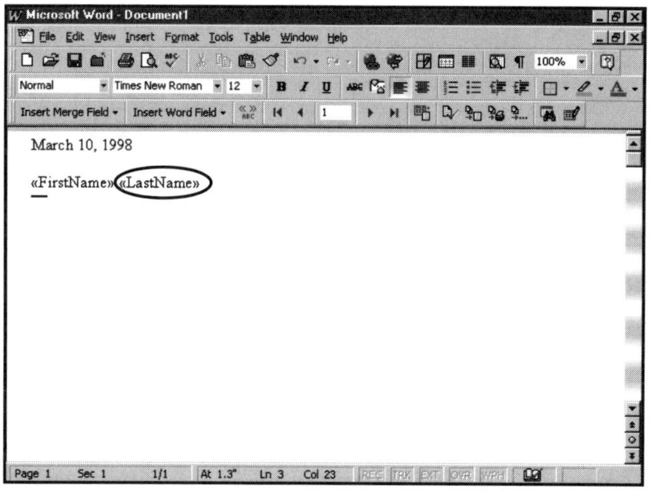


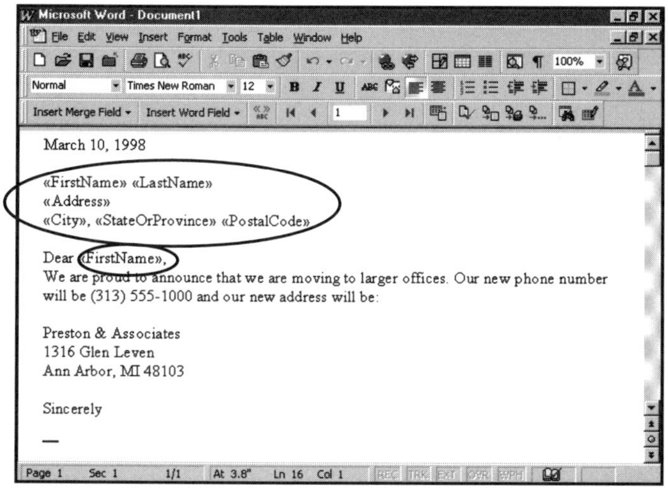


**Quicksand**

Spacing will pose a problem for some students. Careful observation is advised.

**Quicksand**

Close the **Office Assistant** if it opens.

**10** Press Enter to move to the next line of the address. Refer to the figure to create the rest of the document. Insert the fields as shown. (If the Office Assistant pops up during this process, click **Cancel** to close it.)

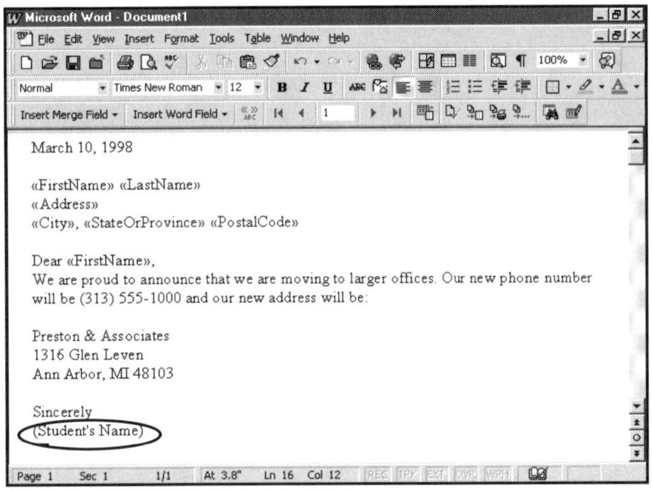


**11** Type your name in the last line.

**Pothole:** The font size on your letter may revert to 10 or whatever default font is set for your computer. If this happens, don't worry about it. The goal of this task is to show you how to merge a database file with a word document and the formatting of the letter is not critical to this purpose.

**12** Click the **Save** button. The **Save As** window opens.

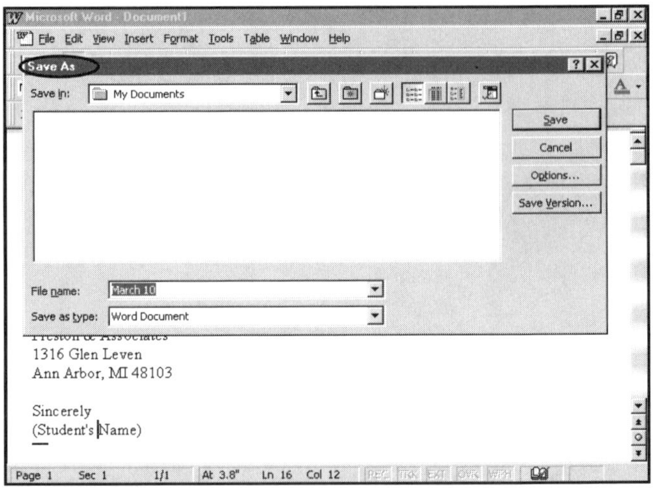


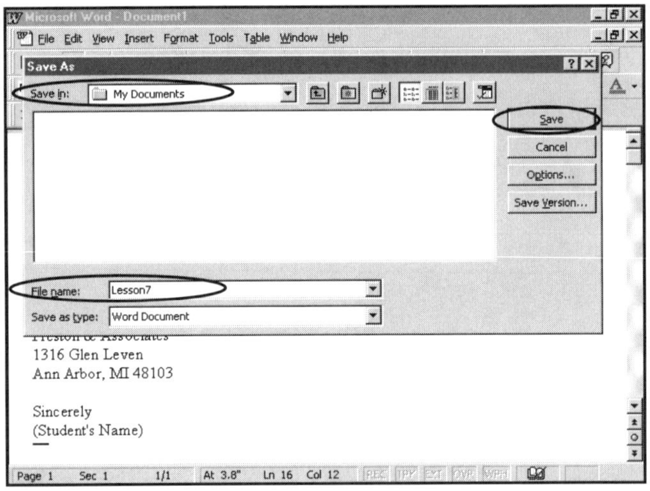


**13** Type **Lesson7** in the **File name** box and use the **Save in** box to select the folder that you are using for your files.

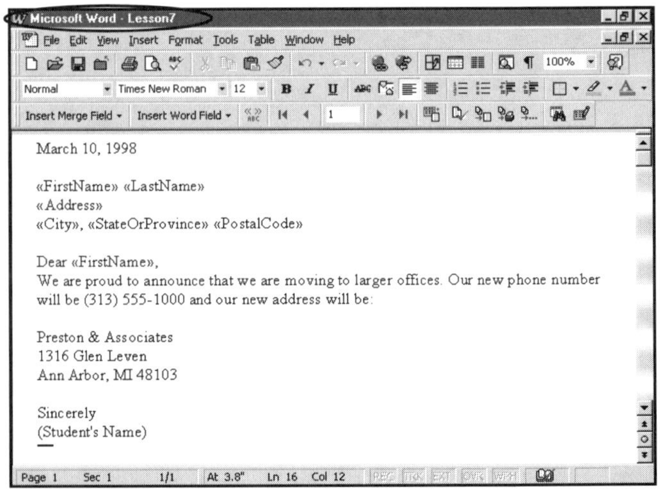


**14** Click **Save**. The document is saved as **Lesson7** for later use.

# Task 2

> **Tip for Instructors**
> The Learn on Demand Module/Lesson "Merging an Access Table with a Word Document" applies to this task.

## Merging an Access Table with a Word Document

### Why would I do this?

Once you have linked the database field names to a Word document, you can easily create a personalized letter to each person in the database. This process creates a file of the merged, personalized letters that you can use as a record to document that the letter was mailed. It is important to test your document with the data before you try to print large quantities, to ensure that the letter looks the way you intended.

In this task, you learn how to merge the database file into the letter, then review the document on screen and print the first two letters.

View Merged Data button

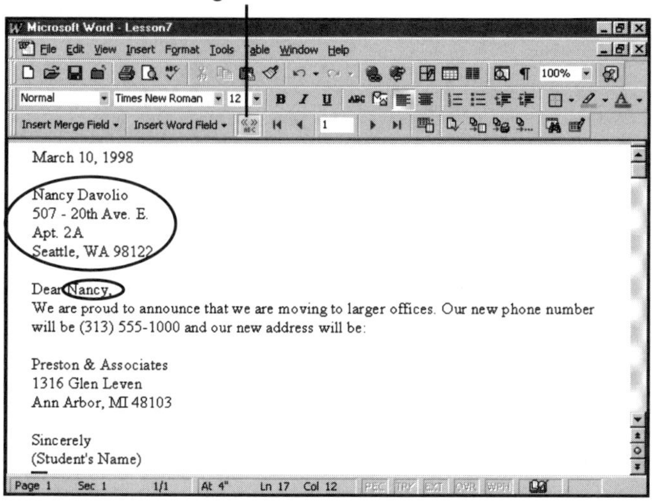


**1** Click the **View Merged Data** button. The data from the first record in the **Addresses** table is inserted into the document.

> **Concept**
> After a merge document has been created, it can be merged as many times as needed.

**2** Click the **Next Record** button. The data from the second record is displayed.

> **On Your Mark**
> How many pre-approved credit card applications have you received? How many sales letters that were addressed to you and the letter actually had your name on it? These were not typed separately; they were generated with a database and a word processor. What applications exist for which you could use this capability?

Mail Merge button

Next Record button

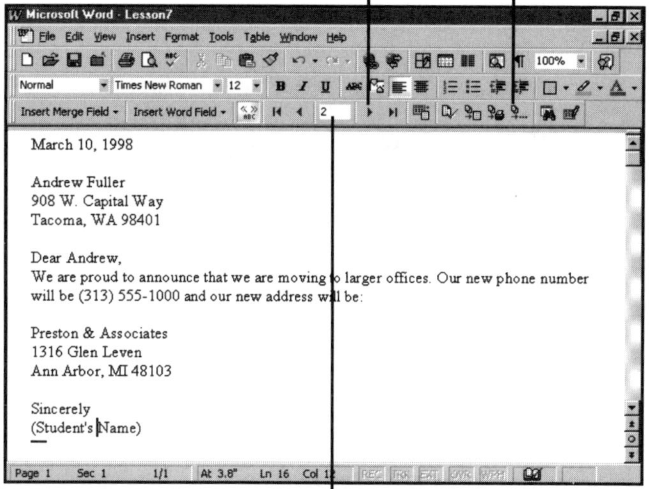


Record Number

> **In Depth:** Notice that the address of the first person takes two lines, while the second person's address takes only one line. Word adjusts for multiple line addresses and for empty fields.

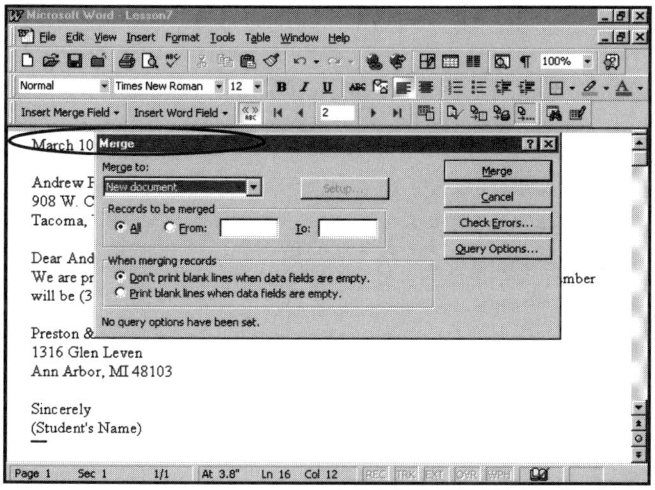


> **Tip for Students**
> If you discover an error in formatting after viewing the merge, you can edit the letter before actually merging.

**3** Click the **Mail Merge** button. The **Merge** dialog box opens.

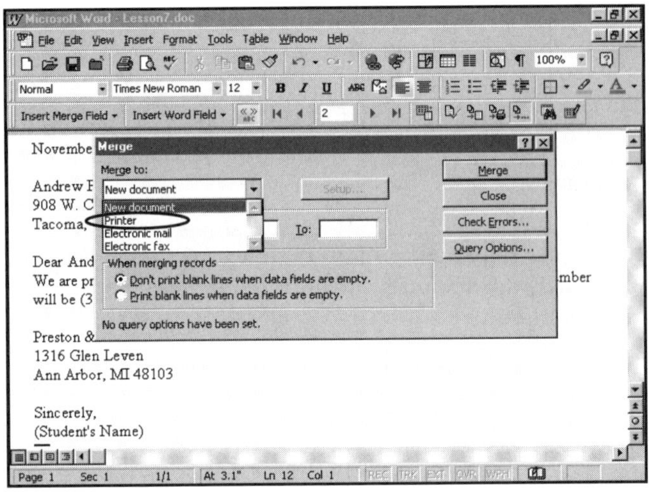


**4** Click the list arrow next to the **Merge to** box. Notice that you can send this letter electronically by e-mail or FAX. Click **Printer**.

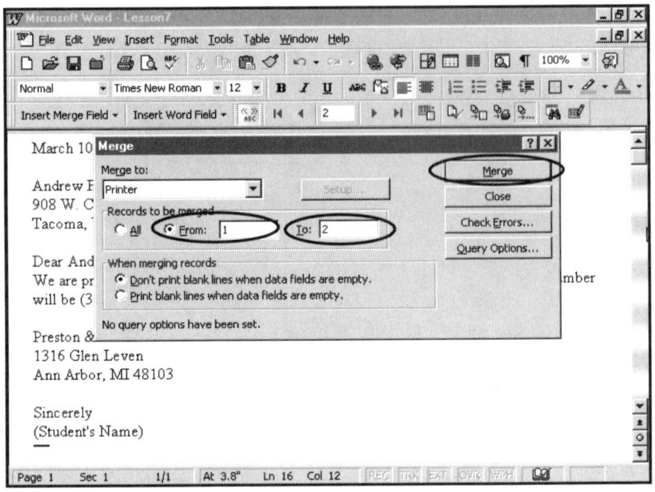


**5** Click the **From:** box in the **Records to be merged** section and type **1**. Type **2** in the **To:** box.

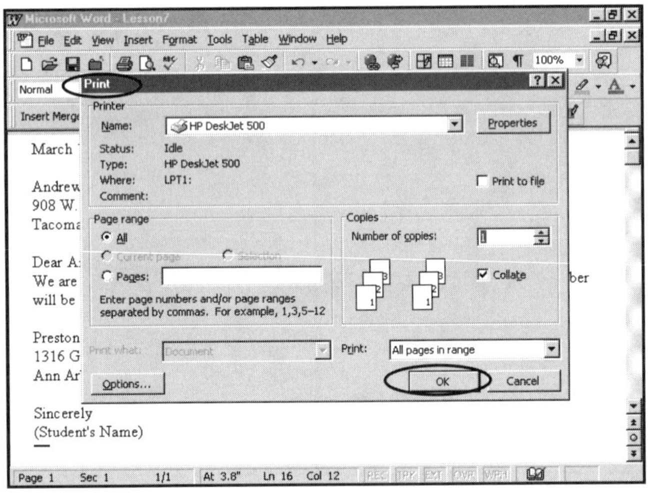


**6** Click the **Merge** button to print the letters to the first two people in the **Addresses** table. The **Print** dialog box opens.

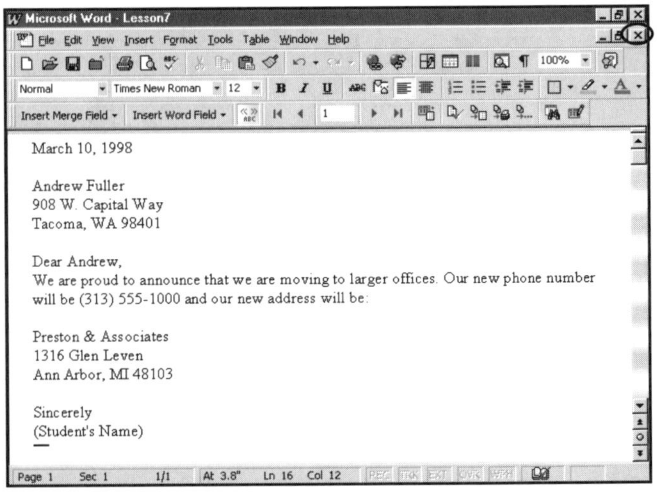


**7** Click **OK** to print the first two letters.

**8** Close the **Lesson7 Word** document. Save any changes when prompted. Close **Microsoft Word**. Leave the **Lesson7 Access** database open for use in the next task.

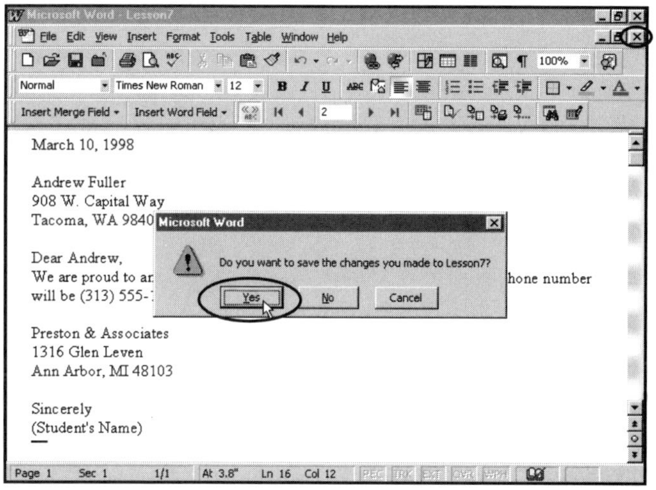


**Q & A**

*Question:* What are the advantages of merging between Word and Access? *Answer:* You can save valuable time by not retyping specific data in many copies of the same Word document; the database can be used in more than one Word document.

# Task 3

## Importing a Table from Excel

**Tip for Instructors**

The Learn on Demand Module/Lesson, "Importing a Table from Excel" applies to this task.

### Why would I do this?

Excel has some database management features such as the ability to sort and filter data. Therefore, many people use Excel as a crude database management program. There will be a time when you need to import data that is stored in an Excel spreadsheet and use it with an Access database.

In this task, you learn how to import an Excel spreadsheet that contains budget information for the U.S. government into the Lesson7 Access database that is open from the previous task. The Lesson7 database is used simply as an example of a how to import data from various sources. The information being imported in the next three tasks is not related to the address table in the database. The open database is used for convenience to demonstrate how to import different sources of information.

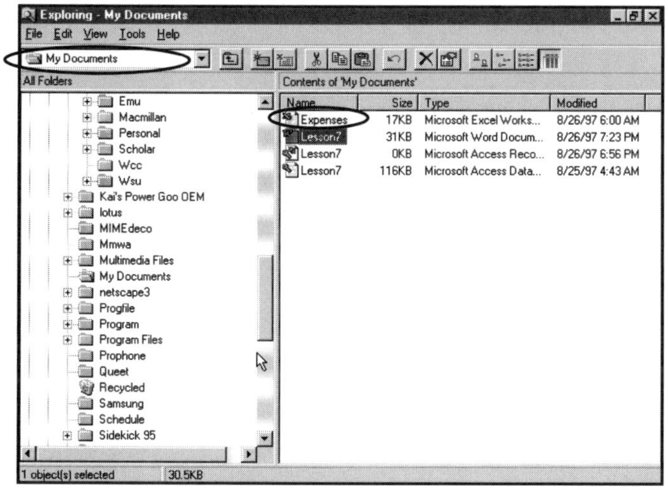


**1** Use Windows Explorer to make a copy of the file **Less0702** and name the copy <u>**Expenses**</u>.

**On Your Mark**

In an earlier lesson, you learned how to obtain database files from other databases. What other programs, besides database programs, have information that you need?

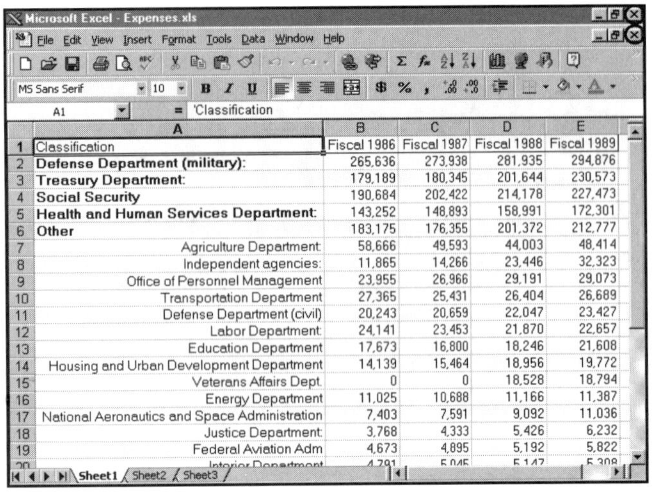


**2** Double-click on the **Expenses** filename to launch Excel and open the file. Scroll the file and examine the data. Notice that each row is a record of a type of government expense. The column headings will become field names. Click the **Close** button to close the file and close Excel.

> **Tip for Students** !
> Before you can use a spreadsheet as a database file, it must be in the database format. In other words, each row represents a record and each column represents a field, like the table view. The first row will become the field names.

**3** Switch to **Access** and the **Lesson7** database.

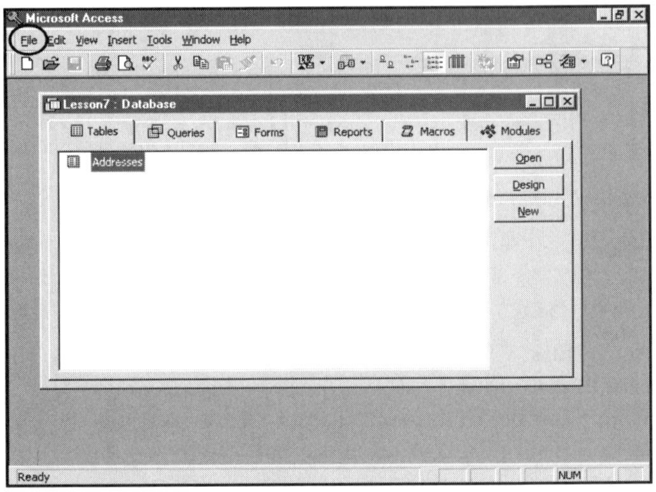


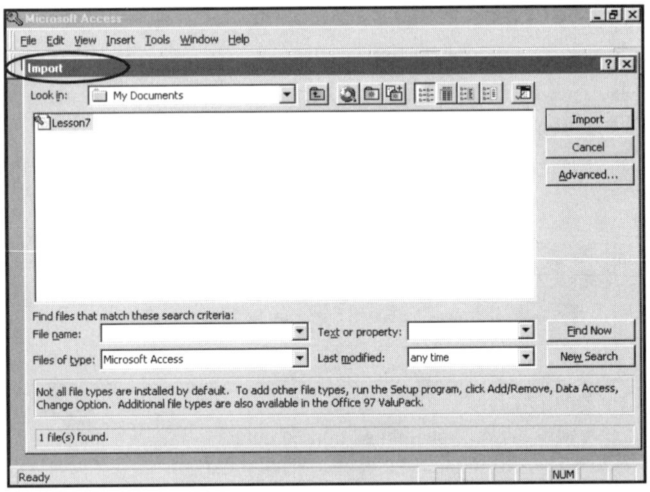


**4** Choose **File**, **Get External Data**, **Import**. The **Import** dialog box opens.

> **Quicksand**
> It might be necessary to explain the **Files of Type** drop-down list box. A brief explanation of the different file types might be helpful.

**SLIDE 7–4**

**5** Click the **list arrow** next to the **Files of type** box and select **Microsoft Excel**.

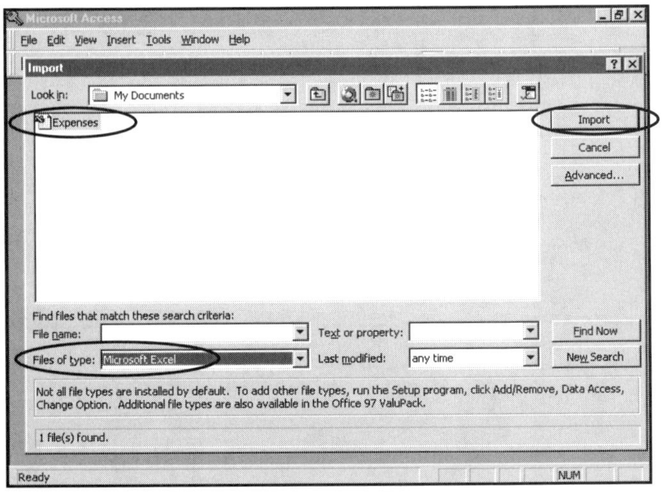

**6** Click the **Expenses** file and then click the **Import** button. The **Import Spreadsheet Wizard** dialog box opens.

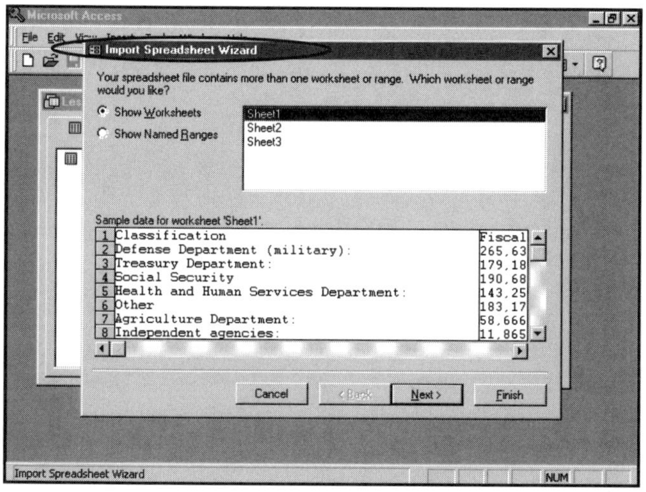


**7** Make sure the **Show Worksheets** option is selected and that **Sheet1** is highlighted.

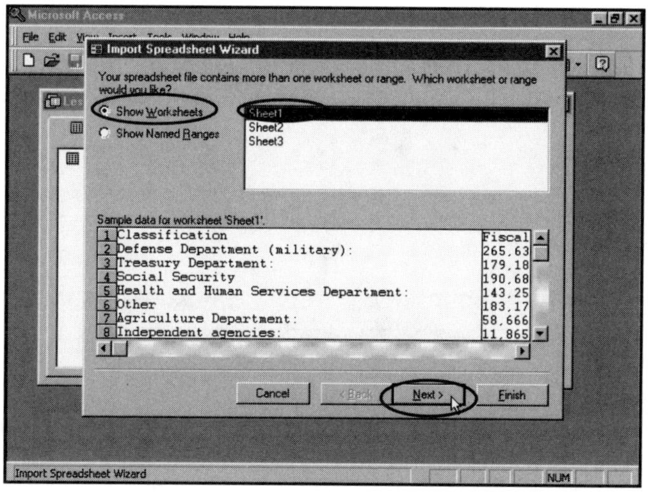


**In Depth:** A spreadsheet must be set up like a database table, if you are going to import it successfully. Check to make sure that the Excel data is arranged in rows and columns where each column is a field type and each row is a record. If necessary, copy the data to a new spreadsheet. Remove blank rows or rows that contain decorative characters such as dashes, colons, exclamation points, or other non- numeric or non-alpha characters.

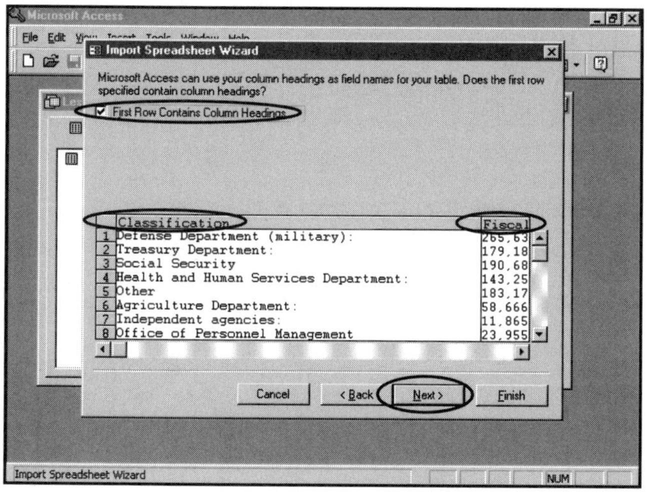


**8** Click **Next**. Click the check box next to **First Row Contains Column Headings**. Notice how the row that contains the words **Classification** and **Fiscal** are converted to headers.

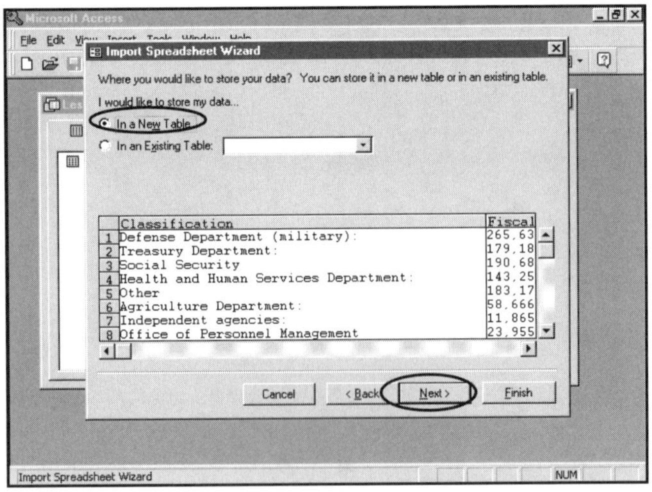


**9** Click <u>N</u>ext. Make sure that the **In a New Table** option is selected.

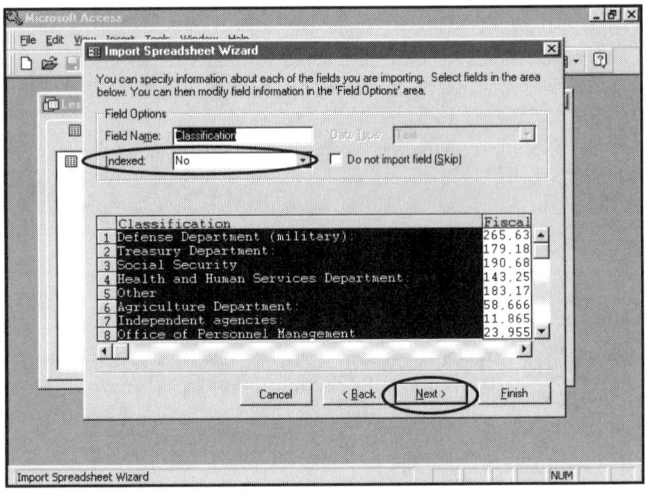


**10** Click <u>N</u>ext. Do not add indexes to any of the fields.

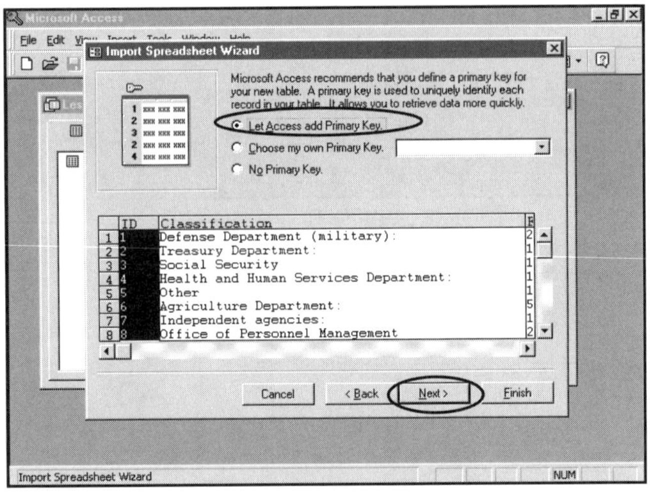


**11** Click <u>N</u>ext. Select **Let <u>A</u>ccess add Primary Key**, if it is not already selected. In this case, there are no unique fields so we can let Access add a field that gives each row a unique number.

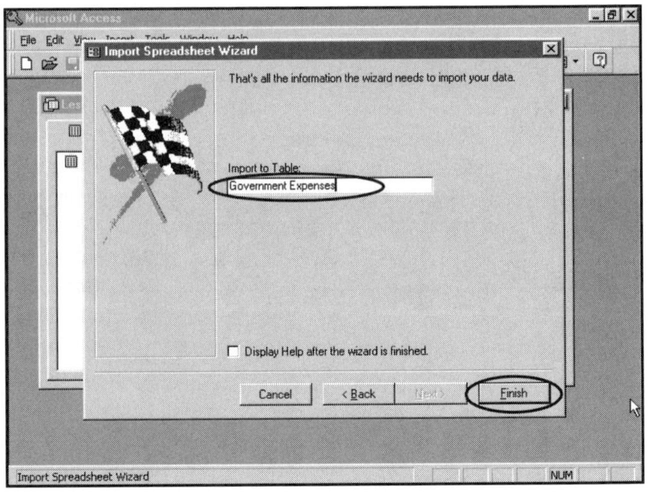


**12** Click <u>N</u>ext. Type <u>**Government Expenses**</u> in the **Import to Table:** box.

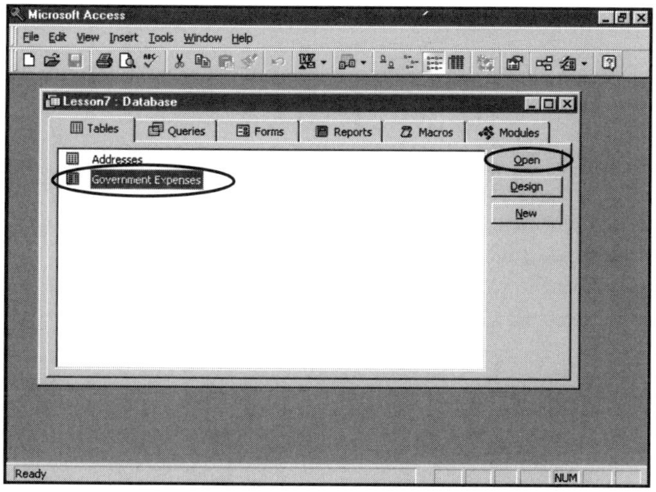


**13** Click **Finish**. Click **OK** when prompted. The **Government Expenses** data is added to the database as a new table.

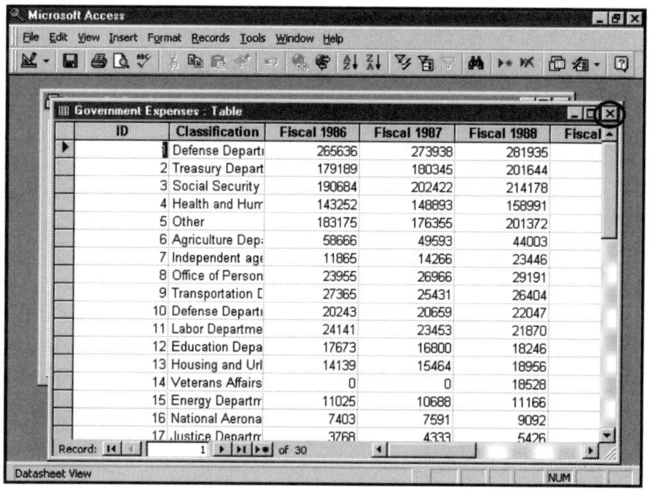


**14** Click the **Open** button. The **Government Expenses** table opens.

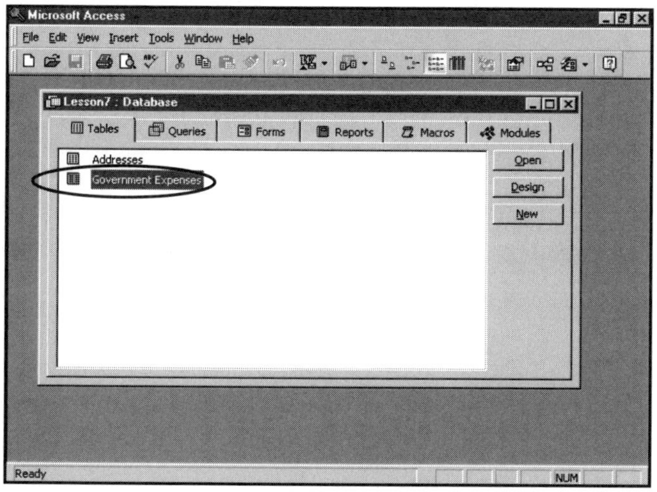


**Q & A** ?

*Question:* How must a spreadsheet be set up before it can be imported into a database? *Answer:* Each row as a record, each column as a field, and the first row as field names.

**15** Click the **Close Window** button. This table is now available for use. Leave the **Lesson7** database open for the next task.

# Task 4

## Importing Tables from Other Database Programs

### Why would I do this?

Importing a table from another personal computer database management program, such as dBASE or FoxPro, is similar to importing a spreadsheet from Excel. If the data is stored in a format that is not directly supported by Access, you can still import the table after you have saved it as a text file. Most database management programs, including most mainframe database programs, can save a table as a text file.

In this task, you learn how to import a table that has already been saved as a text file for you.

**1** Make a copy of the file **Less0703** and name the copy **Parts**.

> **On Your Mark**
> Although Access is one of the newest database programs available, other databases have been used for a very long time. How can you retrieve data that exist in a different database?

> **Tip for Instructors**
> The Learn on Demand Module/Lesson, "Importing Tables from Other Database Programs" applies to this task.

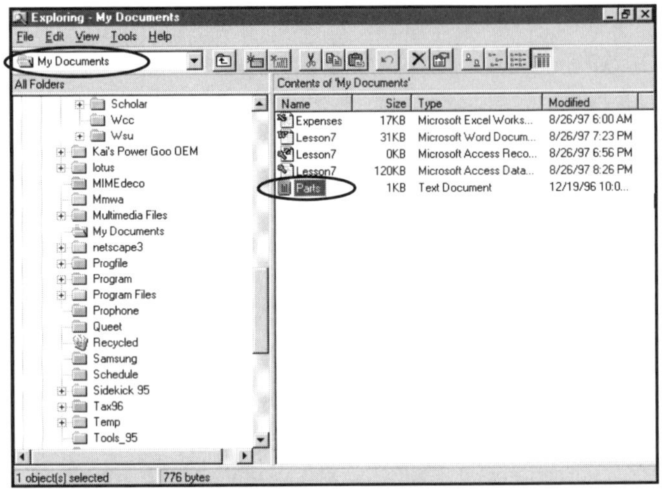


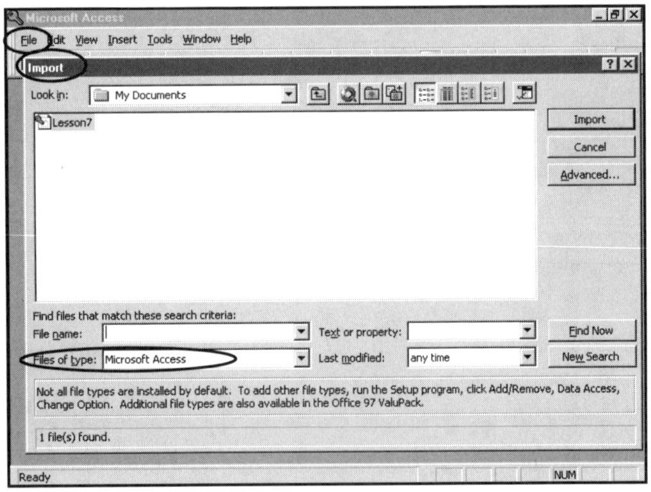


**2** Switch to Access and the **Lesson7** database. Choose **File**, **Get External Data**, **Import**. The **Import** dialog box opens.

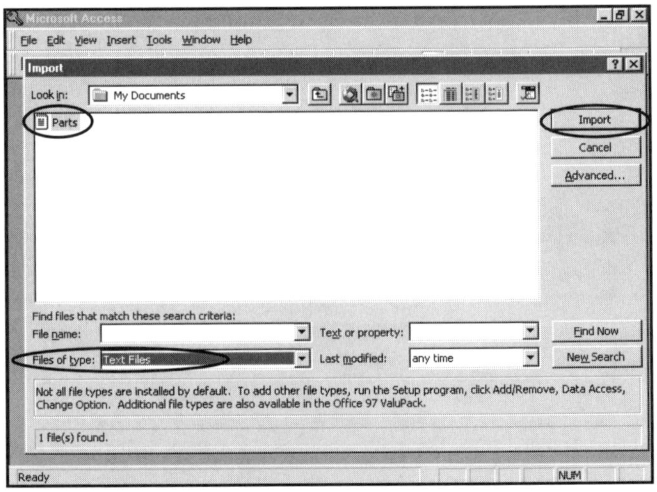


**3** Click the list arrow next to the **Files of type** box and click **Text Files**.

**4** Select the **Parts** file and click the **Import** button. The **Import Text Wizard** dialog box opens.

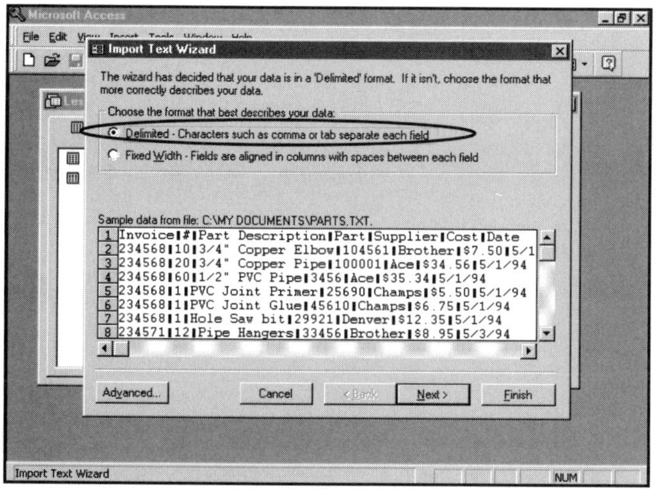


**In Depth:** An important factor in saving the data as a text file is deciding how to separate the fields. One way is to specify that the position of a certain number of characters in each row represents data for a particular field. For example, characters in positions 3 through 18 might be reserved for the Last Name field. This method is called **Fixed width fields.** Another method is to place a particular character between the data for each field. This method is called **Delimited Fields**. The example you are using has delimited fields; that is, fields have been separated one from another by a special character.

**Tip for Instructors**

Go over the information in the In Depth box completely.

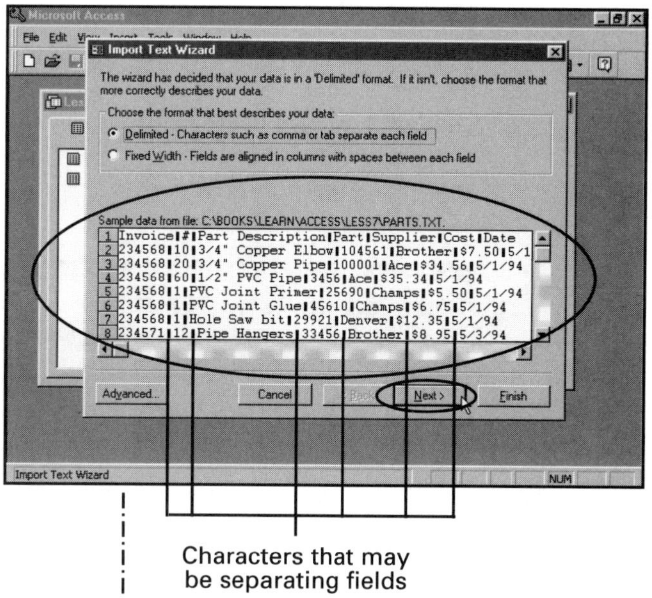


**Tip for Students**

To import an existing database created in another database program, you must first export the original file from the old database as a text file by using one of the previously mentioned methods (see the In Depth box beside Step 3) to delineate between fields.

**5** Examine the sample data from the **Parts** table. The small black rectangles indicate where the program thinks the separation between fields occurs. In this case, it is correct.

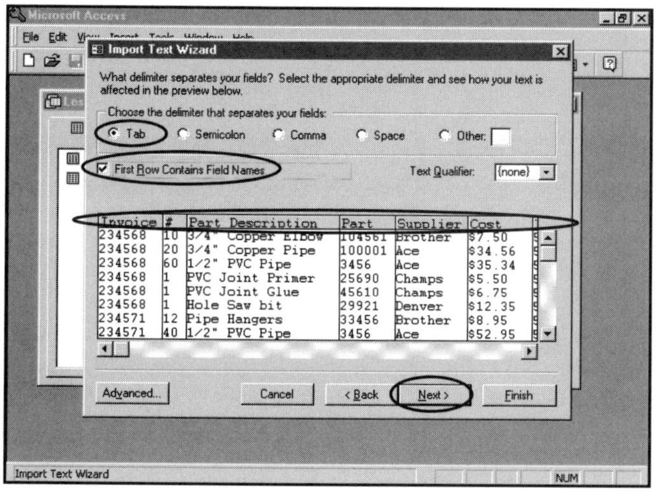


**6** Click **Next**. In the next dialog box, you see that this table uses Tab characters to separate the fields. This has been correctly identified by the program. Click the **First Row Contains Field Names** check box.

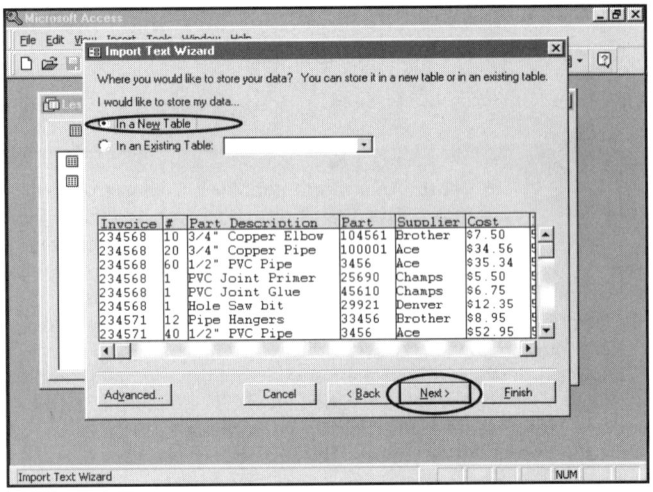


**7** Click **N**ext. Make sure the **In a Ne**w **Table** option is selected.

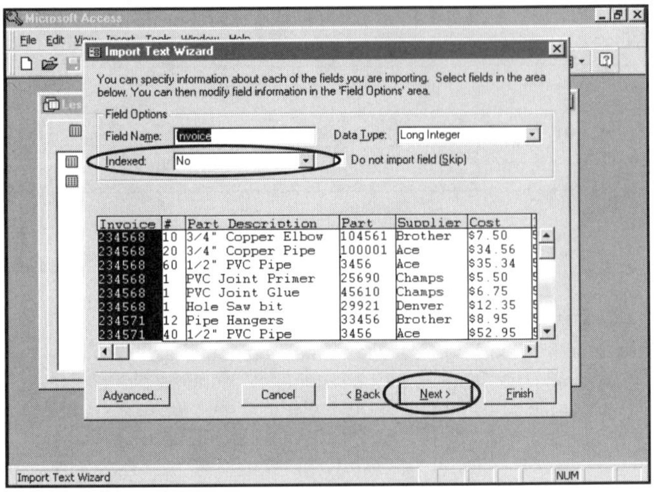


**8** Click **N**ext. This table does not have a key field and none of the fields need to be indexed. No changes are needed.

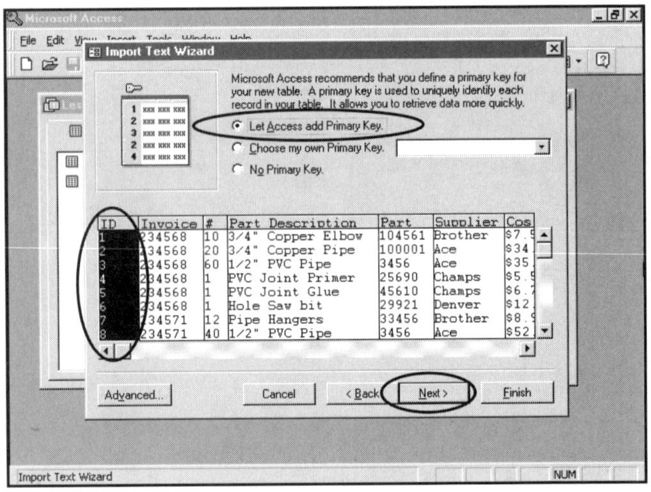


**9** Click **N**ext. If it is not already selected, select the **Let Access add Primary Key** option. The **ID** field is added to the table.

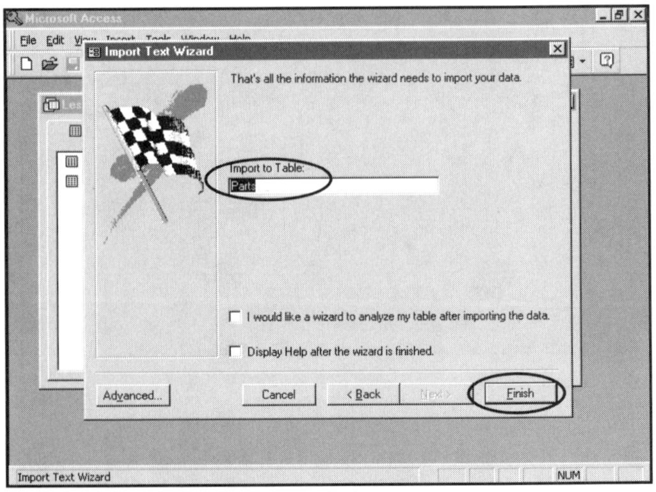


**10** Click **N**ext. Type **Parts** in the **Import to Table** box.

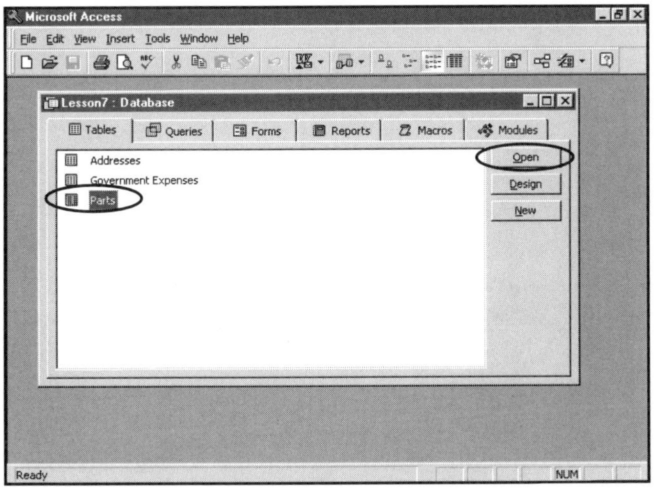


**11** Click **Finish**. Click **OK** when prompted that the table has been imported successfully.

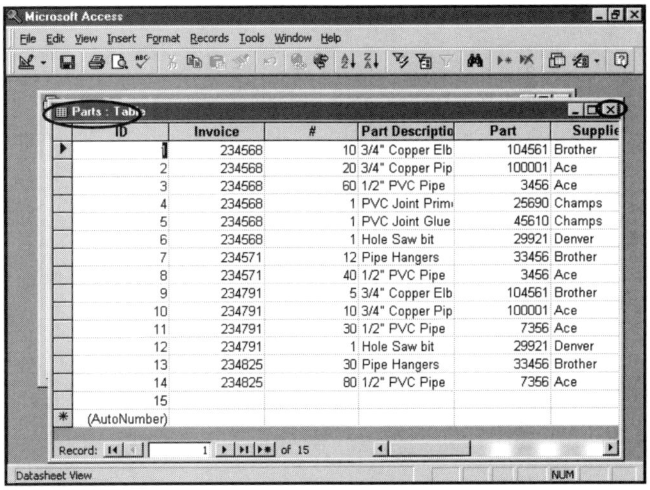


**12** Click **Open** to examine the **Parts** database table. It contains records about items that have been purchased.

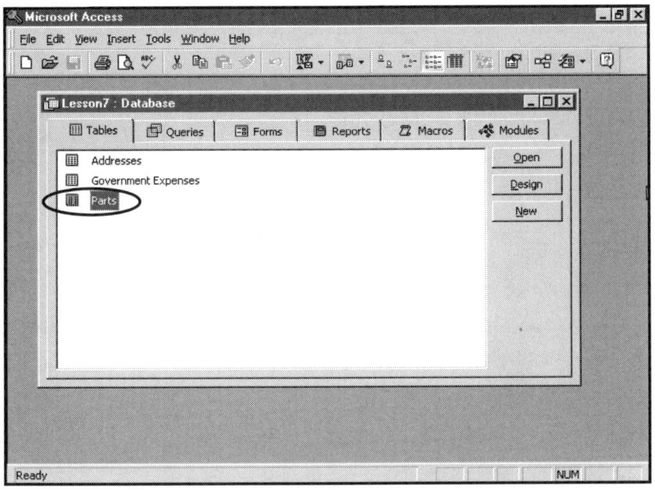


**Q & A** **?**

*Question:* What tool is used to import data from another database program? *Answer:* **Import Text Wizard.**

**13** Click the **Close Window** button. The **Parts** table is now available for use. Leave the **Lesson7** database open for the next task.

# Task 5

## Adding Hyperlinks to the Database

### Why would I do this?

Sometime you may need to make the data in your database available to others in your office or workgroup. Likewise, you may need to link to information that is contained in another file without making the data part of your file. Access 97 is capable of using hyperlinks in its forms, tables, and queries. A *hyperlink* links or connects a word or object in one document to a word or object in another document. This type of connection can be made between spreadsheets, documents, graphic programs, or databases. A hyperlink can be made in a table by specifying that the field is a hyperlink. Clicking a hyperlink quickly jumps you directly to the linked location so you can reference that information.

In this task, you learn how to modify the **Addresses** table to include hyperlink addresses for those individuals who have home pages.

**1** Click the **Addresses** table and click **Design**. The **Addresses** table opens in Design View.

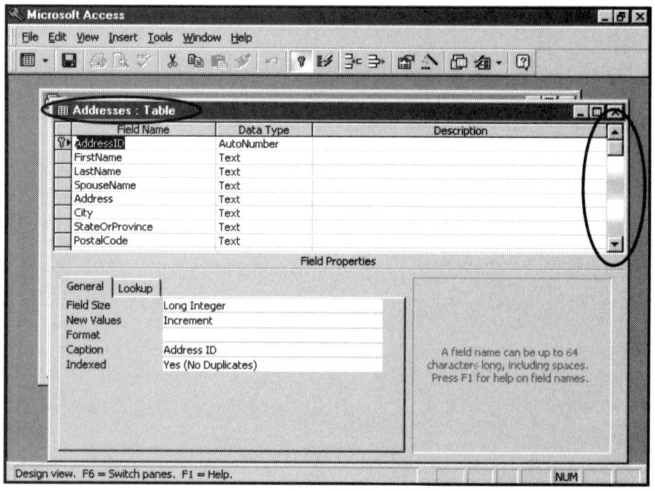


**Tip for Instructors**

The Learn on Demand Module/Lesson, "Adding Hyperlinks to the Database" applies to this task.

**On Your Mark**

Sometimes, you need your file connected to data in another file without making that data part of your database. You can do so by adding a hyperlink to a document. When might you need your database connected to another document?

**Concept**

A *hyperlink* gives the user immediate access to another pertinent file with just a click of the mouse.

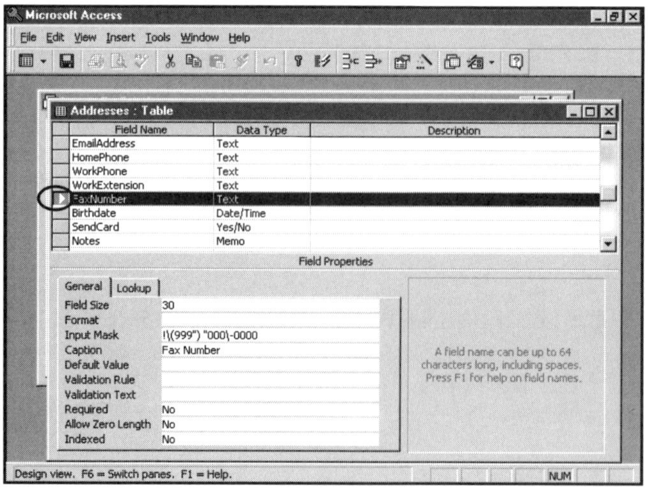


**2** Scroll down the list of field names and click the row selector for the **FaxNumber** field.

**3** Click the **Insert Row** button. A blank row is inserted in the design.

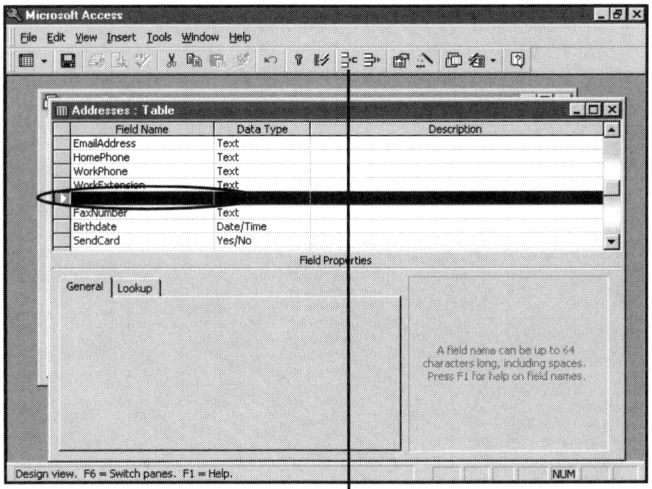


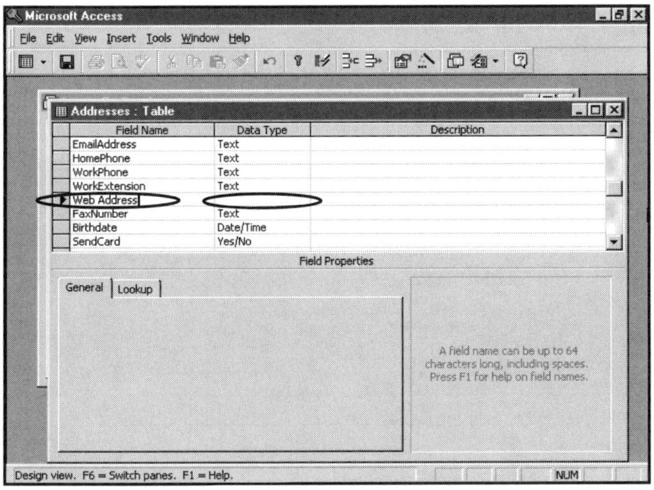


**4** Click in the blank Field Name box and type **Web Address**.

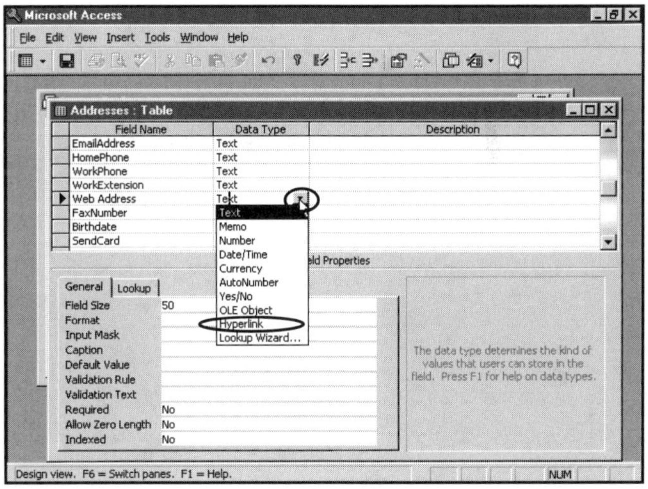


**5** Tab to the **Data Type** box and click the list arrow.

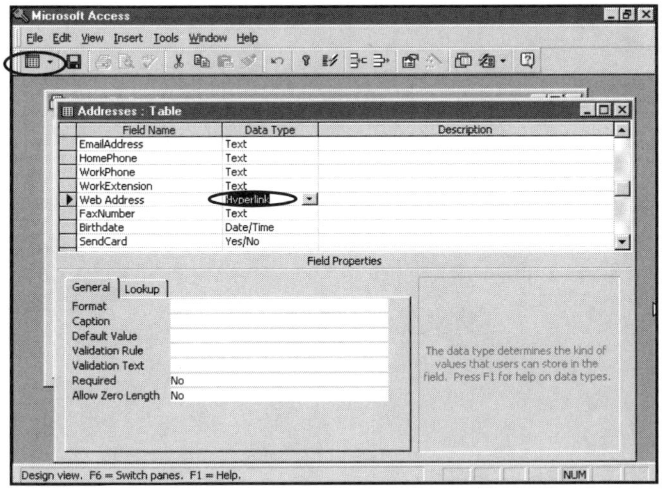


**6** Click **Hyperlink**. This type of field may be used to store Internet links or links to other files.

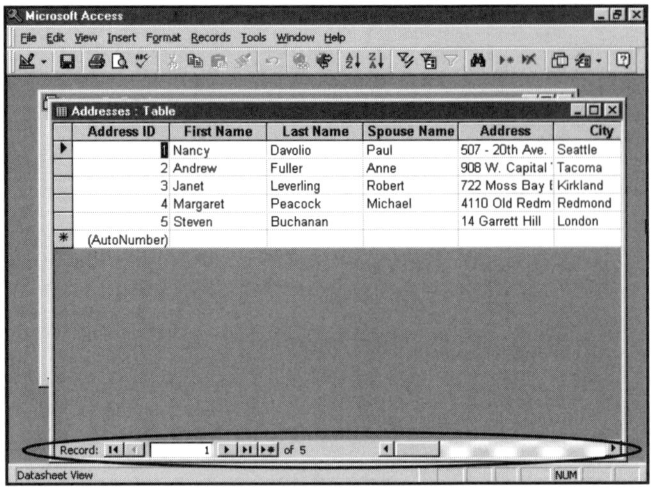


7 Click the **View** button to switch to **Datasheet View**. Click **Yes** to save the changes to the table.

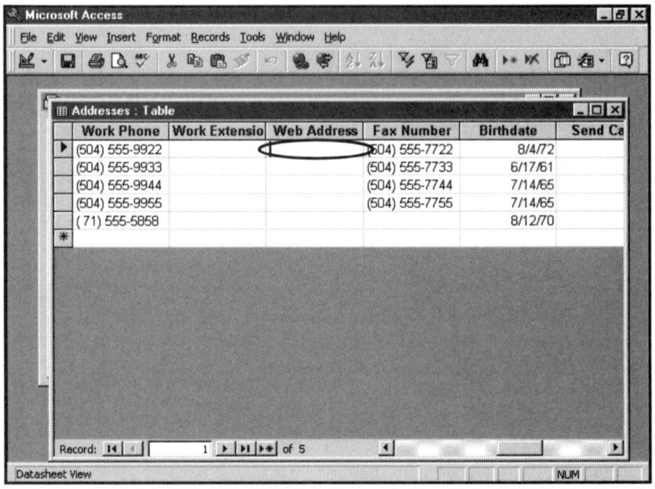


8 Scroll to the right to find the **Web Address** field and click in the box for the first record.

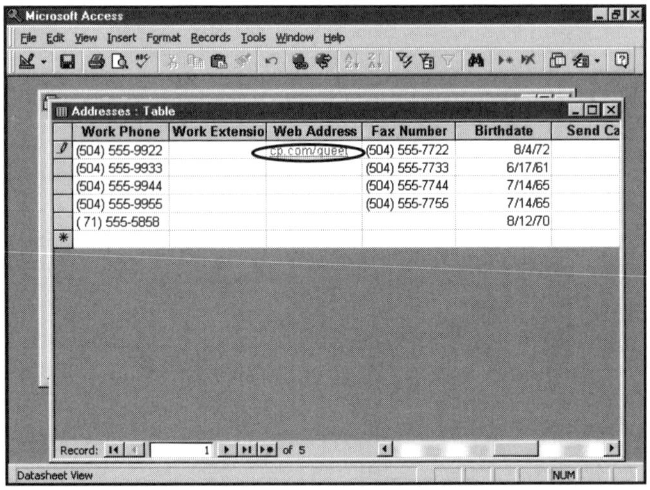


**Quicksand**

It is very important that the Web address be keyed in correctly. Even one typographical error will cause the hyperlink to fail.

9 Type **http://www.mcp.com/queet** in the **Web Address** box for the first record. This is the web address of the Que Education and Training group of Macmillan Publishing Company.

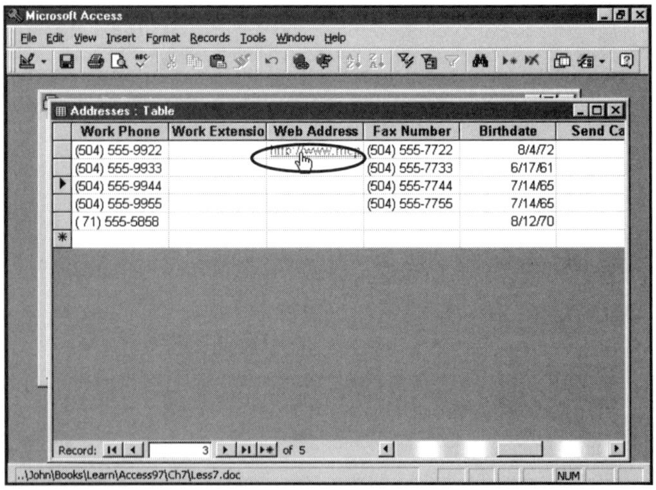


10 Click some other part of the table and then move the pointer back to the web address. The pointer changes to a small hand.

**11** If you have an Internet connection, click the address. Your registered browser opens and connects to this site.

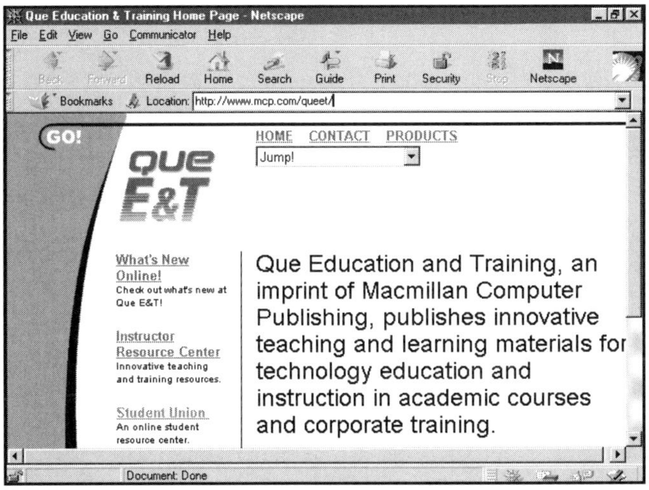


**Q & A** ?

*Question:* What types of hyperlinks might be useful? *Answer:* Web addresses, email addresses, files related to this document.

**Pothole:** The screen you see may look different from the one in the figure. This is a live Internet site, and the screen is subject to change by the company that owns it.

**12** Close the browser. Close the **Lesson7** table.

# Task 6

## Getting Help Using the Office Assistant

### Why would I do this?

This book provides an introduction to many Access topics. There are, however, many more Access features than have been covered here. Fortunately there are many powerful tools at your disposal to help you expand your working knowledge of Access and to answer your specific application questions. There is an entire help manual on disk that comes with Access that can be searched electronically.

In this task, you learn how to use the Office Assistant, one powerful Access help tool, to find out more about the use of the greater than (>) symbol.

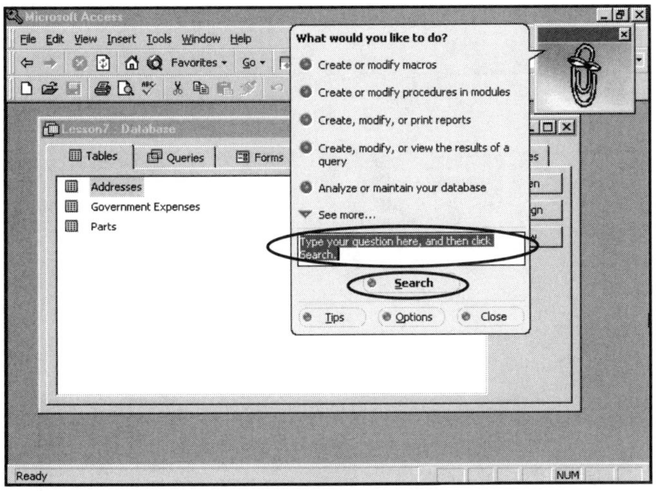


**1** Select **Help**, **Microsoft Access Help**. The Office Assistant opens.

**Tip for Instructors**

There is no Learn on Demand Module/Lesson that applies to this task.

**Tip for Students** !

At times, the **Office Assistant** appears automatically.

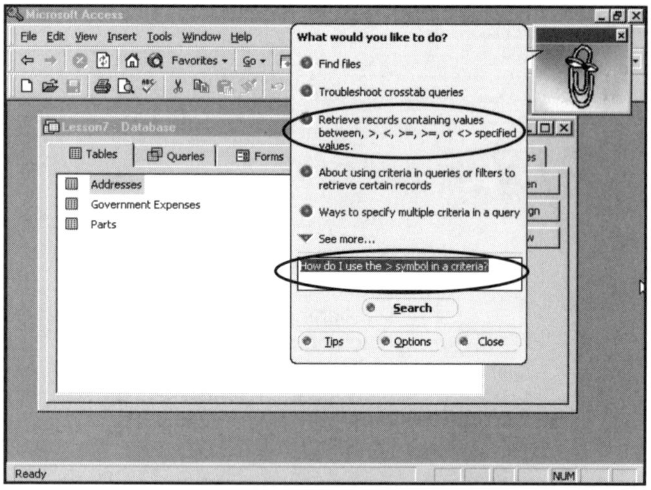


**2** Type **<u>How do I use the > symbol in a criteria?</u>** and click the **<u>S</u>earch** button. The Office Assistant scans your sentence for key words, looks up topics that are related to your request, and displays them.

> **Tip for Students** !
> Grammar is not important when using the **Office Assistant**.

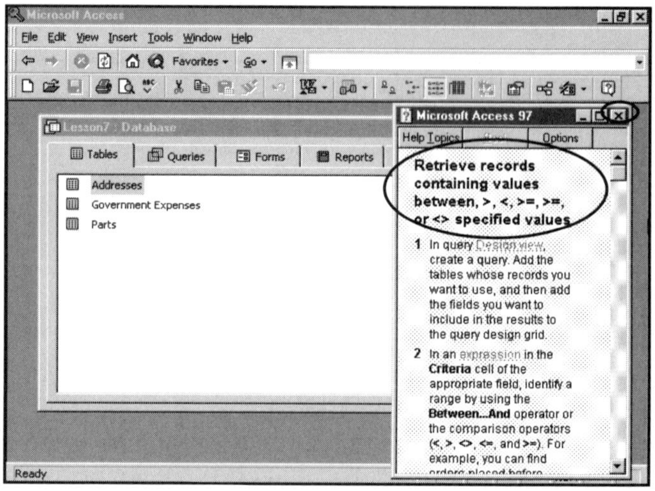


**3** Click the third suggested topic that shows examples of operators used to retrieve records. Read the **Help** screen to see the different types of criteria that you can use to select records for inclusion in a query.

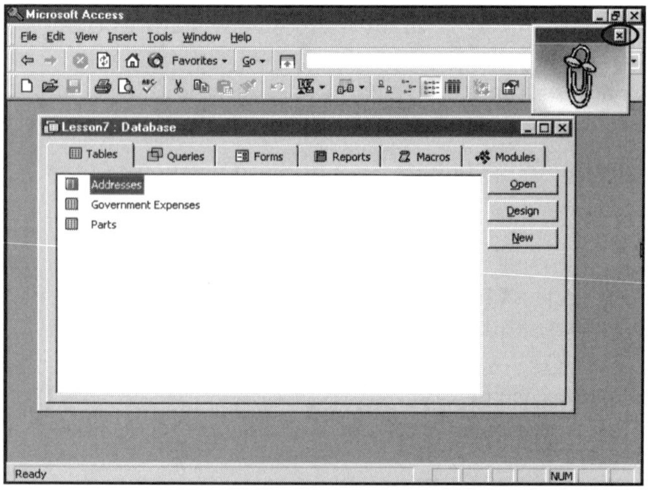


**4** Close the **Help** window.

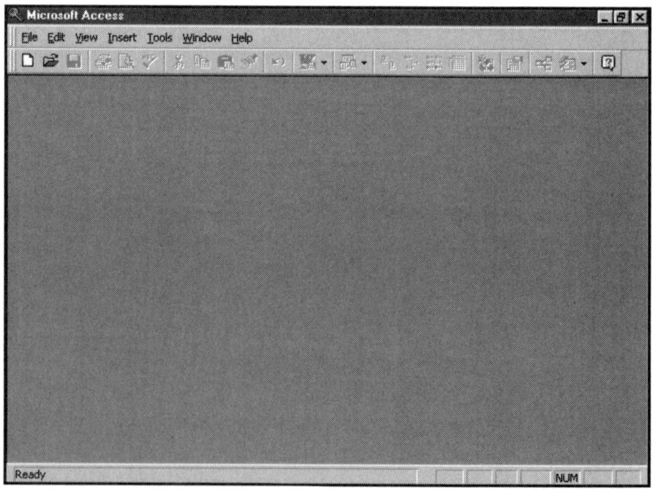


> **Q & A** ?
> *Question:* What is the **Office Assistant**? *Answer:* An interactive help tool.

**5** Close the **Office Assistant**. Close the **Lesson7** Database window, but do not exit Access.

# Task 7

## Getting Help On the Internet

### Why would I do this?

Sometimes the program does not behave as you think it should and the help manual included with the program does not answer your question. Another place to get help is to go to Microsoft's online support on the *Internet*, an interconnection of world wide computer networks, where you can search their knowledge base. If that does not help, you can go to the newsgroups section and post your question. Other users and experts from around the world see your question and post their suggestions or share their experiences.

In this task, you learn how to go to Microsoft's support web page and use several types of help.

**1** Choose **Help**, **Microsoft on the Web**, **Online Support**. If your computer is connected to the Internet, the **Microsoft Technical Support** page opens.

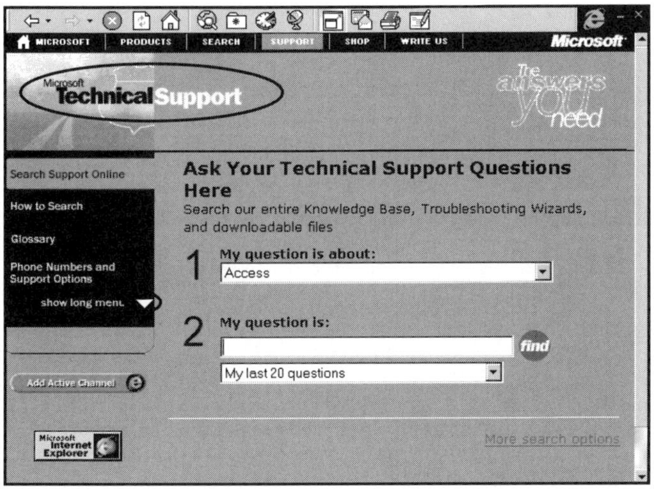


**Tip for Instructors**
There is no Learn on Demand Module/Lesson that applies to this task.

**On Your Mark**
What traditional means of education and help are available? (Reference books, classroom instruction, library, magazines.) What means are available to you that were not 10 years ago?

**Tip for Instructors**
Be aware that many users are not knowledgeable about using the Internet. Be prepared to explain the basics of the Internet, including the World Wide Web (WWW), searching, addresses (URLs), email, and so on.

**Quicksand**
This **Microsoft on the Web** feature will not work if your computer does not have Internet access.

**In Depth:** Pages change rapidly on the Internet and it is likely that Microsoft's Technical Help page will change several times during the useful life of this book. If the pages you see are not the same as those shown in the book, you should still be able to find the same topics that are discussed. The browser that you use may also differ from the one illustrated here (Internet Explorer 4.0 using the Full Screen option).

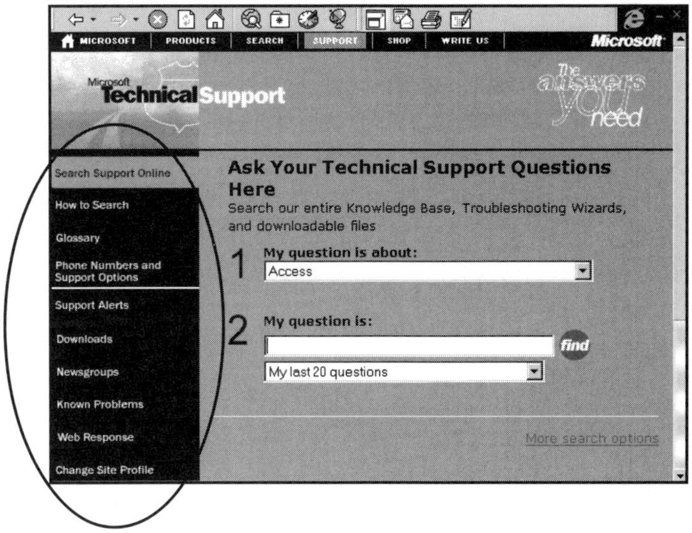


**2** Examine the options at the left side of the screen. If necessary, click the show long menu arrow.

**Quicksand**
Web pages change quite often. Do not be alarmed if the page looks different from the one shown in this book. Refer to the In Depth box.

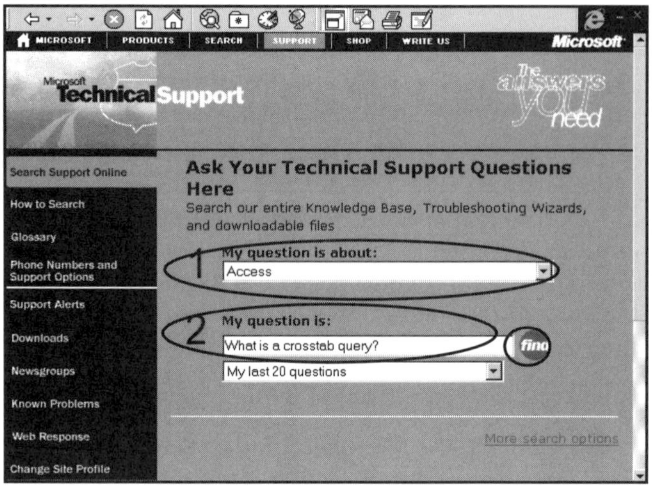


**3** Make sure that **Access** is selected in box 1 and type a question about **Access** into the second box.

**4** Click the **find** button next to the question. Explore the different options that are available from this window.

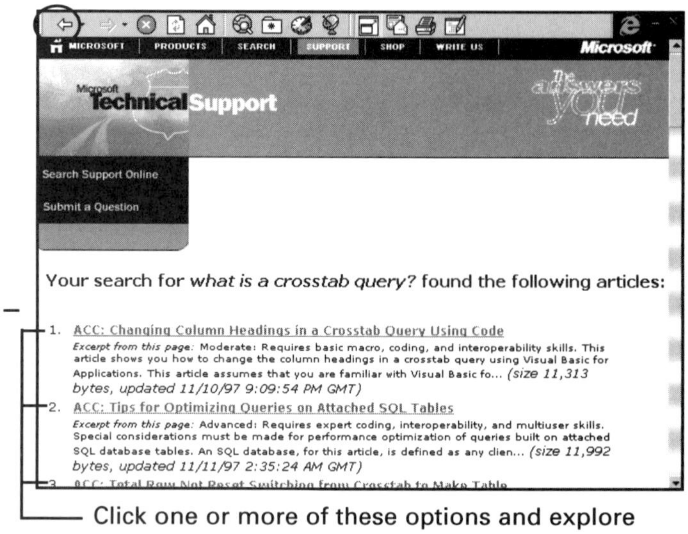


**5** Click the **Back** button repeatedly until you return to the opening page, **Microsoft Technical Support**.

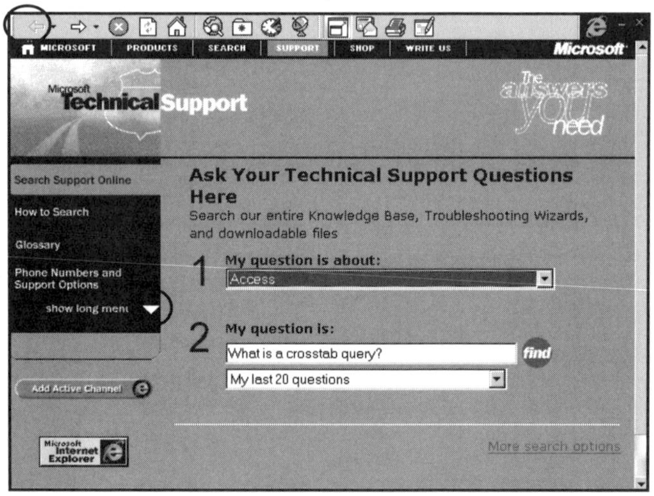


**6** Click the **show long menu** arrow to reveal the **Newsgroups** option. Newsgroups provide the ability to read and ask questions about **Access**. The advice that is given here is from other users and is not guaranteed to be accurate, but it is often a good place to go if you cannot find the answer anywhere else.

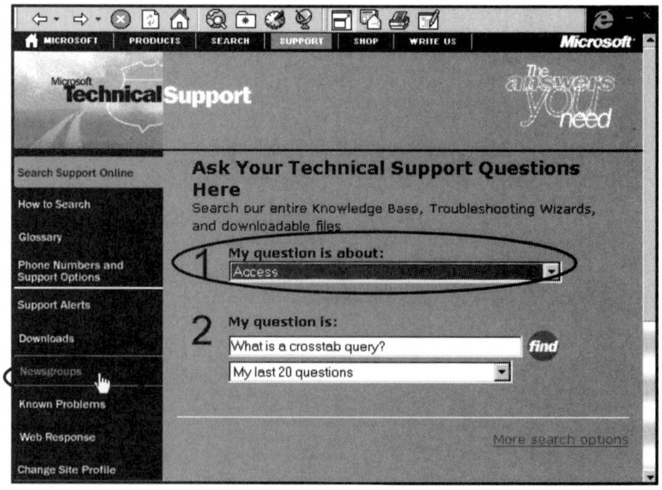

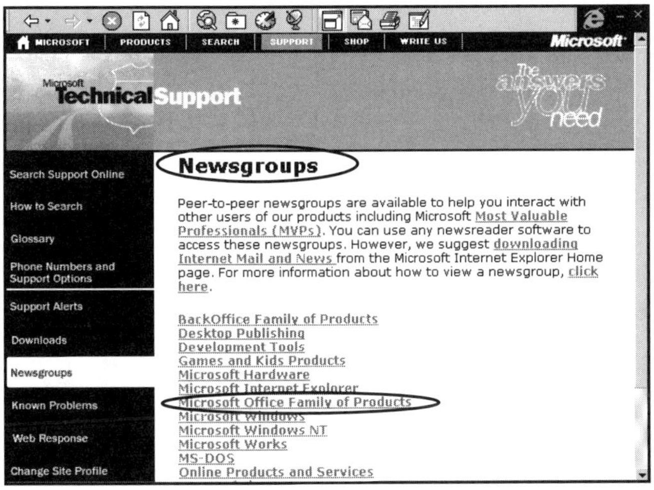


**7** Click **Newsgroups**. The Newsgroup reader that is registered on your computer opens. (You may have a different newsgroup reader installed on your computer. If you do not have a newsgroup reader installed or it is not available at your location, skip the rest of this task.)

> **Tip for Instructors**
>
> Make sure that the computers in your lab have a Newsgroup reader installed. If not, skip this section.

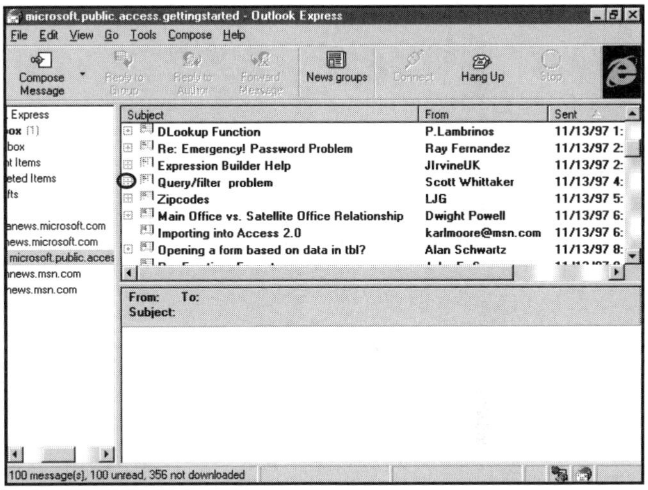


**8** Click the appropriate selections to get to the newsgroups related to **Access**. (The options used change often. At the time of this writing, they were **Microsoft Office Family of Products**, **Access**, and **Access Database Getting Started**.) A list of messages is displayed.(Note: The messages on your screen will be dated with current dates.) Messages with a + sign next to them have responses.

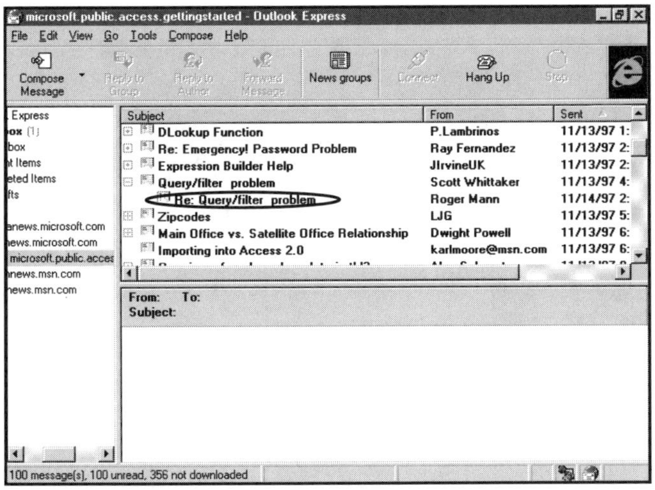


**9** Click the + sign next to one of the messages. The response(s) to the message are listed. The title of a response begins with **Re:**.

**10** Double-click a response to open it. The original message is repeated with each line marked with a > symbol.

Response

Original message

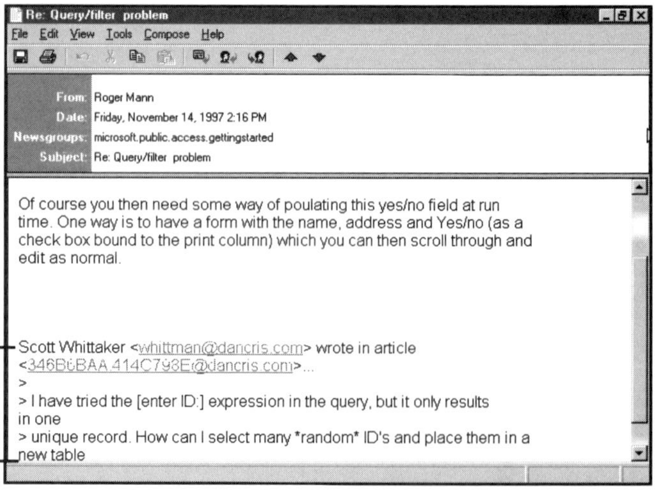


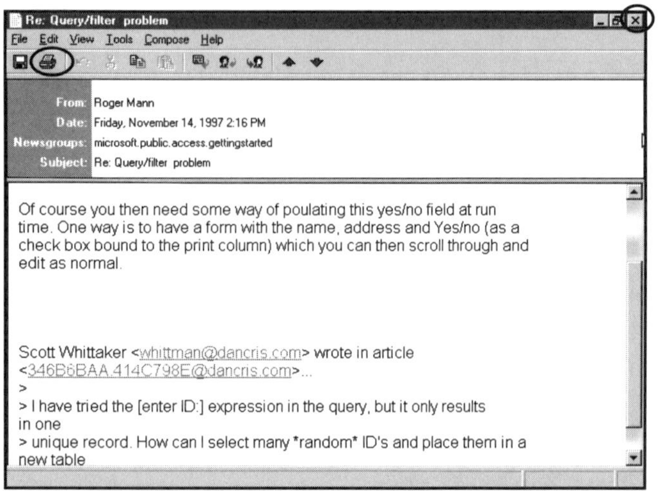


**11** Click the **Print** button on your **Newsreader's** toolbar to print a copy of the message. (Your printer options will be different depending on the browser and your printer setup.)

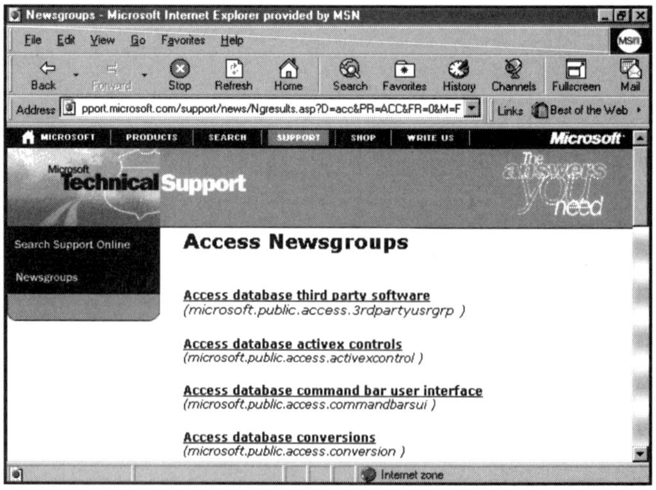


**12** If necessary, click **OK** to print. Close your Newsgroup window to return to your Internet browser.

# Task 8

**Tip for Instructors**
There is no Learn on Demand Module/Lesson that applies to this task.

## Finding Reference Books and Self-Help Textbooks

### Why would I do this?

Computer software is constantly changing, and you will need to upgrade your skills or add new skills. You may not have time to take a class or feel that you do not need to know as much as an entire class would cover. In some cases you may have an occasional need for a very specific tool in Access that is not covered in a class. In these situations, it is valuable to have additional resources available. If you found this book to be easy to use on your own, you may want to use one of the other books in the **Learn** series to teach yourself Word, PowerPoint, Excel, Windows 95, or the Internet.

Another type of book you may consider is a reference book. These are not designed to be read from cover to cover but are used to find detailed instructions on how to perform specific tasks. Most of the large publishing houses have web sites where you can look at descriptions of their books and place orders for them.

In this task, you will take a look at Que's web site as an example. You will also see how to use the Web toolbar in Access with your browser.

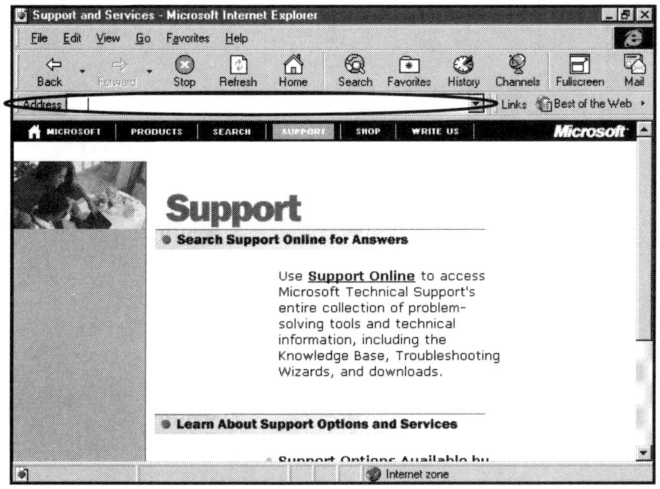


**1** Click the **Address** box. Delete the address that is currently displayed.

**In Depth:** Access97 has a Web toolbar that can be opened and closed by clicking the Web Toolbar button. This toolbar looks like the toolbar you see on a Web page. You can use this bar to enter a URL address and press Enter to activate a search on the Web where information can be accessed electronically.

**On Your Mark**
What traditional means of education and help are available? (Reference books, classroom instruction, library, magazines.)

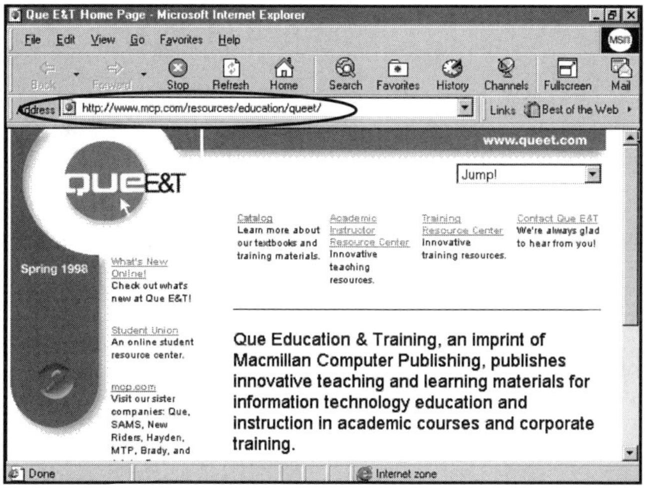


**2** Click the Address box to select the current address. Type **http://www.queet.com/** in the **Address** box and press Enter. The program automatically launches your registered browser, if it is not already running, and opens Que Education and Training's home page.

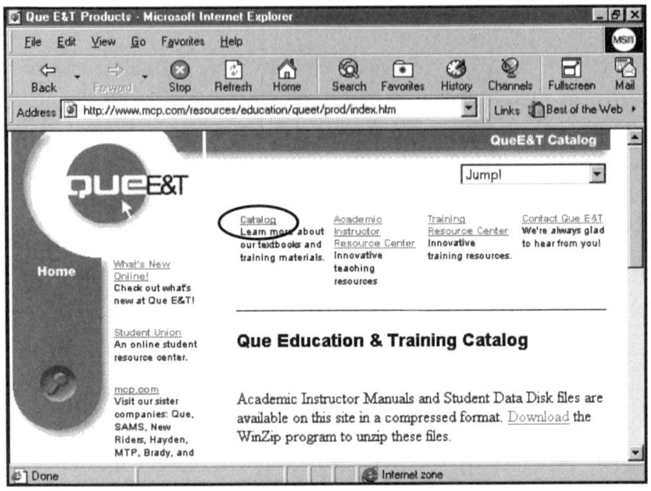


**3** Click the **Catalog** hyperlink to see a list of Que's books.

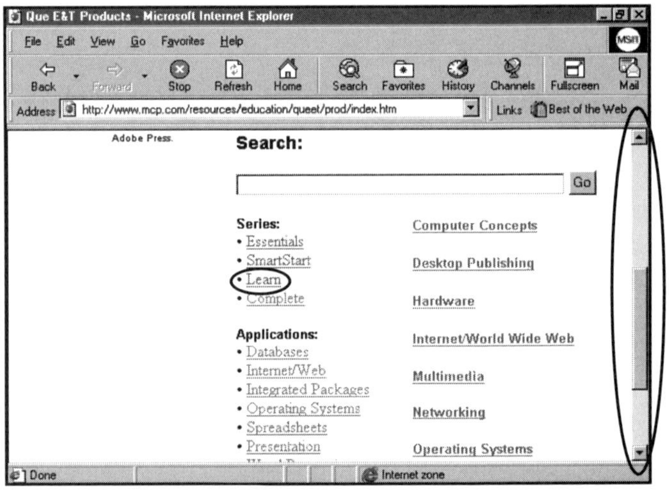


**4** Scroll down the page and find the list of book series that includes the **Learn** series. Click the **Learn** hyperlink.

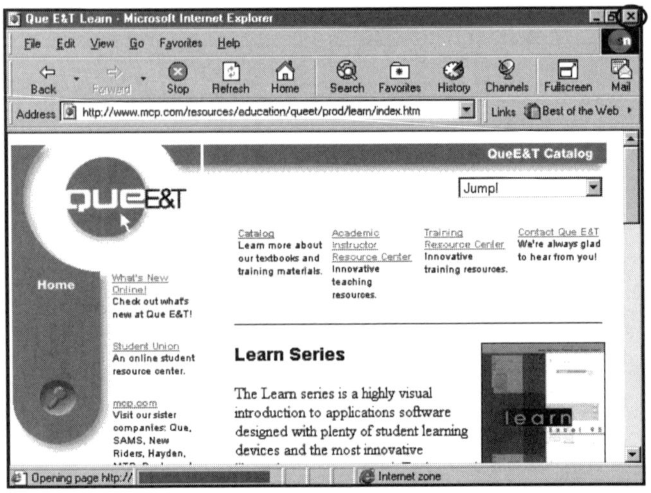


**5** This page displays information about the other books in this series. It also has hyperlinks to other book series by Que that take different approaches in terms of the depth and illustration of the lessons. Close the **browser**.

**Tip for Students**

More specific searches result in shorter responses. For example, you could search for "Access 97" to avoid displaying titles of older versions of Access.

**6** Close **Access**, unless you plan to continue with the following exercises.

**In Depth:** To find other bookstores, use one of the search programs associated with your browser. Look at your browser's toolbar and click the **Search** button. Search for a key word like **Bookstore**.

# Student Exercises

## True-False

For each of the following, circle either T or F to indicate whether the statement is true or false.

(T) F **1.** To merge an Access database with a Word document, you must first create the document and then open the database and merge it with the document.

(T) F **2.** One reason to view your merged document before printing is to ensure that the document looks the way you intended.

T (F) **3.** When you print a merged Word/Access document, you must print all the records, rather than just a few records.

(T) F **4.** The Merge function in Access adjusts for multiple address lines and empty fields when it prints a merged document.

T (F) **5.** Text files cannot be imported into an Access database.

(T) F **6.** When importing a spreadsheet file into Access, it is important that the first row of the spreadsheet is set up with field names, and each subsequent row is a record.

(T) F **7.** An important factor when saving a database as a text file is deciding how to separate the fields. One method is the delimited fields method which places a specified character between fields as the separator.

(T) F **8.** A hyperlink connecting documents, spreadsheets, or databases is a shortcut used to link a word or object in one file to a word or object in another file.

T (F) **9.** The only help system available to Access users comes on a disk that can be searched electronically.

(T) F **10.** The Access Office Assistant allows you to ask questions; it then displays topics related to your request.

# Identifying Parts of the Access Screens

Refer to the figures and identify the numbered parts of the screen. Write the letter of the correct label in the space next to the number.

1. ___*F*___
2. ___*H*___
3. ___*G*___
4. ___*B*___
5. ___*E*___
6. ___*I*___
7. ___*A*___
8. ___*C*___
9. ___*D*___

**A.** Button used to return to previous location
**B.** View Merged Data button
**C.** Print button
**D.** Box where you can indicate the Microsoft program you want help with
**E.** Record number
**F.** Mail Merge toolbar
**G.** Used to insert fields from the database
**H.** Save button
**I.** Mail Merge button

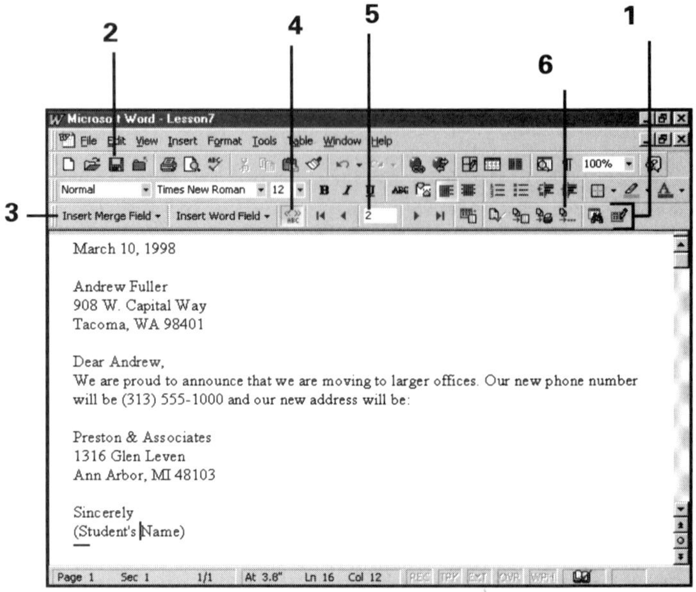


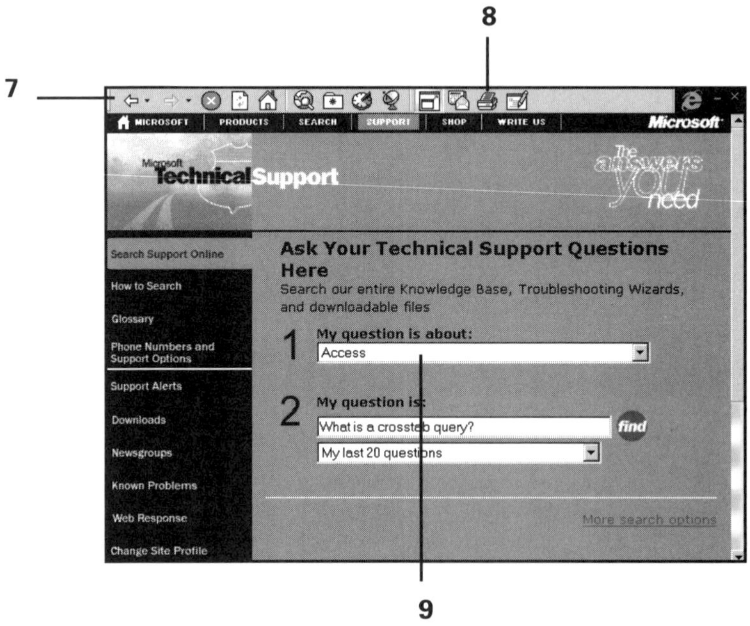

# Matching

Match the statements below to the word or phrase that is the best match from the list. Write the letter of the matching word or phrase in the space provided next to the number.

1. _F_ Office Assistant
2. _K_ Button used to merge data from Access with a form letter or other document designed in Word
3. _H_ Allows you to link an Access database with Word or Excel
4. _G_ In Word, this is used to work with a merged document
5. _E_ Button which opens the Merge dialog box
6. _B_ An example of a web address
7. _C_ Command which allows you to import files into Access
8. _A_ Button used in Word to insert fields from a database into a form letter or document
9. _I_ The title of a response in the on-line help found under Newsgroups starts with this
10. _D_ Online support available from Microsoft

**A.** Insert Merge Field button

**B.** http://www.mcp.com/queet

**C.** File, Get External Data, Import

**D.** Microsoft Access Support Home Page

**E.** View Merge Data button

**F.** Resident Help feature of Access used to search for key words

**G.** Mail Merge toolbar

**H.** Office Links button

**I.** Re:

**J.** >

**K.** Mail Merge button

# Application Exercises

Copy **Less0704** and rename it as **Exercise7** on your disk for use in the following exercises.

## Exercise 1 – Importing a Table from Excel

1. Launch Access and open **Exercise7**.
2. Choose **File**, **Get External Data**, and **Import** from the menu.
3. Specify **Microsoft Excel** in the **Files of type** box and import the **Less0705** Excel file.
4. Import the first sheet and specify that the first row contains column headings.
5. Import both columns of the sheet into a new table.
6. Select the Year column as the primary key.
7. Name the table **Population Projection**.
8. Open the new table and review it.
9. Print the table and then close it. Leave the database open for use in the next exercise.

# Exercise 2 – Importing a Table from an Old dBASE III Database

A common database for personal computers in the 1980s was dBASE III. Many database records from that period are stored in that format. In this exercise you will import data from 1987 that shows information about retail establishments and their employees in Michigan. (Sales and Payroll are in 1000s.)

1. Choose **File**, **Get External Data**, and **Import** from the menu.
2. Specify **dBASE III** in the **Files of type** box and import the **Less0706** dBASE file.
3. Open the table.
4. Click the record selector button to the left of the first record (zip code 00000).
5. Shift-click the record selector next to the tenth record (zip code 48010) to select the first ten records.
6. Choose **File**, **Print**.
7. Click **Selected Record(s)** in the **Print Range** section of the **Print** dialog box.
8. Click **OK**.
9. Close the table. Leave the database open for use in the next exercise.

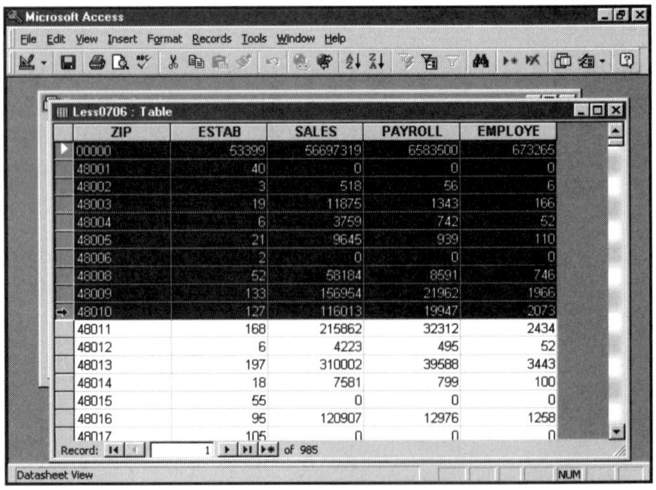


# Exercise 3 – Merging a Word Document and an Access Query

You can merge documents with queries as well as with tables. In this exercise you will use a query that has been created to include only those records which have a birth date in August and have a **Yes** in the **SendCard** field. When this query is used, you combine the filtering capabilities of Access with the Word processing power of Word.

1. Click the **Queries** tab and make sure the **August Birthdays** query is selected.
2. Click the list arrow next to the **OfficeLinks** button on the Standard toolbar and select **Merge it with MS Word**.
3. Create a new document that could be used by an organization to wish someone a happy birthday. Include all of the query's fields in the document except for **AddressID**, **Expr1**, and **SendCard**.

4. Include your name in the document.
5. Save the document as **Birthday**.
6. Print the two letters.
7. Close the document and the database.

## Exercise 4—Getting Help Using the Office Assistant

The **August Birthdays** query in the preceding exercise used the **DatePart** function. In this exercise, you will find out more about this function using the **Office Assistant**.

1. Click the **Office Assistant** button on the Standard toolbar. It is the far right button with the question mark.
2. Type **Tell me more about DatePart** and click **Search**.
3. Select **Extract part of existing date values using a calculated field** and read the description.
4. Click **Options**, **Print Topic**.
5. Close the **Office Assistant**.

## Exercise 5—Getting Help on the Internet

If you cannot find the help you need in the Office Assistant you can try the online help over the Internet. In this exercise you will connect to Microsoft's support site and get more help on the DatePart function.

1. Click **Help, Microsoft on the Web**, and **Online Support**.
2. Make sure that **Access** is in box 1 and type **DatePart** in box 2 on the **Technical Support** page.
3. Click **Find**.
4. Scroll through the list of articles and look for an article named **ACC2: DatePart(), DateDiff() Functions Ignore Global Settings**. (If this article is no longer available when you use this site, return to the previous page and enter another feature of Access that you would like to look up.)
5. Use your browser's Print button to print this two-page description.
6. Close your **browser**.

# Glossary

**Autoform** a form that will list all of the fields in a table.

**Columnar report** a type of report that prints the fields of each record in a single column.

**Combo box** on a form, a text box that presents a drop-down list of options for data that can be selected for a field. With a combo box you also have the option to enter data manually if the options presented do not contain the correct information.

**Comparison operators** used in queries to compare data to a specific condition. Equal is assumed in a criteria unless modified by a comparison operator. Comparison operators include (less than) <, (greater than) >, (equal) =, (less than or equal) <=, (greater than or equal) >=, (not equal) <>, Between . . . And, Like, In.

**Concatenated field** a field that combines two fields or expressions to form a new field.

**Control** a graphical object on a form or report that is used to display data, perform an action, or make a form or report easier to read.

**Criteria** used in a query to restrict data to those records that meet certain conditions.

**Crosstab query** displays summarized values (sums, counts, and averages) from one field in a table and groups them based on at least two other fields.

**Data type** used in a table to specify the kind of information that will be entered in a field. The most common data type is text.

**Database** a management system that allows the user to store, retrieve, analyze, and print large amounts of data.

**Database Wizard** a program that creates a database by guiding you through a series of options.

**Datasheet View** displays the data in rows and columns.

**Date** a data type used to store and display dates.

**Default Values** values that are pre-set. Default values will automatically be filled in when a new record is added unless overwritten.

**Design View** a view of a database object that is used to examine or modify the object.

**Detail section** the area of a form or report where records from the form or report source are displayed.

**Dynaset** the results of running a query.

**Field** a single category of data or information that makes up a record.

**Field selector** the column label at the top of each column in Table view, used to select the whole column.

**Filter** a method used on a form to limit the data to records that meet certain conditions.

**Form** a database object used to display or edit one record at a time.

**Hyperlinks** a connection to other documents, spreadsheets, or databases on your computer or on the Internet.

**Input Mask** a filed property applied in a table, that creates a format so data containing dashes or parentheses is entered in a consistent way. Common examples include social security numbers, zip codes, and phone numbers.

**Internet** an interconnection of worldwide computer networks.

**Label** text in a form or report that is not data, usually the field name.

**Label box** a control on a form or report that contains descriptive text such as a title or caption.

**List box** on a form, a text box that presents a list of options from which to choose data. With a list box, the list always shows on the screen and you can only select from the options that are presented.

**Macros** one of the six objects in a database. Macros are used to automate existing Access commands. Sometimes macros consist of a series of commands that may be attached to buttons on forms, tables, or queries.

**Memo** a data type that is used for unstructured comments.

**Modules** one of the six objects in a database. Modules are programs in the Visual Basic programming language used to customize the database for special needs.

**Navigation buttons** allow you to move through the records by moving to the next record, previous record, to the end, or the beginning of the records.

**Objects** a general term for the six parts of an Access database: tables, queries, forms, reports, macros and modules.

**One-to-many relationship** a relationship where data in a field occurs one time on the first table and many times in the related table.

**Page Footer** the area at the bottom of a form or report that will show the same information on each page when the object is printed.

**Parameter queries** queries that use values to define output as part of the query structure.

**Parameters** values that define output.

**Pivot table** an interactive table that performs calculations; most often used to analyze large amounts of complex data.

**Placeholder** a rectangle that shows the position of an object that is being moved.

**Primary key** used to designate a field that contains a unique value for each record.

**Primary Key field** a field that has unique values for each record that are used to speed up sorting and finding data in a large table and to link tables together.

**Query** one of the six objects in a database. Queries are used to sort, search, and limit the data to just those records that you need to see.

**RAM** a type of computer memory that is fast enough to keep up with the processor but requires constant power to function.

**Record** a group of data pertaining to one event, transaction, or person. The categories of information in a record are called fields.

**Record selector** the small box to the left of each record on the table's Datasheet View that allows you to select all of the fields in a record.

**Relational databases** databases that use related tables.

**Reports** one of the six objects in a database. Reports are used to summarize information for printing and presentation of the data.

**Select query** a query that can be used to filter records, sort, and limit the fields included.

**Tab order** the order the cursor follows in moving from field to field in a form.

**Tables** one of the six objects in a database. Tables store data and are the foundation of the database.

**Template** a pre-designed form or format that can be used instead of creating one of your own.

**Text** a data type in a table that is readable content. May be used to store short phrases or words, or numbers that will not be used in calculations such as phone numbers or social security numbers.

**Text box** a box on a form that shows data from a field or calculation.

**Union query** a union query has the same properties as a select query plus the ability to use fields from more than one table if the tables are related.

**Wildcard** a symbol that is used to search for unspecified characters. An asterisk (*) can be used as the first or last character in a string of characters to match any number of characters.

**Yes/No** a data type in a table used to store data that can only have two logical states.

# Appendix A
# Test Questions and Answers

## Lesson 1 Test Questions

### True/False

For each of the following, check T or F to indicate whether the statement is true or false.

T. ___F. ___**1.** Navigation buttons move Access from one database to another.

T. ___F. ___**2.** You must save each record as it is added.

T. ___F. ___**3.** The Text data type must be used if you want to use an input mask for a field.

T. ___F. ___**4.** The primary key is always an AutoNumber.

T. ___F. ___**5.** The Database Wizard guides you through the process of creating a database.

T. ___F. ___**6.** The Design View is used to modify any of the database components.

T. ___F. ___**7.** A switchboard may be added to make using a database more user-friendly.

T. ___F. ___**8.** Before a record can be added to a newly created database, you must create a form.

T. ___F. ___**9.** You cannot modify a database created through a Database Wizard.

T. ___F. ___**10.** The Undo button can be used if you accidentally delete a record.

### Multiple Choice

Circle the letter of the correct answer for each of the following questions.

**1.** Which of the following would you use to create a database without starting from scratch?

a. Database Wizard

b. Create Database menu option

c. Database Magician

d. None of the above

**2.** Which component is not found in a database?

a. Table

b. Worksheet

c. Report

d. Query

**3.** In a new database, which component must be created first?

a. Form

b. Design

c. Module

d. Table

**4.** Which of the following describes a dialog box?

a. It asks for further information before a procedure can be completed.

b. It enables the computer to speak to you.

c. It is not used on all computers.

d. It tells you that Access is thinking.

**5.** When must you save added records?

a. After each record entry

b. As you close the database

c. Access does it automatically as each is added

d. Every five minutes or so

**6.** Which element makes all of the components of Access easier to utilize?

a. Form

b. Switchboard

c. Wizard

d. Organizer

7. Which of the following is the purpose of an input mask?
   a. To hide the data you just added
   b. To add an automatic format
   c. To block a field from entry
   d. To make the field properties read-only
8. Which of the following is not a data type used in Access?
   a. Text
   b. Number
   c. Yes/No
   d. Notes
9. Which of the following can be shown in a report?
   a. All of the data in a table
   b. One record per page
   c. Only select records
   d. All of the above
10. Which of the following describes the What's This? button?
   a. It displays the definition for an item.
   b. It shows only one definition at a time.
   c. It is used in the Design view of a report or form.
   d. All of the above.

## Completion

In the blank provided, write the correct answer for each of the following statements.

1. The _____ ______ is used to create a new database through a series of dialog boxes.
2. The first component to be created in a database is a(n) ____.
3. ____ ____ enable you to scroll through the records one at a time.
4. Press __ to move to the next field.
5. To use a(n) ____ ____, the data type for a field must be Text.
6. To change the fields or properties, you must be in the ____ View for that table.
7. After you delete a record, it ___ be undeleted.
8. Use ___ ___ to learn more about the design of a form or report.
9. Access is a computerized _____ management system.
10. Access contains __ database templates.

# Lesson 2 Test Questions

## True/False

For each of the following, check T or F to indicate whether the statement is true or false.

T. ___F. ___1. There is a wizard for creation of each component of a database.

T. ___F. ___2. Field properties define the location of a field in a table.

T. ___F. ___3. The Description is a required part of a table creation.

T. ___F. ___4. You can press Enter or Tab to move from column to column in Table Design View.

T. ___F. ___5. Access prompts you to save changes if you change from Design View to Datasheet View.

T. ___F. ___6. If you rename a field from a table, it is automatically renamed in each component in which the field is used.

T. ___F. ___7. When you delete a field, all of the data is still maintained in an unnamed field.

T. ___F. ___8. Select both the label and text box for a field in Design View by pressing Ctrl as you click.

T. ___F. ___9. The tab order for a form cannot be changed unless the fields are rearranged in the table.

T. ___F. ___10. To resize a field in the Report or Form Design View, drag a handle when the mouse is a double arrow.

## Multiple Choice

Circle the letter of the correct answer for each of the following questions.

1. Where does the Description of a field in a table appear?
   a. To the right of the field
   b. To the left of the field
   c. In the status bar when the field is active
   d. In the title bar when the field is active
2. Which of the following describes the primary key?
   a. It must be unique
   b. It aids in indexing of a large database
   c. It makes sorting quicker
   d. All of the above
3. Which of the following can be used to display one record at a time?
   a. AutoForm
   b. Record Restriction button
   c. View, One Record
   d. You cannot do this
4. How do you delete a field?
   a. Click the field name and press Del
   b. Click Edit, Delete Field, and choose the appropriate field
   c. Click the row selector for that field and press Del
   d. Re-create the table
5. In the Form Design View, each field has which of the following?
   a. A field label
   b. A field text box
   c. An AutoNumber assigned to it
   d. Both a and b
6. To move a field in Design view, the mouse must be in what shape?
   a. Arrow
   b. Hand
   c. Double-arrow
   d. Four-headed arrow
7. Which term describes the order in which a cursor moves when entering data?
   a. Tab order
   b. Field order
   c. Tab sequence
   d. Data order
8. Which of the following describes data that appear on each record in a form that is not a part of the table?
   a. Text box
   b. Label
   c. Tag
   d. Field
9. To select more than one box in a form, press which of the following?
   a. Ctrl
   b. Alt
   c. F1
   d. ⇧Shift
10. What is the purpose of handles in the Form/Report Design View?
    a. Show that a box is selected
    b. Enable the user to move the box
    c. Enable the user to resize the box
    d. All of the above

## Completion

In the blank provided, write the correct answer for each of the following statements.

1. Before a database is created, you are asked to ___ it.
2. To alter any of the components in a database, use the ____ View.

3. Click the ____ _____ to choose a field in the Table Design view before deleting or moving it.

4. When you change a field's data type, Access will try to ____ the data in that field.

5. To better organize a report, ____ and ____ can be applied.

6. The Tab Order of a form can be changed through the ____, ______ menu option.

7. The small squares around a selected box are called ____.

8. Press ___ to select the Field label and Field text box together in the Form Design view.

9. In an open report, the mouse pointer looks like a(n) _____.

10. Many times, it is easier to create a report or form with a(n) ____.

# Lesson 3 Test Questions

## True/False

For each of the following, check T or F to indicate whether the statement is true or false.

T. ___F. ___**1.** You cannot add an input mask to a Date/Time data type.

T. ___F. ___**2.** When you change the data type of a field, all data in that field are converted.

T. ___F. ___**3.** To add an input mask, you can type in the mask or use the Build button.

T. ___F. ___**4.** The Expression Builder is used to add an input mask to a field.

T. ___F. ___**5.** A default value can be text, numbers, or a function.

T. ___F. ___**6.** The primary key does not have to be unique.

T. ___F. ___**7.** When using a list box in a form, the only options available are the ones in the list.

T. ___F. ___**8.** The size of a list box is set automatically when you add the items on the list in Design view.

T. ___F. ___**9.** When in Design View, the list items are not shown in a list box or combo box.

T. ___F. ___**10.** A Form Header appears on each page of a form when it is printed.

## Multiple Choice

Circle the letter of the correct answer for each of the following questions.

1. Which of the following is not a preset format of the Input Mask Wizard?
   a. Social Security Number
   b. ZIP Code
   c. Date
   d. Password

2. In the field properties options in Table Design view, what does the ellipsis (...) represent?
   a. Build
   b. Expression Builder
   c. Format Wizard
   d. Function Wizard

3. Which of the following is a good example of a primary key field?
   a. Social Security Number
   b. AutoNumber
   c. Employee ID
   d. All of the above

4. Which of the following enables you to choose from only the items listed in a form?
   a. List box
   b. Combo box
   c. Drop-down list box
   d. Text box

5. Which of the following allows the user to change the properties of a field in a form?
   a. Right-click the field text box and choose Properties
   b. Click View, Properties in the menu
   c. Click the Properties button in the toolbar
   d. Both a and c

6. What are the advantages of a list box?

   a. The items will be spelled correctly.

   b. Only those listed can be chosen.

   c. It saves time in filling in the field.

   d. All of the above.

7. Which of the following appears on every page of a form that is printed?

   a. Form Header

   b. Page Header

   c. Form Footer

   d. Footer

8. The function Date() displays which of the following?

   a. The date of the entry

   b. Whatever date you type in

   c. Today's date, regardless of entry date

   d. The date input mask

9. Which of the following enables you to delete a page break in a report?

   a. Click the page break and press Del

   b. Select Edit, Delete from the menu

   c. Right-click and choose Erase

   d. You cannot delete a page break

10. How can you display all of the data in a column in a table?

    a. Zoom in

    b. Zoom out

    c. Widen the columns

    d. Use page preview.

## Completion

In the blank provided, write the correct answer for each of the following statements.

1. Use the ___ ___ ____ to set the field structure for a field.

2. ____ ____ are entered as soon as you start editing a record.

3. The structure of a field is set in the ____ ______ section of a table.

4. For assistance in setting a default value, use the ___ _____.

5. When widening a column in a table, the mouse pointer must in the shape of a(n) ___ ___.

6. The entries shown in the box are the only possible entries in a(n) _____ ______.

7. In a(n) ___ ___, you can choose from the list or type in your own entry.

8. A(n) _____ header appears only at the top of form when printed.

9. From the ___ menu option, you may add automatic entries such as date, time, and page numbers.

10. _____ displays the current date.

# Lesson 4 Test Questions

## True/False

For each of the following, check T or F to indicate whether the statement is true or false.

T.___F. ___**1.** Freezing a column means that you cannot change any of the data in that column.

T.___F. ___**2.** You can use wildcards when searching for a record with the Find option.

T.___F. ___**3.** The Find option stops on one record at a time.

T.___F. ___**4.** The primary key sorts a table unless a different sort is added and saved.

T.___F. ___**5.** Duplicates are not allowed in an indexed field.

T.___F. ___**6.** A filter can be saved for later usage and is used to extract records that meet certain criteria.

T.___F. ___**7.** The results of a query are known as a dynaset.

T.___F. ___**8.** Within a query, you can use an existing field to create another calculated field.

T.___F. ___**9.** To change the criteria in a query, you must change it manually.

T.___F. ___**10.** Parameters are values that define the output.

## Multiple Choice

Circle the letter of the correct answer for each of the following questions.

1. How can you display only certain fields in a table?
   a. Create a filter
   b. Freeze the columns
   c. Use the Find option
   d. Create an AutoForm
2. Which of the following is appropriate for any field?
   a. Indexed, allowing duplicates
   b. Indexed, allowing no duplicates
   c. Not indexed
   d. All of the above
3. Which of the following will allow you to temporarily limit the records shown?
   a. Create a query
   b. Create a filter
   c. Use the Find option
   d. Freeze the columns
4. What does a filter that looks for one of two criteria in a record use?
   a. Or statement
   b. And statement
   c. If statement
   d. Not statement
5. Which of the following describes a select query?
   a. Limits the records shown
   b. Limits the fields shown
   c. Can calculate new values based on other fields
   d. All of the above
6. To add a field to the grid in a Query Design view, what do you do?
   a. Double-click the field
   b. Drag the name of the field from the table box to the grid
   c. Click the drop-down arrow in an empty column in the grid
   d. All of the above
7. When creating a calculated field, the field name must be enclosed in what?
   a. Brackets
   b. Parentheses
   c. Braces
   d. Asterisks
8. When creating a parameter query, what must the prompting message be enclosed in?
   a. Brackets
   b. Parentheses
   c. Braces
   d. Asterisks
9. What type of query is a query that asks for criteria each time it is used?
   a. Select
   b. Parameter
   c. Union
   d. Question
10. When opening an existing database, which of the following must you know to open that file?
    a. The filename
    b. The folder/subfolder it resides in
    c. The drive it is on
    d. All of the above

## Completion

In the blank provided, write the correct answer for each of the following statements.

1. Use ___ ___ to limit the fields shown in a table.
2. To limit the Find option to only look for the entire Find What text, use ___ ___ in the Match drop-down list box.
3. A(n) ___ can speed up the sorting process of large databases.
4. To look at your data with the same filter over and over, create a(n) _____.

5. Using a(n) ____ makes creating a filter easier.

6. In a filter or query, the ___ statement searches for all records that meet both requirements listed.

7. The ___ window makes entries easier to see in the Query Design view.

8. In a calculated field, the field name must be enclosed in ____.

9. A(n) ____ query enables the user to specify the criteria each time the query is run.

10. Records in _____ order are listed from the highest number/letter to the lowest number/letter.

# Lesson 5 Test Questions

## True/False

For each of the following, check T or F to indicate whether the statement is true or false.

T.___F. ___**1.** Importing a table places a copy of that table in the new database and can be changed only in the original database.

T.___F. ___**2.** A relationship allows two tables to work together.

T.___F. ___**3.** The fields that are related between two tables must have the same field name.

T.___F. ___**4.** A query that uses more than one table is called a union query.

T.___F. ___**5.** When two criteria are on the same row of a Query Design grid, the criteria are in the form of an Or statement.

T.___F. ___**6.** In an Or statement, any records that meet even one of the criteria are displayed.

T.___F. ___**7.** A form using more than one query or table usually has one form as a subform.

T.___F. ___**8.** To use a union query in a report, the tables in the query must be related.

T.___F. ___**9.** Many queries are created for use in a report.

T.___F. ___**10.** The first field used in a relationship is the "one" in a one-to-many relationship.

## Multiple Choice

Circle the letter of the correct answer for each of the following questions.

1. Which of the following is an example of a table that is obtained from another database and can be changed in the new database?
   a. Linked
   b. Imported
   c. Copied
   d. Translated

2. Which of the following are characteristics of relationships?
   a. Allow two tables to work together
   b. Allow fields from two tables to appear in the same report
   c. Create a one-to-many relationship or a many-to-many relationship
   d. All of the above

3. What occurs when you move a table in the relationship window?
   a. It is easier to see the relationship.
   b. The relationships to that table are lost.
   c. The table is deleted from the window.
   d. You must start over.

4. Which of the following can be used to create a relationship between two fields?
   a. Click Edit, Relate
   b. Double-click the first field name
   c. Drag one field name onto another field in another table
   d. Draw a line from one field to another

5. What is a true of a Union query?
   a. Includes fields from more than one table
   b. Combines two tables
   c. Includes two tables that are related
   d. Both a and c

6. In a query, what do criteria that begin with Like suggest?
   a. They can use wildcards
   b. They must match the criteria exactly
   c. They cannot be empty
   d. They use phonics rather than spelling to find matching fields.
7. A form that uses more than one table usually has which of the following?
   a. Link
   b. Subform
   c. Miniform
   d. None of the above
8. From which component are many reports are created?
   a. A form
   b. A table
   c. A query
   d. A macro
9. What does a report based on a parameter query do?
   a. Asks for the parameter entries each time it is viewed
   b. Takes up more memory than other reports
   c. Are very long
   d. Cannot be based on more than one table
10. Which is not a comparison operator?
   a. Sum
   b. Count
   c. If
   d. Average

## Completion

In the blank provided, write the correct answer for each of the following statements.

1. A read-only table is one that has been ___ from another database.
2. You can insert an existing table into another database if you ___ that table.
3. A(n) _____ is matched data between two tables.
4. In a(n) ___ __ ___ relationship, the field in the first table must be unique.
5. A(n) ____ query can use fields from more than one table.
6. A criterion in a query that begins with ___ will accept wildcards.
7. A form with a(n) ___ is like a form within a form.
8. To limit the records in a report, create the report based on a(n) ___.
9. A report asks for information each time it is used if the report is based on a(n) ____ query.
10. To rearrange the tables in a Query Design View, drag the _____.

# Lesson 6 Test Questions

## True/False

For each of the following, check T or F to indicate whether the statement is true or false.

T.___F. ___1. A crosstab query uses only one field when summarizing.

T.___F. ___2. You must create a crosstab query from the Design View.

T.___F. ___3. Two criteria on the same row of a query produce an And statement.

T.___F. ___4. To set a sort on a default field for a query, set it in Design View as a part of the query.

T.___F. ___5. The Totals function in a query adds up the fields you specify.

T.___F. ___6. The default choice for the Totals function is Group By.

T.___F. ___7. A PivotTable is created, housed, and edited in Access only.

T.___F. ___8. 8. After the headings for a PivotTable are set, they cannot be edited.

T.___F. ___9. Summary options in the Report Wizard enable the user to define what type of summary is needed on a report.

T.___F. ___10. To change the settings for a component of a report, use the Properties box.

## Multiple Choice

Circle the letter of the correct answer for each of the following questions.

1. Data can be summarized through which of the following?
   a. Report
   b. Crosstab query
   c. PivotTable
   d. All of the above
2. What do you use to create subtotals and totals in a report?
   a. Totals button
   b. Summary Options
   c. Function Wizard
   d. AutoSum button
3. Which program is a PivotTable created through?
   a. Word
   b. Excel
   c. Access
   d. Both b and c
4. Which is the best option to use to summarize complex data?
   a. Crosstab query
   b. Multilevel crosstab query
   c. PivotTable
   d. Report
5. Which of the following is not found in the Totals function in a query?
   a. If
   b. Average
   c. Sum
   d. Group by
6. What does Save As/Export enable you to do?
   a. Save a query as another query
   b. Save a component to another database
   c. Save a report as another report
   d. All of the above
7. Which type of statement is created when two criteria are on the same row in a Query Design view?
   a. And statement
   b. Or statement
   c. Like statement
   d. Match statement
8. In what manner can you place a field in the Query Design view grid?
   a. Drag the field name to the grid
   b. Double-click the field name
   c. Choose the field from a drop-down list in the grid
   d. All of the above
9. A query that summarizes data from one table based on more than two fields is which of the following?
   a. Crosstab query
   b. Multilevel crosstab query
   c. PivotTable
   d. Union query
10. Which of the following is the simplest way to create a crosstab query?
    a. With the Crosstab Query Wizard
    b. With the Simple Query Wizard
    c. In Design View
    d. In Datasheet View

## Completion

In the blank provided, write the correct answer for each of the following statements.

1. A(n) ____ ____ summarizes data from two tables, depending on how the fields are organized.
2. A(n) ___ ____ displays summarized data from one table, grouped by at least two fields from another table.
3. If more than two fields are used for summary, a(n) _____ _____ _____ is the appropriate query to use.
4. To edit a query, you must be in ____ View.

5. A PivotTable is edited in ____.

6. The ___ button is used to display the results of a query.

7. An Or statement in a query must be placed on _____ row.

8. To use a component in another database, you can ____ it.

9. The Totals button in the Query Design view enables you to use a(n) ____ field summary.

10. ____ can be useful in a report in which data are grouped.

# Lesson 7 Test Questions

## True/False

For each of the following, check T or F to indicate whether the statement is true or false.

T. ___F. ___**1.** A hyperlink can be connected only to files on other computers.

T. ___F. ___**2.** A hyperlink flashes on the screen.

T. ___F. ___**3.** The Office Assistant appears when you access the Contents and Index help option.

T. ___F. ___**4.** Type a normal question to get help with Office Assistant.

T. ___F. ___**5.** If the Microsoft Web page looks different, you did something wrong.

T. ___F. ___**6.** The Web toolbar can be turned on and off by pressing the button on the Standard toolbar.

T. ___F. ___**7.** Merging combines two databases together permanently.

T. ___F. ___**8.** Merge codes are needed in the Word document when merging a file from Word and a table/query from Access.

T. ___F. ___**9.** Access can import any format from Excel as a table.

T. ___F. ___**10.** After data is placed into a database program, it cannot be accessed through an Access database.

## Multiple Choice

Circle the letter of the correct answer for each of the following questions.

1. What can a hyperlink connect to?

   a. A file on a local area network

   b. A URL

   c. A file on the local PC

   d. All of the above

2. The Office Assistant looks like which of the following by default?

   a. Book

   b. On-screen man

   c. On-screen paper clip

   d. Internet site

3. Messages with responses on the news group page are designated with which of the following?

   a. ⊞

   b. ⇥

   c. [?]

   d. ✔

4. Which are books that are meant to contain detailed instructions on specific tasks?

   a. Reference books

   b. Self-help books

   c. Textbooks

   d. Documentation

5. On the Macmillan Computer Publishing Web page, how can books be searched for?

   a. Search words

   b. ISBN

   c. Author

   d. All of the above

6. Which of the following are on the Microsoft Web page?

   a. Tech support

   b. Q&A from users

   c. Downloads

   d. All of the above

7. When importing a text file from another database program, what must the fields be separated by?

   a. A delimiter

   b. Commas

   c. Fixed-width fields

   d. Either a or c

8. What criteria must be met for worksheets to be imported into an Access table?

   a. The data must be laid out in a database format

   b. The file must be saved as an Access table

   c. You must use the Spreadsheet Wizard

   d. They must be created in Excel 97 only

9. An Access table can be combined with a Word document. What is this process called?

   a. Importing

   b. Linking

   c. Merging

   d. Exporting

10. Which of the following is an example merge code?

   a. (FirstName)

   b. {FirstName}

   c. <<FirstName>>

   d. [FirstName]

## Completion

In the blank provided, write the correct answer for each of the following statements.

1. A(n) _______ is a connection between a word or phrase to another file.

2. You can press the ______ key to get help.

3. Microsoft has a(n) ______ _______ Web page for help.

4. The __________ on the Web page are questions and answers from other users.

5. Responses to newsgroup questions begin with ______.

6. http://www.mcp.com/ is the Web address for ___________ ____________ ___________.

7. _______ _______ books are user-friendly and meant to teach how to use software.

8. Combining an Access table/query with a Word document is called ____.

9. When importing an Excel spreadsheet, the ____ must represent records, the _____ fields, and the top row ________.

10. The easiest format to import from another database is _____ format.

# Lesson 1 Test Question Solutions

## True/False Solutions

1. F
2. F
3. T
4. F
5. T
6. T
7. T
8. F
9. F
10. F

## Multiple Choice Solutions

1. A
2. B
3. D
4. A
5. C
6. B
7. B
8. D
9. D
10. D

## Completion Solutions

1. Database Wizard
2. Table
3. Navigation buttons
4. Tab
5. Input mask
6. Design
7. Cannot
8. What's This?
9. Database
10. 22

# Lesson 2 Test Question Solutions

## True/False Solutions

1. T
2. F
3. F
4. T
5. T
6. F
7. F
8. F
9. F
10. T

## Multiple Choice Solutions

1. C
2. D
3. A
4. C
5. D
6. B
7. A
8. B
9. D
10. D

## Completion Solutions

1. Save
2. Design
3. Row selector
4. Convert
5. Sorting, grouping
6. View, tab order
7. handles
8. Shift
9. Hourglass
10. Wizard

# Lesson 3 Test Question Solutions

## True/False Solutions

1. F
2. T
3. T
4. F
5. T
6. F
7. T
8. F
9. T
10. F

## Multiple Choice Solutions

1. C
2. A
3. D
4. A
5. D
6. D
7. B
8. C
9. A
10. C

## Completion Solutions

1. Input Mask Wizard
2. Default values
3. Field Properties
4. Expression Builder
5. Two-sided arrow
6. List box
7. Combo box
8. Form
9. Insert
10. Date()

# Lesson 4 Test Question Solutions

## True/False Solutions

1. F
2. T
3. T
4. T
5. F
6. F
7. T
8. T
9. F
10. T

## Multiple Choice Solutions

1. b
2. d
3. b
4. a
5. d
6. d
7. a
8. a
9. b
10. d

## Completion Solutions

1. Freeze columns
2. Whole field
3. Index
4. Query
5. AutoForm
6. And
7. Zoom
8. Brackets
9. Parameter
10. Descending

# Lesson 5 Test Question Solutions

## True/False Solutions

1. F
2. T
3. F
4. T
5. F
6. T
7. T
8. T
9. T
10. T

## Multiple Choice Solutions

1. b
2. d
3. a
4. c
5. d
6. a
7. b
8. c
9. a
10. c

## Completion Solutions

1. Linked
2. Import
3. Relationship
4. One-to-many
5. Union
6. Like
7. Subform
8. Query
9. Parameter
10. Title bar

# Lesson 6 Test Question Solutions

## True/False Solutions

1. F
2. F
3. T
4. T
5. F
6. T
7. F
8. F
9. T
10. T

## Multiple Choice Solutions

1. d
2. b
3. d
4. c
5. a
6. d
7. a
8. d
9. b
10. a

## Completion Solutions

1. Pivot table
2. Crosstab query
3. Multilevel crosstab query
4. Design
5. Excel
6. Run
7. Different
8. Export
9. Single
10. Subtotals

# Lesson 7 Test Question Solutions

## True/False Solutions

1. F
2. F
3. T
4. T
5. F
6. T
7. F
8. T
9. F
10. F

## Multiple Choice Solutions

1. d
2. c
3. a
4. a
5. d
6. d
7. d
8. a
9. c
10. c

## Completion Solutions

1. Hyperlink
2. F1
3. Technical support
4. Newsgroups
5. Re:
6. Macmillan Computer Publishing
7. Self-help
8. Merging
9. Row, Columns, Fieldnames
10. Text

# Instructor's Notes

# Instructor's Notes

# Instructor's Notes

# Instructor's Notes

# Instructor's Notes

# Index

## Symbols



## A



## B



## C

# D



# E



# F

# G-H



# I-J

## K-L



## M



## N



## O



## P

# Q



# R



# S

## T



## U



## V



## W-Z

By opening this package, you are agreeing to be bound by the following agreement:

Some of the software included with this product may be copyrighted, in which case all rights are reserved by the respective copyright holder. You are licensed to use software copyrighted by the publisher and its licensors on a single computer. You may copy and/or modify the software as needed to facilitate your use of it on a single computer. Making copies of the software for any other purpose is a violation of the United States copyright laws.

This software is sold as is without warranty of any kind, either expressed or implied, including but not limited to the implied warranties of merchantability and fitness for a particular purpose. Neither the publisher nor its dealers or distributors assumes any liability for any alleged or actual damages arising from the use of this program. (Some states do not allow for the exclusion of implied warranties, so the exclusion may not apply to you.)